Shojo Beat

honey and clover

Vol. 5
Story & Art by
Chica Umino

honey and clover

Volume 5
CONTENTS

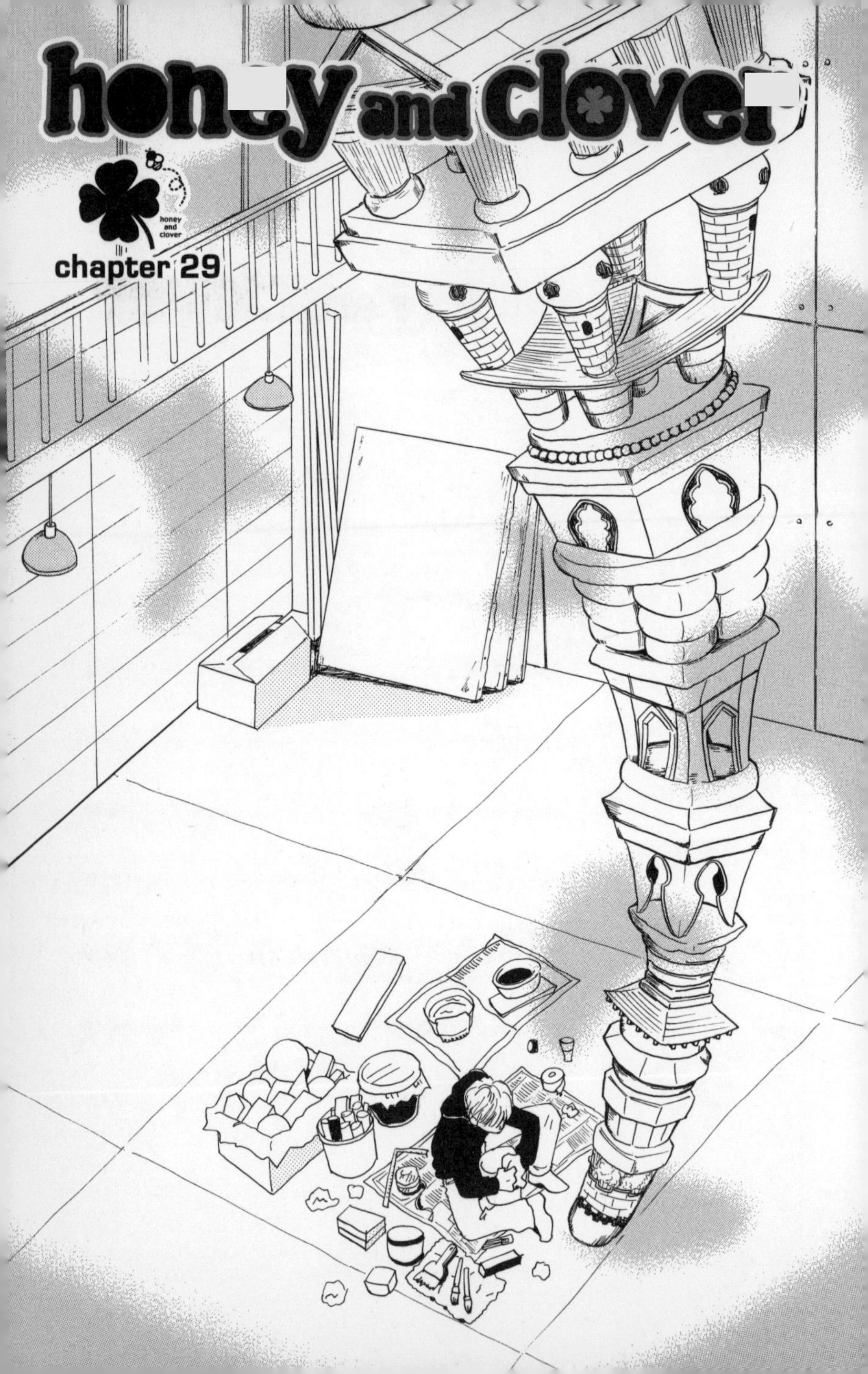
honey
and
clover
chapter 29

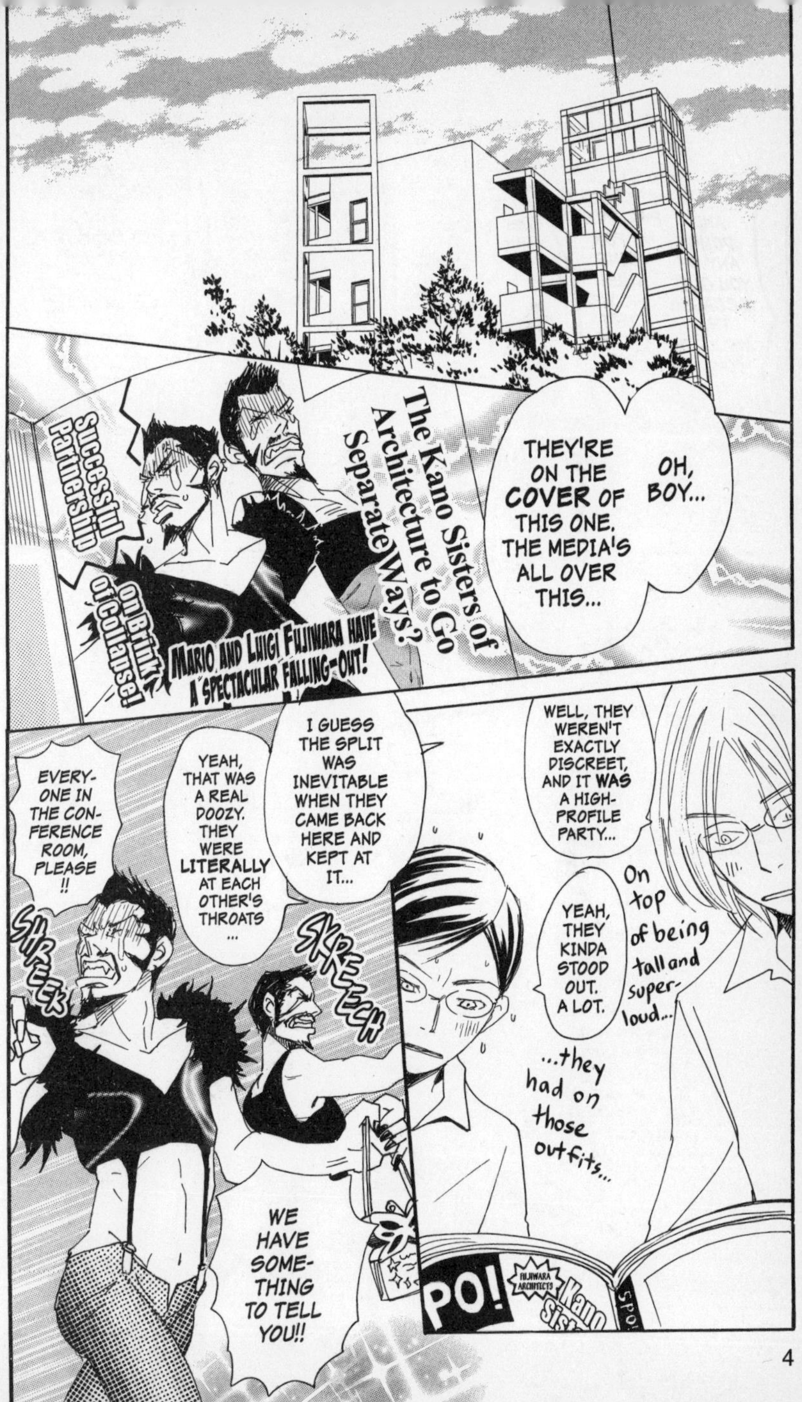
OH, BOY...
THEY'RE ON THE COVER OF THIS ONE. THE MEDIA'S ALL OVER THIS...
The Kano Sisters of Architecture to Go Separate Ways?
Successful Partnership On Brink of Collapse!
MARIO AND LUIGI FUJIWARA HAVE A SPECTACULAR FALLING-OUT!
WELL, THEY WEREN'T EXACTLY DISCREET, AND IT WAS A HIGH-PROFILE PARTY...
YEAH, THEY KINDA STOOD OUT. A LOT.
On top of being tall and super-loud...
...they had on those outfits...
PO!
FUJIWARA ARCHITECTS
Kano
I GUESS THE SPLIT WAS INEVITABLE WHEN THEY CAME BACK HERE AND KEPT AT IT...
YEAH, THAT WAS A REAL DOOZY. THEY WERE LITERALLY AT EACH OTHER'S THROATS ...
EVERY-ONE IN THE CON-FERENCE ROOM, PLEASE!!
SKREECH
SHREEK
WE HAVE SOME-THING TO TELL YOU!!

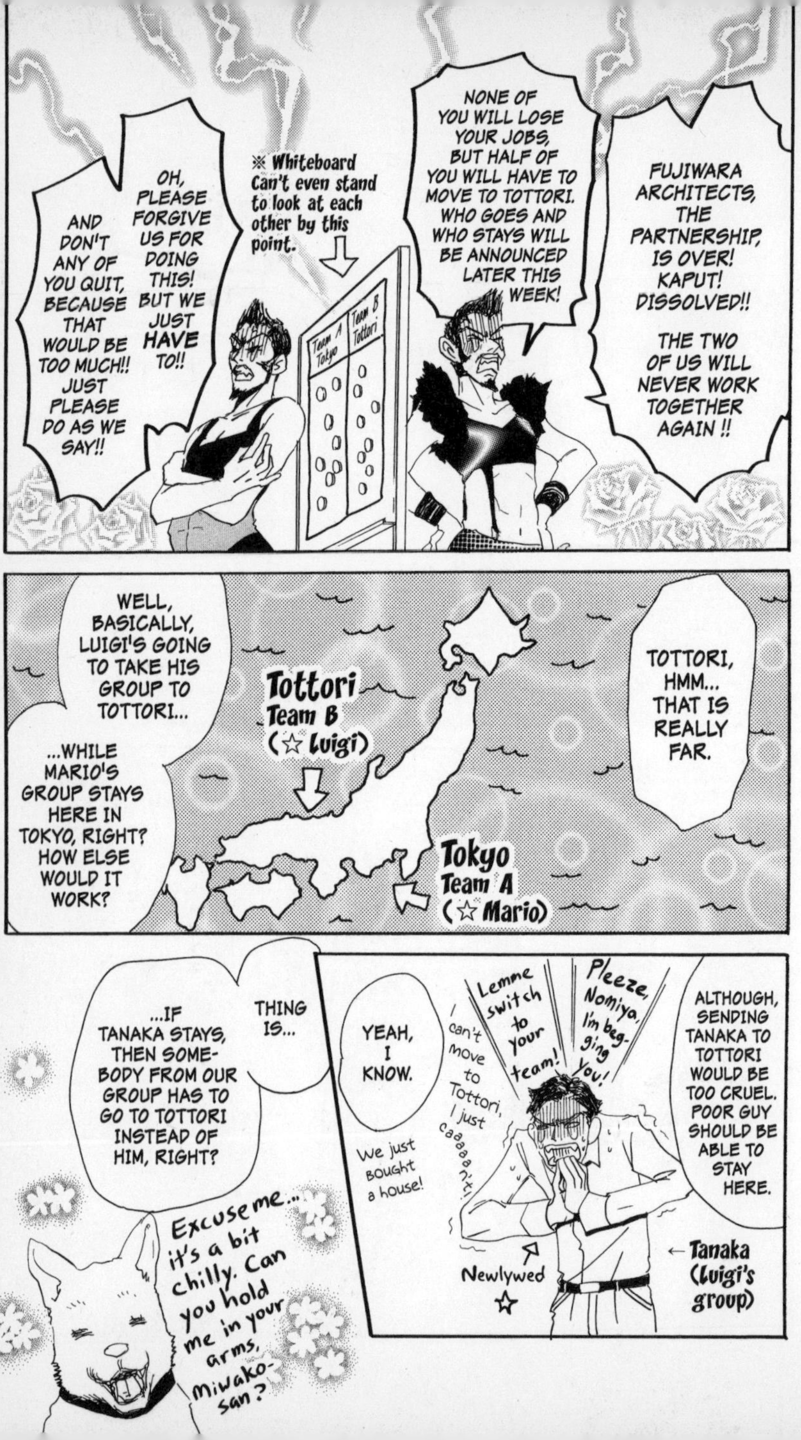
FUJIWARA ARCHITECTS, THE PARTNERSHIP, IS OVER! KAPUT! DISSOLVED!!
THE TWO OF US WILL NEVER WORK TOGETHER AGAIN !!
NONE OF YOU WILL LOSE YOUR JOBS, BUT HALF OF YOU WILL HAVE TO MOVE TO TOTTORI. WHO GOES AND WHO STAYS WILL BE ANNOUNCED LATER THIS WEEK!
※ Whiteboard Can't even stand to look at each other by this point.
Team B Tottori
Team A Tokyo
OH, PLEASE FORGIVE US FOR DOING THIS! BUT WE JUST HAVE TO!!
AND DON'T ANY OF YOU QUIT, BECAUSE THAT WOULD BE TOO MUCH!! JUST PLEASE DO AS WE SAY!!
TOTTORI, HMM... THAT IS REALLY FAR.
Tottori Team B (☆ Luigi)
Tokyo Team A (☆ Mario)
WELL, BASICALLY, LUIGI'S GOING TO TAKE HIS GROUP TO TOTTORI...
...WHILE MARIO'S GROUP STAYS HERE IN TOKYO, RIGHT? HOW ELSE WOULD IT WORK?
ALTHOUGH, SENDING TANAKA TO TOTTORI WOULD BE TOO CRUEL. POOR GUY SHOULD BE ABLE TO STAY HERE.
← Tanaka (Luigi's group)
Pleeze, Nomiya, I'm begging you!
Lemme switch to your team!
I can't move to Tottori, I just caaaaan't!
We just bought a house!
Newlywed ☆
YEAH, I KNOW.
THING IS...
...IF TANAKA STAYS, THEN SOMEBODY FROM OUR GROUP HAS TO GO TO TOTTORI INSTEAD OF HIM, RIGHT?
Excuse me... it's a bit chilly. Can you hold me in your arms, Miwako-san?

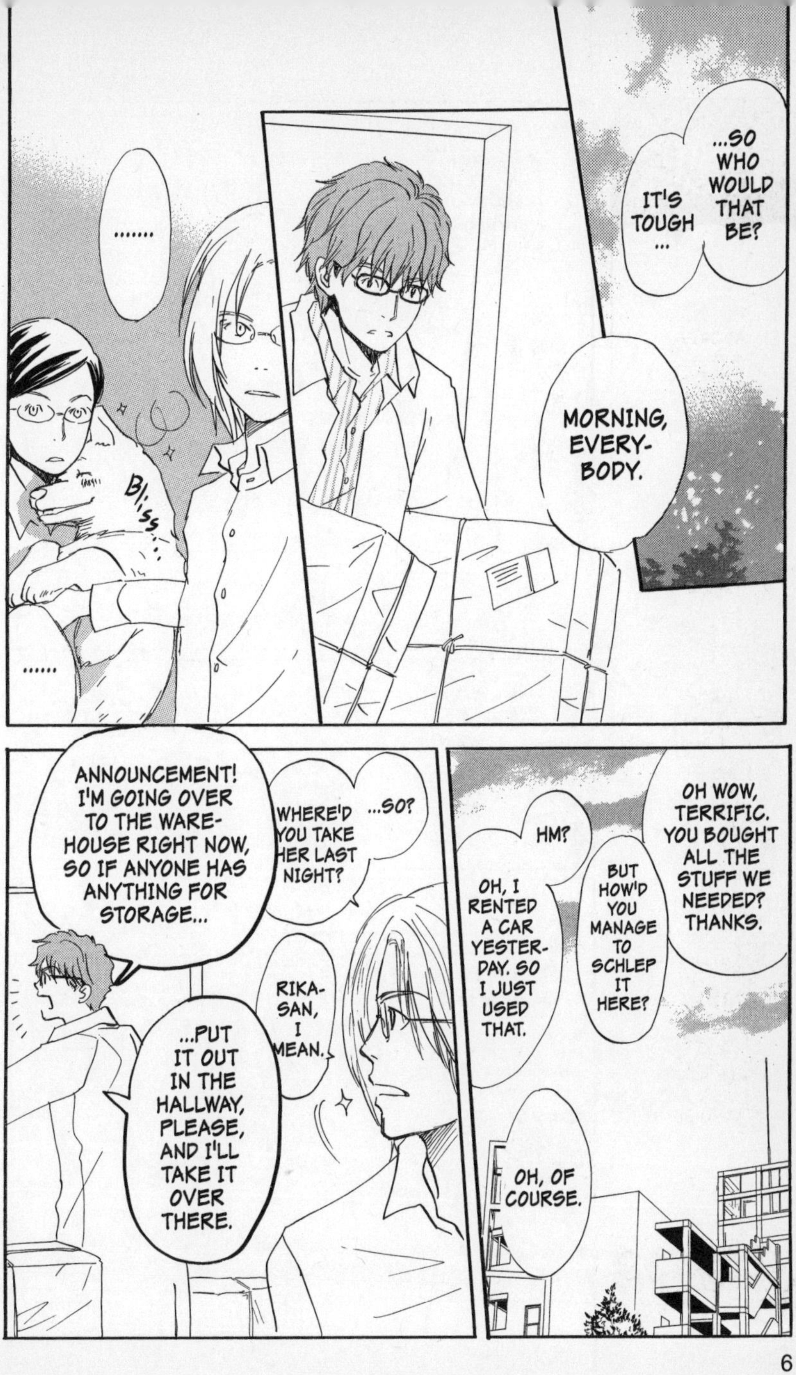
...SO WHO WOULD THAT BE?
IT'S TOUGH...
MORNING, EVERYBODY.
......
BLISS...
......
OH WOW, TERRIFIC. YOU BOUGHT ALL THE STUFF WE NEEDED? THANKS.
BUT HOW'D YOU MANAGE TO SCHLEP IT HERE?
HM?
OH, I RENTED A CAR YESTERDAY. SO I JUST USED THAT.
OH, OF COURSE.
...SO?
WHERE'D YOU TAKE HER LAST NIGHT?
RIKA-SAN, I MEAN.
ANNOUNCEMENT! I'M GOING OVER TO THE WAREHOUSE RIGHT NOW, SO IF ANYONE HAS ANYTHING FOR STORAGE...
...PUT IT OUT IN THE HALLWAY, PLEASE, AND I'LL TAKE IT OVER THERE.

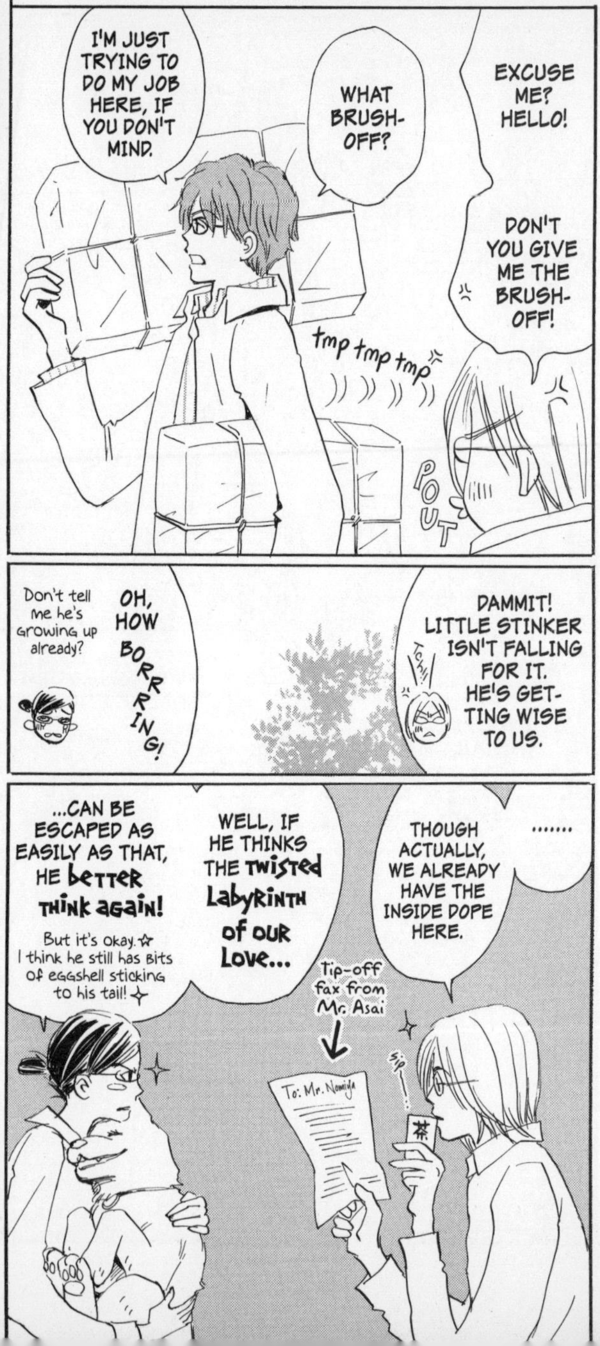
EXCUSE ME? HELLO!
DON'T YOU GIVE ME THE BRUSH-OFF!
tmp tmp tmp
POUT
WHAT BRUSH-OFF?
I'M JUST TRYING TO DO MY JOB HERE, IF YOU DON'T MIND.
DAMMIT! LITTLE STINKER ISN'T FALLING FOR IT. HE'S GETTING WISE TO US.
Tch!!
OH, HOW BORRRRING!
Don't tell me he's growing up already?
....
THOUGH ACTUALLY, WE ALREADY HAVE THE INSIDE DOPE HERE.
Tip-off fax from Mr. Asai
To: Mr. Nomiya
sip
WELL, IF HE THINKS THE TWISTED LABYRINTH OF OUR LOVE...
...CAN BE ESCAPED AS EASILY AS THAT, HE BETTER THINK AGAIN!
But it's okay.☆ I think he still has bits of eggshell sticking to his tail!

I love dresses!

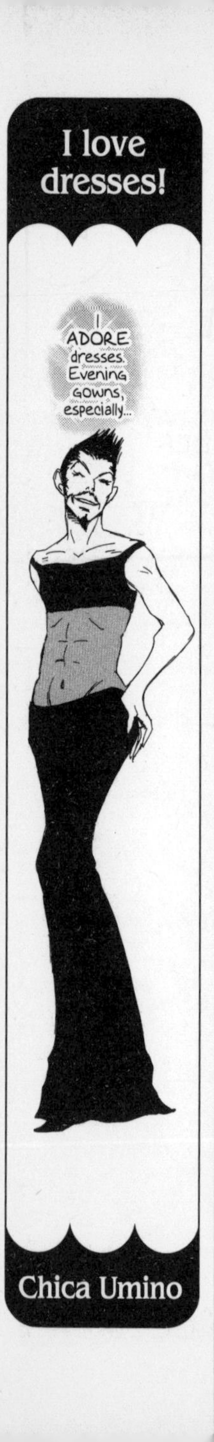
I ADORE dresses. Evening gowns, especially...

Chica Umino

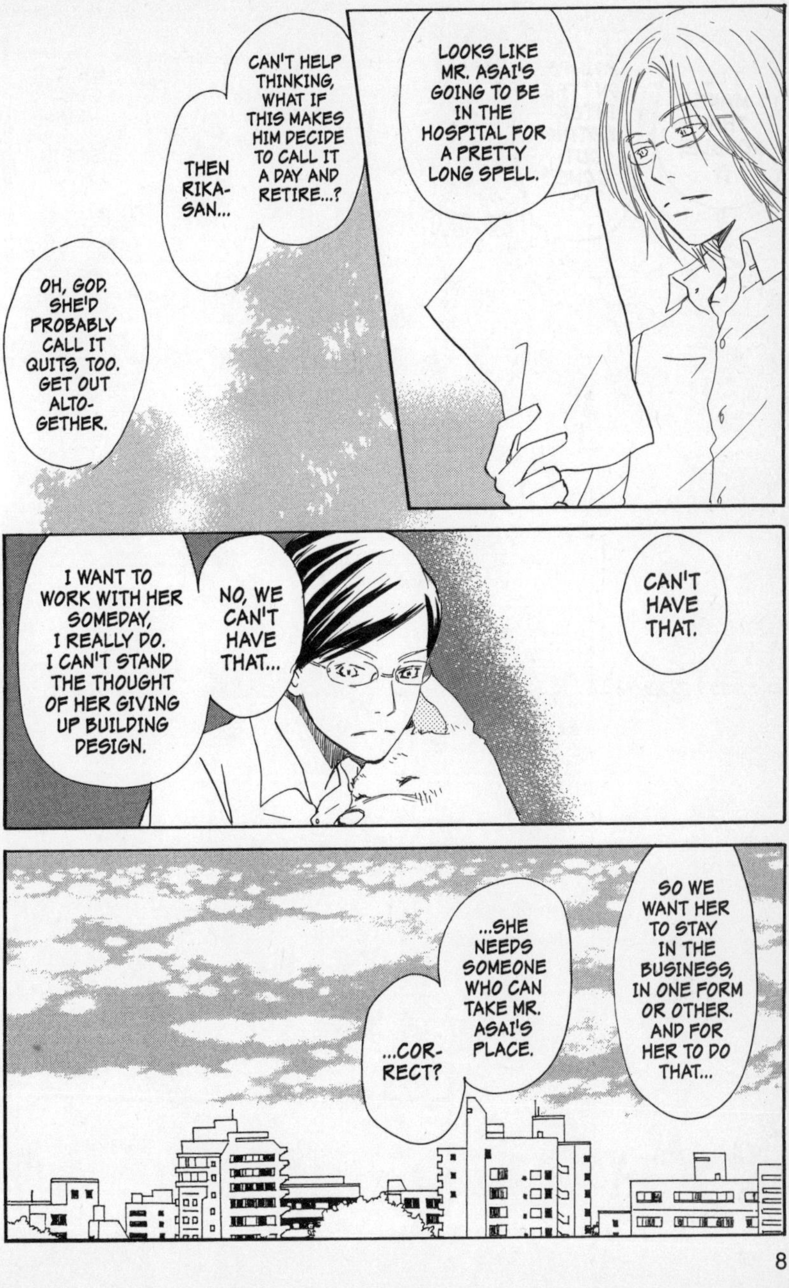
LOOKS LIKE MR. ASAI'S GOING TO BE IN THE HOSPITAL FOR A PRETTY LONG SPELL.
CAN'T HELP THINKING, WHAT IF THIS MAKES HIM DECIDE TO CALL IT A DAY AND RETIRE...?
THEN RIKA-SAN...
OH, GOD. SHE'D PROBABLY CALL IT QUITS, TOO. GET OUT ALTO-GETHER.
CAN'T HAVE THAT.
NO, WE CAN'T HAVE THAT...
I WANT TO WORK WITH HER SOMEDAY, I REALLY DO. I CAN'T STAND THE THOUGHT OF HER GIVING UP BUILDING DESIGN.
SO WE WANT HER TO STAY IN THE BUSINESS, IN ONE FORM OR OTHER. AND FOR HER TO DO THAT...
...SHE NEEDS SOMEONE WHO CAN TAKE MR. ASAI'S PLACE.
...COR-RECT?

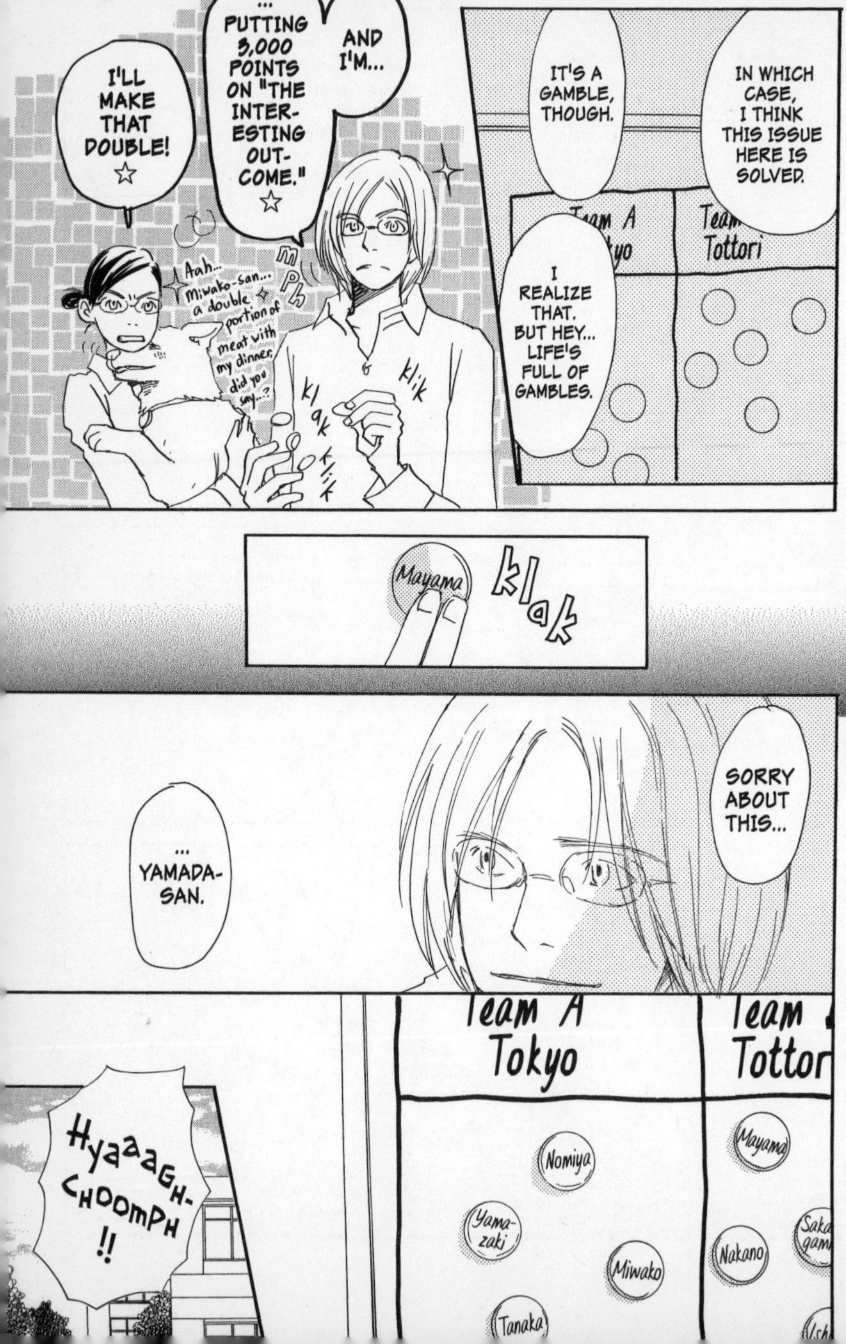
IN WHICH CASE, I THINK THIS ISSUE HERE IS SOLVED.
IT'S A GAMBLE, THOUGH.
I REALIZE THAT. BUT HEY... LIFE'S FULL OF GAMBLES.
Tottori
AND I'M...
... PUTTING 3,000 POINTS ON "THE INTERESTING OUTCOME." ☆
I'LL MAKE THAT DOUBLE! ☆
mph
Aah... Miwako-san... a double portion of meat with my dinner, did you say...?
klik
klak
klik
Mayama
klak
SORRY ABOUT THIS...
... YAMADA-SAN.
Team A Tokyo
Mayama
Nomiya
Yama-zaki
Nakano
Miwako
Tanaka
Hyaaagh-choomph!!

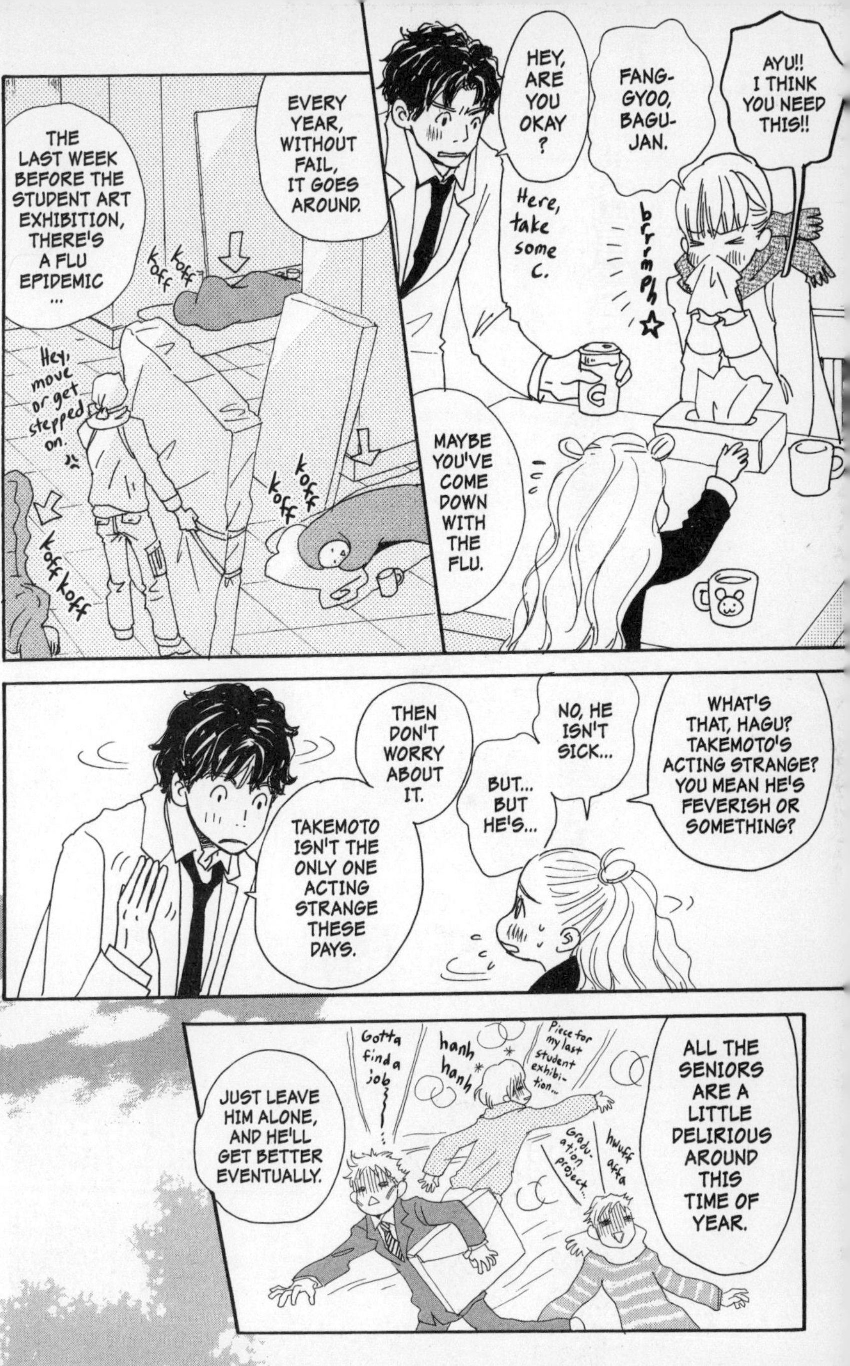
AYU!! I THINK YOU NEED THIS!!
FANG-GYOO, BAGU-JAN.
HEY, ARE YOU OKAY?
brrrmph☆
Here, take some C.
MAYBE YOU'VE COME DOWN WITH THE FLU.
EVERY YEAR, WITHOUT FAIL, IT GOES AROUND.
THE LAST WEEK BEFORE THE STUDENT ART EXHIBITION, THERE'S A FLU EPIDEMIC...
koff koff
Hey, move or get stepped on.
koff koff
koff koff
WHAT'S THAT, HAGU? TAKEMOTO'S ACTING STRANGE? YOU MEAN HE'S FEVERISH OR SOMETHING?
NO, HE ISN'T SICK...
BUT... BUT HE'S...
THEN DON'T WORRY ABOUT IT.
TAKEMOTO ISN'T THE ONLY ONE ACTING STRANGE THESE DAYS.
ALL THE SENIORS ARE A LITTLE DELIRIOUS AROUND THIS TIME OF YEAR.
hwuff affa
Piece for my last student exhibition...
Graduation project...
hanh hanh
Gotta find a job
JUST LEAVE HIM ALONE, AND HE'LL GET BETTER EVENTUALLY.

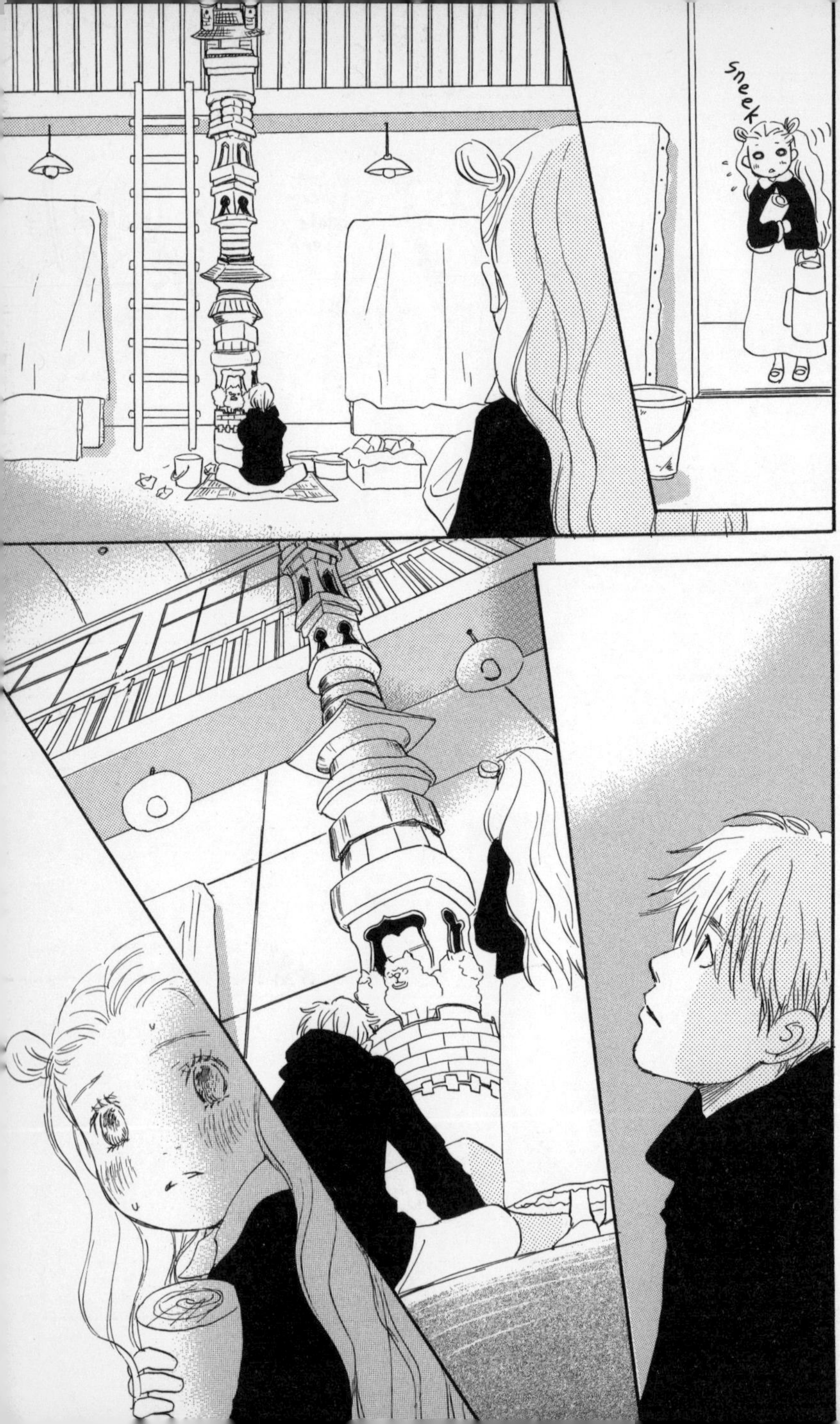
sneek

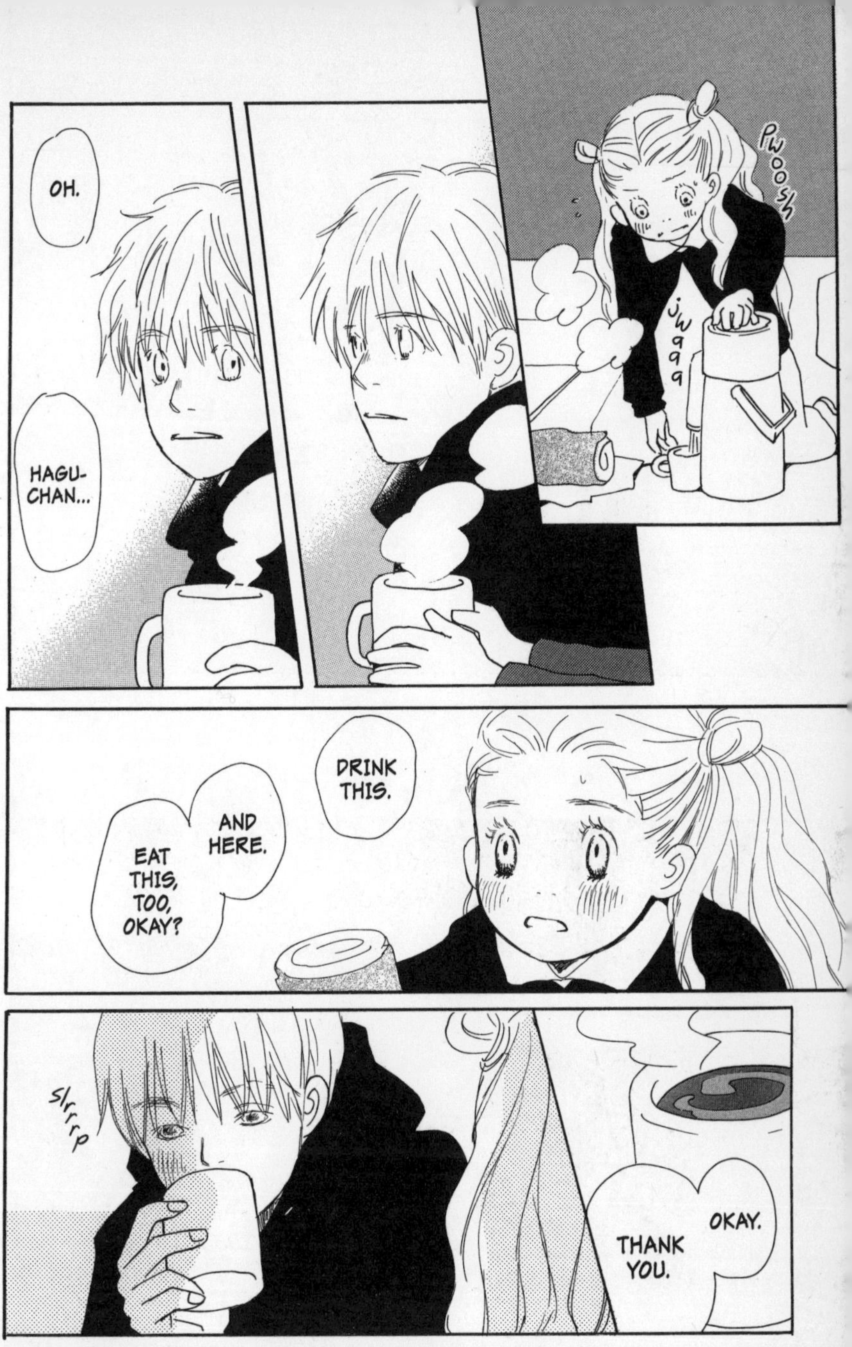
Pwoosh
jwggg
OH.
HAGU-CHAN...
DRINK THIS.
AND HERE.
EAT THIS, TOO, OKAY?
OKAY.
THANK YOU.
slrrrp

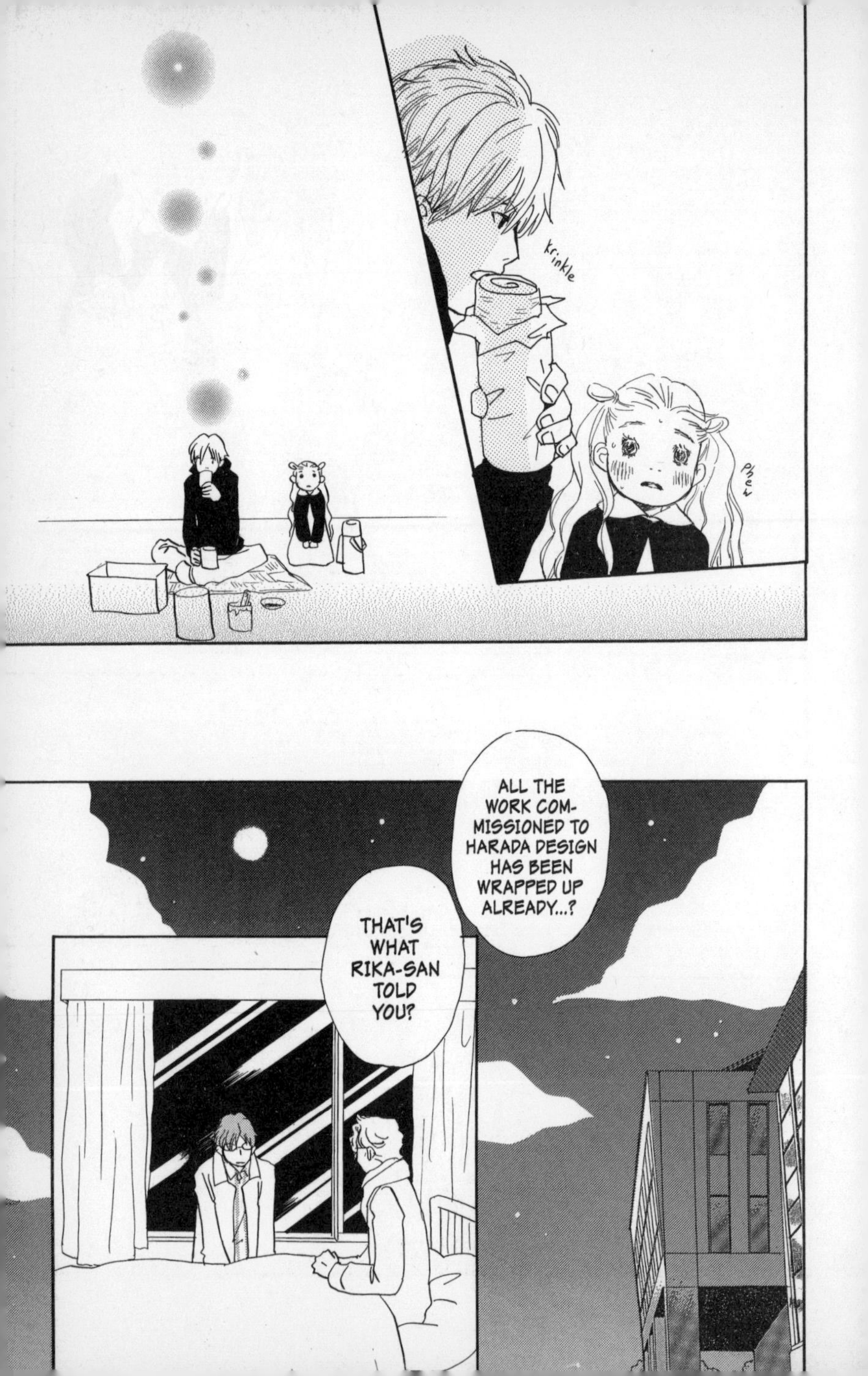
krinkle
Phew
ALL THE WORK COMMISSIONED TO HARADA DESIGN HAS BEEN WRAPPED UP ALREADY...?
THAT'S WHAT RIKA-SAN TOLD YOU?

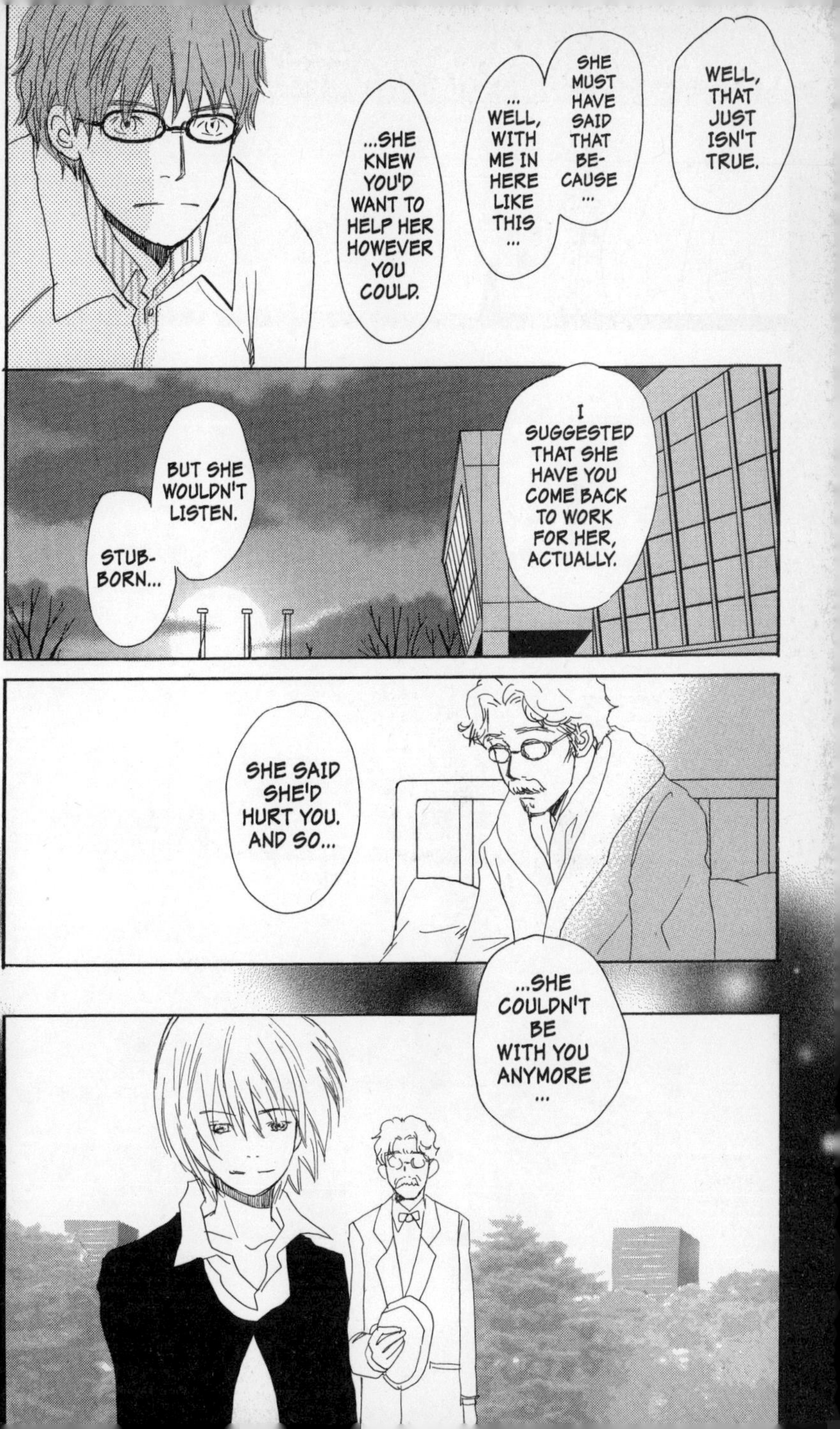
WELL, THAT JUST ISN'T TRUE.
SHE MUST HAVE SAID THAT BE-CAUSE ...
... WELL, WITH ME IN HERE LIKE THIS ...
...SHE KNEW YOU'D WANT TO HELP HER HOWEVER YOU COULD.
I SUGGESTED THAT SHE HAVE YOU COME BACK TO WORK FOR HER, ACTUALLY.
BUT SHE WOULDN'T LISTEN.
STUB-BORN...
SHE SAID SHE'D HURT YOU. AND SO...
...SHE COULDN'T BE WITH YOU ANYMORE ...

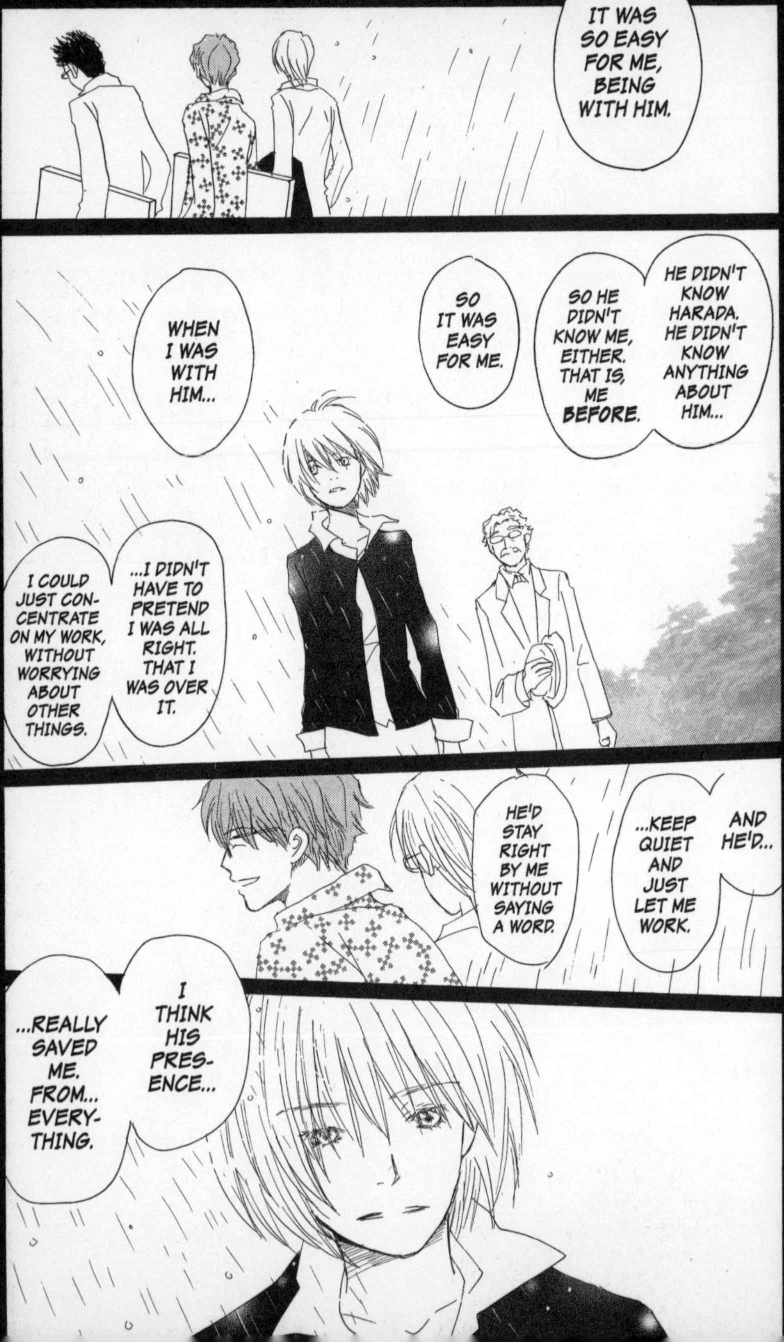
IT WAS SO EASY FOR ME, BEING WITH HIM.
HE DIDN'T KNOW HARADA. HE DIDN'T KNOW ANYTHING ABOUT HIM...
SO HE DIDN'T KNOW ME, EITHER. THAT IS, ME **BEFORE.**
SO IT WAS EASY FOR ME.
WHEN I WAS WITH HIM...
...I DIDN'T HAVE TO PRETEND I WAS ALL RIGHT. THAT I WAS OVER IT.
I COULD JUST CONCENTRATE ON MY WORK, WITHOUT WORRYING ABOUT OTHER THINGS.
AND HE'D...
...KEEP QUIET AND JUST LET ME WORK.
HE'D STAY RIGHT BY ME WITHOUT SAYING A WORD.
I THINK HIS PRESENCE...
...REALLY SAVED ME. FROM... EVERYTHING.

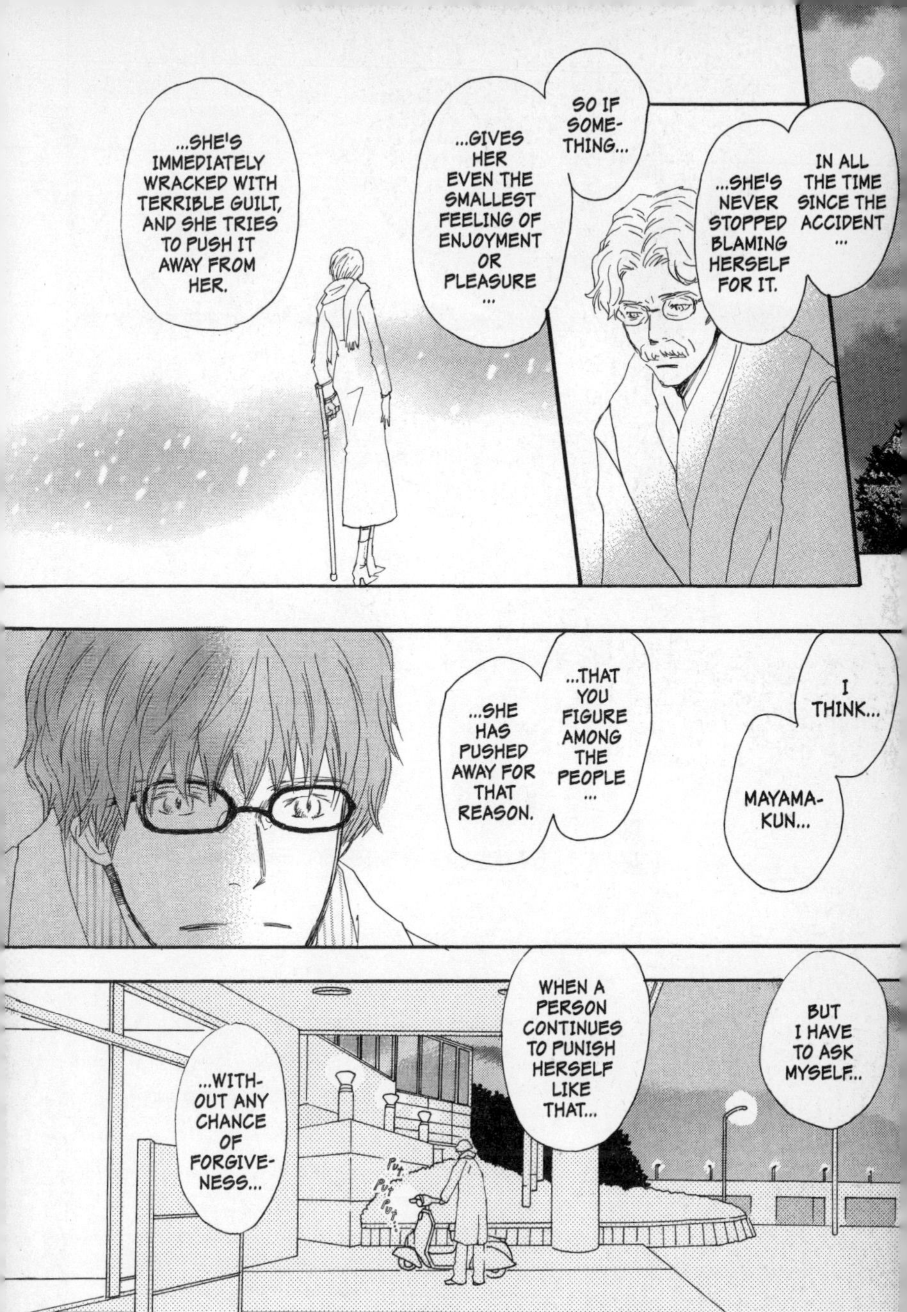
IN ALL THE TIME SINCE THE ACCIDENT...
...SHE'S NEVER STOPPED BLAMING HERSELF FOR IT.
SO IF SOME-THING...
...GIVES HER EVEN THE SMALLEST FEELING OF ENJOYMENT OR PLEASURE...
...SHE'S IMMEDIATELY WRACKED WITH TERRIBLE GUILT, AND SHE TRIES TO PUSH IT AWAY FROM HER.
I THINK...
MAYAMA-KUN...
...THAT YOU FIGURE AMONG THE PEOPLE...
...SHE HAS PUSHED AWAY FOR THAT REASON.
BUT I HAVE TO ASK MYSELF...
WHEN A PERSON CONTINUES TO PUNISH HERSELF LIKE THAT...
...WITH-OUT ANY CHANCE OF FORGIVE-NESS...
Put Put Put...

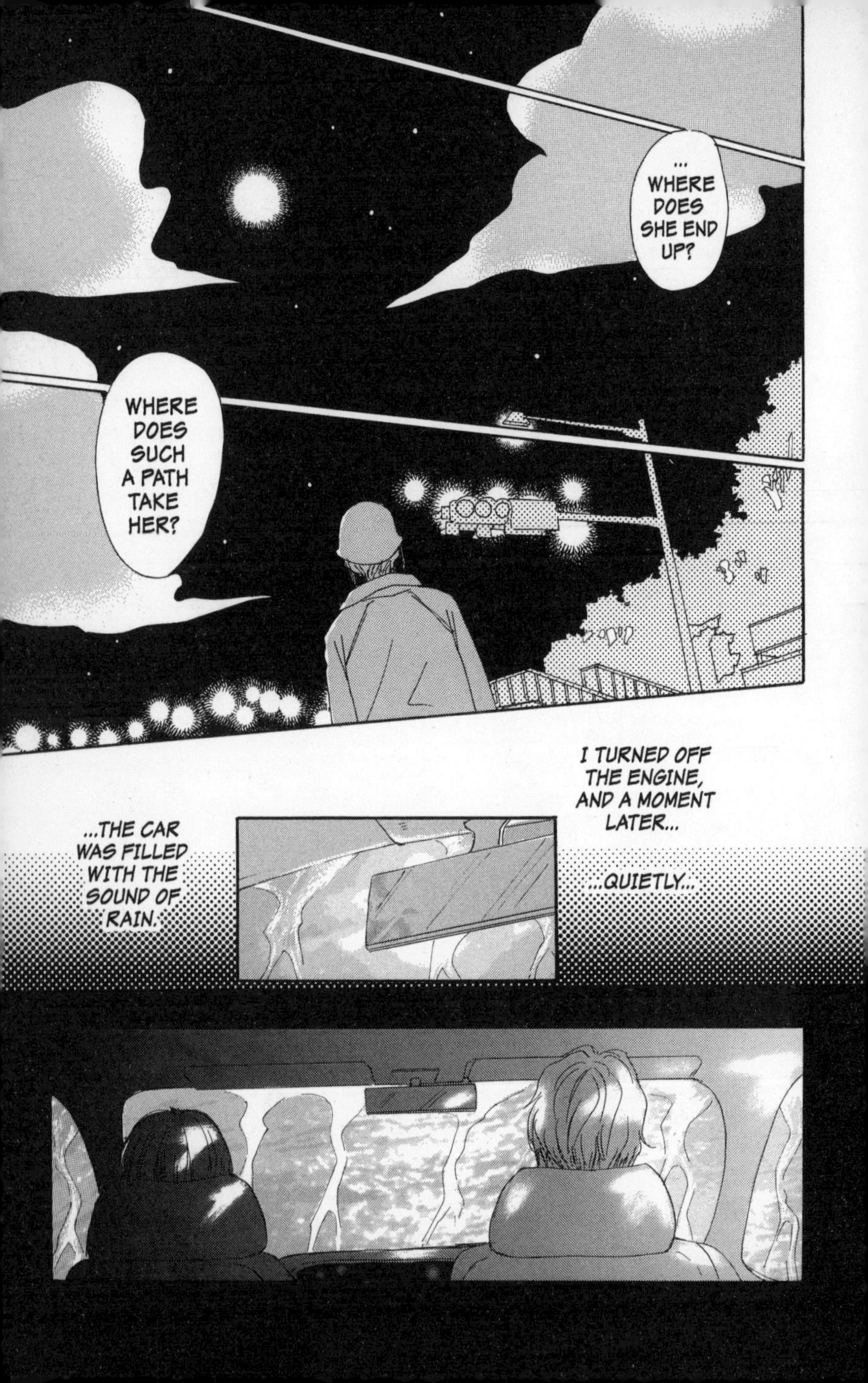
...WHERE DOES SHE END UP?
WHERE DOES SUCH A PATH TAKE HER?
I TURNED OFF THE ENGINE, AND A MOMENT LATER...
...QUIETLY...
...THE CAR WAS FILLED WITH THE SOUND OF RAIN.

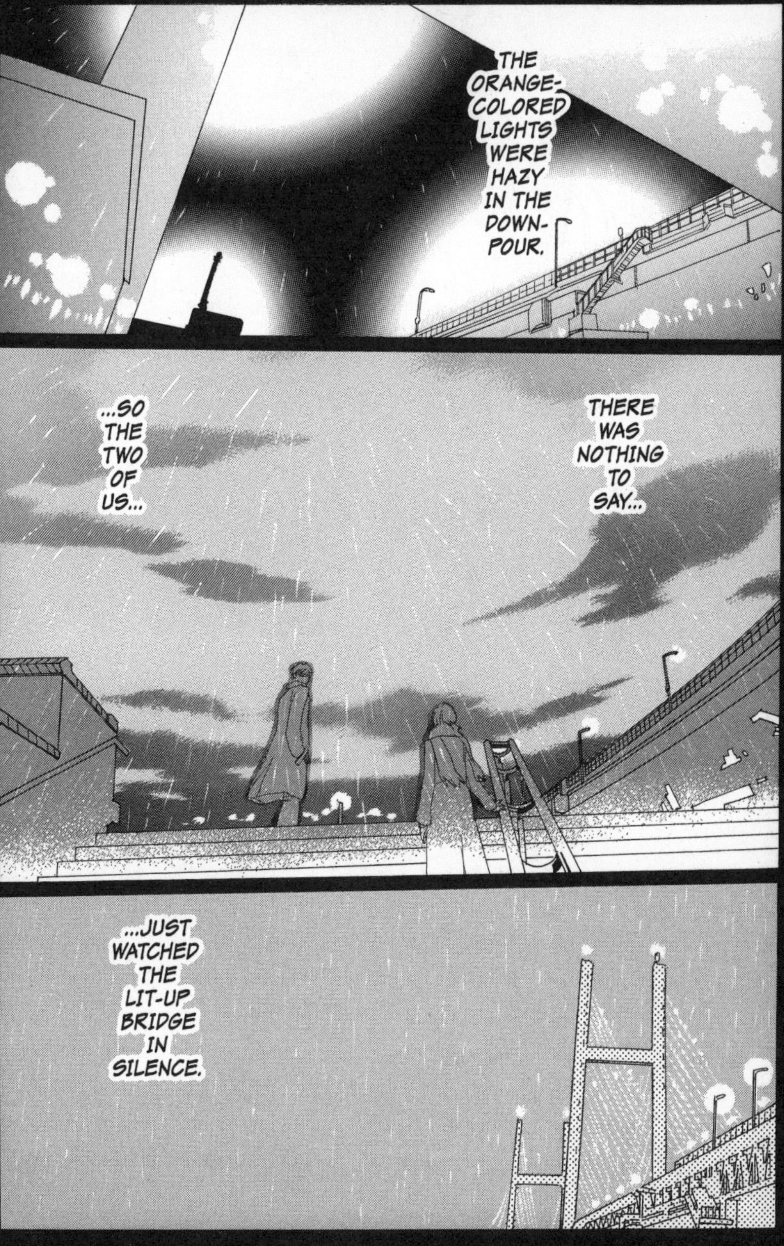
THE ORANGE-COLORED LIGHTS WERE HAZY IN THE DOWN-POUR.
THERE WAS NOTHING TO SAY...
...SO THE TWO OF US...
...JUST WATCHED THE LIT-UP BRIDGE IN SILENCE.

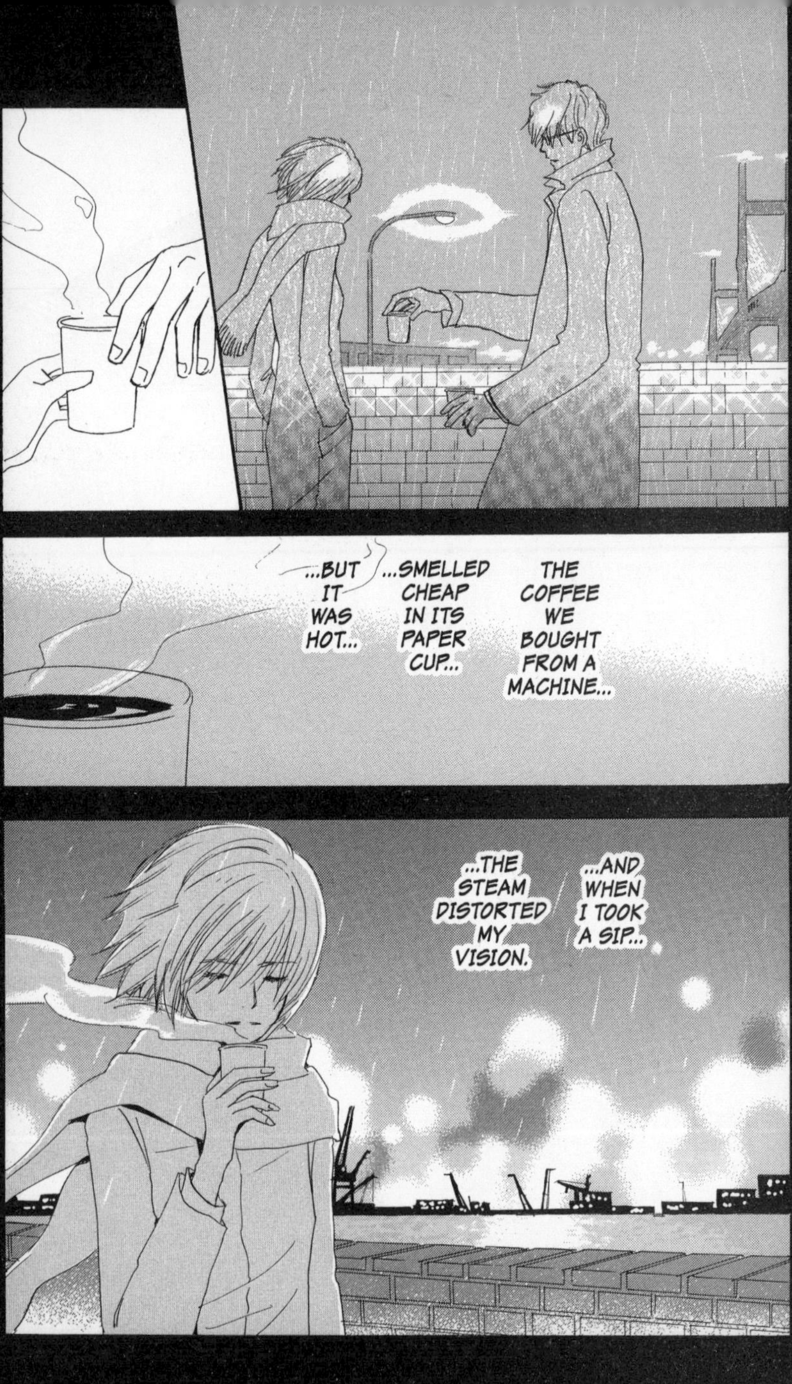
THE COFFEE WE BOUGHT FROM A MACHINE...
...SMELLED CHEAP IN ITS PAPER CUP...
...BUT IT WAS HOT...
...AND WHEN I TOOK A SIP...
...THE STEAM DISTORTED MY VISION.

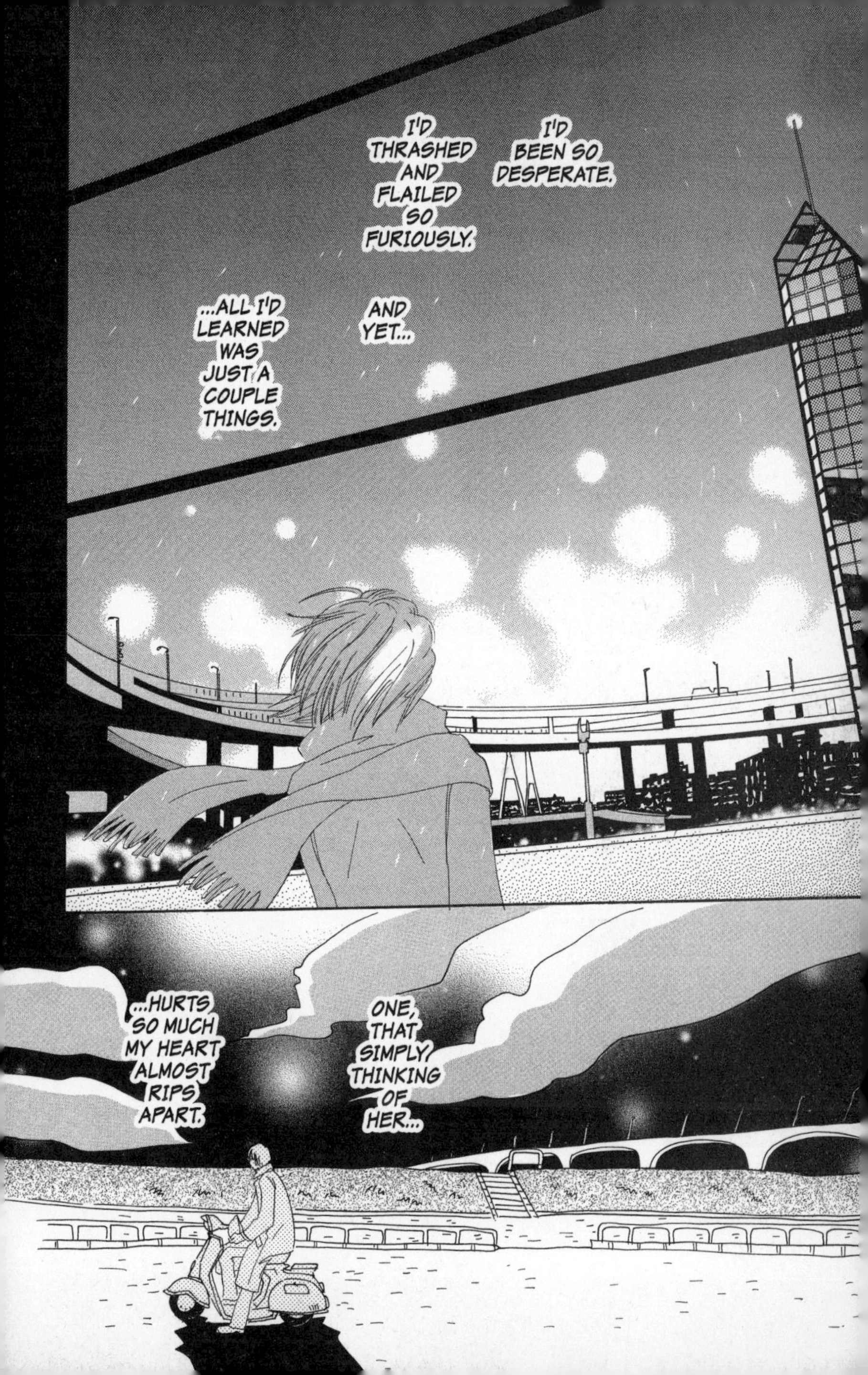
I'D BEEN SO DESPERATE.
I'D THRASHED AND FLAILED SO FURIOUSLY.
AND YET...
...ALL I'D LEARNED WAS JUST A COUPLE THINGS.
ONE, THAT SIMPLY THINKING OF HER...
...HURTS SO MUCH MY HEART ALMOST RIPS APART.

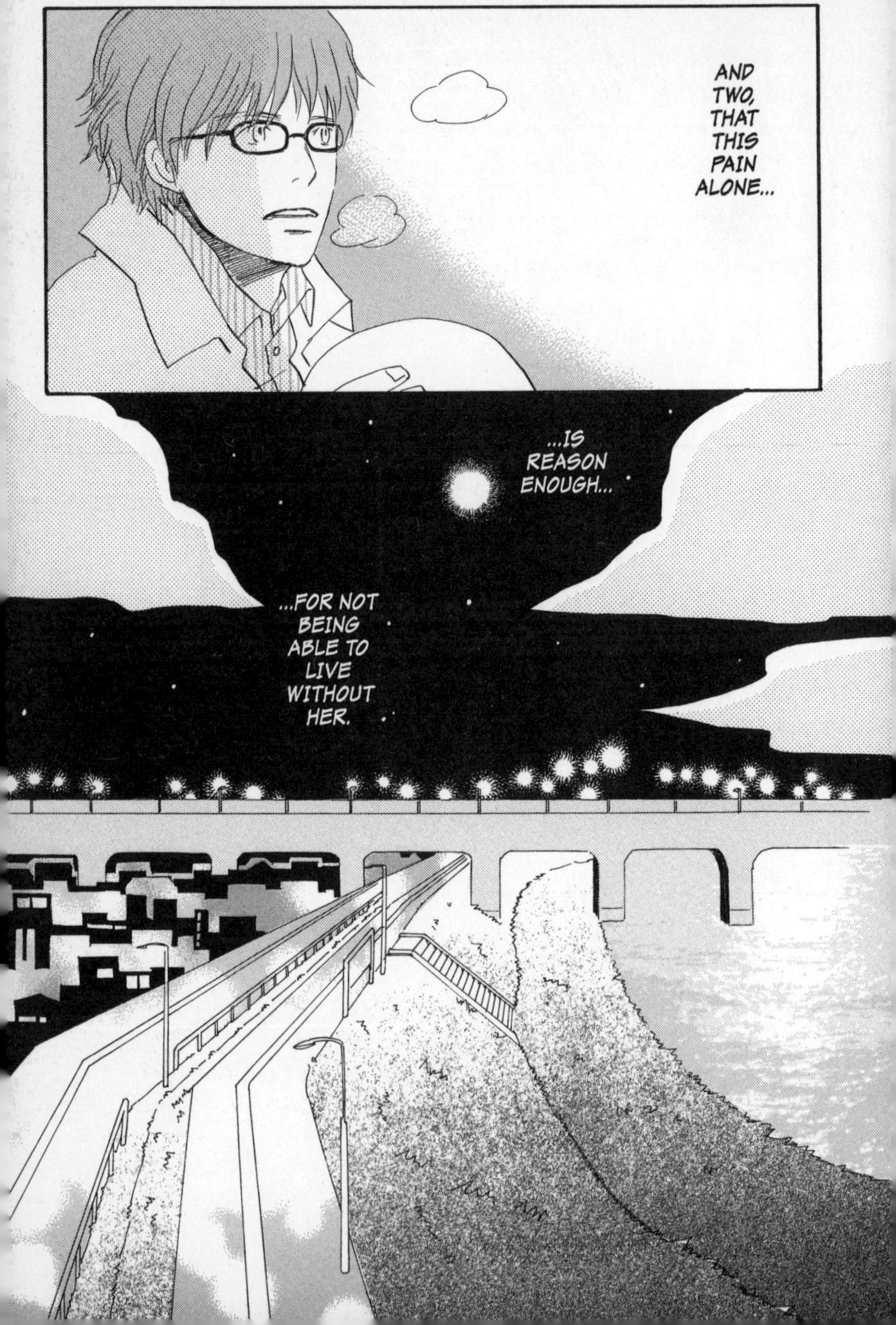
AND TWO, THAT THIS PAIN ALONE...
...IS REASON ENOUGH...
...FOR NOT BEING ABLE TO LIVE WITHOUT HER.

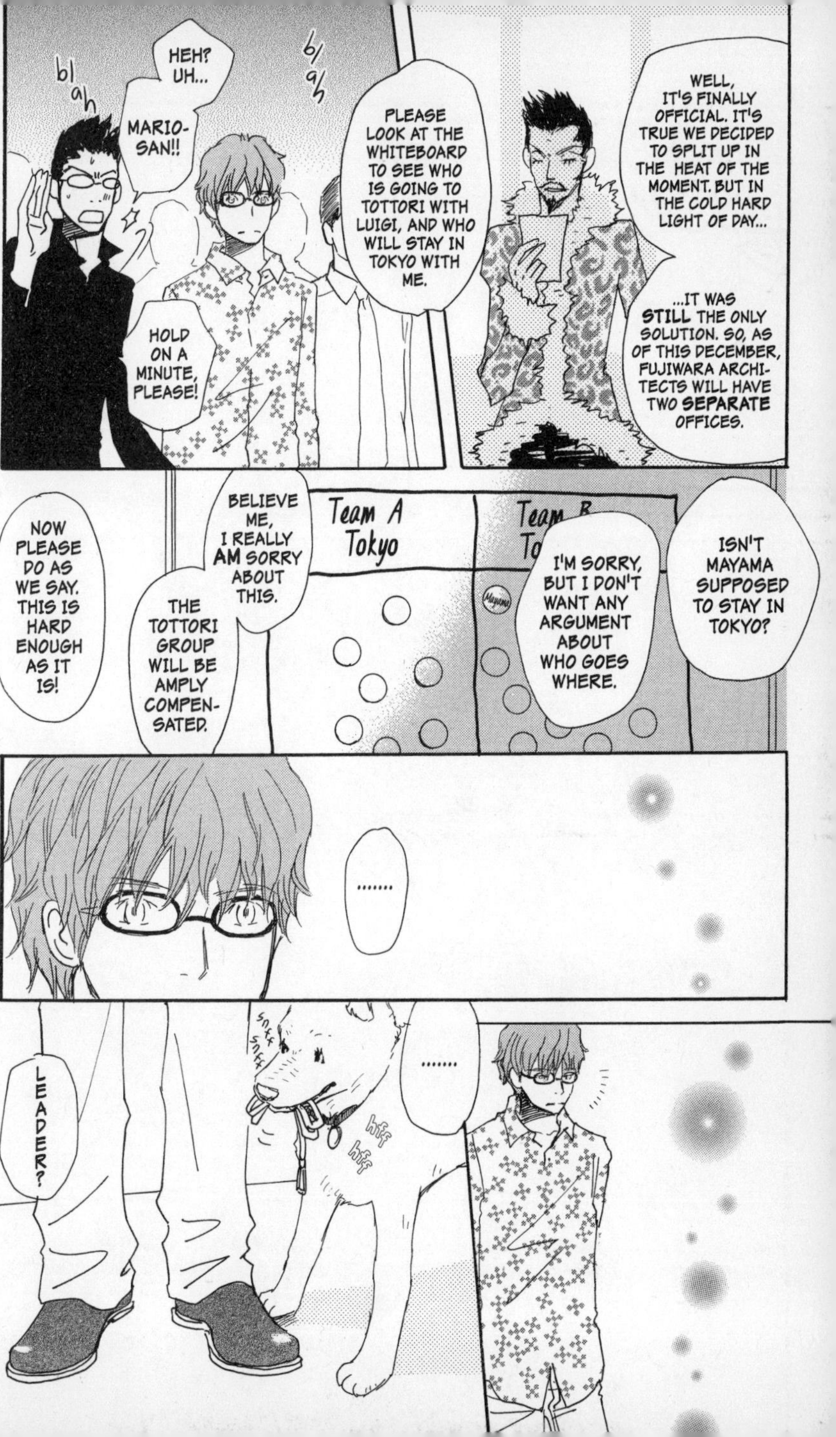

WELL, IT'S FINALLY OFFICIAL. IT'S TRUE WE DECIDED TO SPLIT UP IN THE HEAT OF THE MOMENT. BUT IN THE COLD HARD LIGHT OF DAY...
...IT WAS STILL THE ONLY SOLUTION. SO, AS OF THIS DECEMBER, FUJIWARA ARCHITECTS WILL HAVE TWO SEPARATE OFFICES.
PLEASE LOOK AT THE WHITEBOARD TO SEE WHO IS GOING TO TOTTORI WITH LUIGI, AND WHO WILL STAY IN TOKYO WITH ME.
blah
blah
HEH? UH...
MARIO-SAN!!
HOLD ON A MINUTE, PLEASE!
ISN'T MAYAMA SUPPOSED TO STAY IN TOKYO?
I'M SORRY, BUT I DON'T WANT ANY ARGUMENT ABOUT WHO GOES WHERE.
Team A Tokyo
Mayama
BELIEVE ME, I REALLY AM SORRY ABOUT THIS.
THE TOTTORI GROUP WILL BE AMPLY COMPENSATED.
NOW PLEASE DO AS WE SAY. THIS IS HARD ENOUGH AS IT IS!
....
....
sniff sniff
hff hff
LEADER?

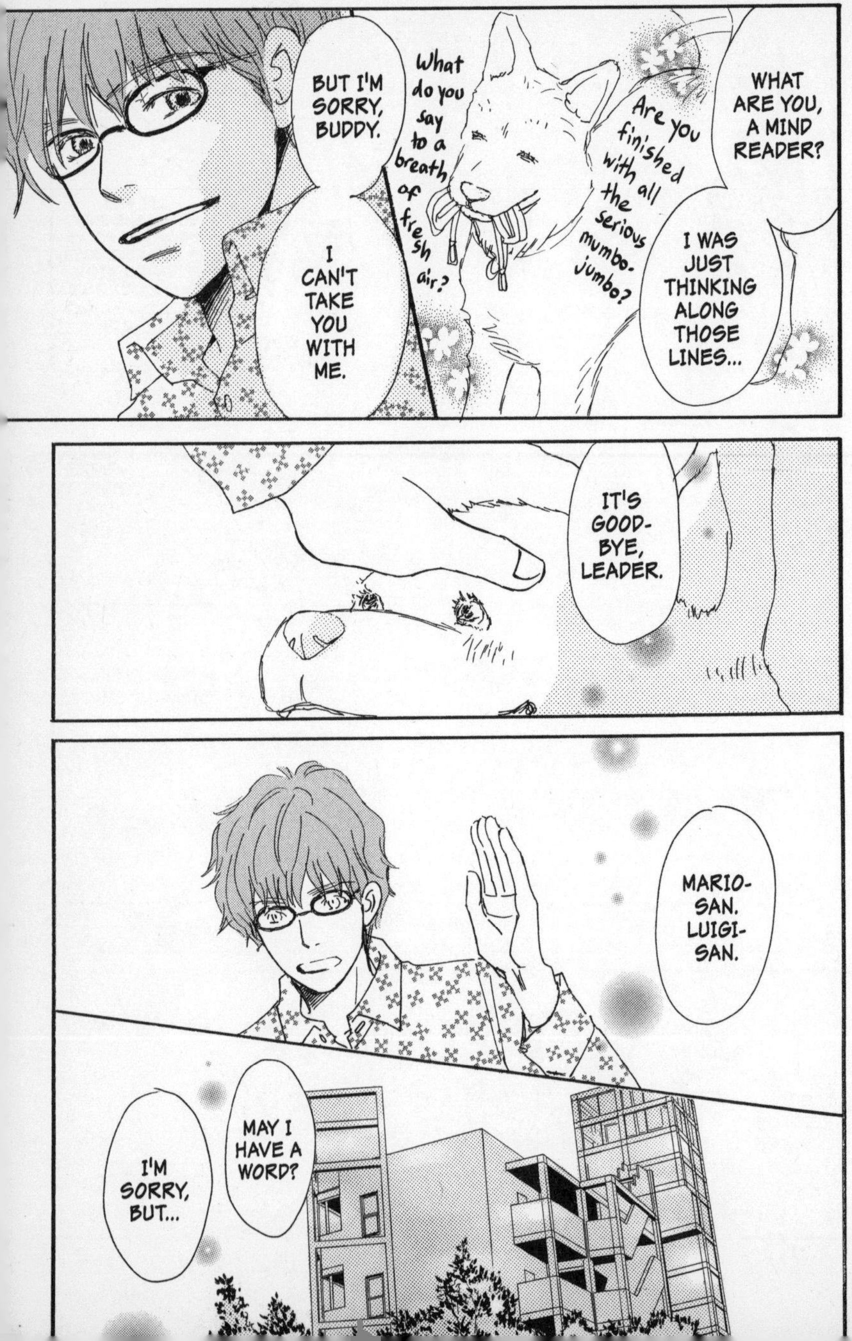
Are you finished with all the serious mumbo-jumbo?
What do you say to a breath of fresh air?
WHAT ARE YOU, A MIND READER?
I WAS JUST THINKING ALONG THOSE LINES...
BUT I'M SORRY, BUDDY.
I CAN'T TAKE YOU WITH ME.
IT'S GOOD-BYE, LEADER.
MARIO-SAN. LUIGI-SAN.
MAY I HAVE A WORD?
I'M SORRY, BUT...

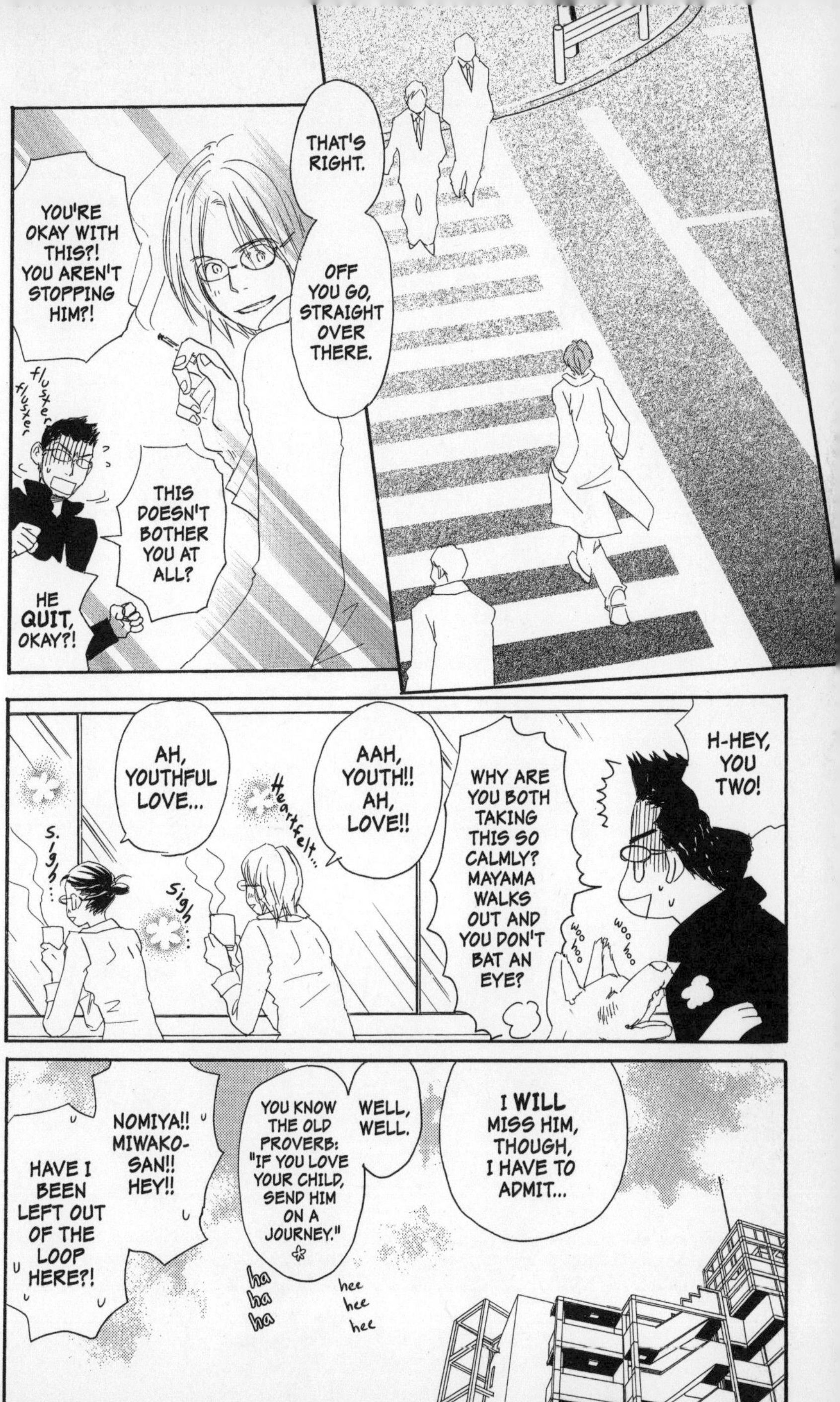
THAT'S RIGHT.
OFF YOU GO, STRAIGHT OVER THERE.
YOU'RE OKAY WITH THIS?! YOU AREN'T STOPPING HIM?!
fluster fluster
THIS DOESN'T BOTHER YOU AT ALL?
HE QUIT, OKAY?!
H-HEY, YOU TWO!
WHY ARE YOU BOTH TAKING THIS SO CALMLY? MAYAMA WALKS OUT AND YOU DON'T BAT AN EYE?
woo hoo
woo hoo
AAH, YOUTH!! AH, LOVE!!
Heartfelt...
AH, YOUTHFUL LOVE...
sigh...
s.igh...
I WILL MISS HIM, THOUGH, I HAVE TO ADMIT...
WELL, WELL.
YOU KNOW THE OLD PROVERB: "IF YOU LOVE YOUR CHILD, SEND HIM ON A JOURNEY."
hee hee hee
ha ha ha
NOMIYA!! MIWAKO-SAN!! HEY!!
HAVE I BEEN LEFT OUT OF THE LOOP HERE?!

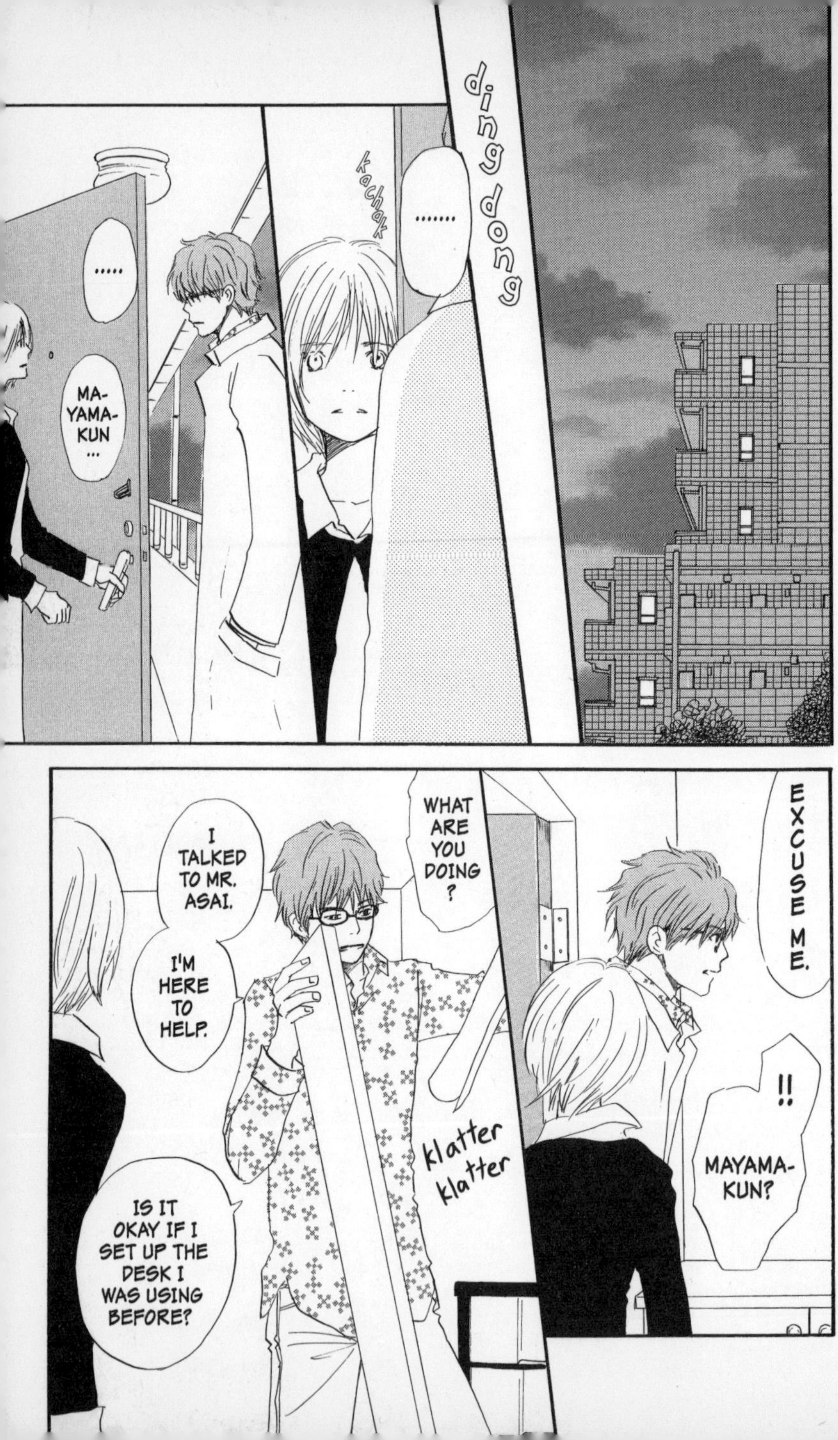
ding dong
kachak
....
......
MA-YAMA-KUN ...
EXCUSE ME.
!!
MAYAMA-KUN?
WHAT ARE YOU DOING?
klatter klatter
I TALKED TO MR. ASAI.
I'M HERE TO HELP.
IS IT OKAY IF I SET UP THE DESK I WAS USING BEFORE?

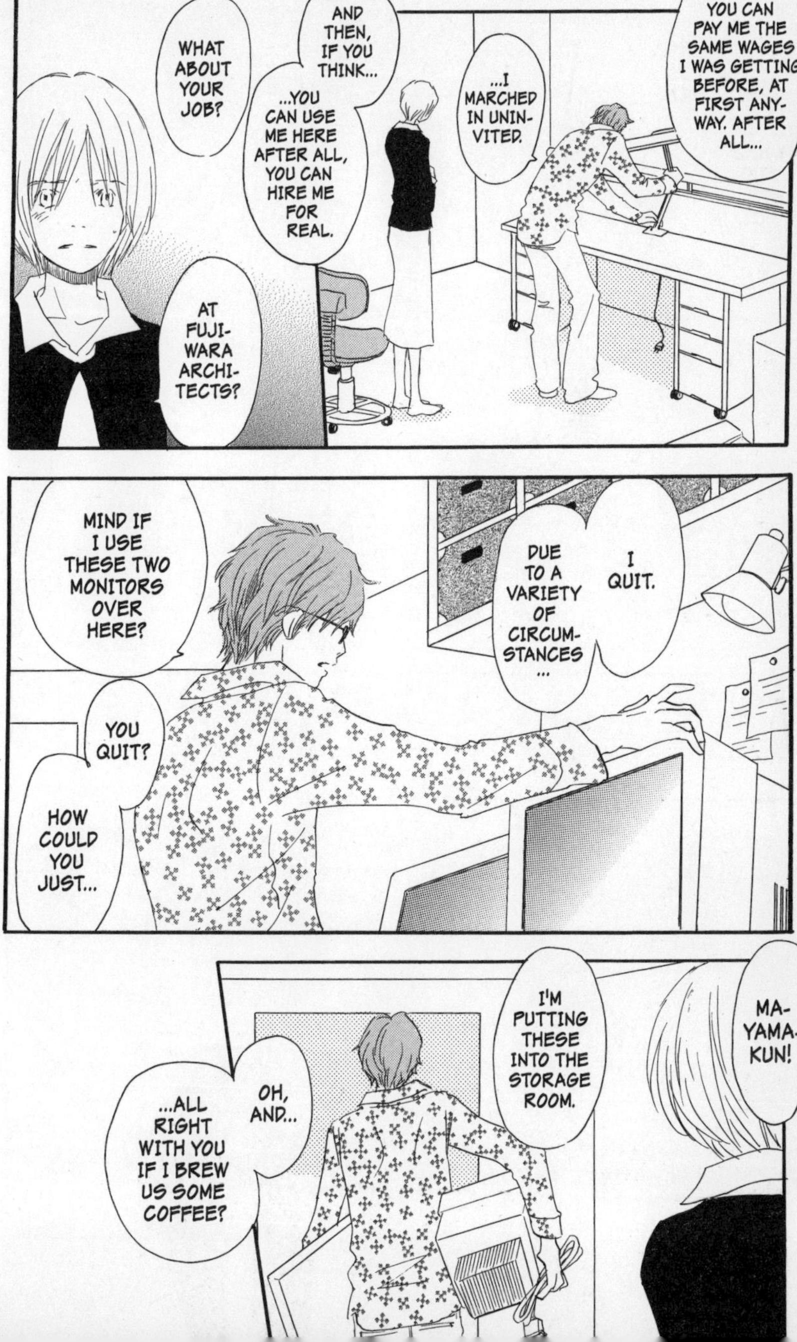
YOU CAN PAY ME THE SAME WAGES I WAS GETTING BEFORE, AT FIRST ANYWAY. AFTER ALL...
...I MARCHED IN UNINVITED.
AND THEN, IF YOU THINK...
...YOU CAN USE ME HERE AFTER ALL, YOU CAN HIRE ME FOR REAL.
WHAT ABOUT YOUR JOB?
AT FUJIWARA ARCHITECTS?
I QUIT.
DUE TO A VARIETY OF CIRCUMSTANCES...
MIND IF I USE THESE TWO MONITORS OVER HERE?
YOU QUIT?
HOW COULD YOU JUST...
MAYAMA-KUN!
I'M PUTTING THESE INTO THE STORAGE ROOM.
OH, AND...
...ALL RIGHT WITH YOU IF I BREW US SOME COFFEE?

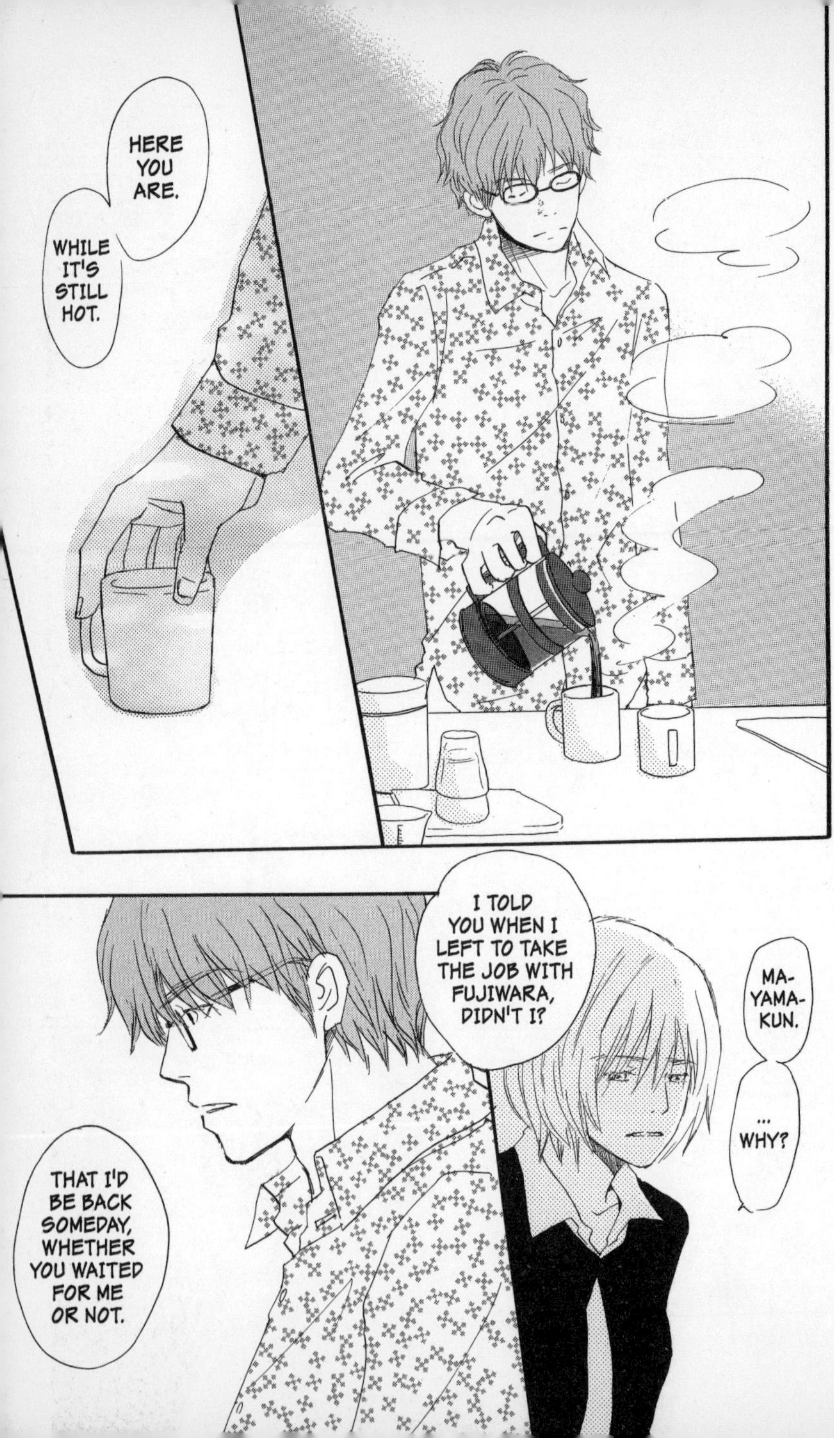
HERE YOU ARE.
WHILE IT'S STILL HOT.
MA-YAMA-KUN.
... WHY?
I TOLD YOU WHEN I LEFT TO TAKE THE JOB WITH FUJIWARA, DIDN'T I?
THAT I'D BE BACK SOMEDAY, WHETHER YOU WAITED FOR ME OR NOT.

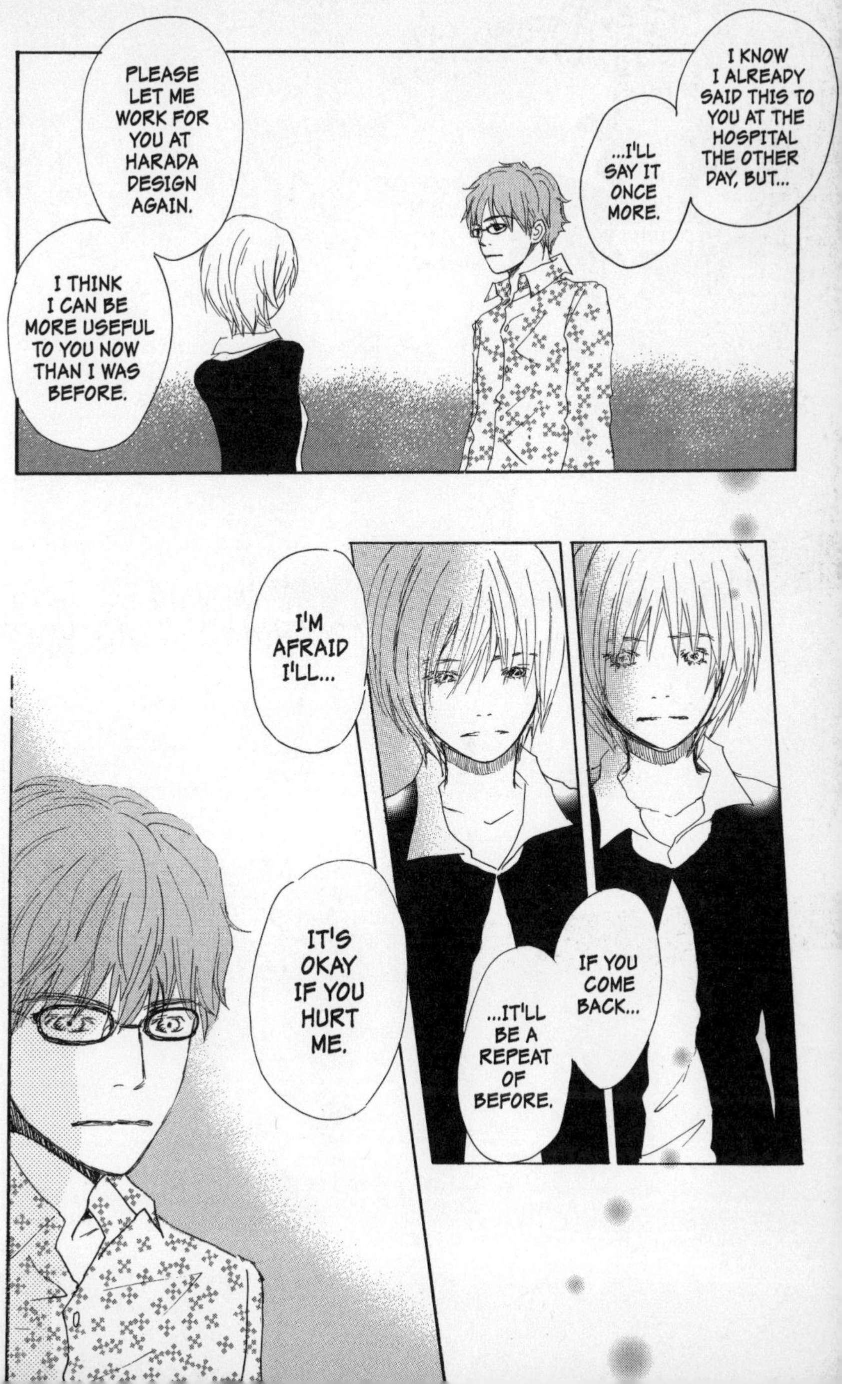
I KNOW I ALREADY SAID THIS TO YOU AT THE HOSPITAL THE OTHER DAY, BUT...
...I'LL SAY IT ONCE MORE.
PLEASE LET ME WORK FOR YOU AT HARADA DESIGN AGAIN.
I THINK I CAN BE MORE USEFUL TO YOU NOW THAN I WAS BEFORE.
I'M AFRAID I'LL...
IF YOU COME BACK...
...IT'LL BE A REPEAT OF BEFORE.
IT'S OKAY IF YOU HURT ME.

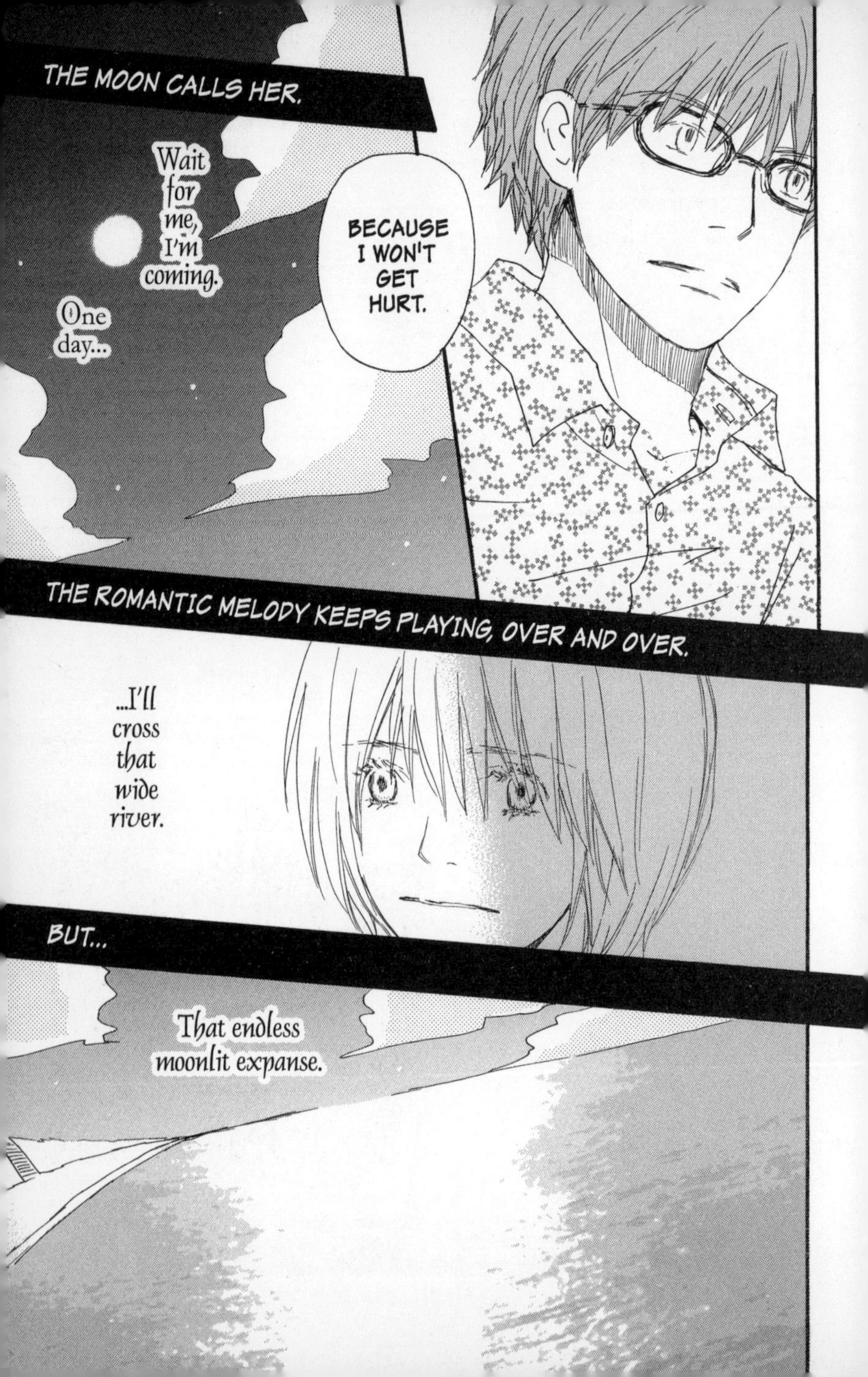
THE MOON CALLS HER.
BECAUSE I WON'T GET HURT.
Wait for me, I'm coming.
One day...
THE ROMANTIC MELODY KEEPS PLAYING, OVER AND OVER.
...I'll cross that wide river.
BUT...
That endless moonlit expanse.

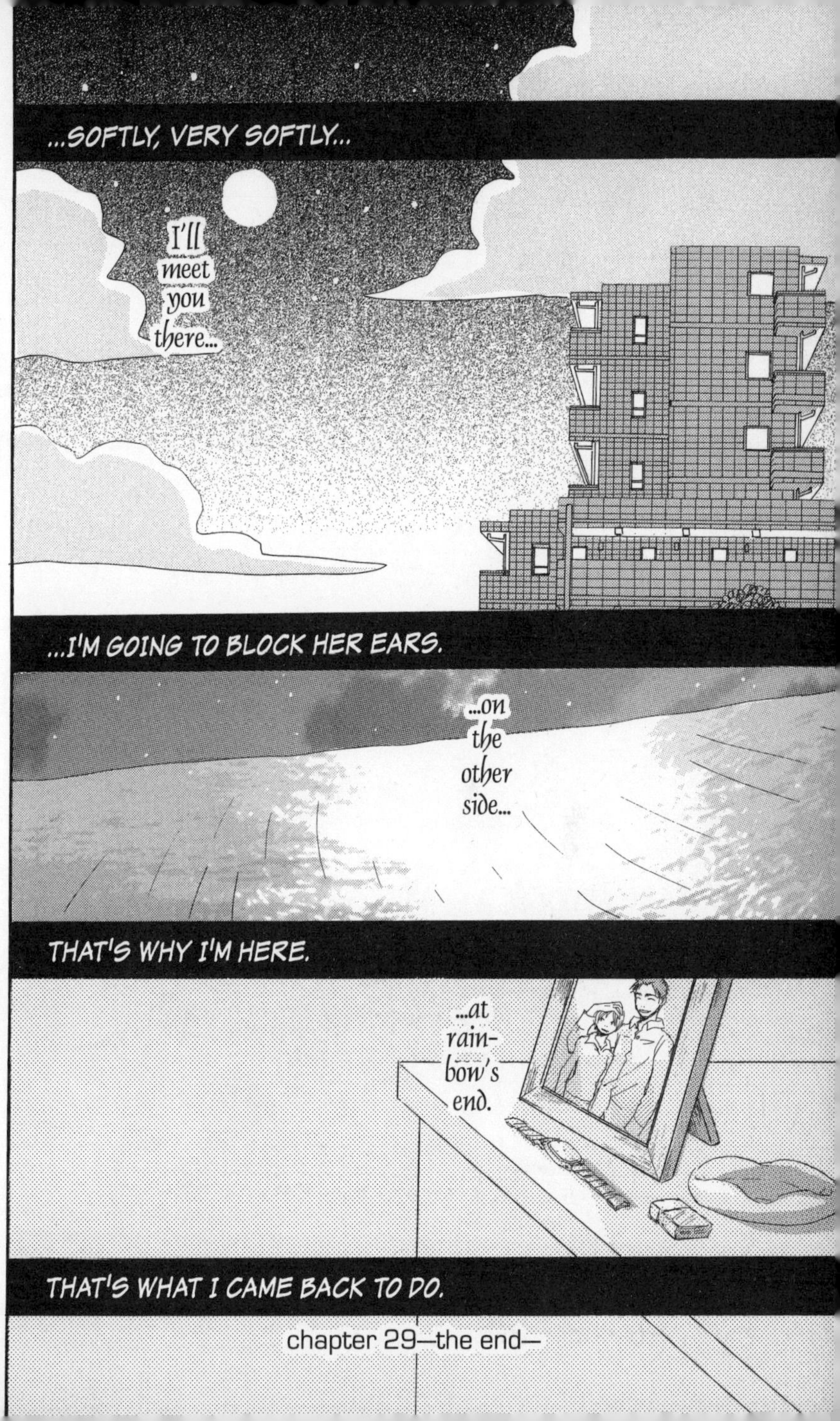
...SOFTLY, VERY SOFTLY...
I'll meet you there...
...I'M GOING TO BLOCK HER EARS.
...on the other side...
THAT'S WHY I'M HERE.
...at rainbow's end.
THAT'S WHAT I CAME BACK TO DO.
chapter 29—the end—

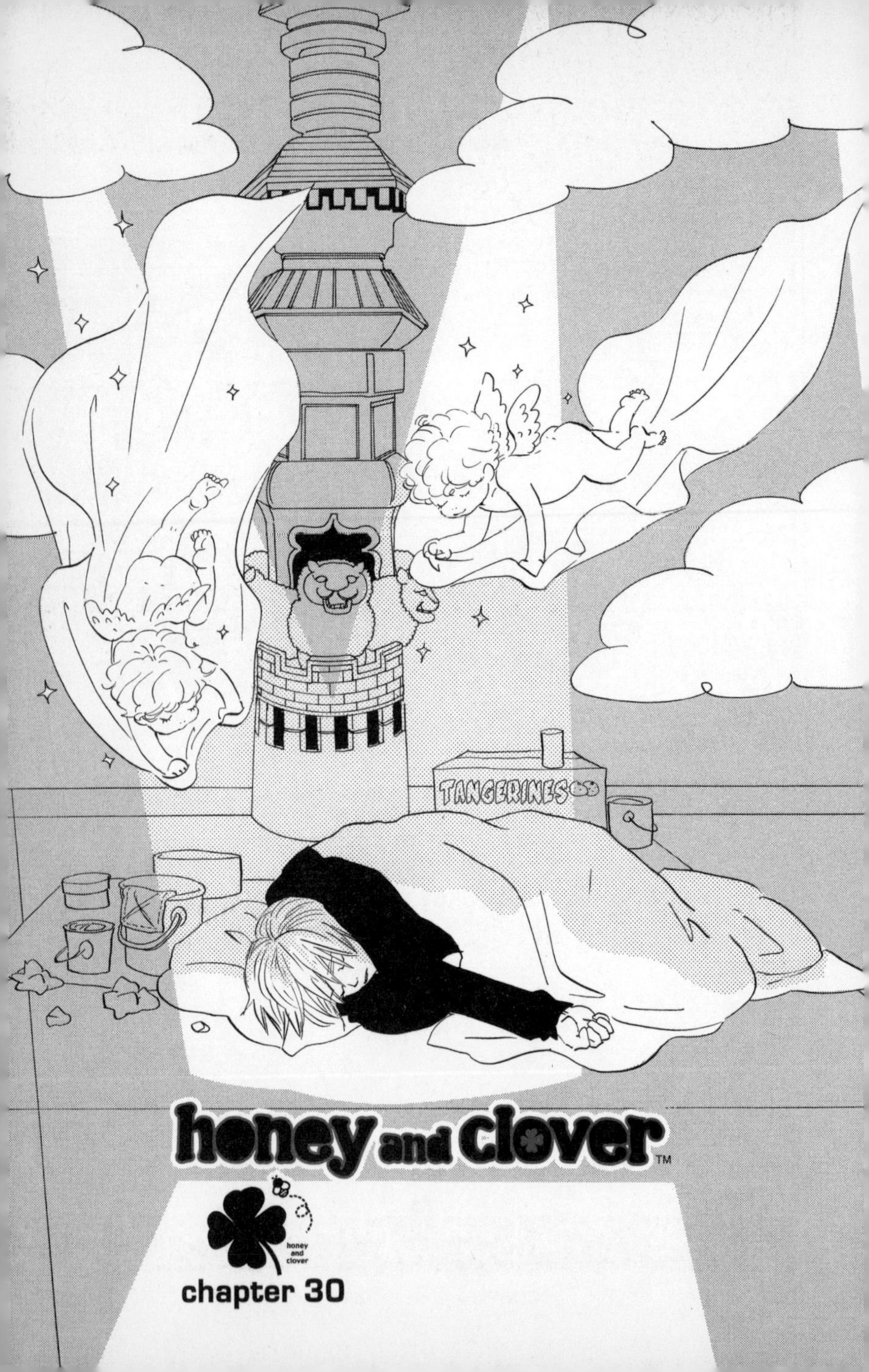
TANGERINES

honey and clover™

chapter 30

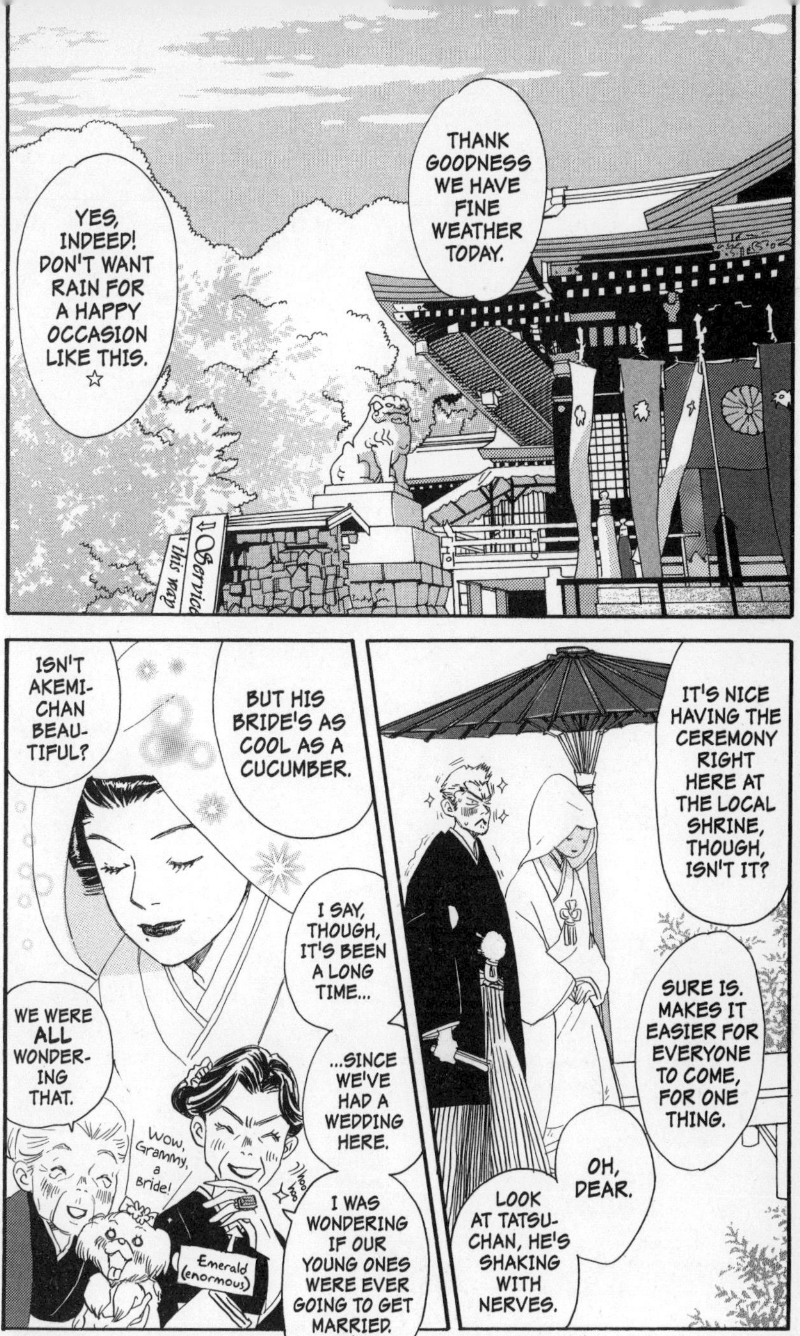
THANK GOODNESS WE HAVE FINE WEATHER TODAY.
YES, INDEED! DON'T WANT RAIN FOR A HAPPY OCCASION LIKE THIS. ☆
this way
IT'S NICE HAVING THE CEREMONY RIGHT HERE AT THE LOCAL SHRINE, THOUGH, ISN'T IT?
SURE IS. MAKES IT EASIER FOR EVERYONE TO COME, FOR ONE THING.
OH, DEAR.
LOOK AT TATSU-CHAN, HE'S SHAKING WITH NERVES.
BUT HIS BRIDE'S AS COOL AS A CUCUMBER.
ISN'T AKEMI-CHAN BEAU-TIFUL?
I SAY, THOUGH, IT'S BEEN A LONG TIME...
...SINCE WE'VE HAD A WEDDING HERE.
WE WERE ALL WONDER-ING THAT.
I WAS WONDERING IF OUR YOUNG ONES WERE EVER GOING TO GET MARRIED. ☆
Wow, Grammy, a Bride!
Emerald (enormous)

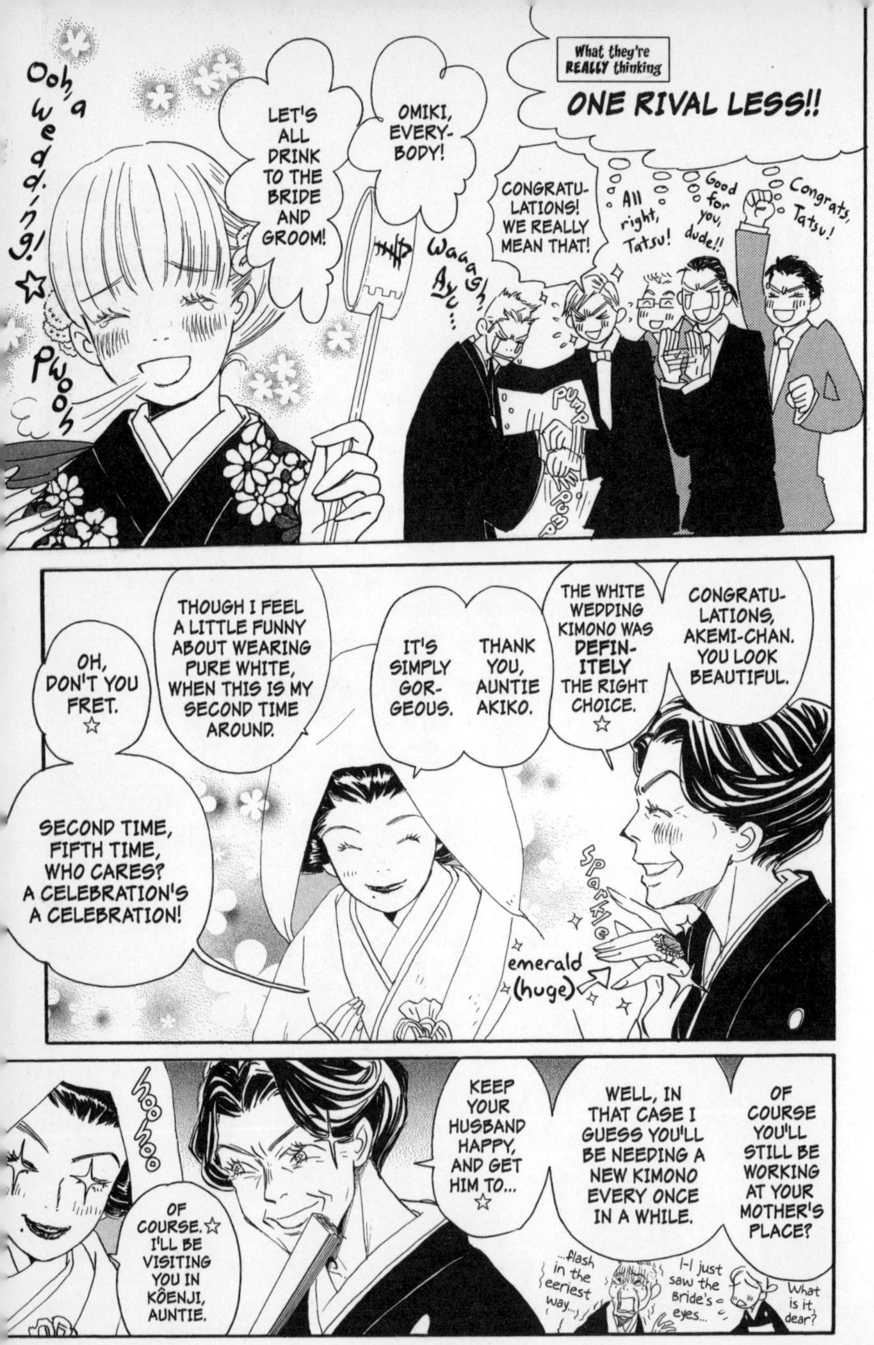
What they're REALLY thinking
ONE RIVAL LESS!!
Congrats, Tatsu!
Good for you, dude!!
All right, Tatsu!
CONGRATULATIONS! WE REALLY MEAN THAT!
Waaagh
Ayu...
pump
pump
OMIKI, EVERYBODY!
LET'S ALL DRINK TO THE BRIDE AND GROOM!
Ooh, a wedding! ☆
Pwooh
CONGRATULATIONS, AKEMI-CHAN. YOU LOOK BEAUTIFUL.
THE WHITE WEDDING KIMONO WAS DEFINITELY THE RIGHT CHOICE. ☆
THANK YOU, AUNTIE AKIKO.
IT'S SIMPLY GORGEOUS.
THOUGH I FEEL A LITTLE FUNNY ABOUT WEARING PURE WHITE, WHEN THIS IS MY SECOND TIME AROUND.
OH, DON'T YOU FRET. ☆
SECOND TIME, FIFTH TIME, WHO CARES? A CELEBRATION'S A CELEBRATION!
Sparkle
emerald (huge)
OF COURSE YOU'LL STILL BE WORKING AT YOUR MOTHER'S PLACE?
WELL, IN THAT CASE I GUESS YOU'LL BE NEEDING A NEW KIMONO EVERY ONCE IN A WHILE.
KEEP YOUR HUSBAND HAPPY, AND GET HIM TO... ☆
What is it, dear?
I-I just saw the bride's eyes...
...flash in the eeriest way...
hoo hoo
OF COURSE. ☆ I'LL BE VISITING YOU IN KÔENJI, AUNTIE.

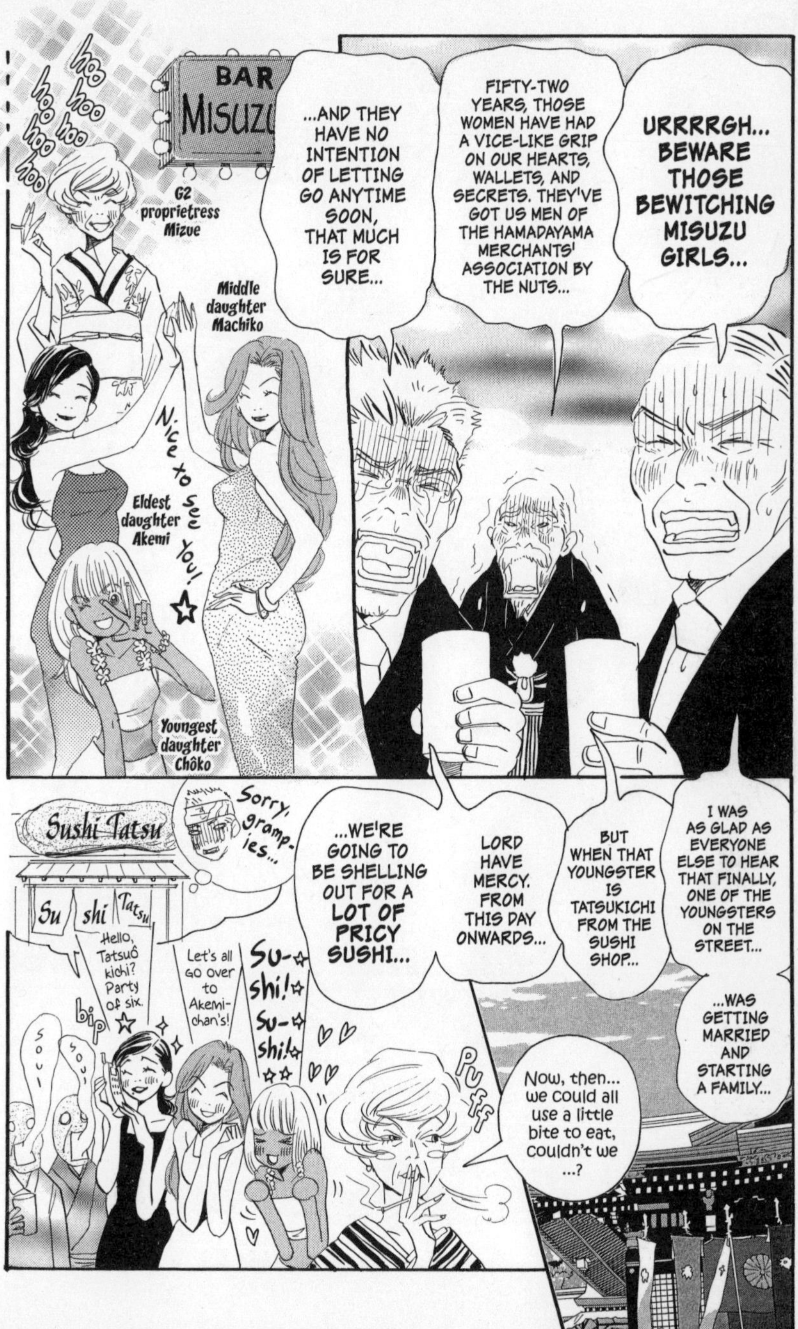
URRRRGH... BEWARE THOSE BEWITCHING MISUZU GIRLS...
FIFTY-TWO YEARS, THOSE WOMEN HAVE HAD A VICE-LIKE GRIP ON OUR HEARTS, WALLETS, AND SECRETS. THEY'VE GOT US MEN OF THE HAMADAYAMA MERCHANTS' ASSOCIATION BY THE NUTS...
...AND THEY HAVE NO INTENTION OF LETTING GO ANYTIME SOON, THAT MUCH IS FOR SURE...
BAR MISUZU
hoo hoo hoo hoo hoo hoo
G2 proprietress Mizue
Middle daughter Machiko
Nice to see you! ☆
Eldest daughter Akemi
Youngest daughter Chôko
I WAS AS GLAD AS EVERYONE ELSE TO HEAR THAT FINALLY, ONE OF THE YOUNGSTERS ON THE STREET...
...WAS GETTING MARRIED AND STARTING A FAMILY...
BUT WHEN THAT YOUNGSTER IS TATSUKICHI FROM THE SUSHI SHOP...
LORD HAVE MERCY. FROM THIS DAY ONWARDS...
...WE'RE GOING TO BE SHELLING OUT FOR A LOT OF PRICY SUSHI...
Now, then... we could all use a little bite to eat, couldn't we ...?
Puff
Sushi Tatsu
Sorry, gramp-ies...
Su shi Tatsu
Su-☆ shi!☆ Su-☆ shi!☆ ☆☆
Let's all go over to Akemi-chan's!
Hello, Tatsukichi? Party of six.
bip ☆
sou sou

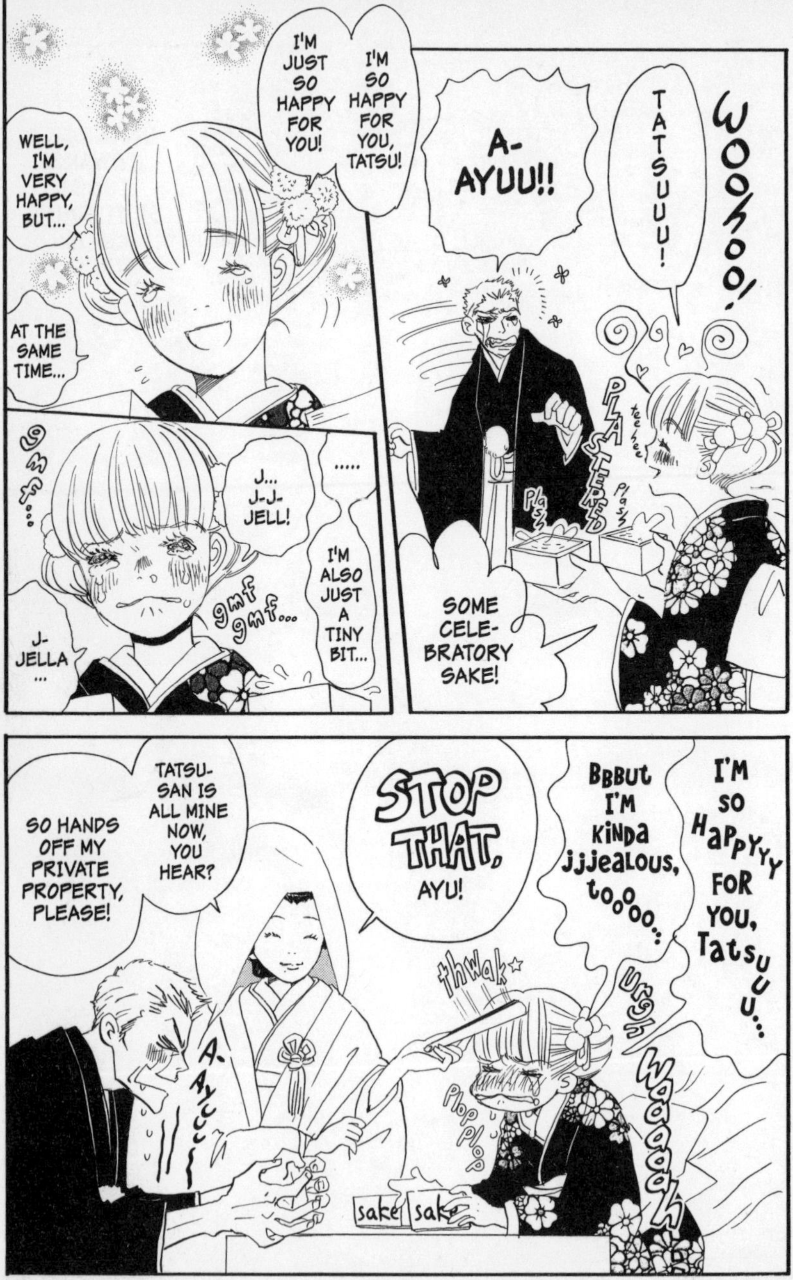
WOOHOO!
TATSUUU!
A-AYUU!!
PLASTERED
tee hee
Plash
Plash
SOME CELEBRATORY SAKE!
I'M SO HAPPY FOR YOU, TATSU!
I'M JUST SO HAPPY FOR YOU!
WELL, I'M VERY HAPPY, BUT...
AT THE SAME TIME...
.....
J... J-J-JELL!
I'M ALSO JUST A TINY BIT...
gmf gmf...
gmf...
J-JELLA...
I'M SO HAPPYYY FOR YOU, TatsUUU...
BBBut I'M KINDA jjjealous, tooOOO...
urgh
Waaaah
thwak
STOP THAT, AYU!
Plop plop
sake
sake
TATSU-SAN IS ALL MINE NOW, YOU HEAR?
SO HANDS OFF MY PRIVATE PROPERTY, PLEASE!
A-AYUUU

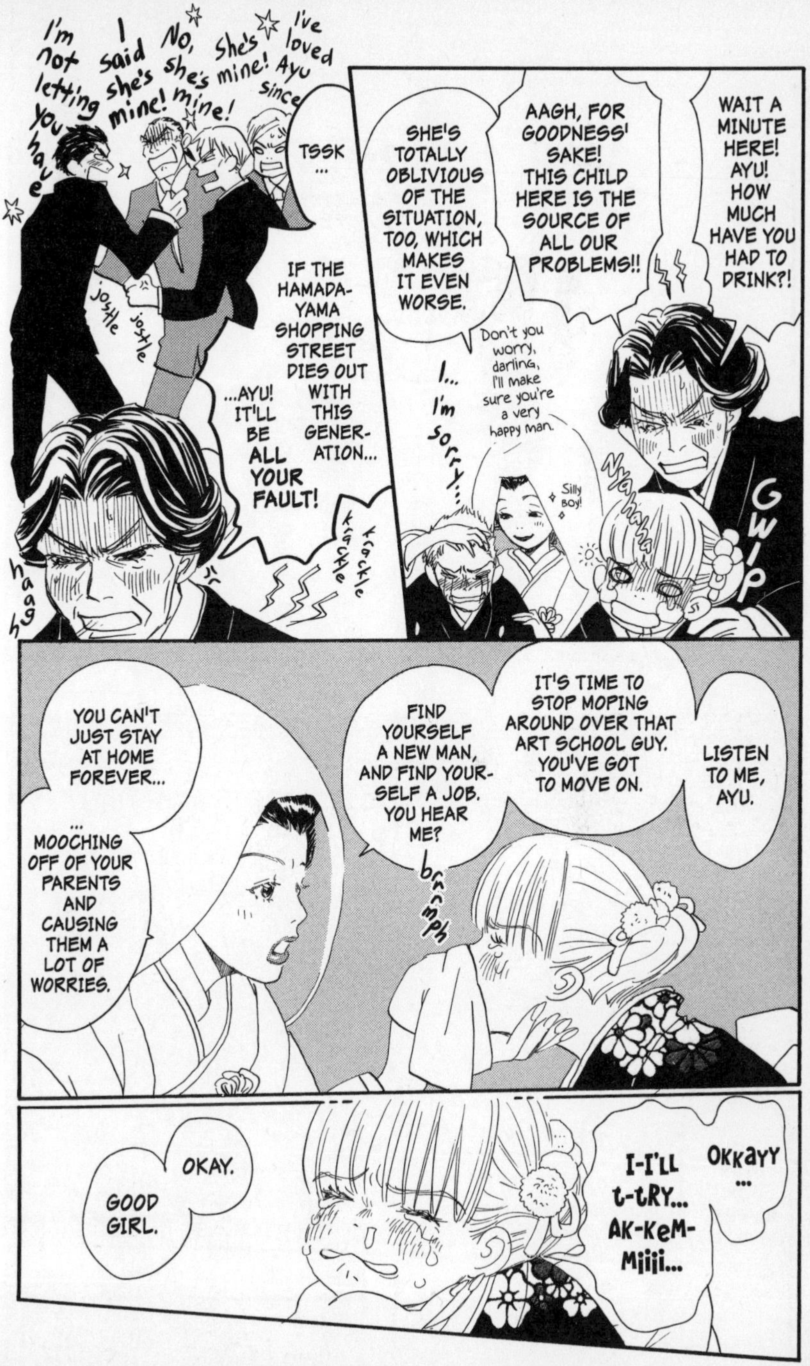
WAIT A MINUTE HERE! AYU! HOW MUCH HAVE YOU HAD TO DRINK?!
AAGH, FOR GOODNESS' SAKE! THIS CHILD HERE IS THE SOURCE OF ALL OUR PROBLEMS!!
SHE'S TOTALLY OBLIVIOUS OF THE SITUATION, TOO, WHICH MAKES IT EVEN WORSE.
GWIP
Nyahaha
Don't you worry, darling, I'll make sure you're a very happy man.
Silly boy!
I... I'm sorry...
TSSK...
I've loved Ayu since
She's mine!
No, she's mine!
I said she's mine!
I'm not letting you have
jostle jostle
IF THE HAMADA-YAMA SHOPPING STREET DIES OUT WITH THIS GENERATION...
...AYU! IT'LL BE ALL YOUR FAULT!
krackle krackle
haagh
LISTEN TO ME, AYU.
IT'S TIME TO STOP MOPING AROUND OVER THAT ART SCHOOL GUY. YOU'VE GOT TO MOVE ON.
FIND YOURSELF A NEW MAN, AND FIND YOURSELF A JOB. YOU HEAR ME?
brrrmph
YOU CAN'T JUST STAY AT HOME FOREVER...
...MOOCHING OFF OF YOUR PARENTS AND CAUSING THEM A LOT OF WORRIES.
OKKAYY...
I-I'LL t-tRY... AK-KeM-Miiii...
OKAY.
GOOD GIRL.

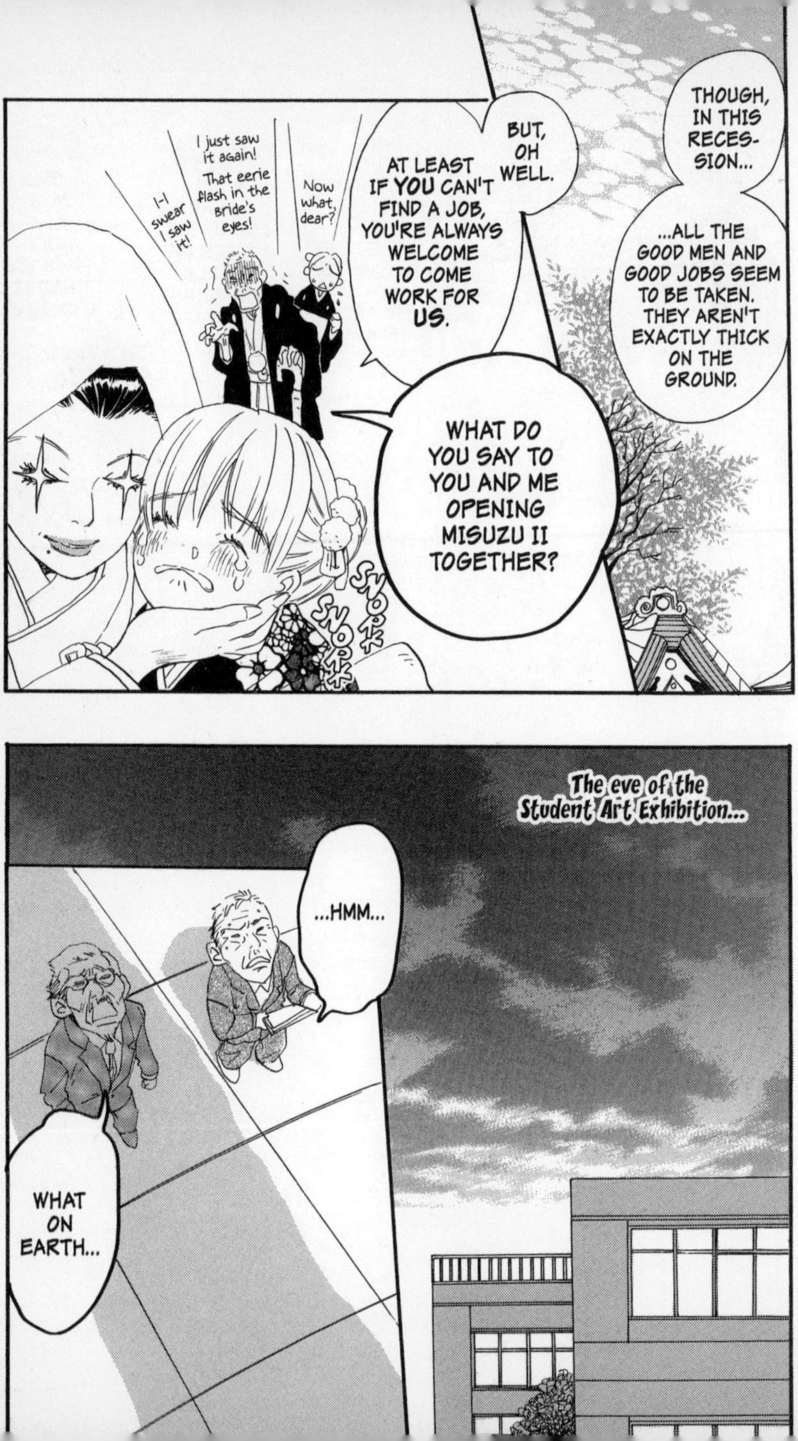
THOUGH, IN THIS RECES-SION...
...ALL THE GOOD MEN AND GOOD JOBS SEEM TO BE TAKEN. THEY AREN'T EXACTLY THICK ON THE GROUND.
BUT, OH WELL.
AT LEAST IF YOU CAN'T FIND A JOB, YOU'RE ALWAYS WELCOME TO COME WORK FOR US.
WHAT DO YOU SAY TO YOU AND ME OPENING MISUZU II TOGETHER?
Now what, dear?
I just saw it again!
That eerie flash in the Bride's eyes!
I-I swear I saw it!
SNORK SNORK
The eve of the Student Art Exhibition...
...HMM...
WHAT ON EARTH...

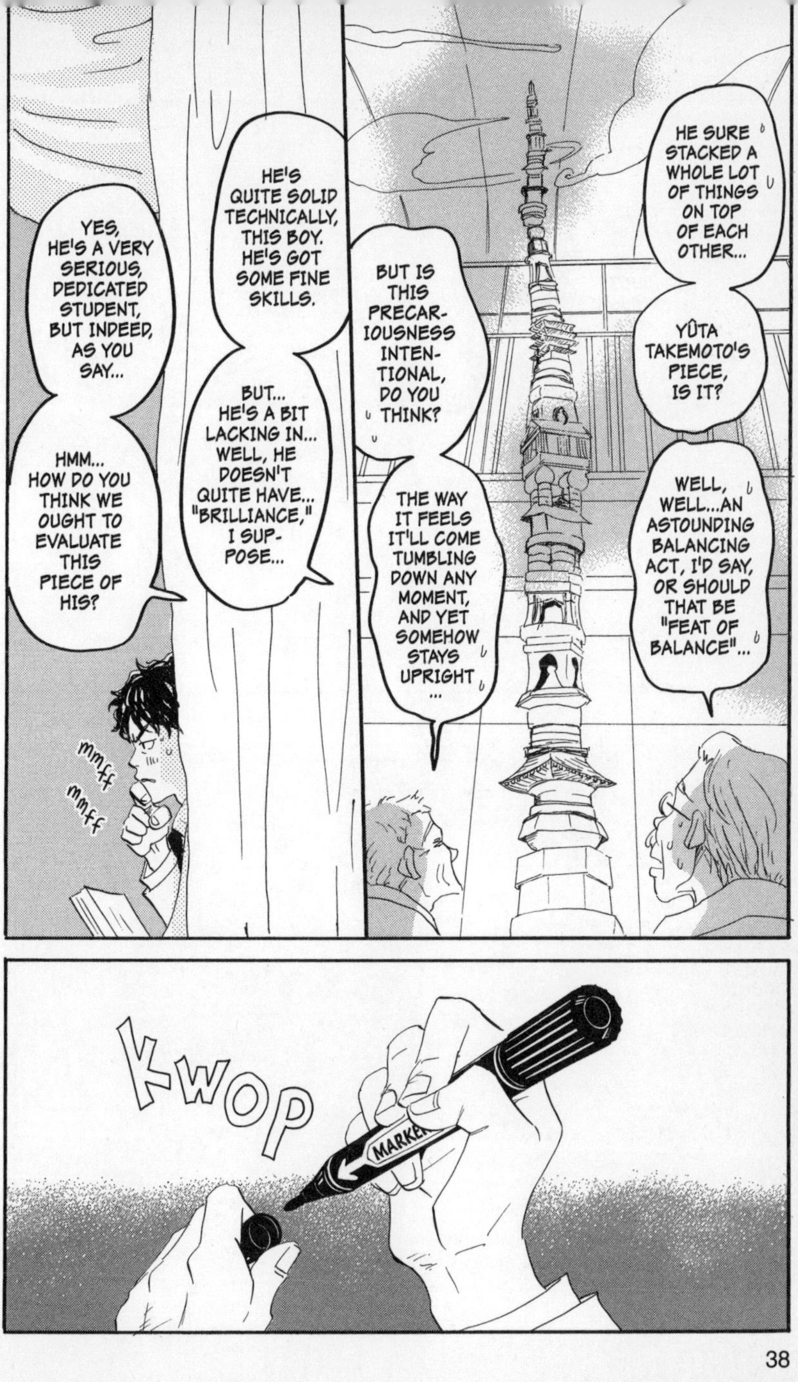
HE SURE STACKED A WHOLE LOT OF THINGS ON TOP OF EACH OTHER...
YÛTA TAKEMOTO'S PIECE, IS IT?
WELL, WELL...AN ASTOUNDING BALANCING ACT, I'D SAY, OR SHOULD THAT BE "FEAT OF BALANCE"...
BUT IS THIS PRECARIOUSNESS INTENTIONAL, DO YOU THINK?
THE WAY IT FEELS IT'LL COME TUMBLING DOWN ANY MOMENT, AND YET SOMEHOW STAYS UPRIGHT...
HE'S QUITE SOLID TECHNICALLY, THIS BOY. HE'S GOT SOME FINE SKILLS.
BUT... HE'S A BIT LACKING IN... WELL, HE DOESN'T QUITE HAVE... "BRILLIANCE," I SUPPOSE...
YES, HE'S A VERY SERIOUS, DEDICATED STUDENT, BUT INDEED, AS YOU SAY...
HMM... HOW DO YOU THINK WE OUGHT TO EVALUATE THIS PIECE OF HIS?
mmff mmff
KWOP
MARKER

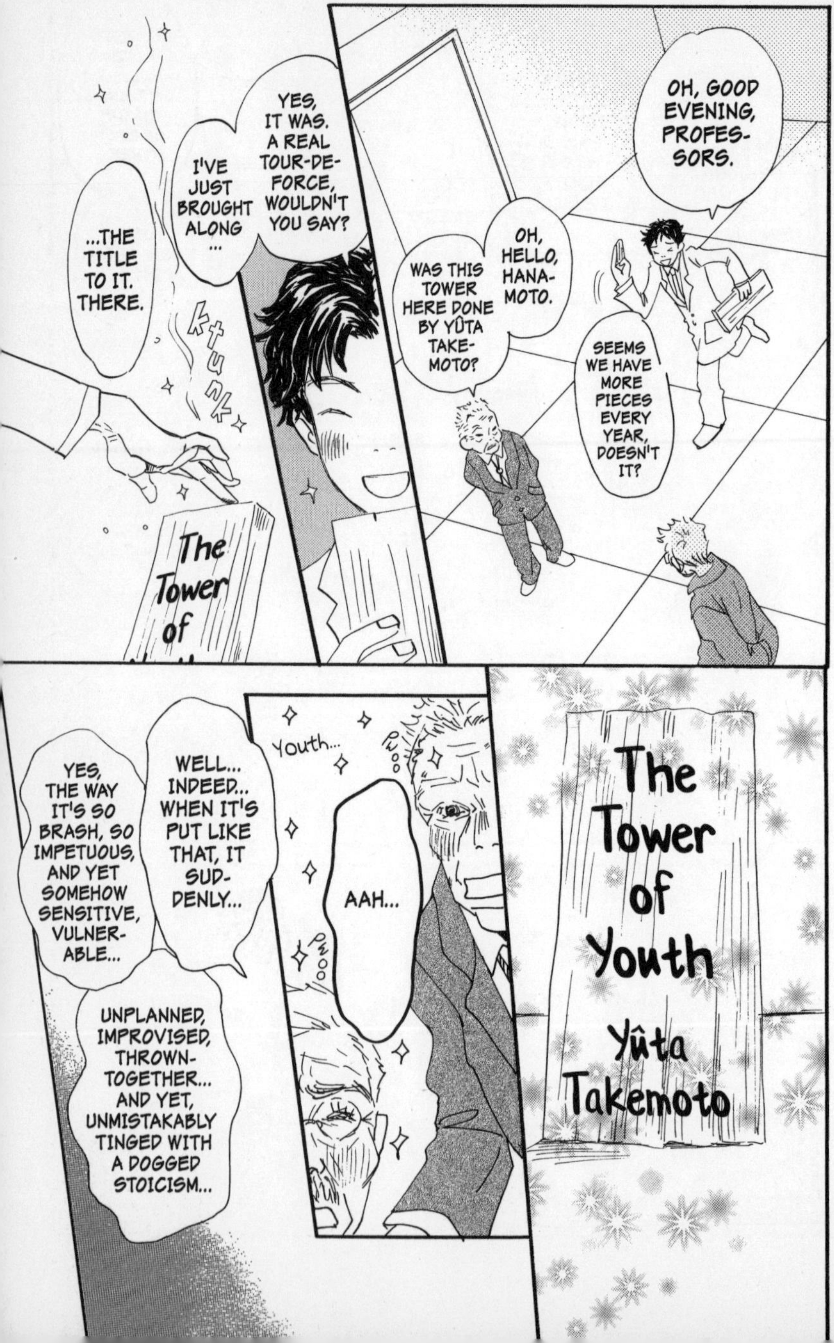
OH, GOOD EVENING, PROFES-SORS.
OH, HELLO, HANA-MOTO.
SEEMS WE HAVE MORE PIECES EVERY YEAR, DOESN'T IT?
WAS THIS TOWER HERE DONE BY YÛTA TAKE-MOTO?
YES, IT WAS. A REAL TOUR-DE-FORCE, WOULDN'T YOU SAY?
I'VE JUST BROUGHT ALONG ...
...THE TITLE TO IT. THERE.
ktunk
The Tower of
The Tower of Youth Yûta Takemoto
Youth...
PWOO
AAH...
PWOO
WELL... INDEED... WHEN IT'S PUT LIKE THAT, IT SUD-DENLY...
YES, THE WAY IT'S SO BRASH, SO IMPETUOUS, AND YET SOMEHOW SENSITIVE, VULNER-ABLE...
UNPLANNED, IMPROVISED, THROWN-TOGETHER... AND YET, UNMISTAKABLY TINGED WITH A DOGGED STOICISM...

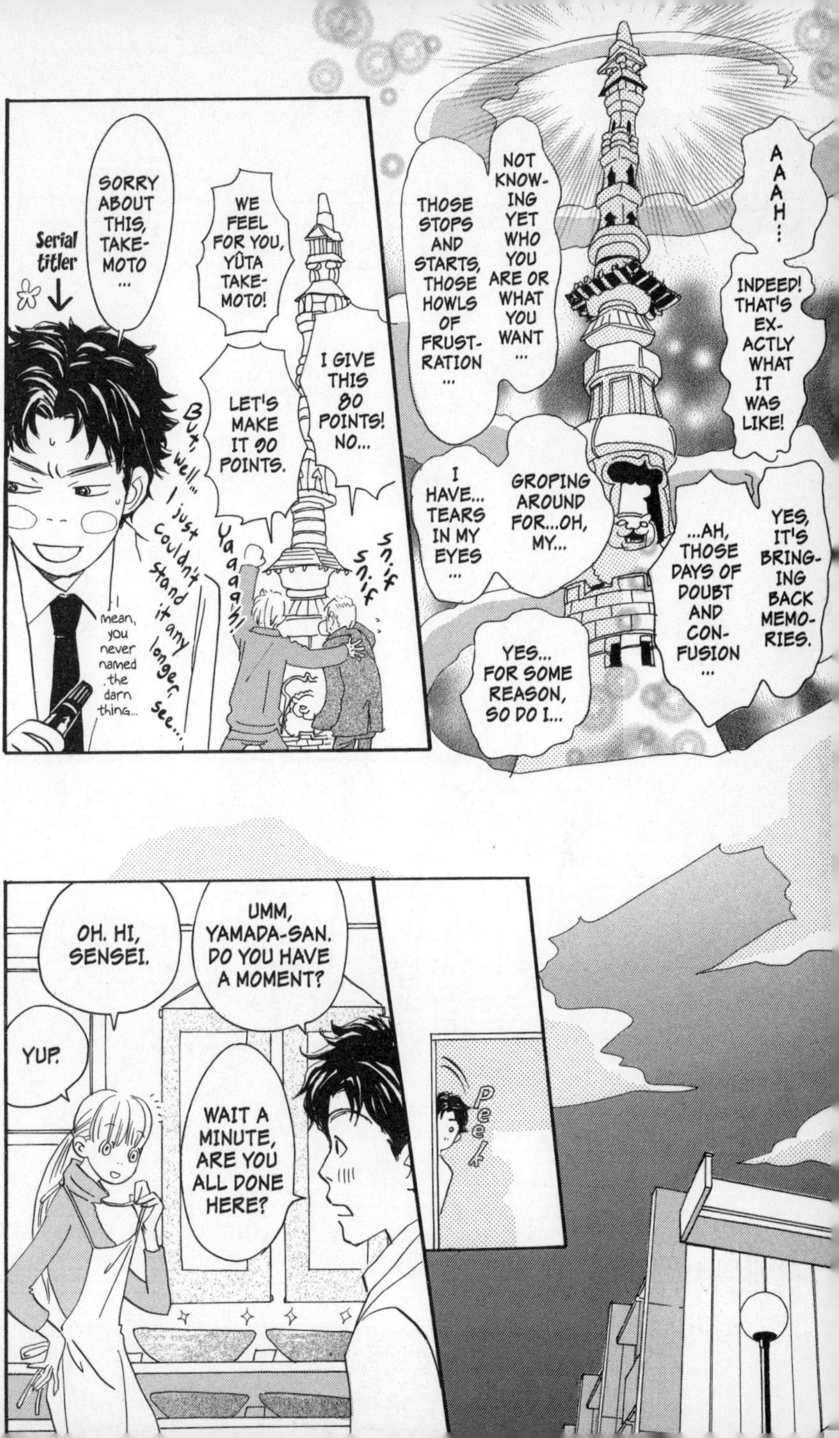
AAAAH...
INDEED! THAT'S EXACTLY WHAT IT WAS LIKE!
NOT KNOWING YET WHO YOU ARE OR WHAT YOU WANT...
THOSE STOPS AND STARTS, THOSE HOWLS OF FRUSTRATION...
YES, IT'S BRINGING BACK MEMORIES.
...AH, THOSE DAYS OF DOUBT AND CONFUSION...
GROPING AROUND FOR...OH, MY...
I HAVE... TEARS IN MY EYES...
YES... FOR SOME REASON, SO DO I...
WE FEEL FOR YOU, YÛTA TAKEMOTO!
SORRY ABOUT THIS, TAKEMOTO...
Serial titler
I GIVE THIS 80 POINTS! NO...
LET'S MAKE IT 90 POINTS.
snif snif
Yaaaagh!
But, well... I just couldn't stand it any longer, see...
I mean, you never named the darn thing...
Peek
UMM, YAMADA-SAN. DO YOU HAVE A MOMENT?
OH. HI, SENSEI.
WAIT A MINUTE, ARE YOU ALL DONE HERE?
YUP.

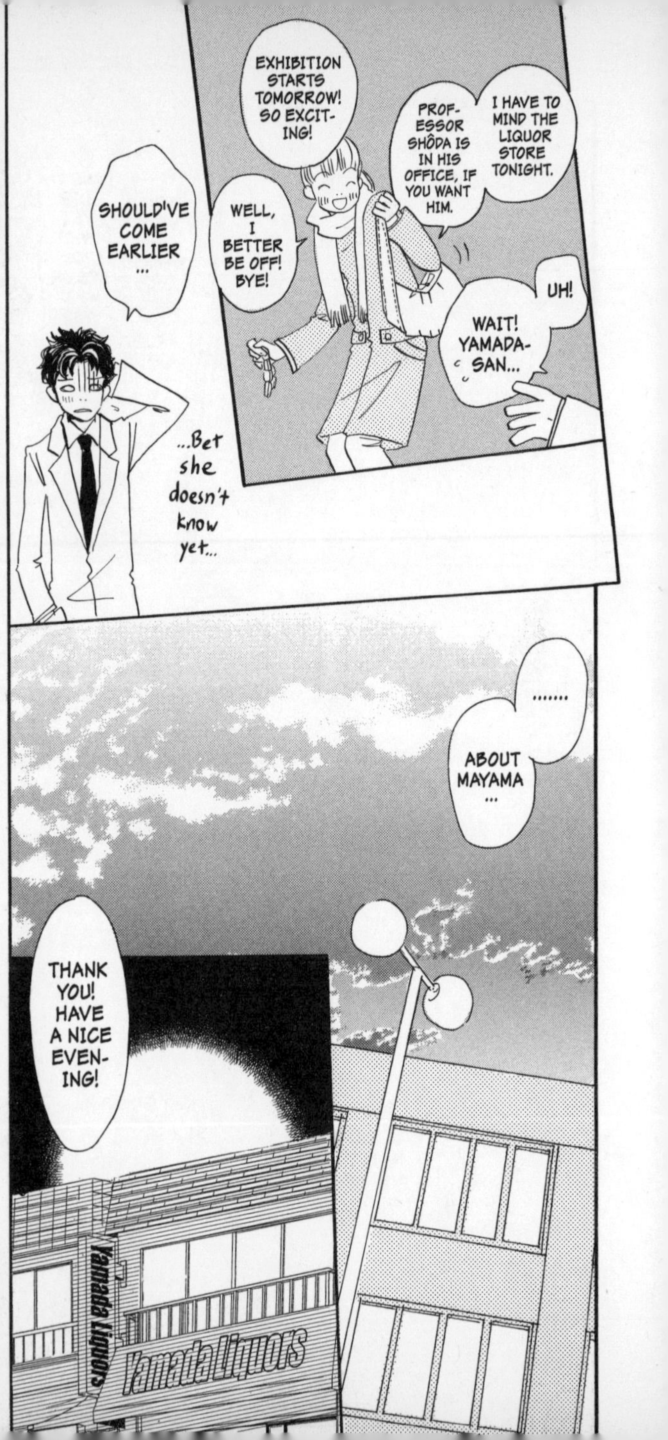
EXHIBITION STARTS TOMORROW! SO EXCIT-ING!
I HAVE TO MIND THE LIQUOR STORE TONIGHT.
PROF-ESSOR SHÔDA IS IN HIS OFFICE, IF YOU WANT HIM.
WELL, I BETTER BE OFF! BYE!
UH!
WAIT! YAMADA-SAN...
SHOULD'VE COME EARLIER ...
...Bet she doesn't know yet...
....
ABOUT MAYAMA ...
THANK YOU! HAVE A NICE EVEN-ING!
Yamada Liquors
Yamada Liquors

I love Hanami!

For cherry blossoms I always go to a park in my neighbor-hood.

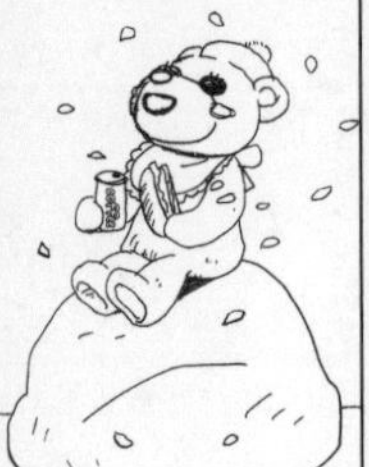

Yakisoba-Bread and canned coffee go very well together.

Chica Umino

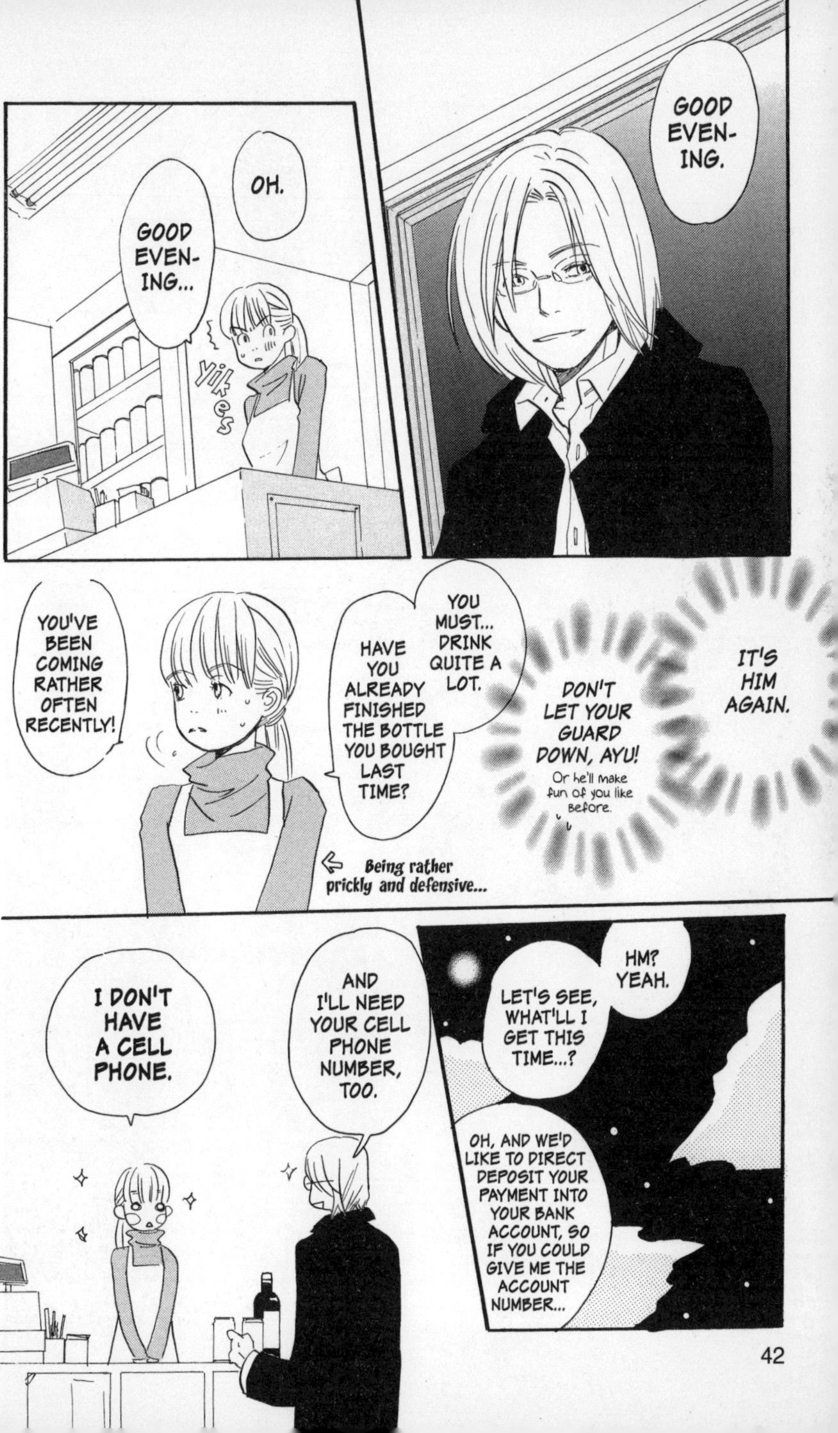
GOOD EVEN-ING.
OH.
GOOD EVEN-ING...
yikes
IT'S HIM AGAIN.
DON'T LET YOUR GUARD DOWN, AYU!
Or he'll make fun of you like before.
YOU MUST... DRINK QUITE A LOT.
HAVE YOU ALREADY FINISHED THE BOTTLE YOU BOUGHT LAST TIME?
YOU'VE BEEN COMING RATHER OFTEN RECENTLY!
Being rather prickly and defensive...
HM? YEAH.
LET'S SEE, WHAT'LL I GET THIS TIME...?
OH, AND WE'D LIKE TO DIRECT DEPOSIT YOUR PAYMENT INTO YOUR BANK ACCOUNT, SO IF YOU COULD GIVE ME THE ACCOUNT NUMBER...
AND I'LL NEED YOUR CELL PHONE NUMBER, TOO.
I DON'T HAVE A CELL PHONE.

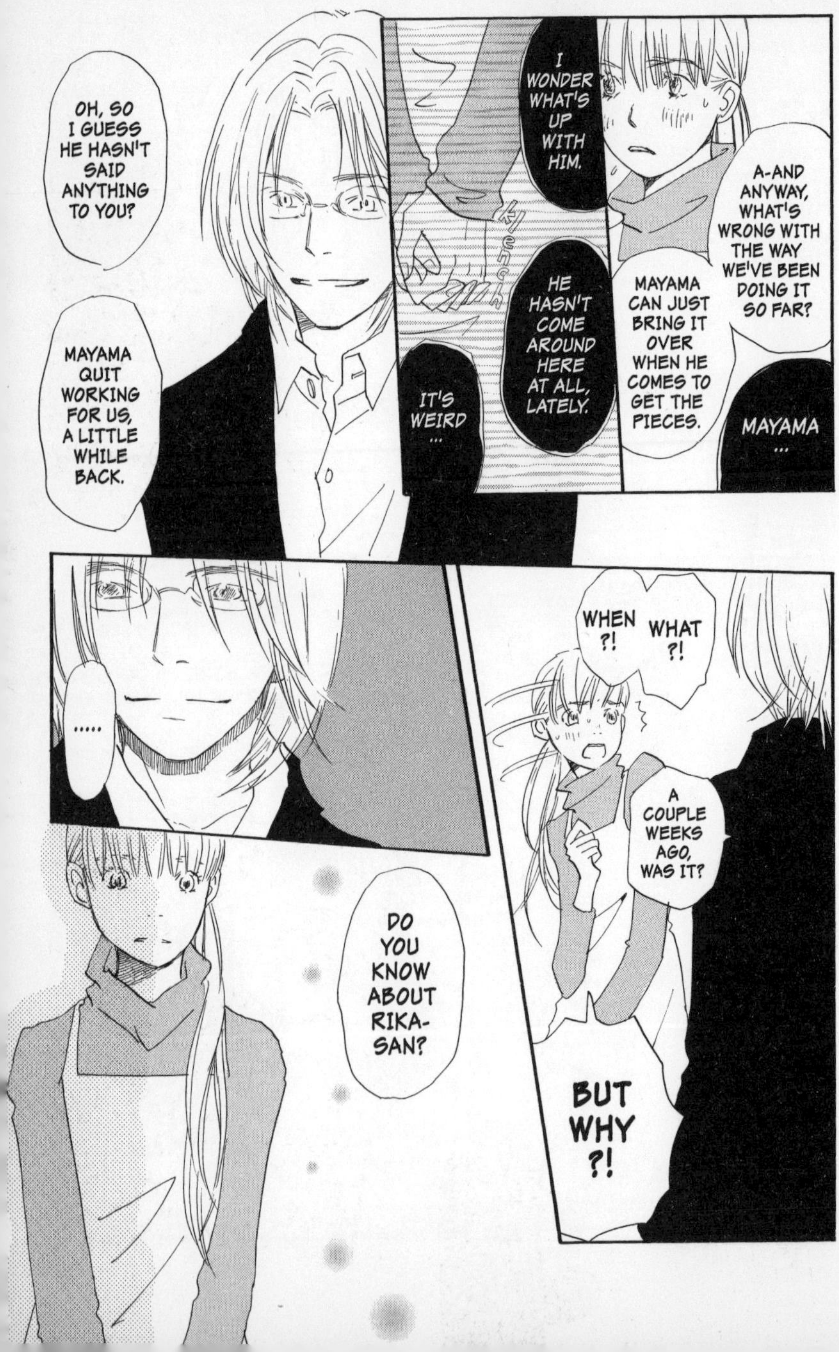
A-AND ANYWAY, WHAT'S WRONG WITH THE WAY WE'VE BEEN DOING IT SO FAR?
MAYAMA CAN JUST BRING IT OVER WHEN HE COMES TO GET THE PIECES.
MAYAMA ...
I WONDER WHAT'S UP WITH HIM.
klench
HE HASN'T COME AROUND HERE AT ALL, LATELY.
IT'S WEIRD ...
OH, SO I GUESS HE HASN'T SAID ANYTHING TO YOU?
MAYAMA QUIT WORKING FOR US, A LITTLE WHILE BACK.
WHAT ?!
WHEN ?!
A COUPLE WEEKS AGO, WAS IT?
BUT WHY ?!
.....
DO YOU KNOW ABOUT RIKA-SAN?

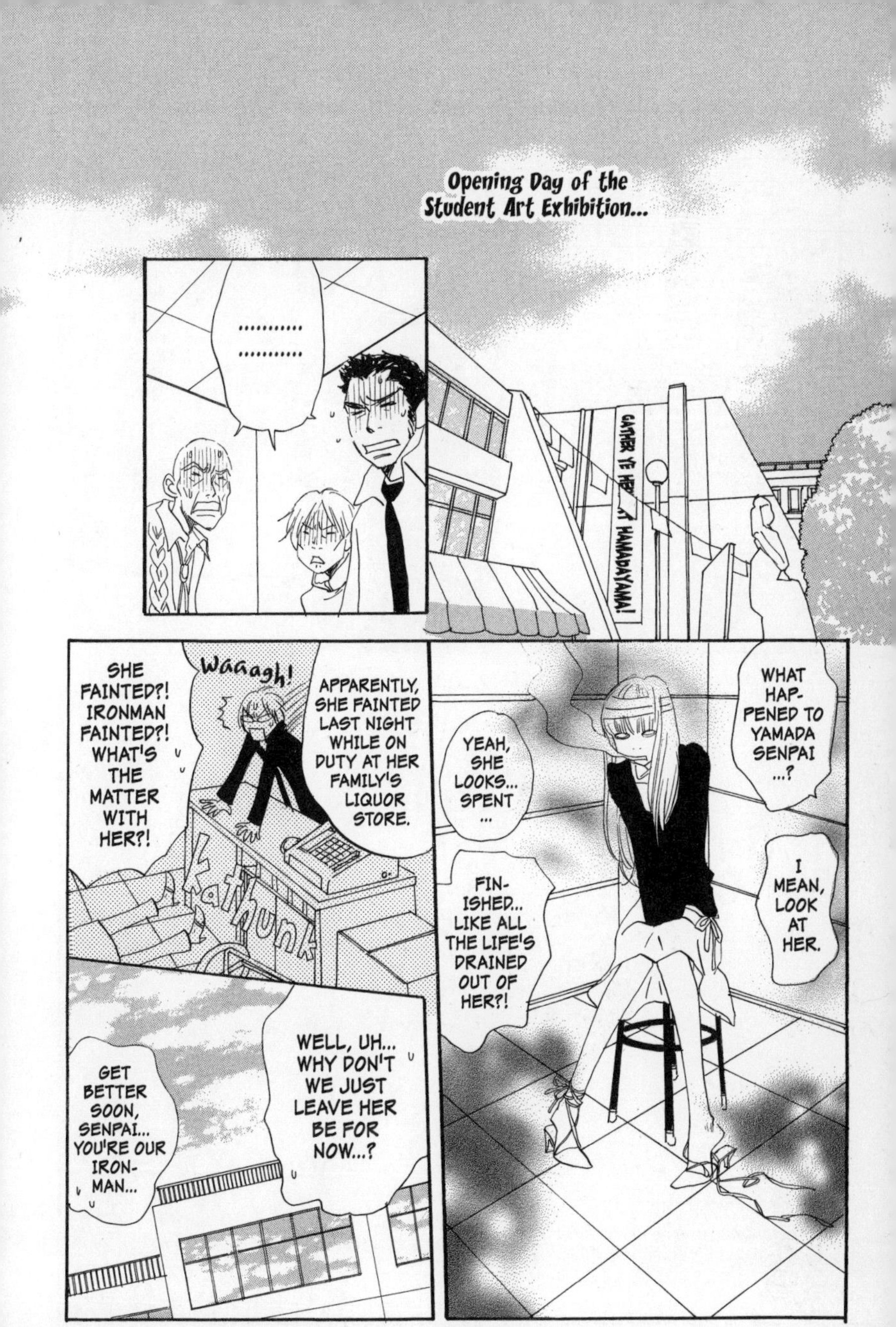
Opening Day of the Student Art Exhibition...
....
....
WHAT HAP-PENED TO YAMADA SENPAI ...?
YEAH, SHE LOOKS... SPENT ...
I MEAN, LOOK AT HER.
FIN-ISHED... LIKE ALL THE LIFE'S DRAINED OUT OF HER?!
APPARENTLY, SHE FAINTED LAST NIGHT WHILE ON DUTY AT HER FAMILY'S LIQUOR STORE.
Waaagh!
SHE FAINTED?! IRONMAN FAINTED?! WHAT'S THE MATTER WITH HER?!
kathunk
WELL, UH... WHY DON'T WE JUST LEAVE HER BE FOR NOW...?
GET BETTER SOON, SENPAI... YOU'RE OUR IRON-MAN...

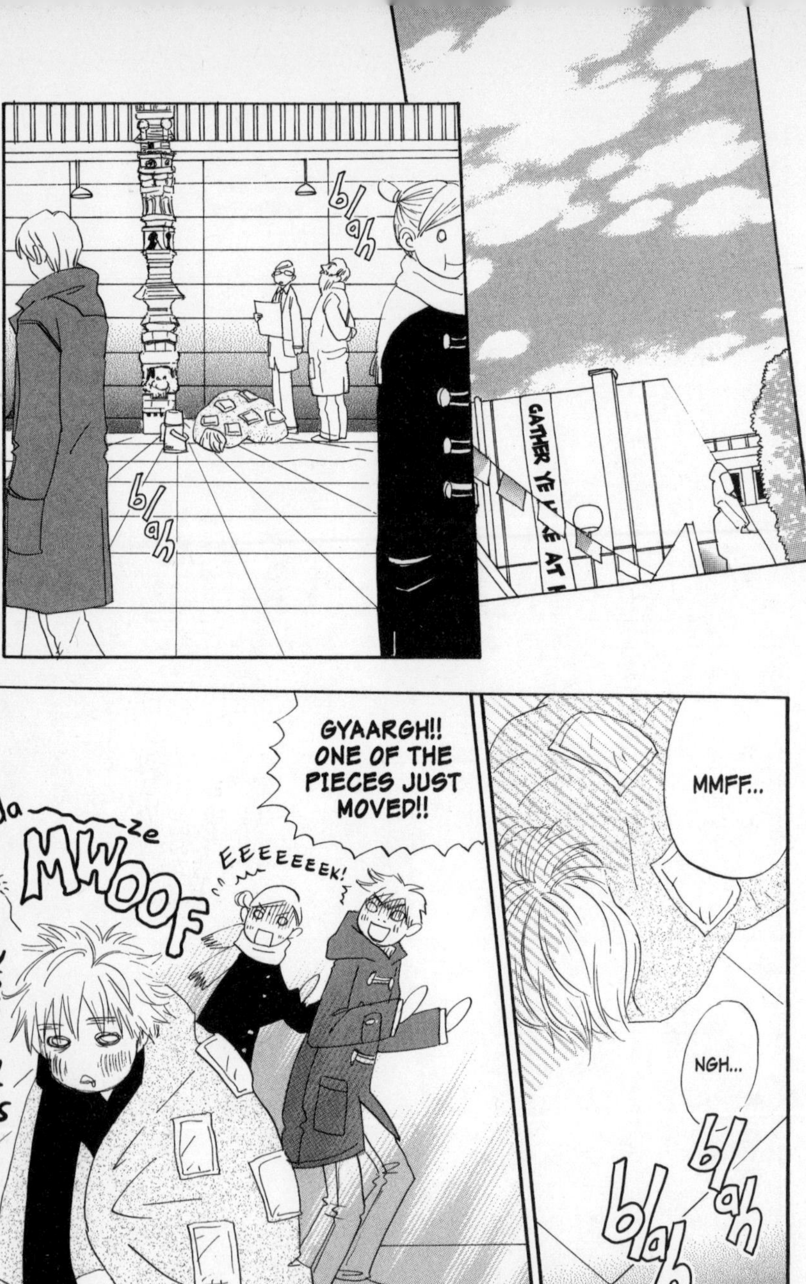
GATHER YE
blah
blah
MMFF...
NGH...
blah
blah
GYAARGH!! ONE OF THE PIECES JUST MOVED!!
EEEEEEEEK!
da~ze
MWOOF
MUSS MUSS

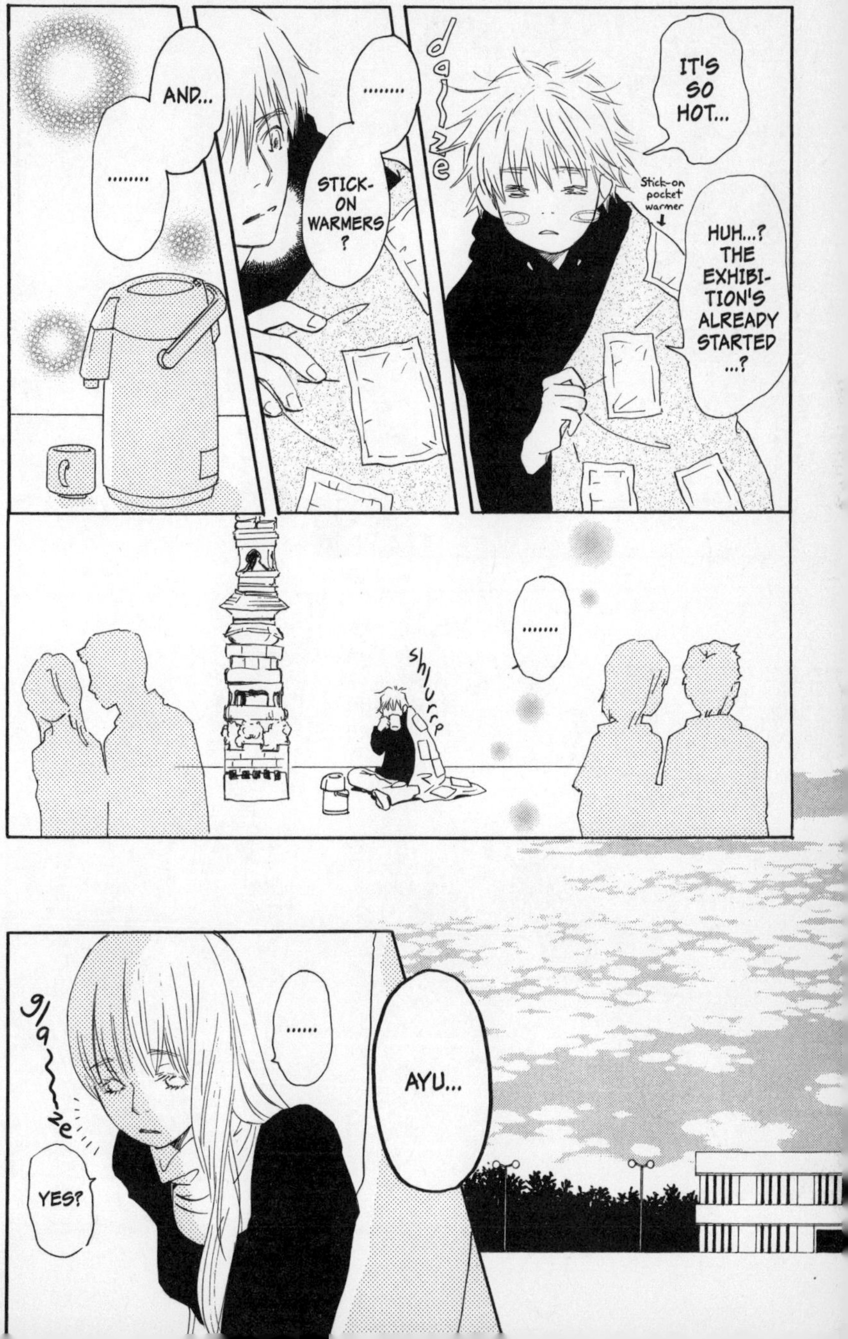
IT'S SO HOT...
da~ze
Stick-on pocket warmer
HUH...? THE EXHIBITION'S ALREADY STARTED...?
....
STICK-ON WARMERS?
AND...
....
....
shlurrp
AYU...
......
gla~ze
YES?

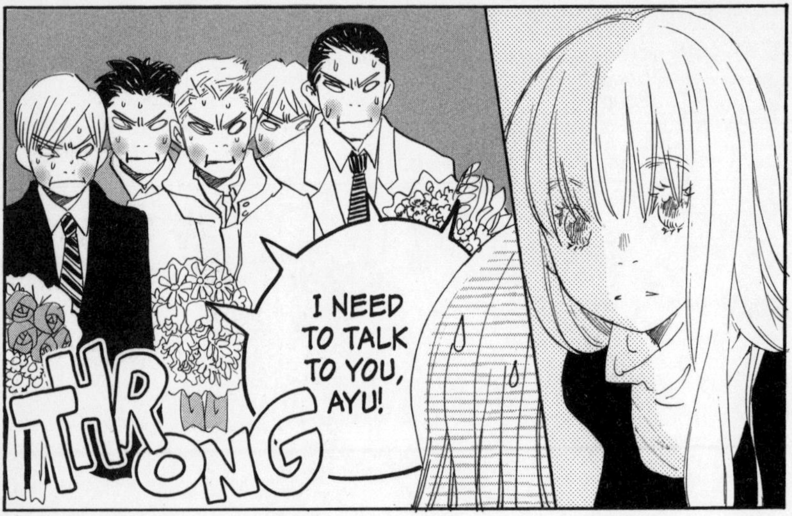
I NEED TO TALK TO YOU, AYU!
THRONG

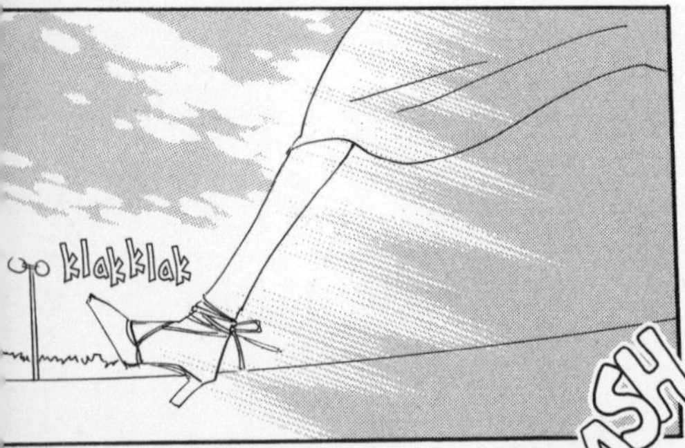
klakklak

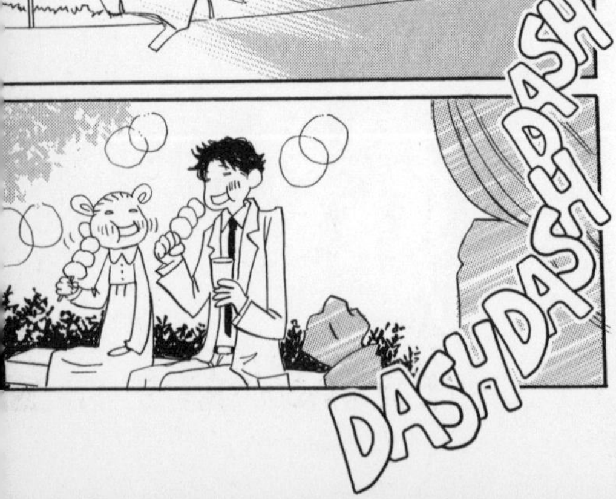
DASHDASHDASH

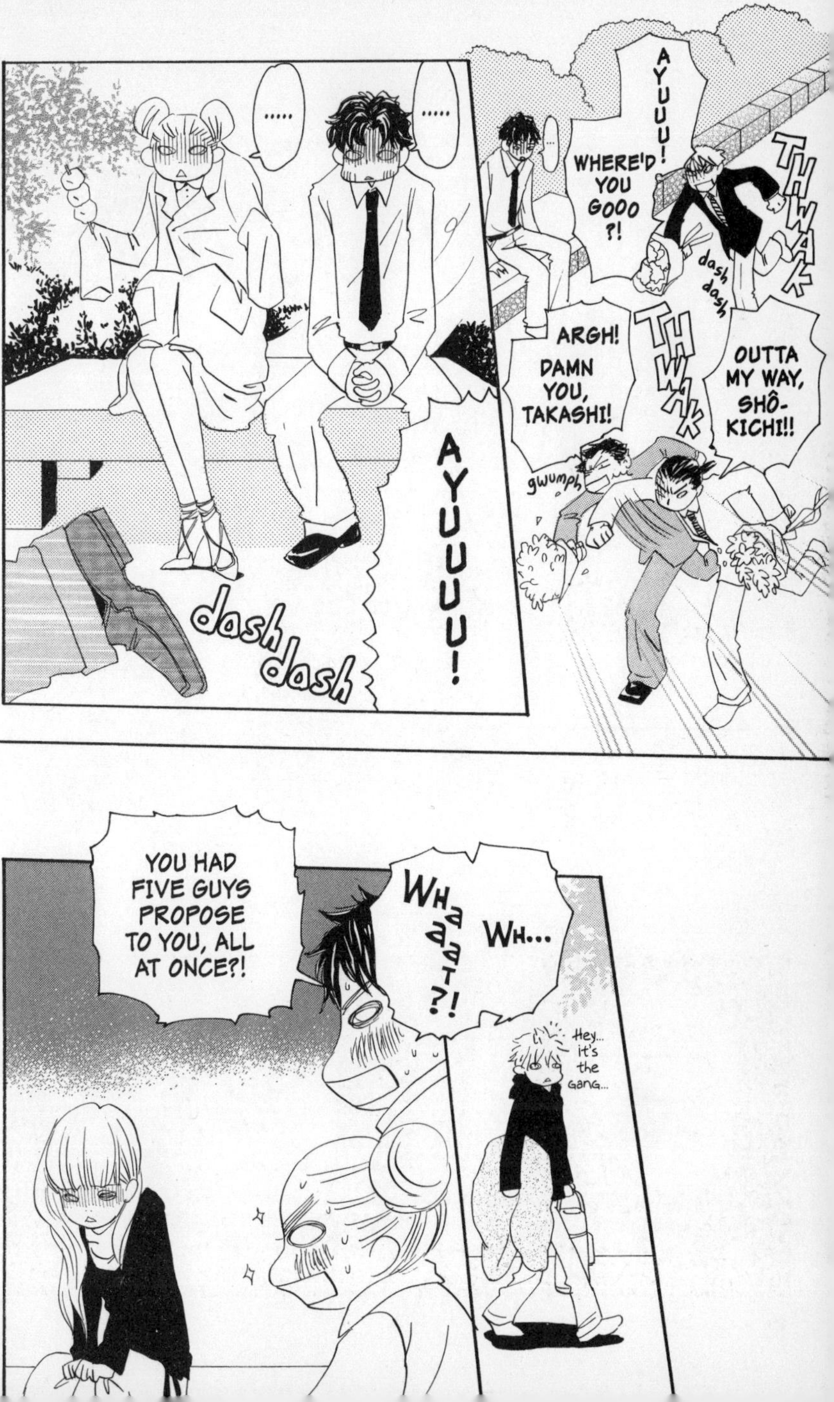
AYUUUU!
WHERE'D YOU GOOO ?!
THWAK
dash dash
…
OUTTA MY WAY, SHÔ-KICHI!!
THWAK
ARGH! DAMN YOU, TAKASHI!
gwumph
AYUUUUU!
......
......
dash dash
Hey... it's the gang...
WH...
WHaaaT?!
YOU HAD FIVE GUYS PROPOSE TO YOU, ALL AT ONCE?!

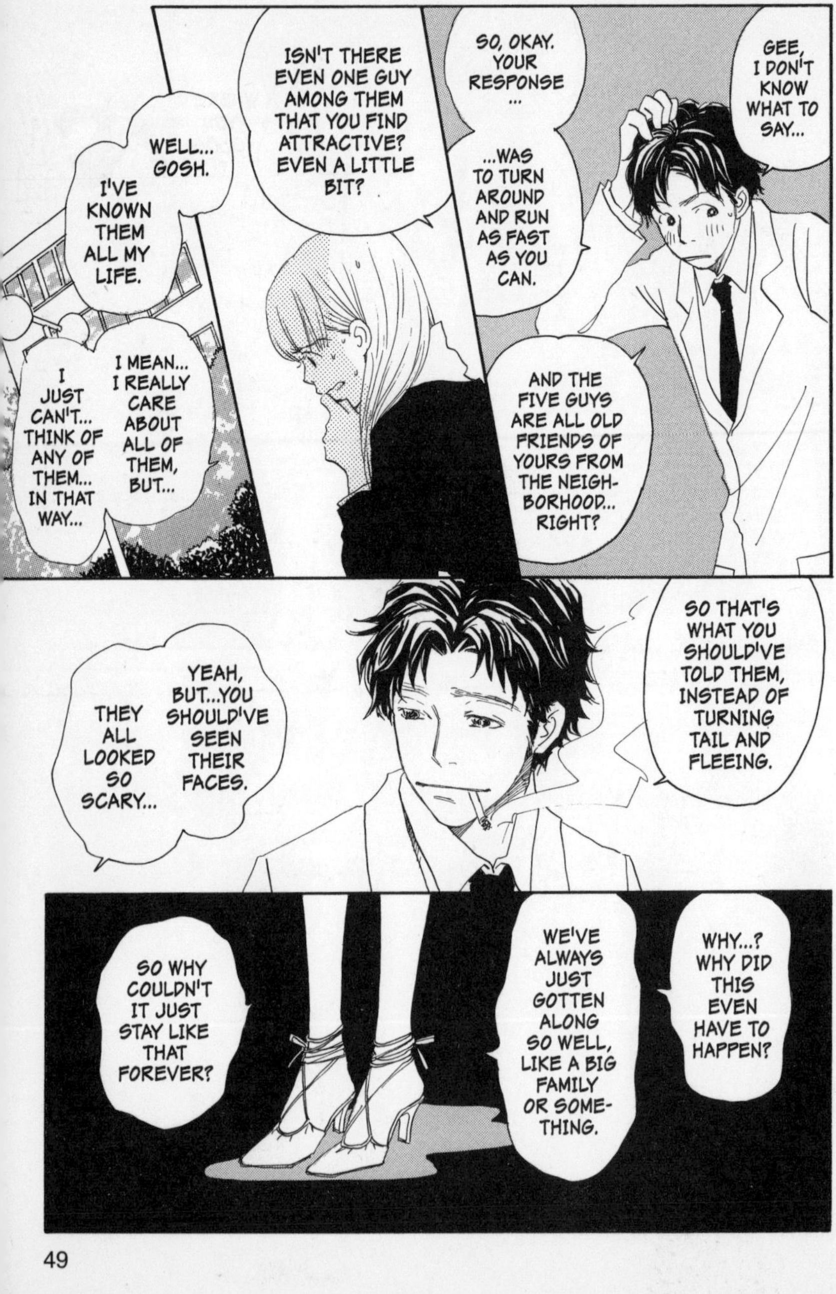
GEE, I DON'T KNOW WHAT TO SAY...
SO, OKAY. YOUR RESPONSE ...
...WAS TO TURN AROUND AND RUN AS FAST AS YOU CAN.
AND THE FIVE GUYS ARE ALL OLD FRIENDS OF YOURS FROM THE NEIGHBORHOOD... RIGHT?
ISN'T THERE EVEN ONE GUY AMONG THEM THAT YOU FIND ATTRACTIVE? EVEN A LITTLE BIT?
WELL... GOSH.
I'VE KNOWN THEM ALL MY LIFE.
I MEAN... I REALLY CARE ABOUT ALL OF THEM, BUT...
I JUST CAN'T... THINK OF ANY OF THEM... IN THAT WAY...
SO THAT'S WHAT YOU SHOULD'VE TOLD THEM, INSTEAD OF TURNING TAIL AND FLEEING.
YEAH, BUT...YOU SHOULD'VE SEEN THEIR FACES.
THEY ALL LOOKED SO SCARY...
WHY...? WHY DID THIS EVEN HAVE TO HAPPEN?
WE'VE ALWAYS JUST GOTTEN ALONG SO WELL, LIKE A BIG FAMILY OR SOME-THING.
SO WHY COULDN'T IT JUST STAY LIKE THAT FOREVER?

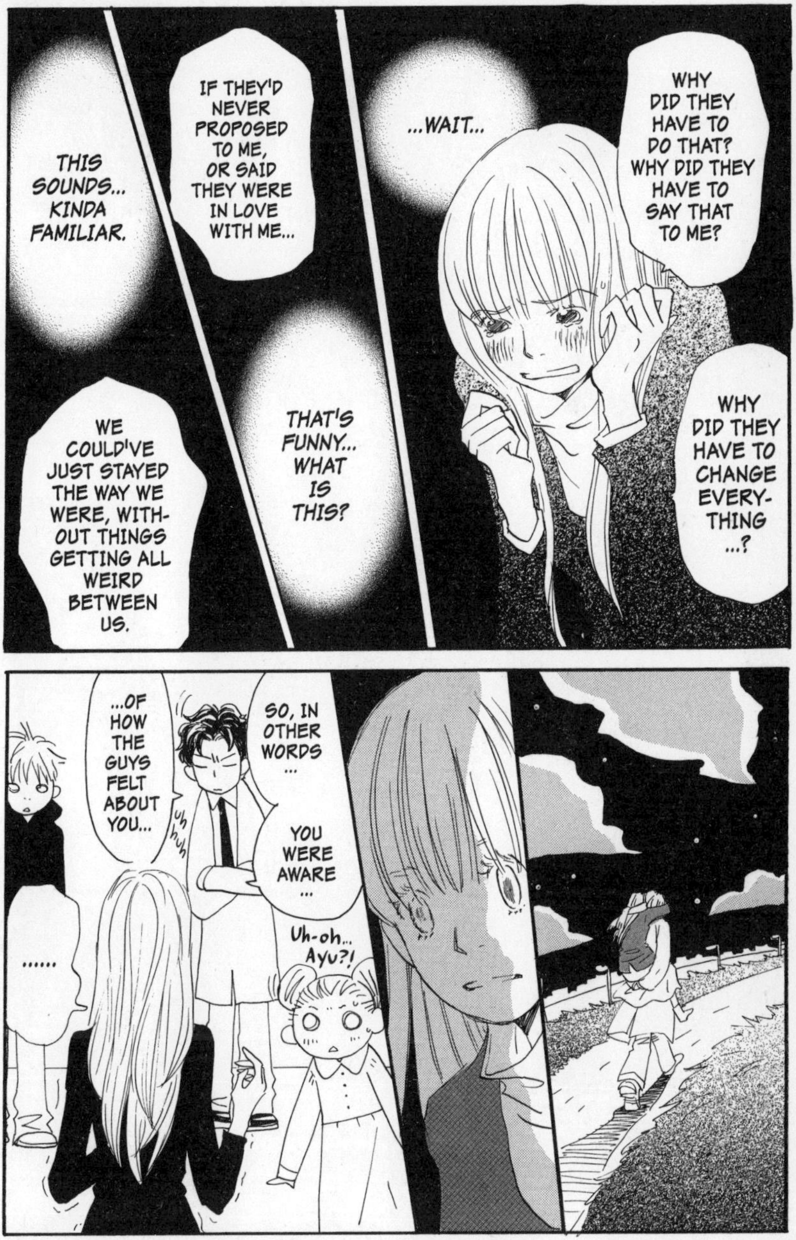
WHY DID THEY HAVE TO DO THAT? WHY DID THEY HAVE TO SAY THAT TO ME?
WHY DID THEY HAVE TO CHANGE EVERY-THING...?
...WAIT...
IF THEY'D NEVER PROPOSED TO ME, OR SAID THEY WERE IN LOVE WITH ME...
THAT'S FUNNY... WHAT IS THIS?
WE COULD'VE JUST STAYED THE WAY WE WERE, WITH-OUT THINGS GETTING ALL WEIRD BETWEEN US.
THIS SOUNDS... KINDA FAMILIAR.
SO, IN OTHER WORDS...
YOU WERE AWARE...
...OF HOW THE GUYS FELT ABOUT YOU...
uh huh
Uh-oh... Ayu?!
......

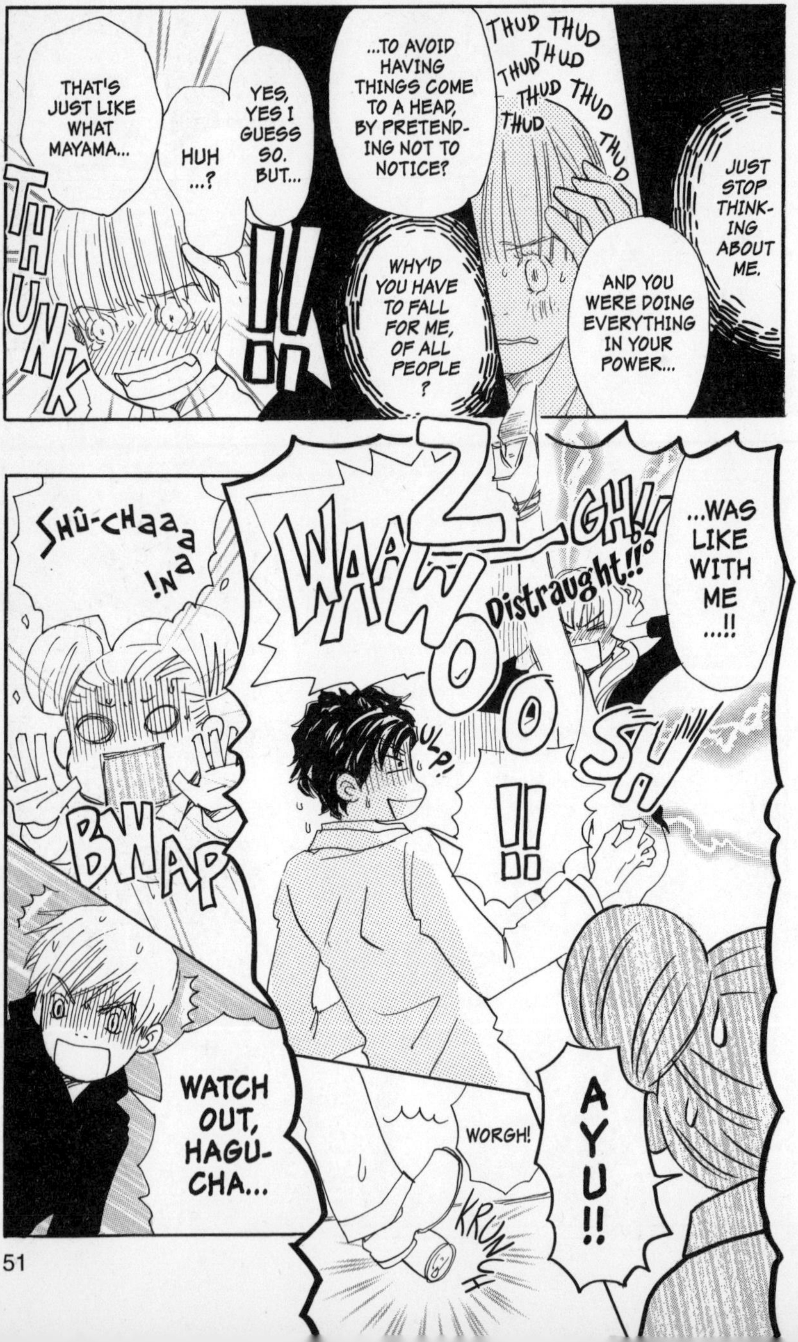
JUST STOP THINKING ABOUT ME.
AND YOU WERE DOING EVERYTHING IN YOUR POWER...
THUD THUD THUD THUD THUD THUD THUD THUD
...TO AVOID HAVING THINGS COME TO A HEAD, BY PRETENDING NOT TO NOTICE?
WHY'D YOU HAVE TO FALL FOR ME, OF ALL PEOPLE?
YES, YES I GUESS SO. BUT...
!!
HUH...?
THAT'S JUST LIKE WHAT MAYAMA...
THUNK
...WAS LIKE WITH ME...!!
Distraught!!
WOOOSH!!
ULP!
SHÛ-CHAaaaaN!
BWAP
AYU!!
WORGH!
KRUNCH
WATCH OUT, HAGU-CHA...

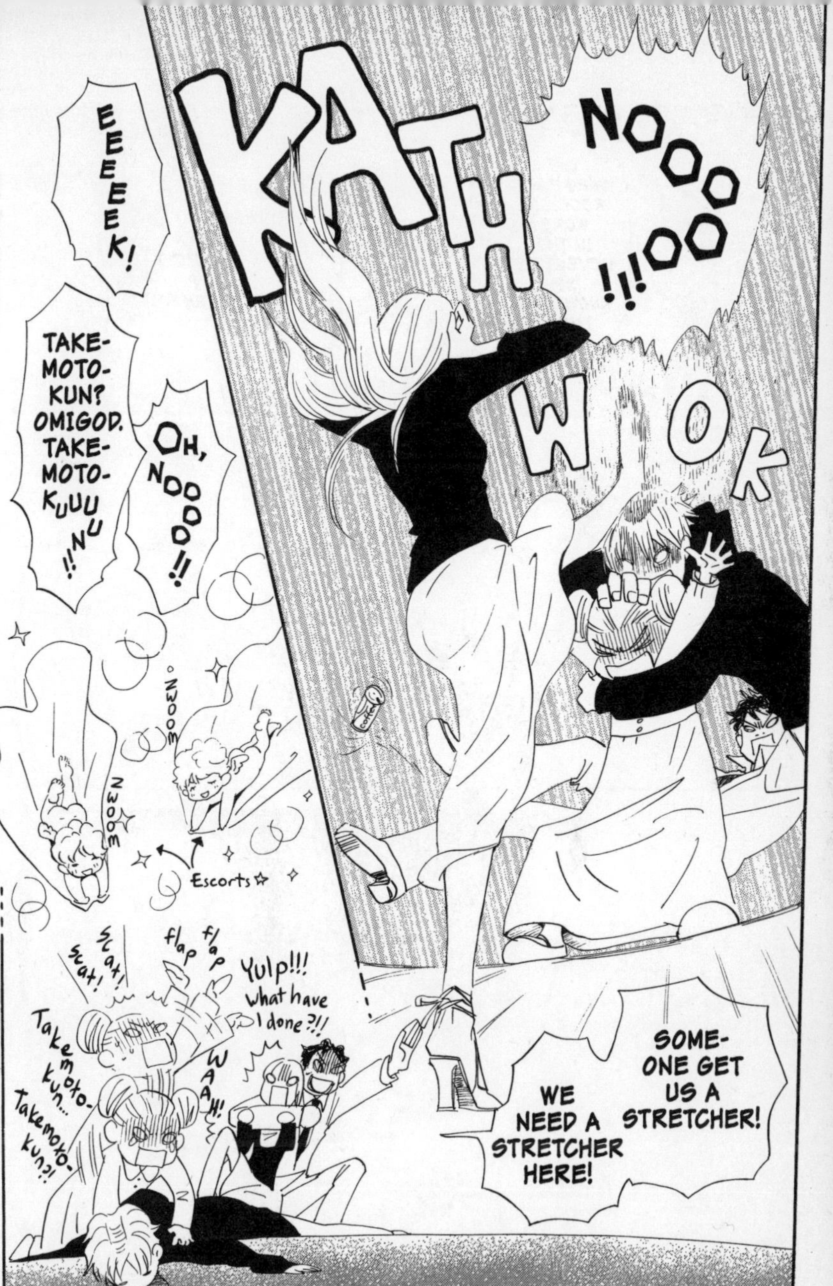

NOOOOOO!!
KATH
WOK
OH, NOOOOO!!
EEEEEK!
TAKE-MOTO-KUN? OMIGOD. TAKE-MOTO-KUUUUN!!
ZWOOM
ZWOOM
Escorts☆
SOME-ONE GET US A STRETCHER!
WE NEED A STRETCHER HERE!
Yulp!!! what have I done?!!
WAAH!
flap flap
Scat! scat!
Takemoto-kun...
Takemoto-kun?!

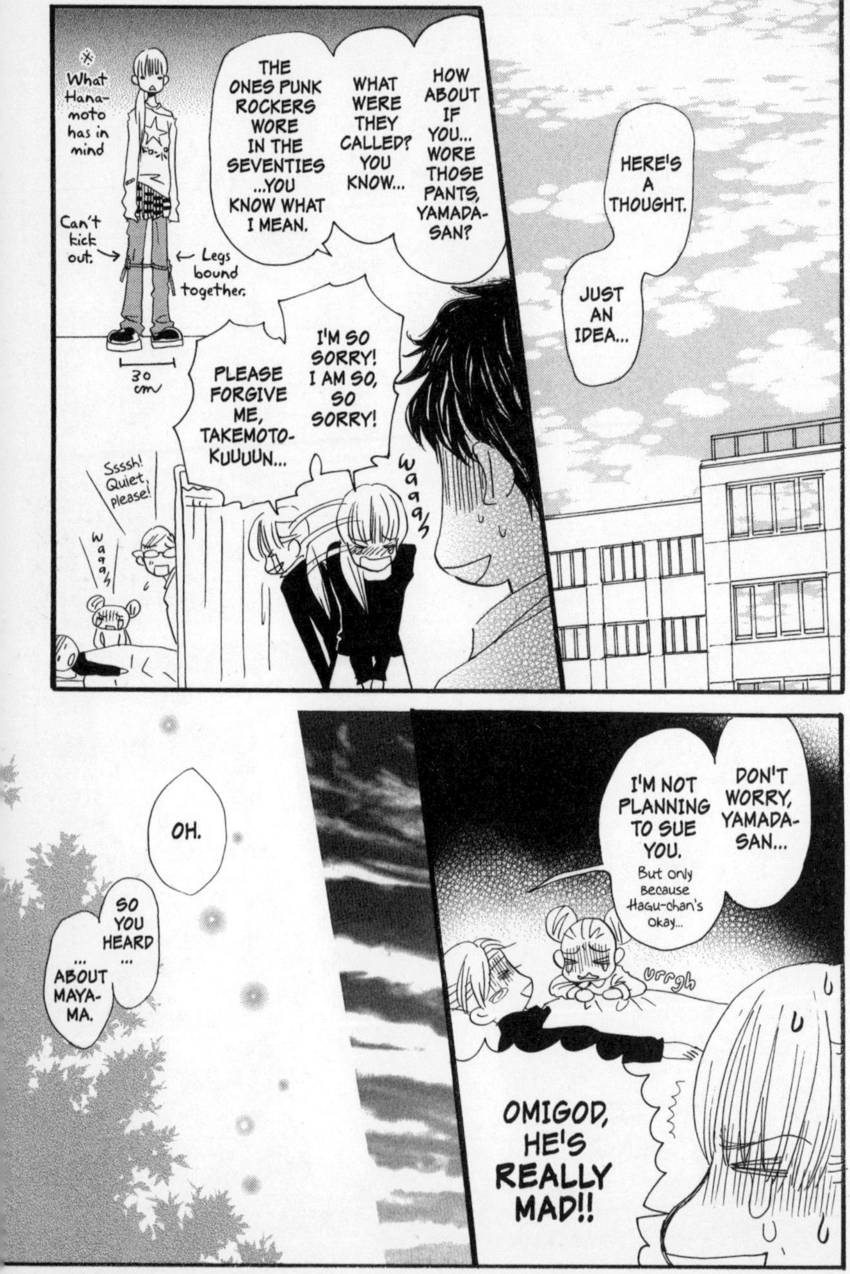
HERE'S A THOUGHT.
JUST AN IDEA...
HOW ABOUT IF YOU... WORE THOSE PANTS, YAMADA-SAN?
WHAT WERE THEY CALLED? YOU KNOW...
THE ONES PUNK ROCKERS WORE IN THE SEVENTIES ...YOU KNOW WHAT I MEAN.
※ What Hanamoto has in mind
Can't kick out.
Legs bound together.
30 cm
I'M SO SORRY! I AM SO, SO SORRY!
PLEASE FORGIVE ME, TAKEMOTO-KUUUUN...
waaagh
Ssssh! Quiet, please!
waaagh
DON'T WORRY, YAMADA-SAN...
I'M NOT PLANNING TO SUE YOU.
But only because Hagu-chan's okay...
urrgh
OMIGOD, HE'S REALLY MAD!!
OH.
SO YOU HEARD ... ABOUT MAYAMA.

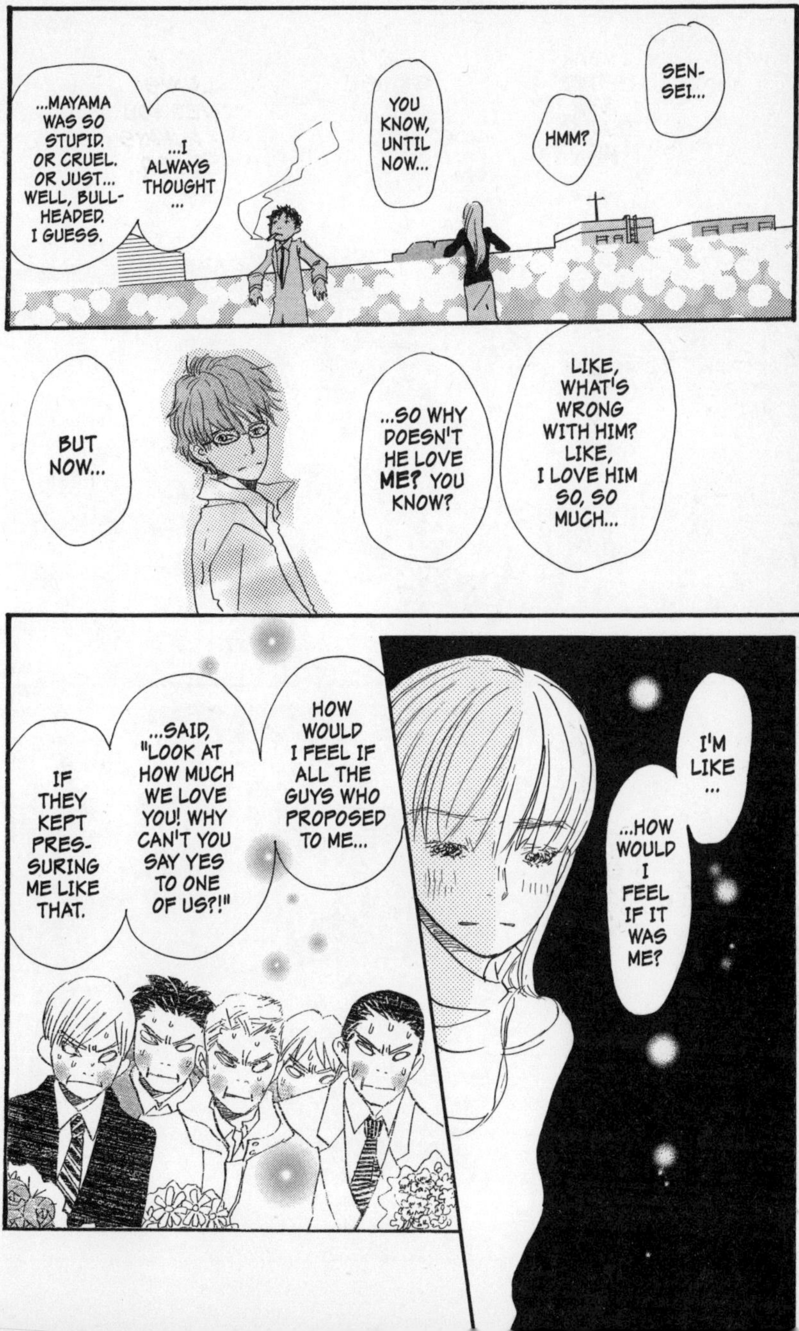
SEN-SEI...
HMM?
YOU KNOW, UNTIL NOW...
...I ALWAYS THOUGHT ...
...MAYAMA WAS SO STUPID. OR CRUEL. OR JUST... WELL, BULL-HEADED. I GUESS.
LIKE, WHAT'S WRONG WITH HIM? LIKE, I LOVE HIM SO, SO MUCH...
...SO WHY DOESN'T HE LOVE ME? YOU KNOW?
BUT NOW...
I'M LIKE ...
...HOW WOULD I FEEL IF IT WAS ME?
HOW WOULD I FEEL IF ALL THE GUYS WHO PROPOSED TO ME...
...SAID, "LOOK AT HOW MUCH WE LOVE YOU! WHY CAN'T YOU SAY YES TO ONE OF US?!"
IF THEY KEPT PRES-SURING ME LIKE THAT.

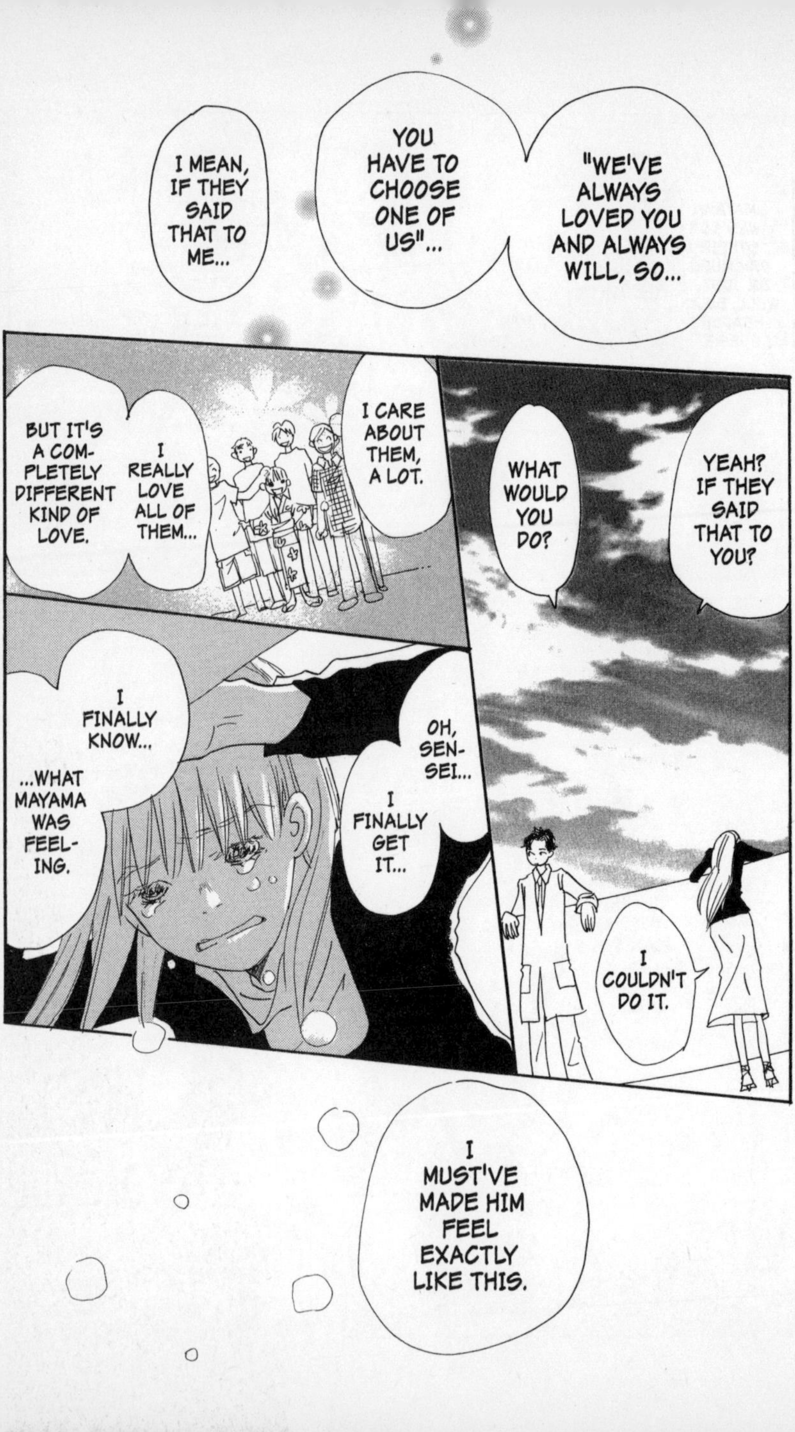
"WE'VE ALWAYS LOVED YOU AND ALWAYS WILL, SO...
YOU HAVE TO CHOOSE ONE OF US"...
I MEAN, IF THEY SAID THAT TO ME...
YEAH? IF THEY SAID THAT TO YOU?
WHAT WOULD YOU DO?
I COULDN'T DO IT.
I CARE ABOUT THEM, A LOT.
I REALLY LOVE ALL OF THEM...
BUT IT'S A COM-PLETELY DIFFERENT KIND OF LOVE.
OH, SEN-SEI...
I FINALLY GET IT...
I FINALLY KNOW...
...WHAT MAYAMA WAS FEEL-ING.
I MUST'VE MADE HIM FEEL EXACTLY LIKE THIS.

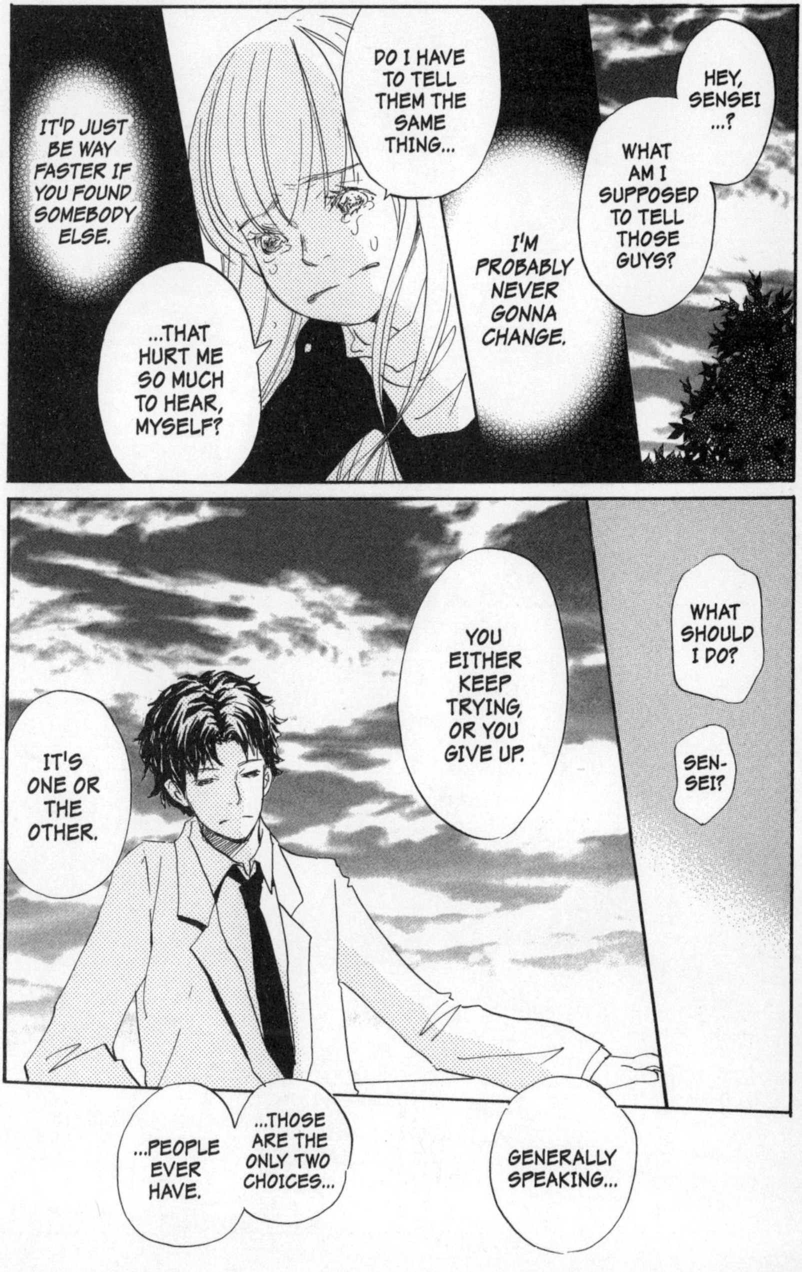
HEY, SENSEI ...?
WHAT AM I SUPPOSED TO TELL THOSE GUYS?
I'M PROBABLY NEVER GONNA CHANGE.
DO I HAVE TO TELL THEM THE SAME THING...
...THAT HURT ME SO MUCH TO HEAR, MYSELF?
IT'D JUST BE WAY FASTER IF YOU FOUND SOMEBODY ELSE.
WHAT SHOULD I DO?
SEN-SEI?
YOU EITHER KEEP TRYING, OR YOU GIVE UP.
IT'S ONE OR THE OTHER.
GENERALLY SPEAKING...
...THOSE ARE THE ONLY TWO CHOICES...
...PEOPLE EVER HAVE.

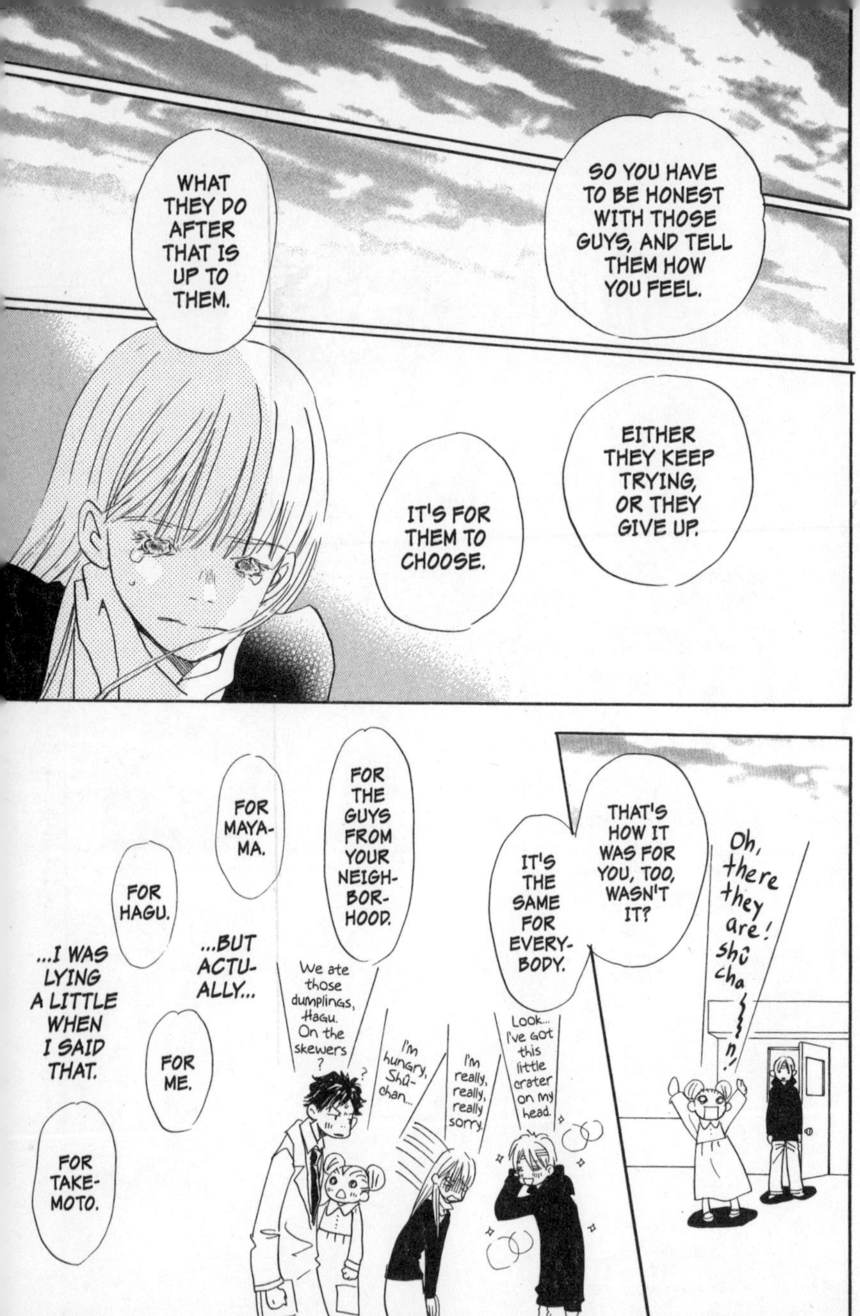
SO YOU HAVE TO BE HONEST WITH THOSE GUYS, AND TELL THEM HOW YOU FEEL.
WHAT THEY DO AFTER THAT IS UP TO THEM.
EITHER THEY KEEP TRYING, OR THEY GIVE UP.
IT'S FOR THEM TO CHOOSE.
Oh, there they are! Shû-cha~n!
THAT'S HOW IT WAS FOR YOU, TOO, WASN'T IT?
IT'S THE SAME FOR EVERYBODY.
Look... I've got this little crater on my head.
I'm really, really, really sorry.
I'm hungry, Shû-chan...
We ate those dumplings, Hagu. On the skewers?
?
FOR THE GUYS FROM YOUR NEIGHBORHOOD.
FOR MAYAMA.
FOR HAGU.
...BUT ACTUALLY...
FOR ME.
...I WAS LYING A LITTLE WHEN I SAID THAT.
FOR TAKEMOTO.

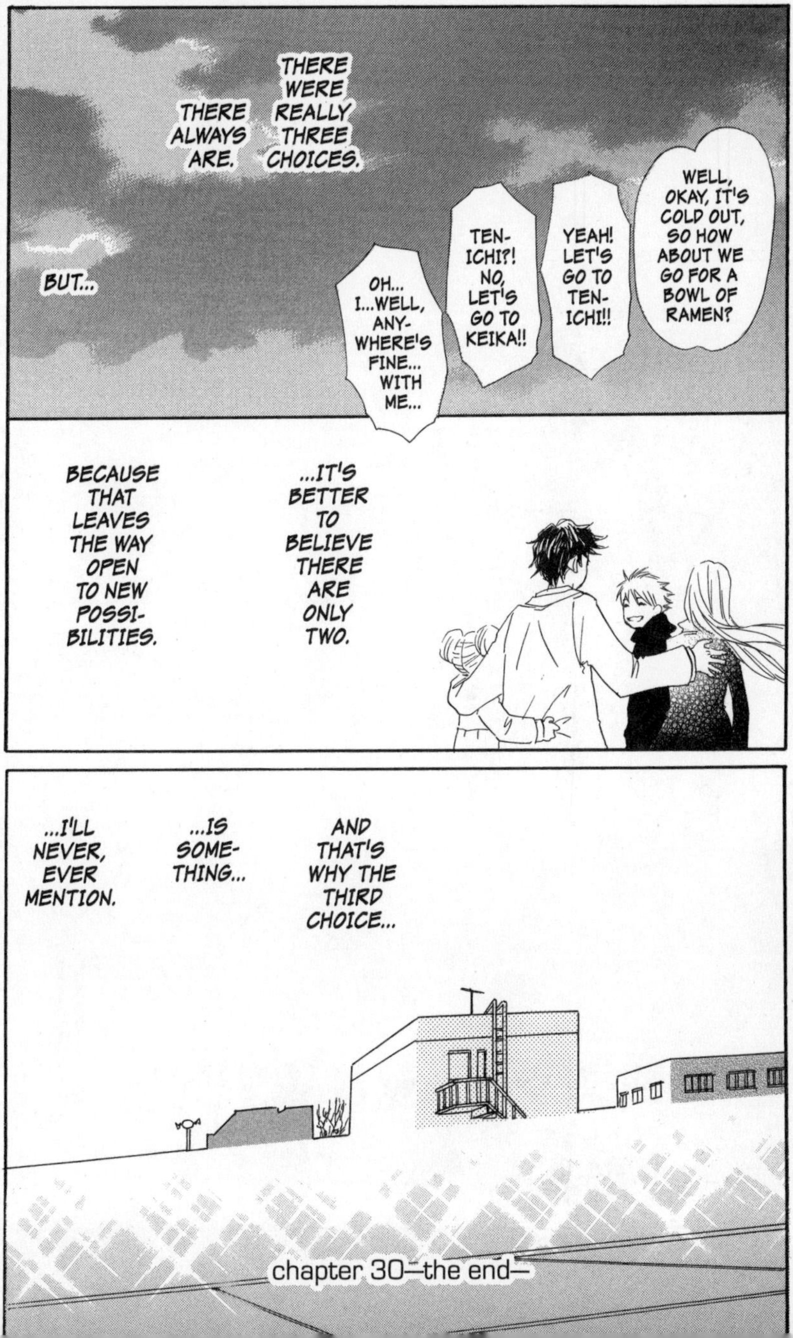
WELL, OKAY, IT'S COLD OUT, SO HOW ABOUT WE GO FOR A BOWL OF RAMEN?
YEAH! LET'S GO TO TEN-ICHI!!
TEN-ICHI?! NO, LET'S GO TO KEIKA!!
OH... I...WELL, ANY-WHERE'S FINE... WITH ME...
THERE WERE REALLY THREE CHOICES.
THERE ALWAYS ARE.
BUT...
...IT'S BETTER TO BELIEVE THERE ARE ONLY TWO.
BECAUSE THAT LEAVES THE WAY OPEN TO NEW POSSI-BILITIES.
AND THAT'S WHY THE THIRD CHOICE...
...IS SOME-THING...
...I'LL NEVER, EVER MENTION.
chapter 30—the end—

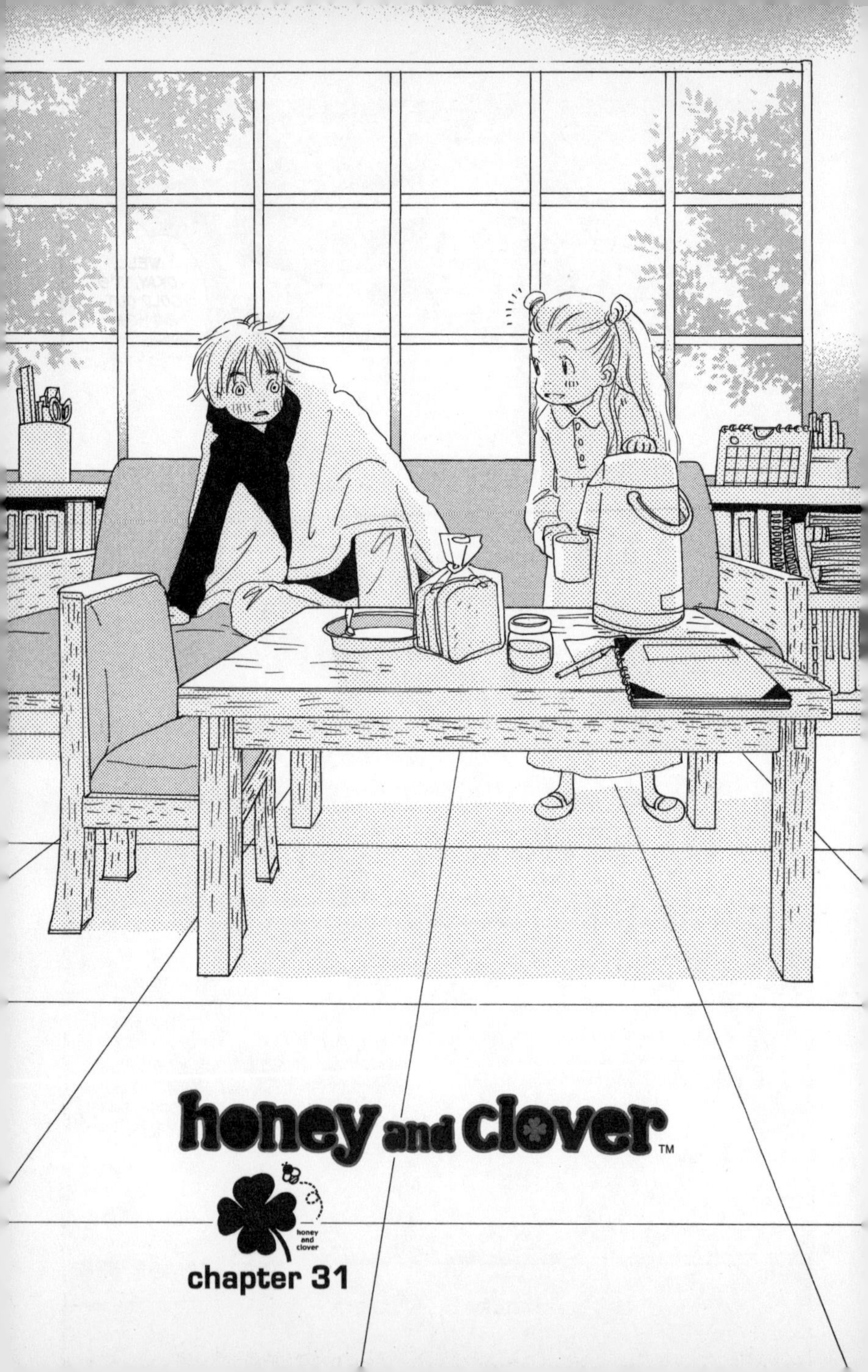
honey and clover™
honey and clover
chapter 31

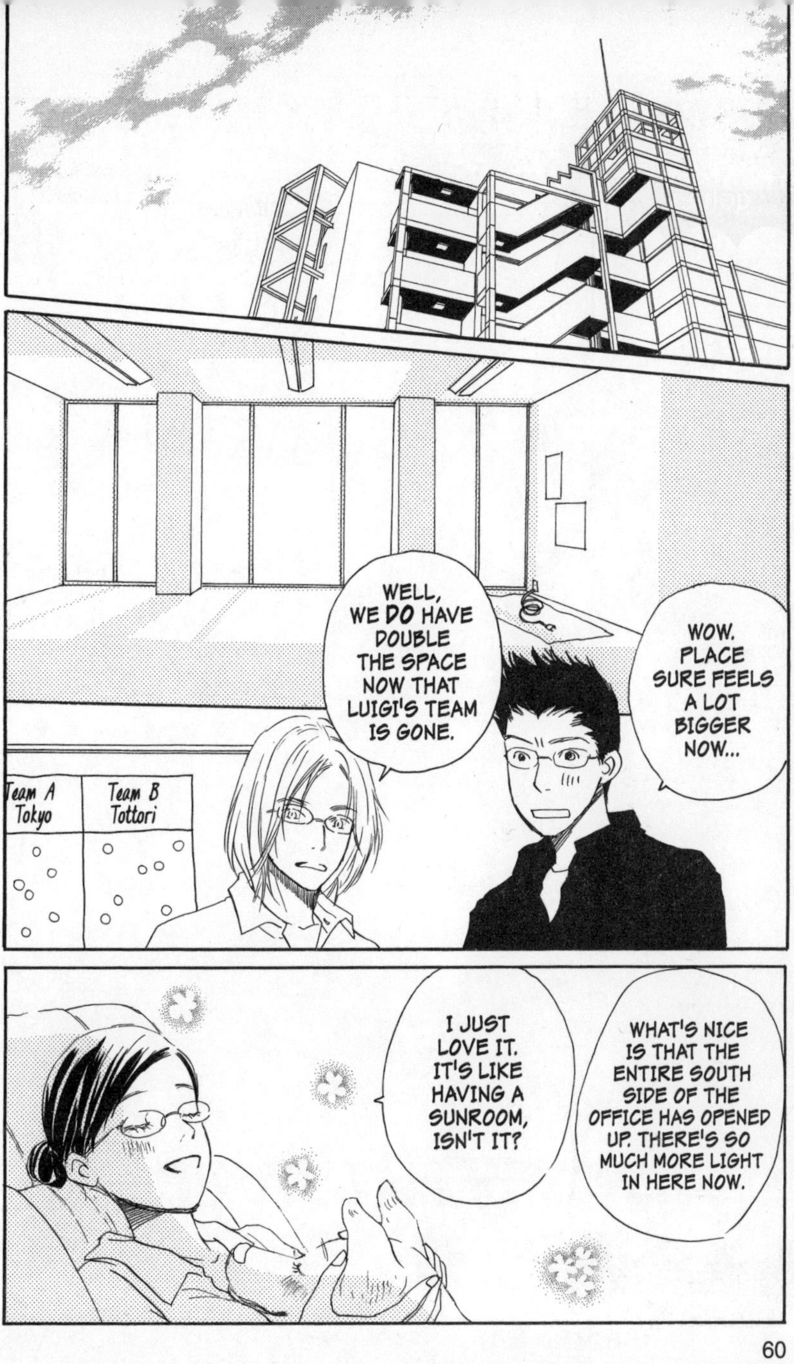
WOW. PLACE SURE FEELS A LOT BIGGER NOW...
WELL, WE DO HAVE DOUBLE THE SPACE NOW THAT LUIGI'S TEAM IS GONE.
Team B Tottori
Team A Tokyo
WHAT'S NICE IS THAT THE ENTIRE SOUTH SIDE OF THE OFFICE HAS OPENED UP. THERE'S SO MUCH MORE LIGHT IN HERE NOW.
I JUST LOVE IT. IT'S LIKE HAVING A SUNROOM, ISN'T IT?

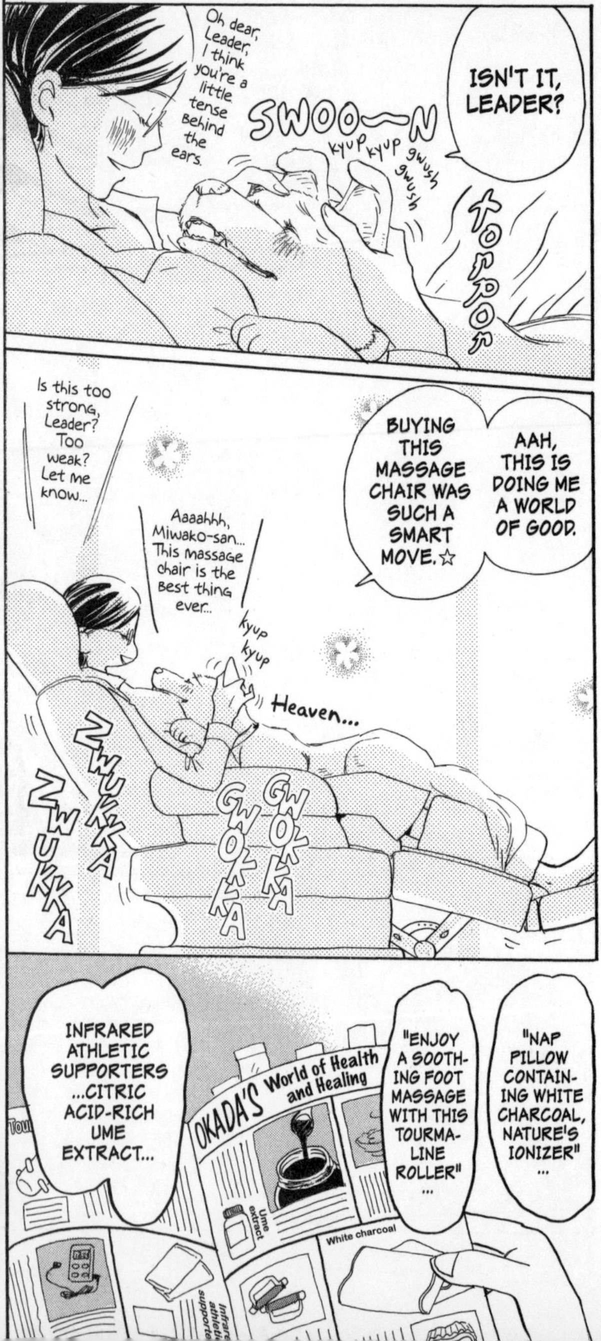
ISN'T IT, LEADER?
Oh dear, Leader, I think you're a little tense behind the ears.
SWOO—N
kyup kyup
gwush gwush
TOPPON
AAH, THIS IS DOING ME A WORLD OF GOOD.
BUYING THIS MASSAGE CHAIR WAS SUCH A SMART MOVE.☆
Is this too strong, Leader? Too weak? Let me know...
Aaaahh, Miwako-san... This massage chair is the best thing ever...
kyup kyup
Heaven...
GWOKKA GWOKKA
ZWUKKA ZWUKKA
"NAP PILLOW CONTAINING WHITE CHARCOAL, NATURE'S IONIZER"...
"ENJOY A SOOTHING FOOT MASSAGE WITH THIS TOURMALINE ROLLER"...
INFRARED ATHLETIC SUPPORTERS ...CITRIC ACID-RICH UME EXTRACT...
OKADA'S World of Health and Healing
Ume extract
White charcoal

I love takikomi gohan!

Oh, this takes me back...

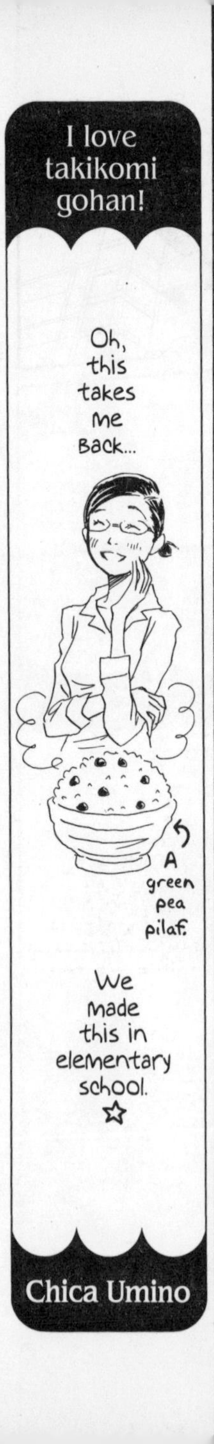
A green pea pilaf.

We made this in elementary school. ☆

Chica Umino

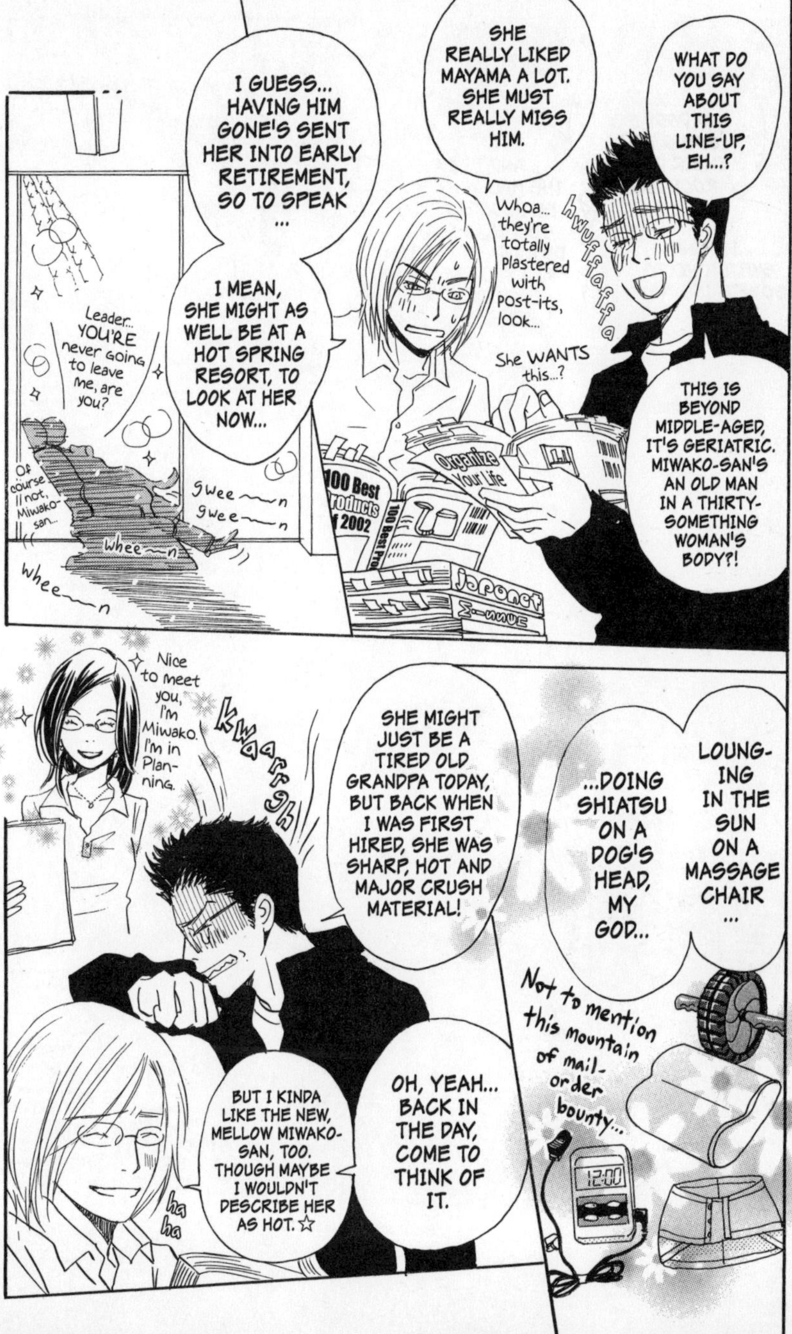
WHAT DO YOU SAY ABOUT THIS LINE-UP, EH...?
hwuffaffa
SHE REALLY LIKED MAYAMA A LOT. SHE MUST REALLY MISS HIM.
Whoa... they're totally plastered with post-its, look...
She WANTS this...?
THIS IS BEYOND MIDDLE-AGED, IT'S GERIATRIC. MIWAKO-SAN'S AN OLD MAN IN A THIRTY-SOMETHING WOMAN'S BODY?!
Organize Your Life
100 Best Products of 2002
japonet
I GUESS... HAVING HIM GONE'S SENT HER INTO EARLY RETIREMENT, SO TO SPEAK...
I MEAN, SHE MIGHT AS WELL BE AT A HOT SPRING RESORT, TO LOOK AT HER NOW...
Leader... YOU'RE never going to leave me, are you?
Of course not, Miwako-san...
gwee—n
gwee—n
whee—n
whee—n
LOUNGING IN THE SUN ON A MASSAGE CHAIR...
...DOING SHIATSU ON A DOG'S HEAD, MY GOD...
SHE MIGHT JUST BE A TIRED OLD GRANDPA TODAY, BUT BACK WHEN I WAS FIRST HIRED, SHE WAS SHARP, HOT AND MAJOR CRUSH MATERIAL!
Kwaarrgh
Nice to meet you, I'm Miwako. I'm in Planning.
Not to mention this mountain of mail-order bounty...
12:00
OH, YEAH... BACK IN THE DAY, COME TO THINK OF IT.
BUT I KINDA LIKE THE NEW, MELLOW MIWAKO-SAN, TOO. THOUGH MAYBE I WOULDN'T DESCRIBE HER AS HOT.☆
ha ha

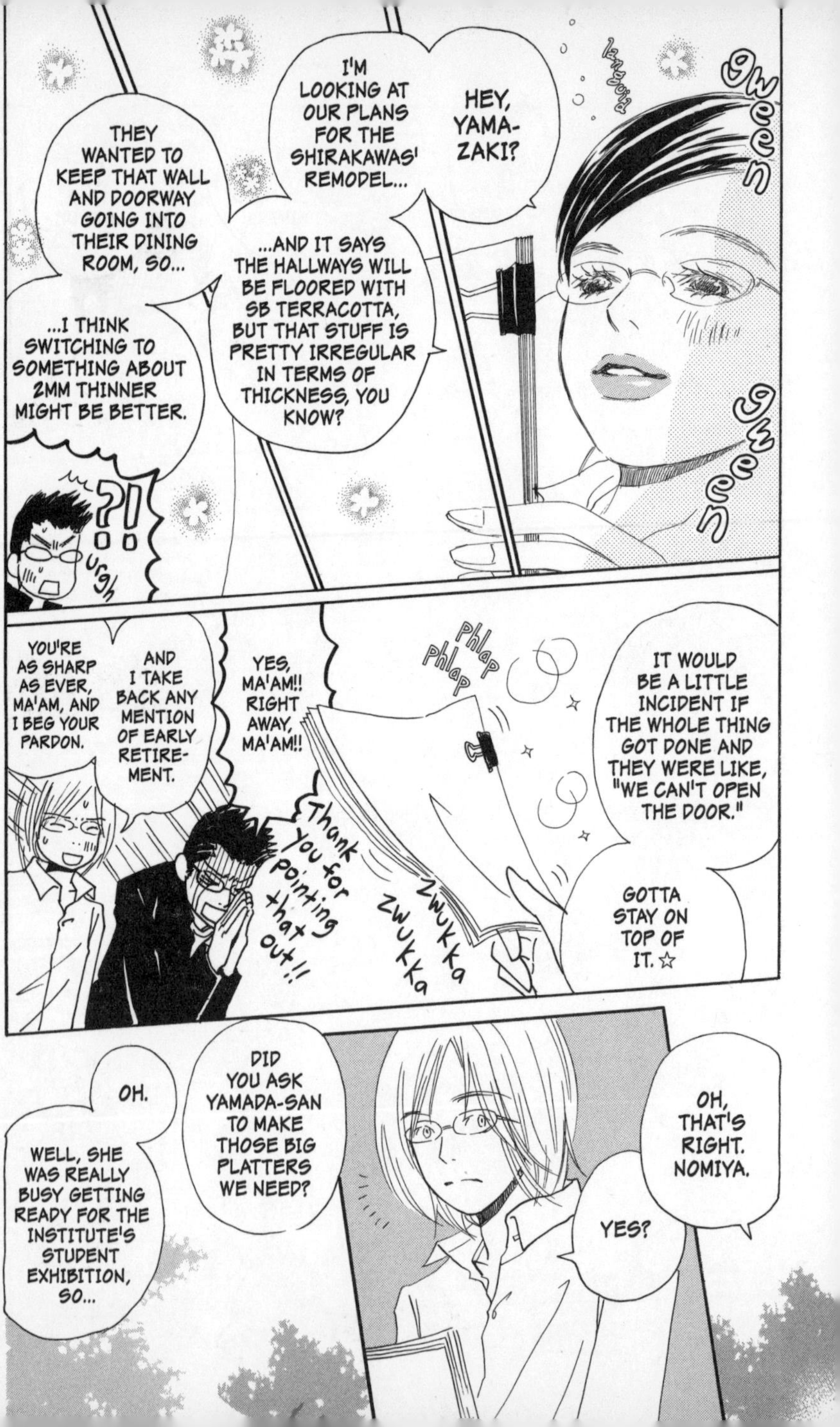
gween
gween
HEY, YAMA-ZAKI?
I'M LOOKING AT OUR PLANS FOR THE SHIRAKAWAS' REMODEL...
...AND IT SAYS THE HALLWAYS WILL BE FLOORED WITH SB TERRACOTTA, BUT THAT STUFF IS PRETTY IRREGULAR IN TERMS OF THICKNESS, YOU KNOW?
THEY WANTED TO KEEP THAT WALL AND DOORWAY GOING INTO THEIR DINING ROOM, SO...
...I THINK SWITCHING TO SOMETHING ABOUT 2MM THINNER MIGHT BE BETTER.
?!
urgh
IT WOULD BE A LITTLE INCIDENT IF THE WHOLE THING GOT DONE AND THEY WERE LIKE, "WE CAN'T OPEN THE DOOR."
GOTTA STAY ON TOP OF IT. ☆
Phlap Phlap
Zwukka Zwukka
YES, MA'AM!! RIGHT AWAY, MA'AM!!
Thank you for pointing that out!!
AND I TAKE BACK ANY MENTION OF EARLY RETIRE-MENT.
YOU'RE AS SHARP AS EVER, MA'AM, AND I BEG YOUR PARDON.
OH, THAT'S RIGHT. NOMIYA.
YES?
DID YOU ASK YAMADA-SAN TO MAKE THOSE BIG PLATTERS WE NEED?
OH.
WELL, SHE WAS REALLY BUSY GETTING READY FOR THE INSTITUTE'S STUDENT EXHIBITION, SO...

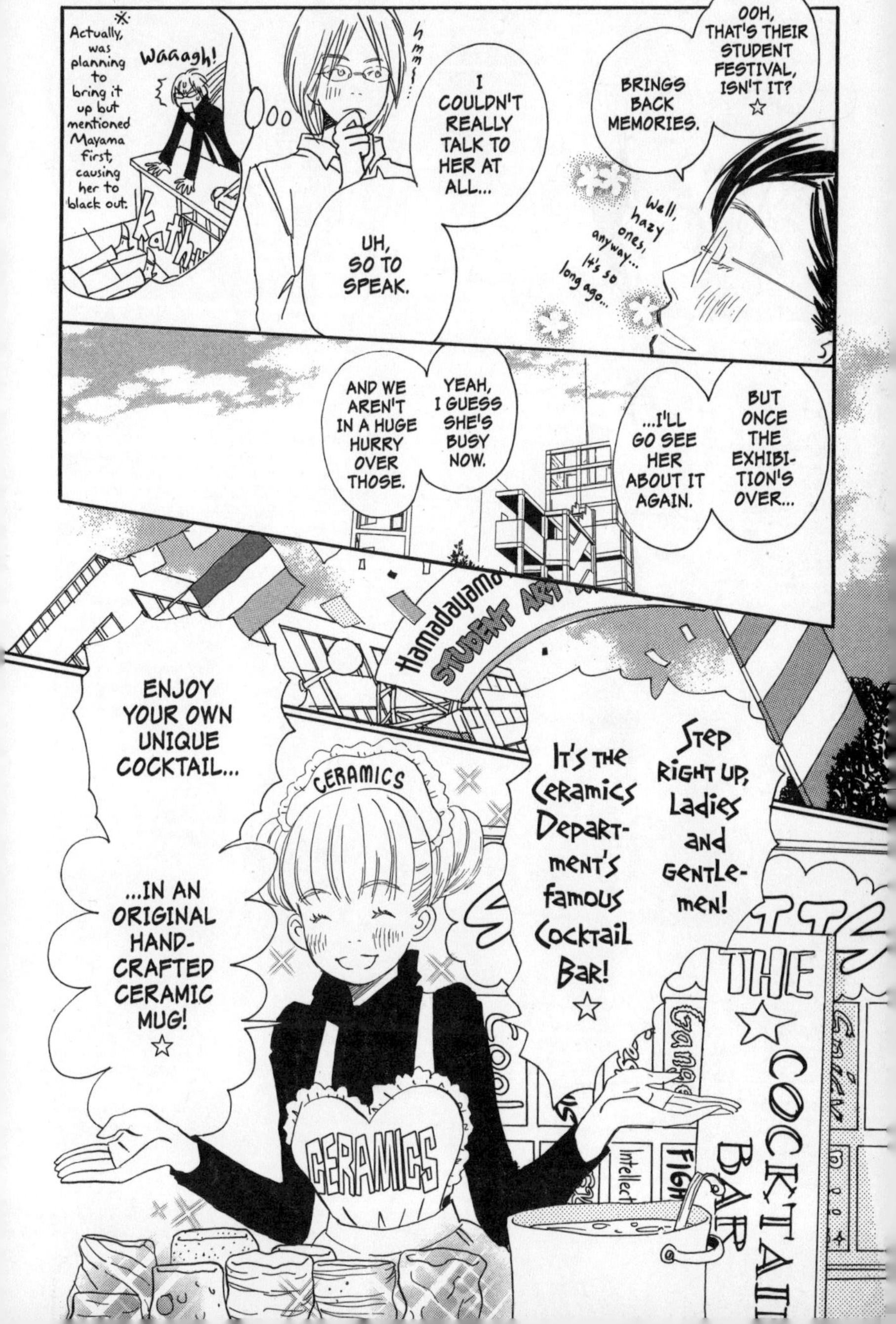
OOH, THAT'S THEIR STUDENT FESTIVAL, ISN'T IT? ☆
BRINGS BACK MEMORIES.
Well, hazy ones, anyway... It's so long ago...
hmm~
I COULDN'T REALLY TALK TO HER AT ALL...
UH, SO TO SPEAK.
※ Actually, was planning to bring it up but mentioned Mayama first, causing her to black out.
Waaagh!
BUT ONCE THE EXHIBITION'S OVER...
...I'LL GO SEE HER ABOUT IT AGAIN.
YEAH, I GUESS SHE'S BUSY NOW.
AND WE AREN'T IN A HUGE HURRY OVER THOSE.
Step right up, Ladies and Gentlemen!
It's the Ceramics Department's famous Cocktail Bar! ☆
THE ☆ COCKTAIL BAR
CERAMICS
ENJOY YOUR OWN UNIQUE COCKTAIL...
...IN AN ORIGINAL HAND-CRAFTED CERAMIC MUG! ☆
CERAMICS

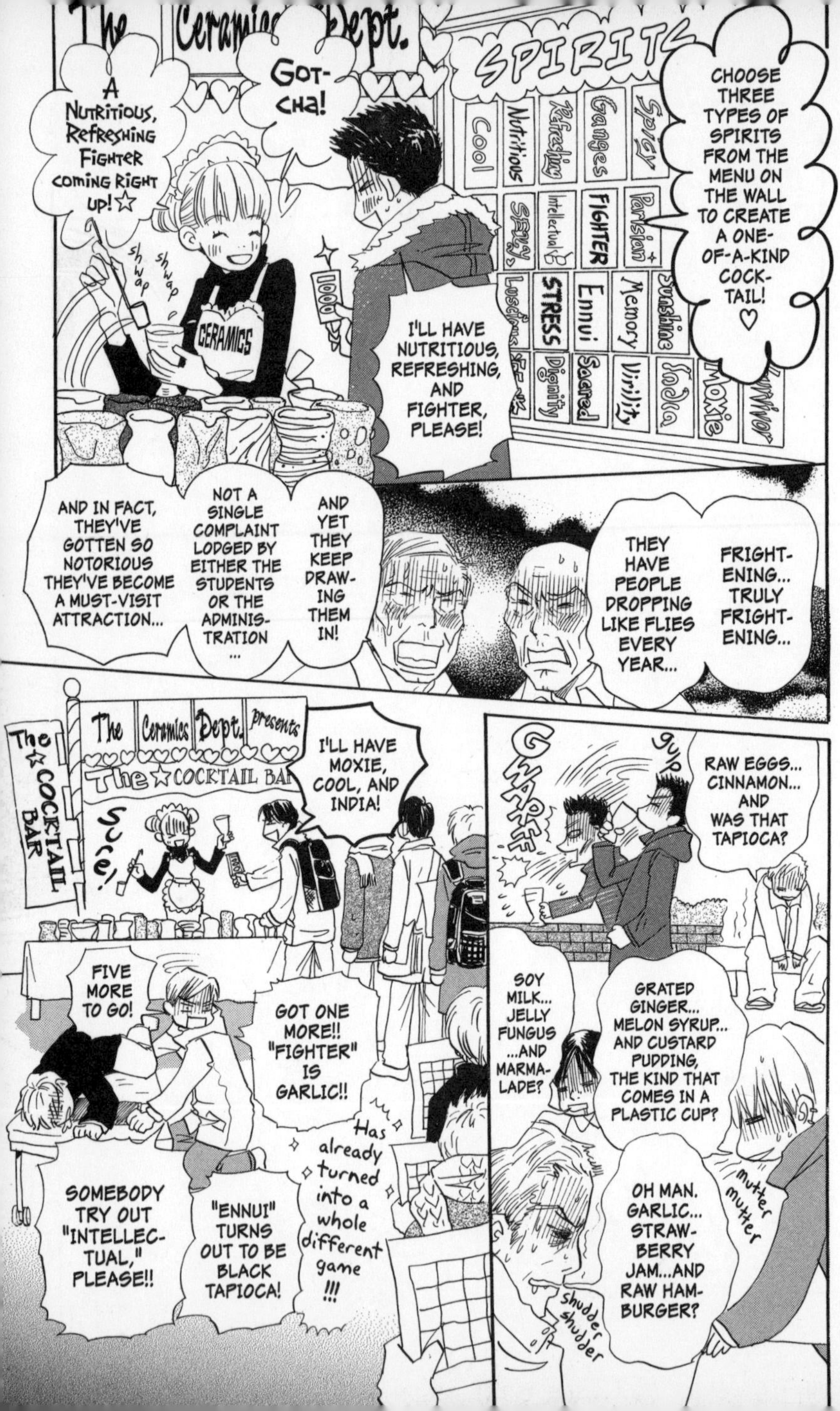
CHOOSE THREE TYPES OF SPIRITS FROM THE MENU ON THE WALL TO CREATE A ONE-OF-A-KIND COCKTAIL! ♡
SPIRITS
Spicy
Ganges
Refreshing
Nutritious
Cool
Parisian
FIGHTER
Intellectual
Sexy
Sunshine
Memory
Ennui
STRESS
Vodka
Virility
Sacred
Dignity
Moxie
Survivor
I'LL HAVE NUTRITIOUS, REFRESHING, AND FIGHTER, PLEASE!
1000
GOT-CHA!
The Ceramics Dept.
A NUTRITIOUS, REFRESHING FIGHTER COMING RIGHT UP! ☆
shwap shwap
CERAMICS
FRIGHTENING... TRULY FRIGHTENING...
THEY HAVE PEOPLE DROPPING LIKE FLIES EVERY YEAR...
AND YET THEY KEEP DRAWING THEM IN!
NOT A SINGLE COMPLAINT LODGED BY EITHER THE STUDENTS OR THE ADMINISTRATION...
AND IN FACT, THEY'VE GOTTEN SO NOTORIOUS THEY'VE BECOME A MUST-VISIT ATTRACTION...
RAW EGGS... CINNAMON... AND WAS THAT TAPIOCA?
gulp
GWAFF
The Ceramics Dept. presents
The ☆ COCKTAIL BAR
I'LL HAVE MOXIE, COOL, AND INDIA!
Sure!
The ☆ COCKTAIL BAR
mutter mutter
OH MAN. GARLIC... STRAWBERRY JAM...AND RAW HAMBURGER?
shudder shudder
GRATED GINGER... MELON SYRUP... AND CUSTARD PUDDING, THE KIND THAT COMES IN A PLASTIC CUP?
SOY MILK... JELLY FUNGUS ...AND MARMALADE?
Has already turned into a whole different game !!!
GOT ONE MORE!! "FIGHTER" IS GARLIC!!
FIVE MORE TO GO!
"ENNUI" TURNS OUT TO BE BLACK TAPIOCA!
SOMEBODY TRY OUT "INTELLECTUAL," PLEASE!!

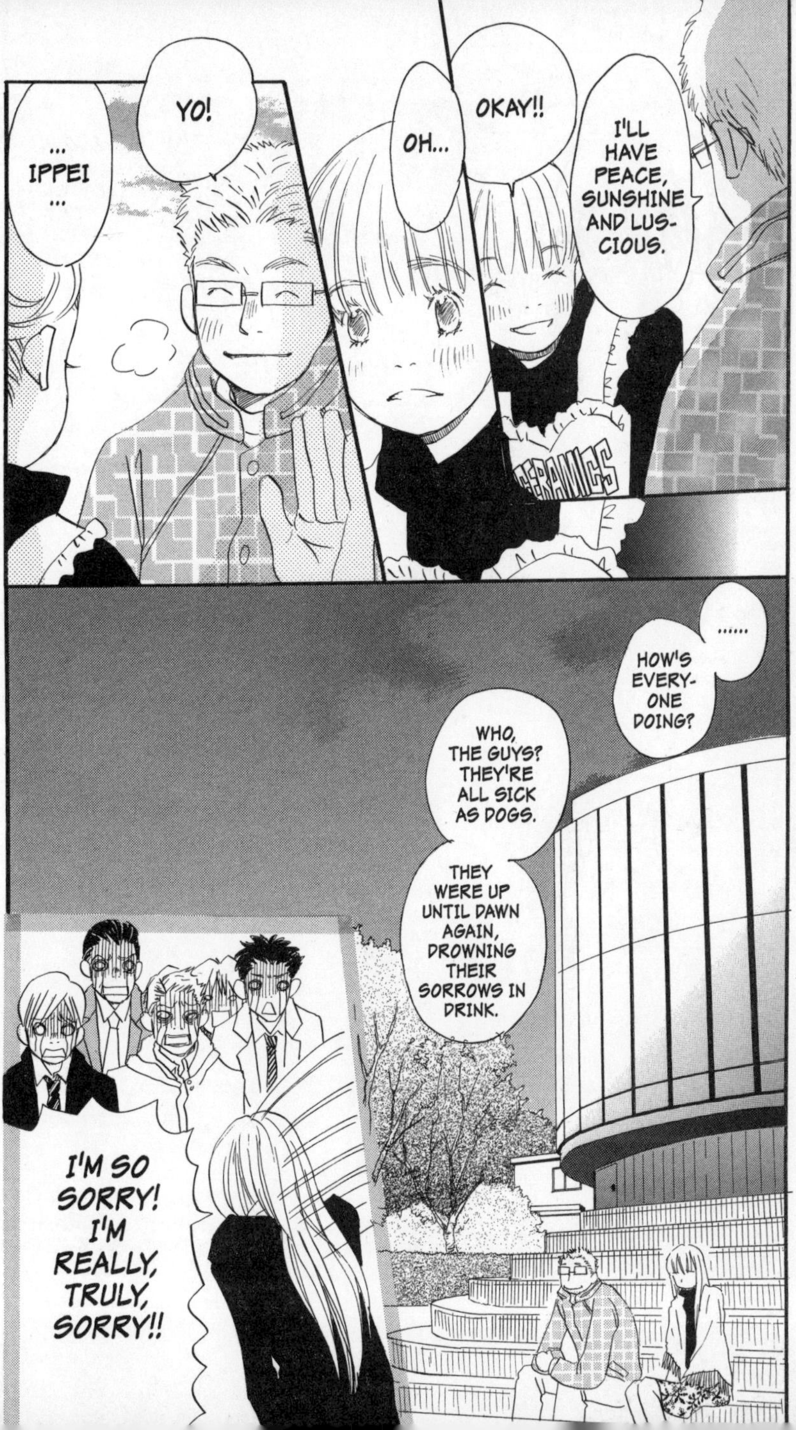
I'LL HAVE PEACE, SUNSHINE AND LUS-CIOUS.
OKAY!!
OH...
YO!
... IPPEI ...
......
HOW'S EVERY-ONE DOING?
WHO, THE GUYS? THEY'RE ALL SICK AS DOGS.
THEY WERE UP UNTIL DAWN AGAIN, DROWNING THEIR SORROWS IN DRINK.
I'M SO SORRY! I'M REALLY, TRULY, SORRY!!

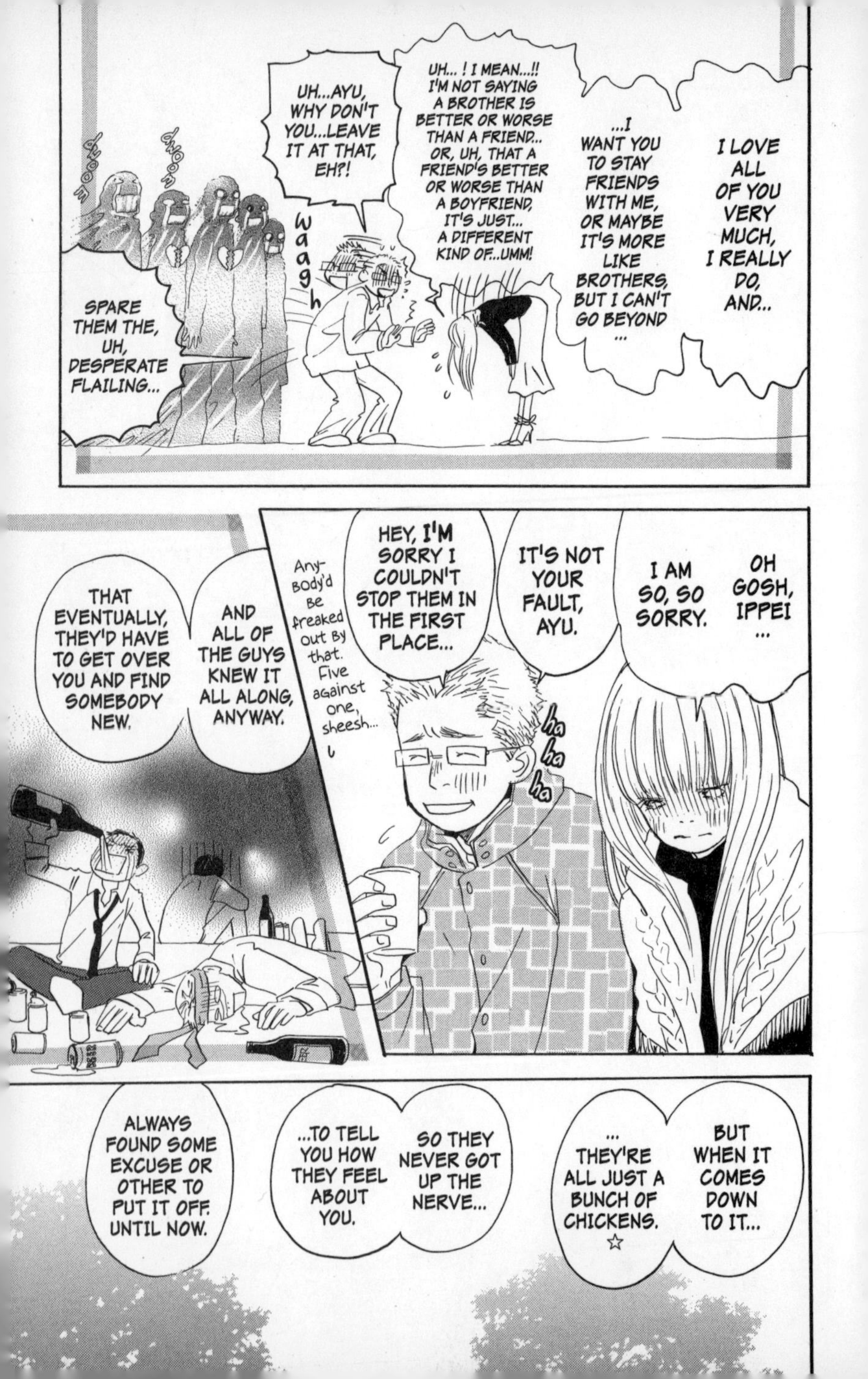
I LOVE ALL OF YOU VERY MUCH, I REALLY DO, AND...
...I WANT YOU TO STAY FRIENDS WITH ME, OR MAYBE IT'S MORE LIKE BROTHERS, BUT I CAN'T GO BEYOND ...
UH... ! I MEAN...!! I'M NOT SAYING A BROTHER IS BETTER OR WORSE THAN A FRIEND... OR, UH, THAT A FRIEND'S BETTER OR WORSE THAN A BOYFRIEND, IT'S JUST... A DIFFERENT KIND OF...UMM!
UH...AYU, WHY DON'T YOU...LEAVE IT AT THAT, EH?!
waagh
SPARE THEM THE, UH, DESPERATE FLAILING...
dwoom
dwoom
OH GOSH, IPPEI ...
I AM SO, SO SORRY.
IT'S NOT YOUR FAULT, AYU.
HEY, I'M SORRY I COULDN'T STOP THEM IN THE FIRST PLACE...
ha ha ha
Any-body'd be freaked out by that. Five against one, sheesh...
AND ALL OF THE GUYS KNEW IT ALL ALONG, ANYWAY.
THAT EVENTUALLY, THEY'D HAVE TO GET OVER YOU AND FIND SOMEBODY NEW.
BUT WHEN IT COMES DOWN TO IT...
... THEY'RE ALL JUST A BUNCH OF CHICKENS. ☆
SO THEY NEVER GOT UP THE NERVE...
...TO TELL YOU HOW THEY FEEL ABOUT YOU.
ALWAYS FOUND SOME EXCUSE OR OTHER TO PUT IT OFF. UNTIL NOW.

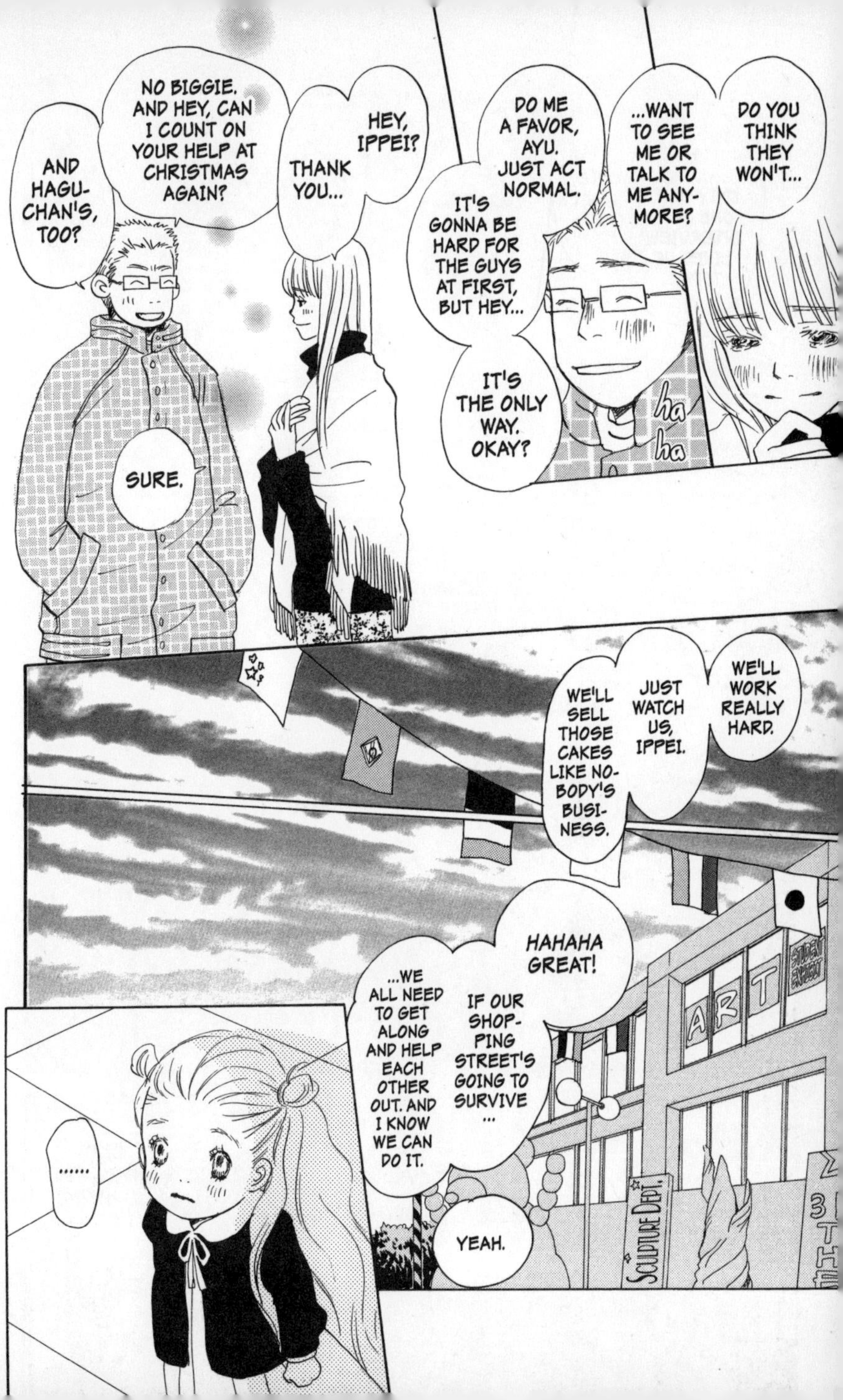
DO YOU THINK THEY WON'T...
...WANT TO SEE ME OR TALK TO ME ANYMORE?
DO ME A FAVOR, AYU. JUST ACT NORMAL.
IT'S GONNA BE HARD FOR THE GUYS AT FIRST, BUT HEY...
ha ha
IT'S THE ONLY WAY. OKAY?
HEY, IPPEI?
THANK YOU...
NO BIGGIE. AND HEY, CAN I COUNT ON YOUR HELP AT CHRISTMAS AGAIN?
AND HAGU-CHAN'S, TOO?
SURE.
WE'LL WORK REALLY HARD.
JUST WATCH US, IPPEI.
WE'LL SELL THOSE CAKES LIKE NOBODY'S BUSINESS.
HAHAHA GREAT!
IF OUR SHOPPING STREET'S GOING TO SURVIVE...
...WE ALL NEED TO GET ALONG AND HELP EACH OTHER OUT. AND I KNOW WE CAN DO IT.
YEAH.
STUDENT EXHIBIT
ART
SCULPTURE DEPT.
......

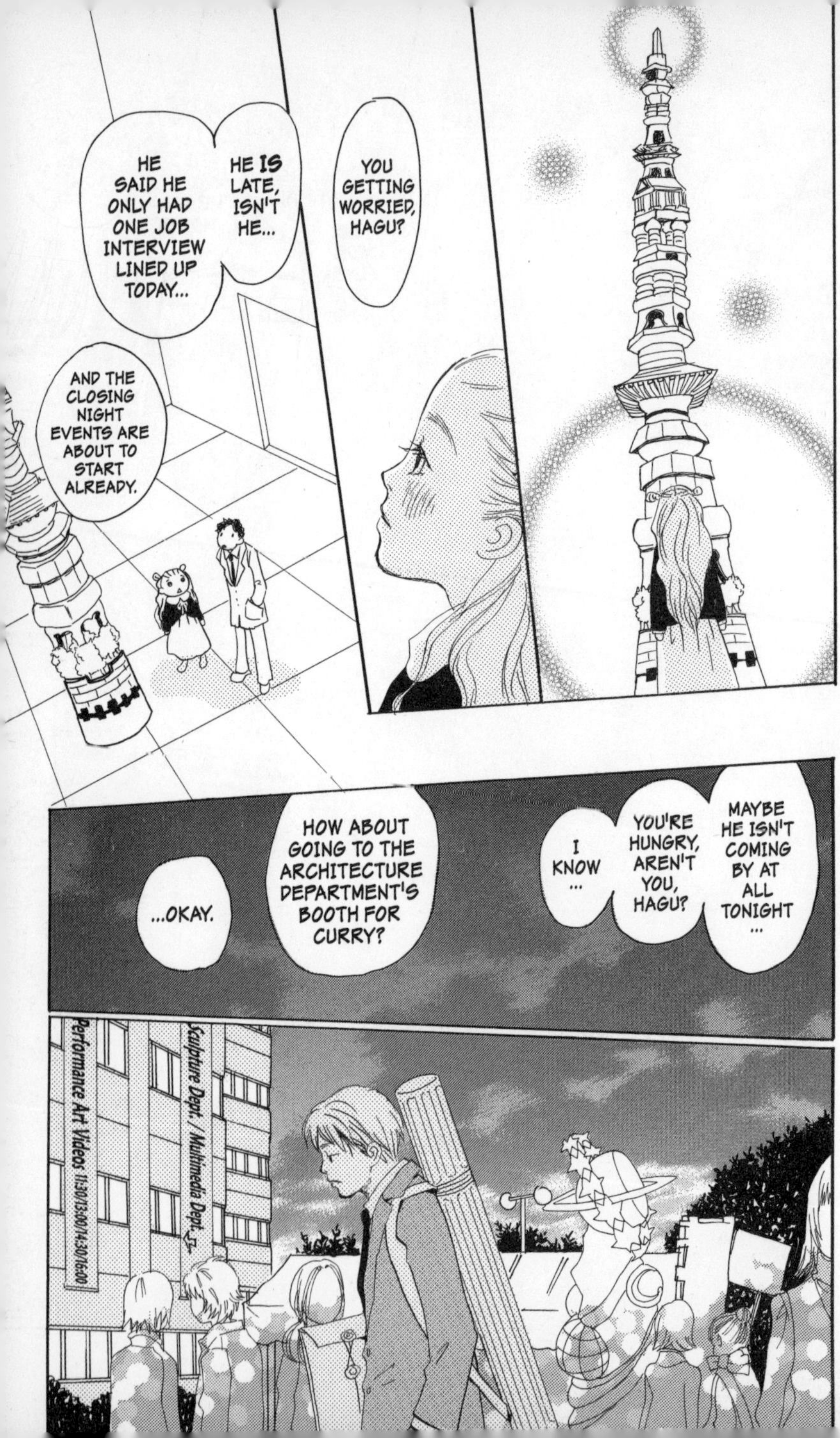
YOU GETTING WORRIED, HAGU?
HE IS LATE, ISN'T HE...
HE SAID HE ONLY HAD ONE JOB INTERVIEW LINED UP TODAY...
AND THE CLOSING NIGHT EVENTS ARE ABOUT TO START ALREADY.
MAYBE HE ISN'T COMING BY AT ALL TONIGHT ...
YOU'RE HUNGRY, AREN'T YOU, HAGU?
I KNOW ...
HOW ABOUT GOING TO THE ARCHITECTURE DEPARTMENT'S BOOTH FOR CURRY?
...OKAY.
Sculpture Dept. / Multimedia Dept.
Performance Art Videos 11:30/13:00/14:30/16:00

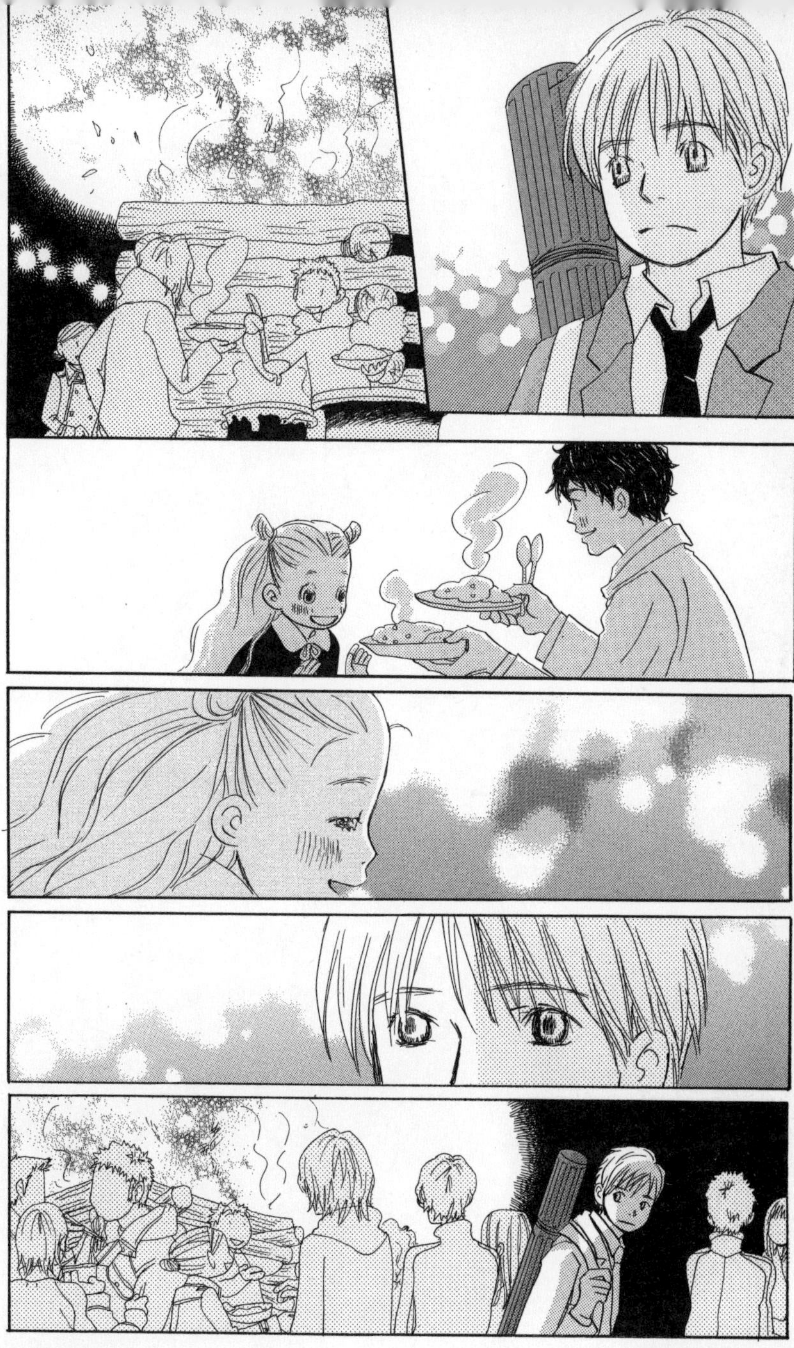

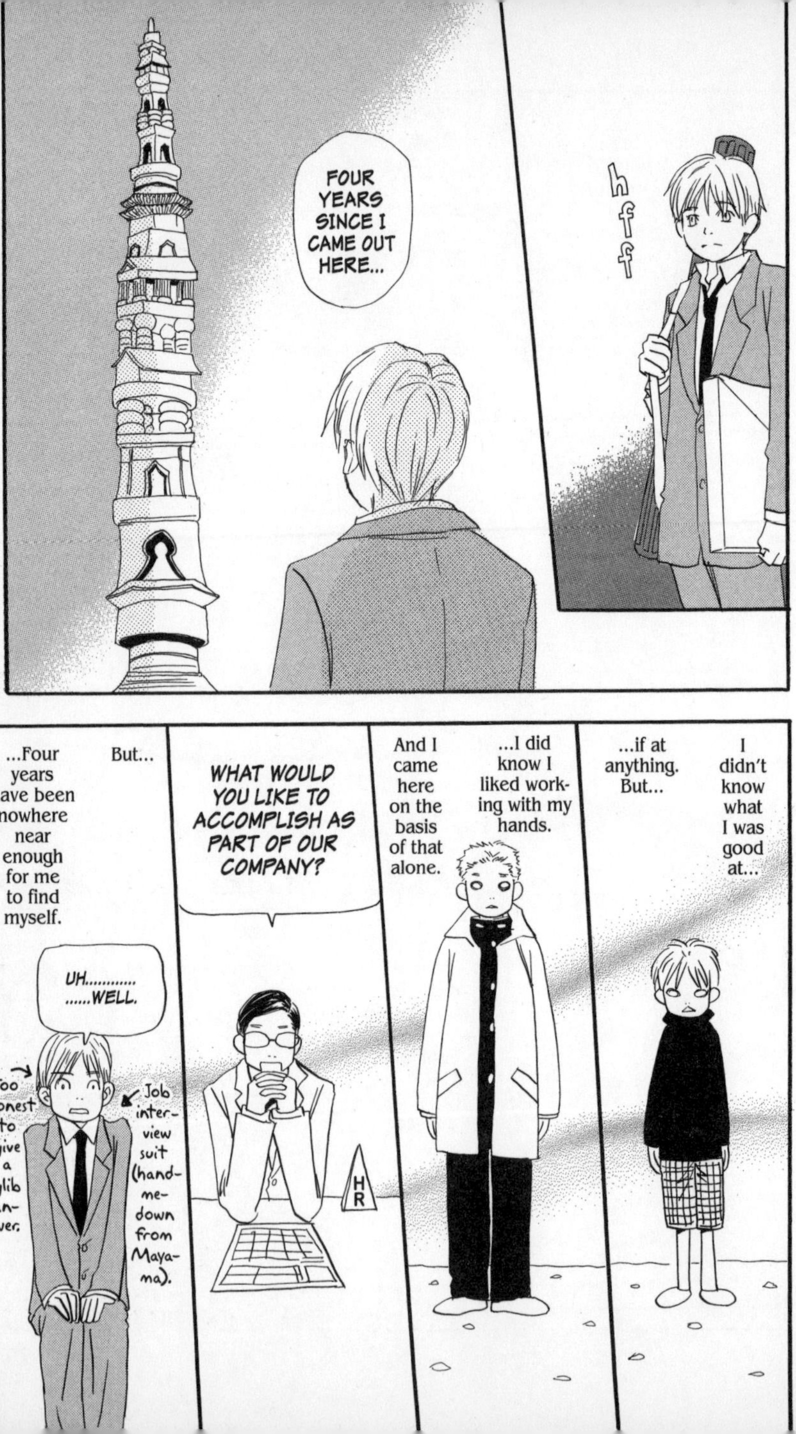
hff
FOUR YEARS SINCE I CAME OUT HERE...
I didn't know what I was good at...
...if at anything. But...
...I did know I liked working with my hands.
And I came here on the basis of that alone.
WHAT WOULD YOU LIKE TO ACCOMPLISH AS PART OF OUR COMPANY?
HR
But...
...Four years have been nowhere near enough for me to find myself.
UH........... ......WELL.
Job interview suit (hand-me-down from Mayama).
Too honest to give a glib answer.

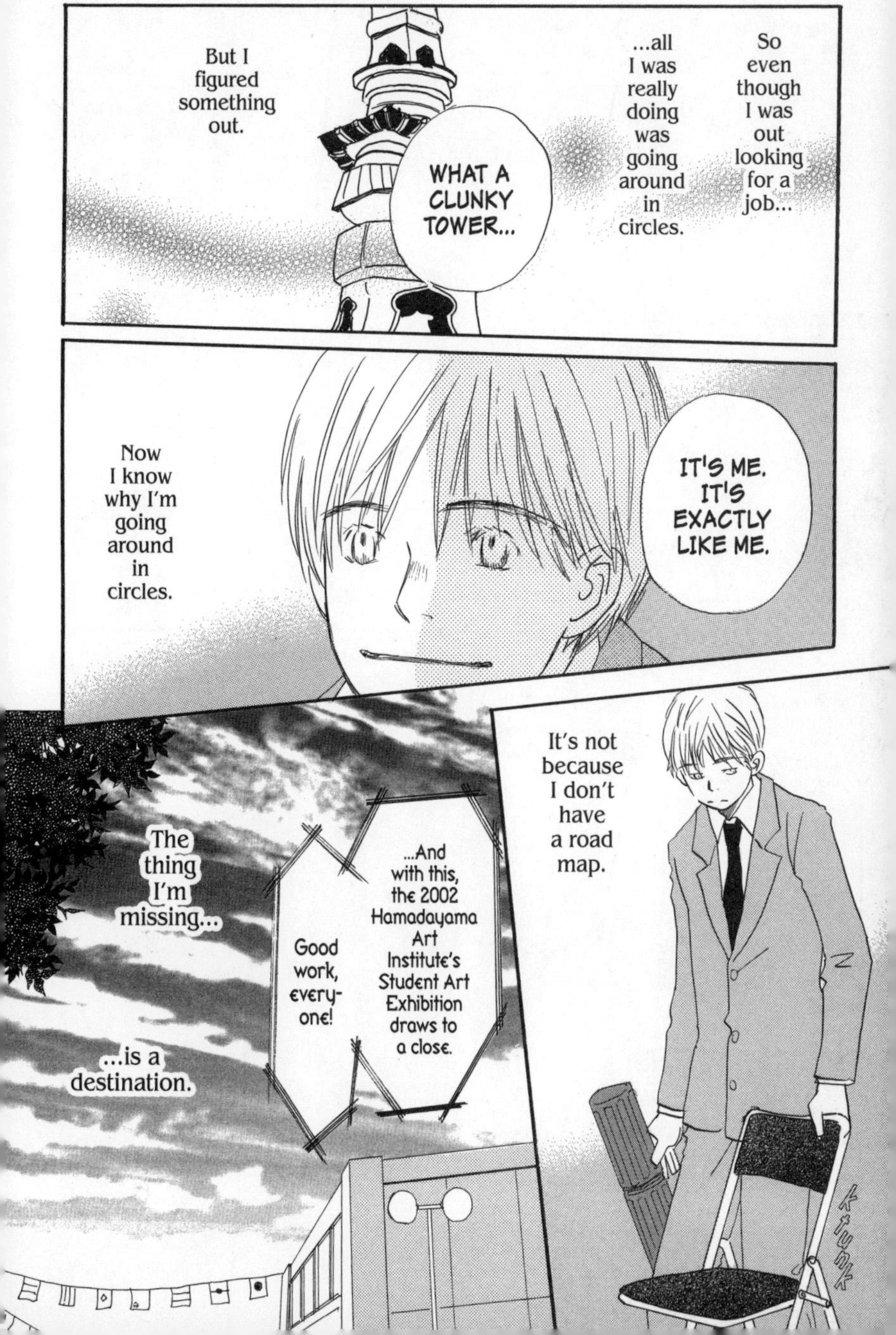
So even though I was out looking for a job...
...all I was really doing was going around in circles.
WHAT A CLUNKY TOWER...
But I figured something out.
IT'S ME. IT'S EXACTLY LIKE ME.
Now I know why I'm going around in circles.
It's not because I don't have a road map.
ktunk
...And with this, the 2002 Hamadayama Art Institute's Student Art Exhibition draws to a close.
Good work, every-one!
The thing I'm missing...
...is a destination.

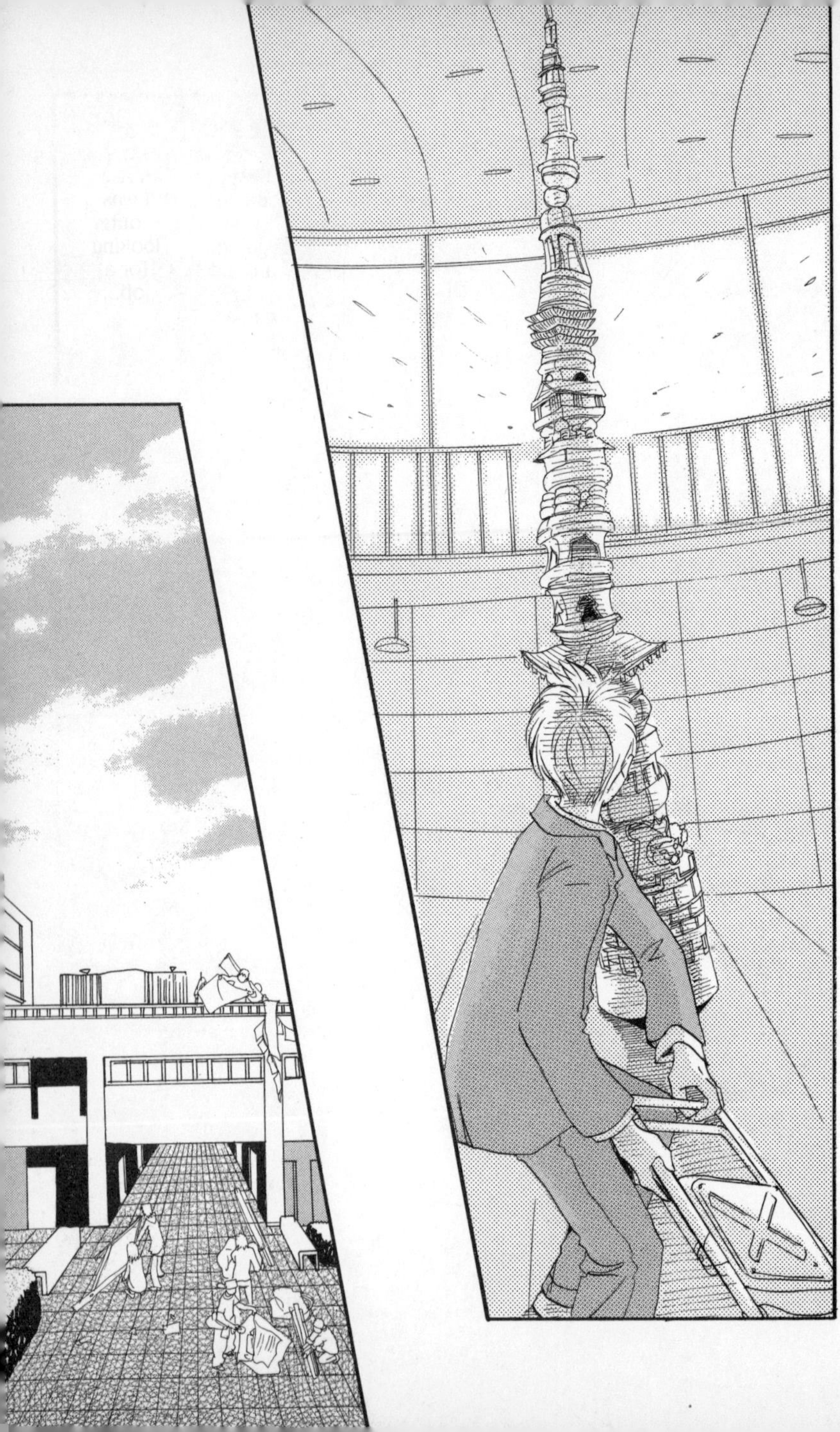

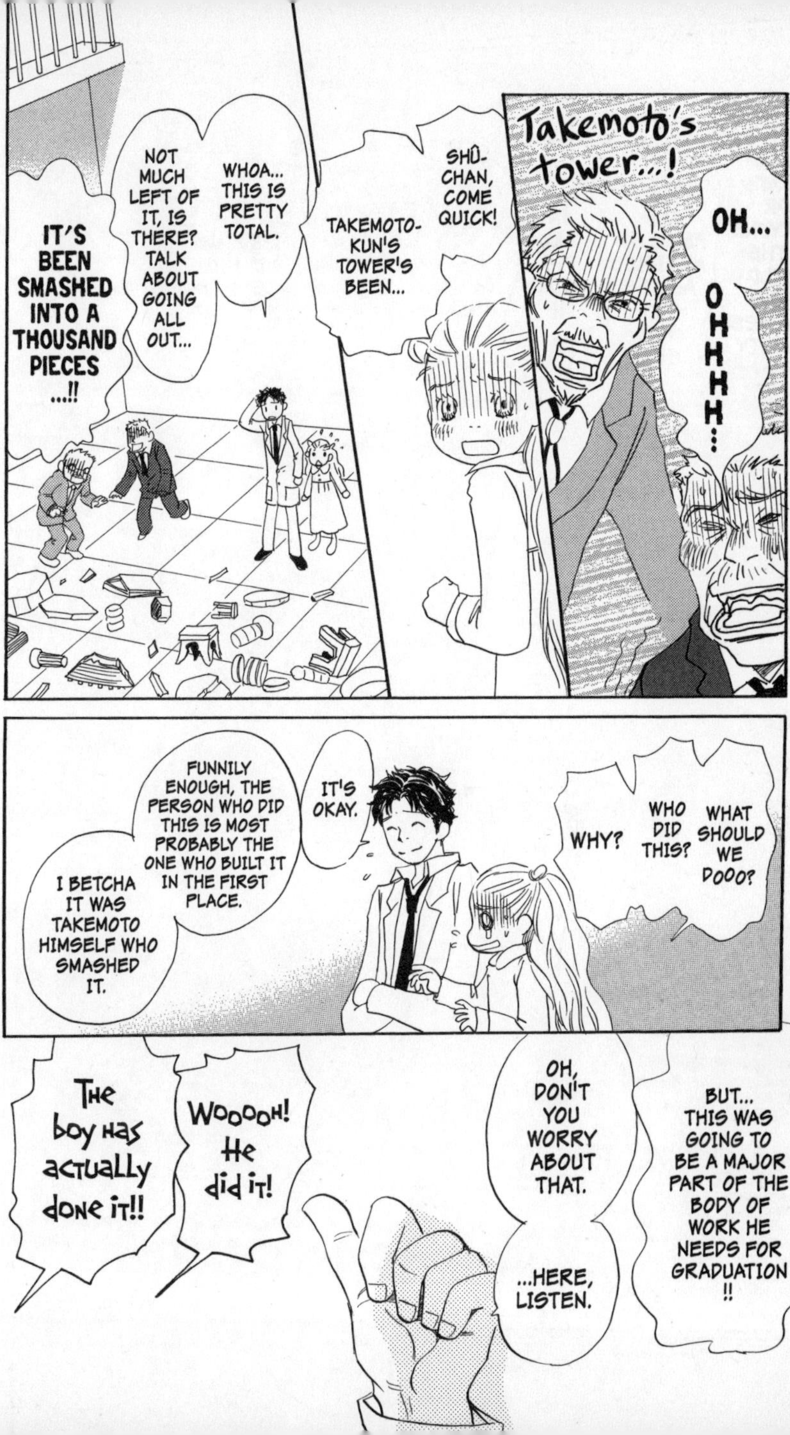
Takemoto's tower...!
OH... OHHHH...
SHÛ-CHAN, COME QUICK!
TAKEMOTO-KUN'S TOWER'S BEEN...
WHOA... THIS IS PRETTY TOTAL.
NOT MUCH LEFT OF IT, IS THERE? TALK ABOUT GOING ALL OUT...
IT'S BEEN SMASHED INTO A THOUSAND PIECES ...!!
WHAT SHOULD WE DOOO?
WHO DID THIS?
WHY?
IT'S OKAY.
FUNNILY ENOUGH, THE PERSON WHO DID THIS IS MOST PROBABLY THE ONE WHO BUILT IT IN THE FIRST PLACE.
I BETCHA IT WAS TAKEMOTO HIMSELF WHO SMASHED IT.
BUT... THIS WAS GOING TO BE A MAJOR PART OF THE BODY OF WORK HE NEEDS FOR GRADUATION !!
OH, DON'T YOU WORRY ABOUT THAT.
...HERE, LISTEN.
WOOOOH! He did it!
The boy has actually done it!!

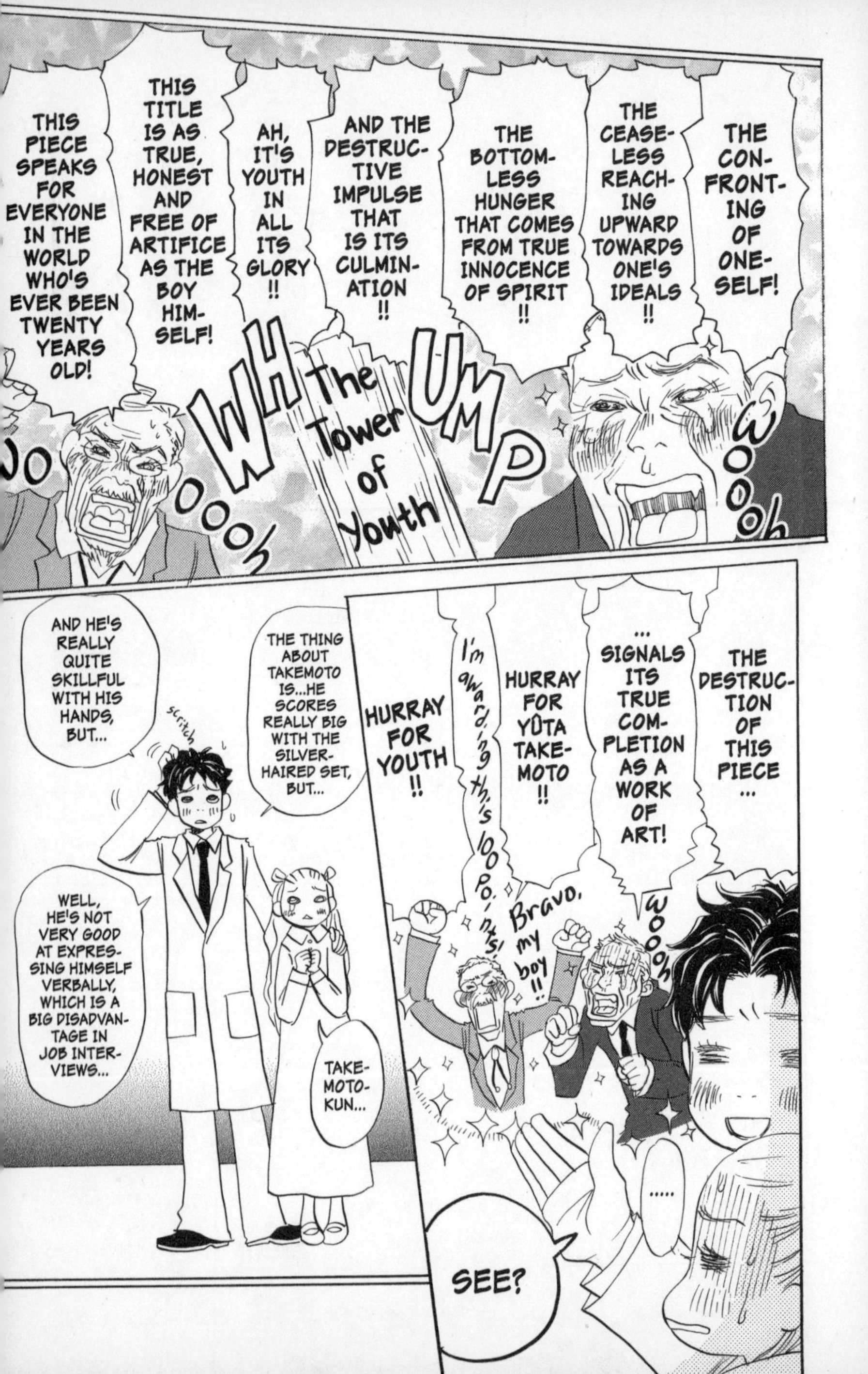
THE CONFRONTING OF ONESELF!
THE CEASELESS REACHING UPWARD TOWARDS ONE'S IDEALS!!
THE BOTTOMLESS HUNGER THAT COMES FROM TRUE INNOCENCE OF SPIRIT!!
AND THE DESTRUCTIVE IMPULSE THAT IS ITS CULMINATION!!
AH, IT'S YOUTH IN ALL ITS GLORY!!
THIS TITLE IS AS TRUE, HONEST AND FREE OF ARTIFICE AS THE BOY HIMSELF!
THIS PIECE SPEAKS FOR EVERYONE IN THE WORLD WHO'S EVER BEEN TWENTY YEARS OLD!
WOOOoh
WHUMP
The Tower of Youth
WOOOoh
THE DESTRUCTION OF THIS PIECE...
...SIGNALS ITS TRUE COMPLETION AS A WORK OF ART!
HURRAY FOR YŪTA TAKEMOTO!!
I'm awarding this 100 points!
HURRAY FOR YOUTH!!
Bravo, my boy!!
WOOOoh
.....
SEE?
THE THING ABOUT TAKEMOTO IS...HE SCORES REALLY BIG WITH THE SILVER-HAIRED SET, BUT...
AND HE'S REALLY QUITE SKILLFUL WITH HIS HANDS, BUT...
scritch
WELL, HE'S NOT VERY GOOD AT EXPRESSING HIMSELF VERBALLY, WHICH IS A BIG DISADVANTAGE IN JOB INTERVIEWS...
TAKEMOTO-KUN...

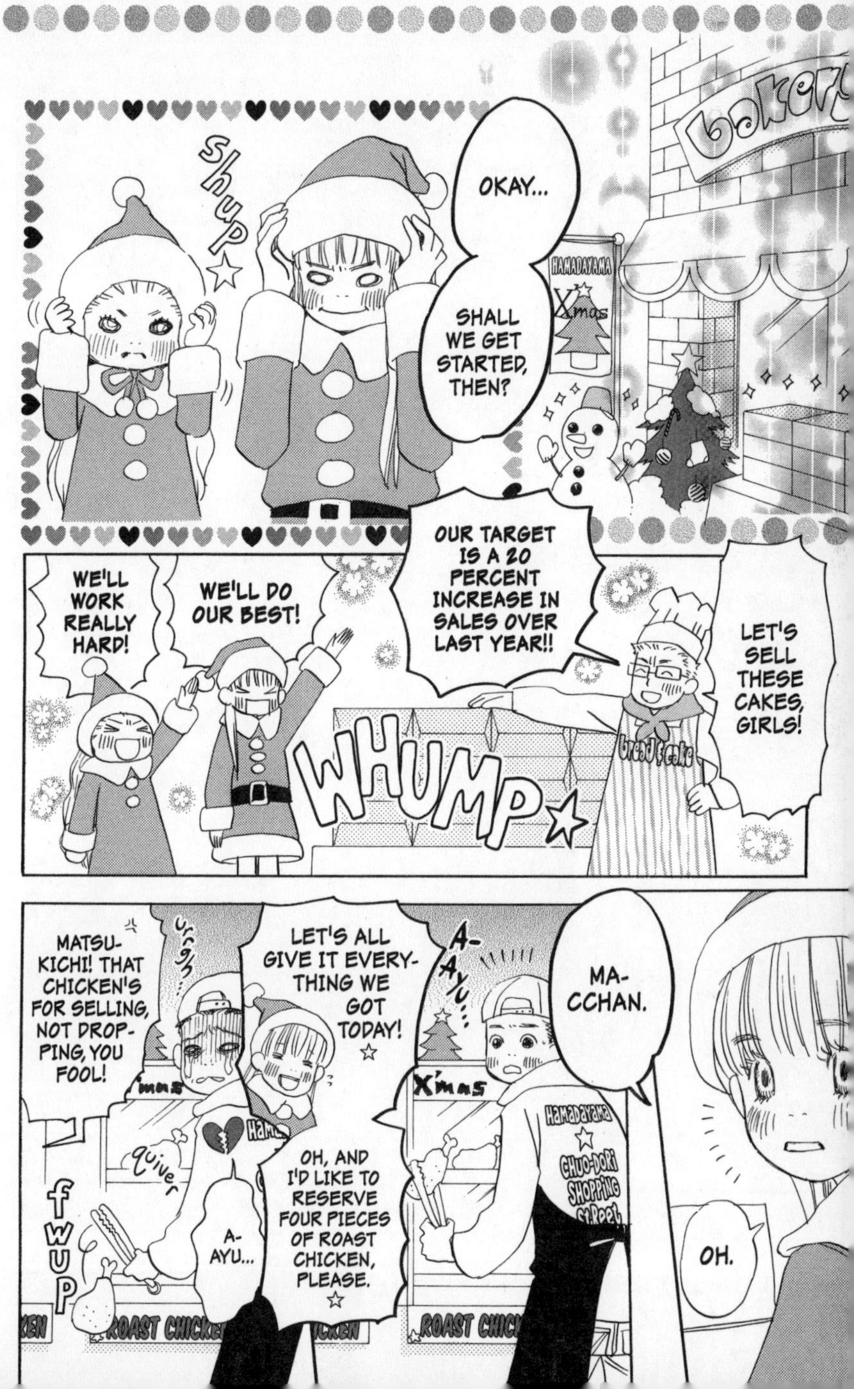
bakery
OKAY... SHALL WE GET STARTED, THEN?
shup☆
HAMADAYAMA X'mas
LET'S SELL THESE CAKES, GIRLS!
bread & cake
OUR TARGET IS A 20 PERCENT INCREASE IN SALES OVER LAST YEAR!!
WHUMP☆
WE'LL DO OUR BEST!
WE'LL WORK REALLY HARD!
MA-CHAN.
OH.
A-AYU...
HAMADAYAMA ☆ CHUO-DORI SHOPPING STREET
X'mas
ROAST CHICK
LET'S ALL GIVE IT EVERYTHING WE GOT TODAY! ☆
OH, AND I'D LIKE TO RESERVE FOUR PIECES OF ROAST CHICKEN, PLEASE. ☆
urgh...
MATSU-KICHI! THAT CHICKEN'S FOR SELLING, NOT DROP-PING, YOU FOOL!
A-AYU...
quiver
fwup
ROAST CHICKEN

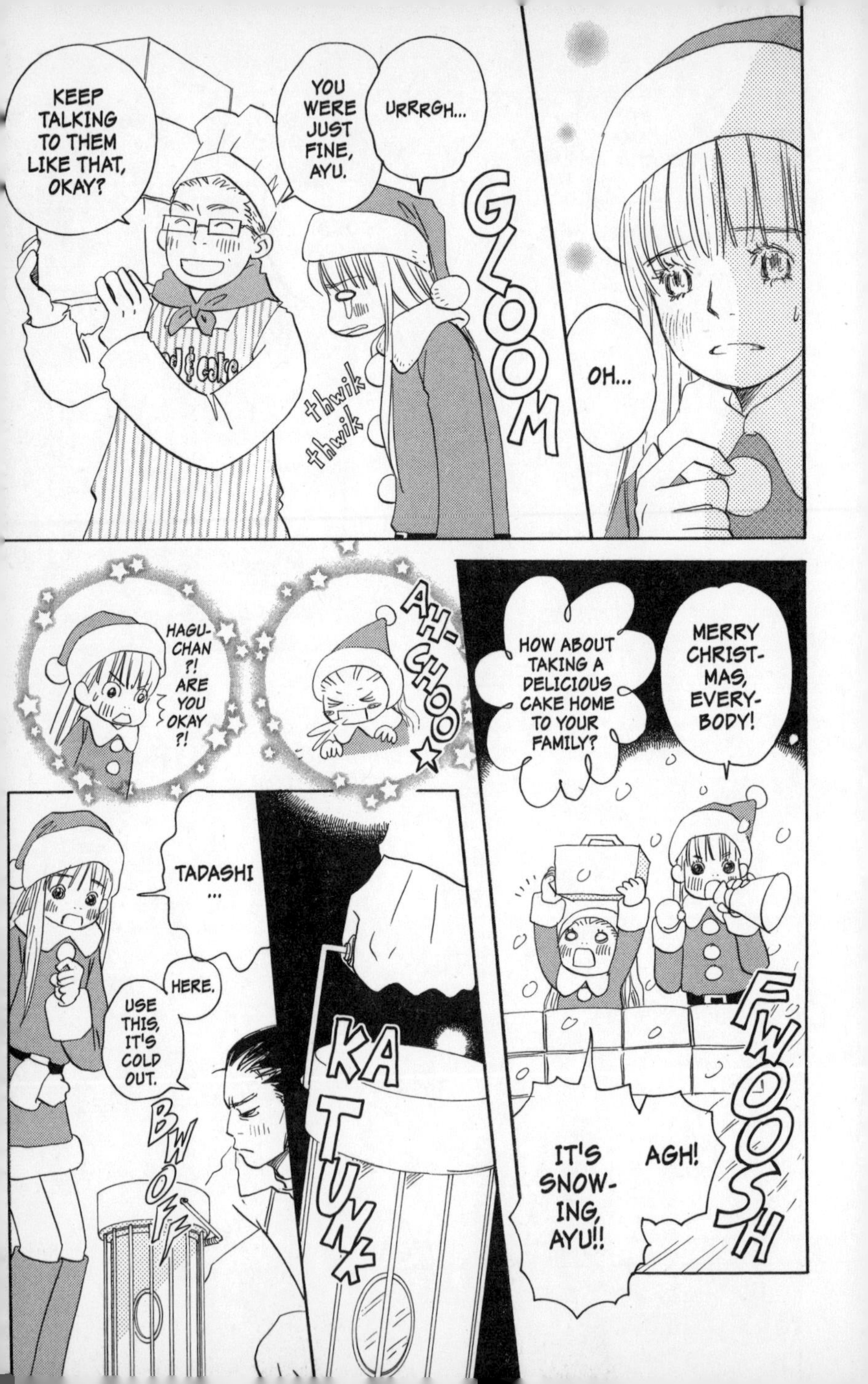
OH...
URRRGH...
YOU WERE JUST FINE, AYU.
KEEP TALKING TO THEM LIKE THAT, OKAY?
GLOOM
thwik thwik
MERRY CHRISTMAS, EVERYBODY!
HOW ABOUT TAKING A DELICIOUS CAKE HOME TO YOUR FAMILY?
FWOOSH
AGH!
IT'S SNOWING, AYU!!
AH-CHOO☆
HAGU-CHAN?! ARE YOU OKAY?!
KA TUNK
TADASHI...
HERE.
USE THIS, IT'S COLD OUT.
BWOMM

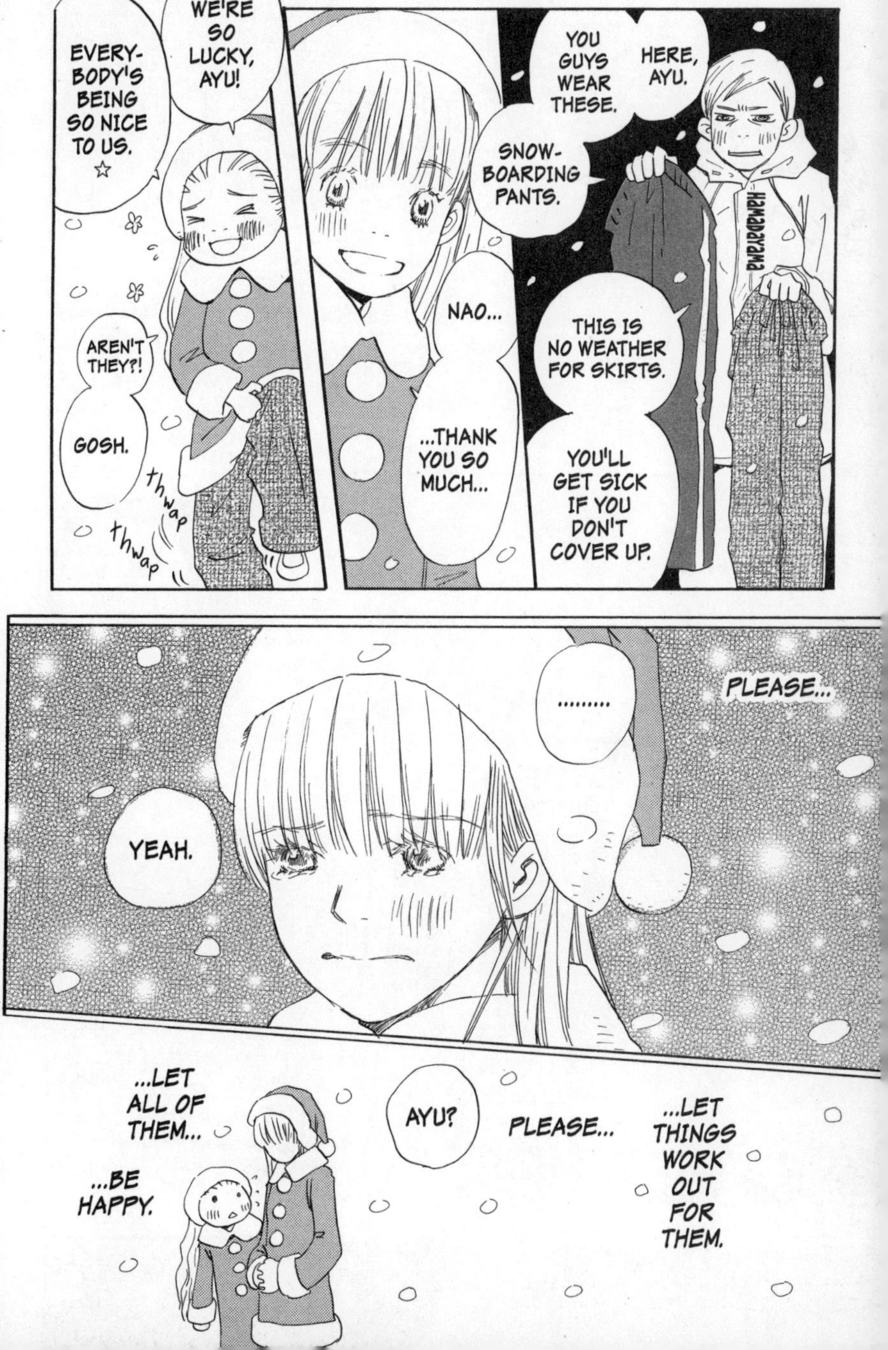
HERE, AYU.
YOU GUYS WEAR THESE.
SNOW-BOARDING PANTS.
HAMADAYAMA
THIS IS NO WEATHER FOR SKIRTS.
YOU'LL GET SICK IF YOU DON'T COVER UP.
NAO...
...THANK YOU SO MUCH...
WE'RE SO LUCKY, AYU!
EVERY-BODY'S BEING SO NICE TO US. ☆
AREN'T THEY?!
GOSH.
thwap
thwap
PLEASE...
....
YEAH.
...LET THINGS WORK OUT FOR THEM.
PLEASE...
AYU?
...LET ALL OF THEM...
...BE HAPPY.

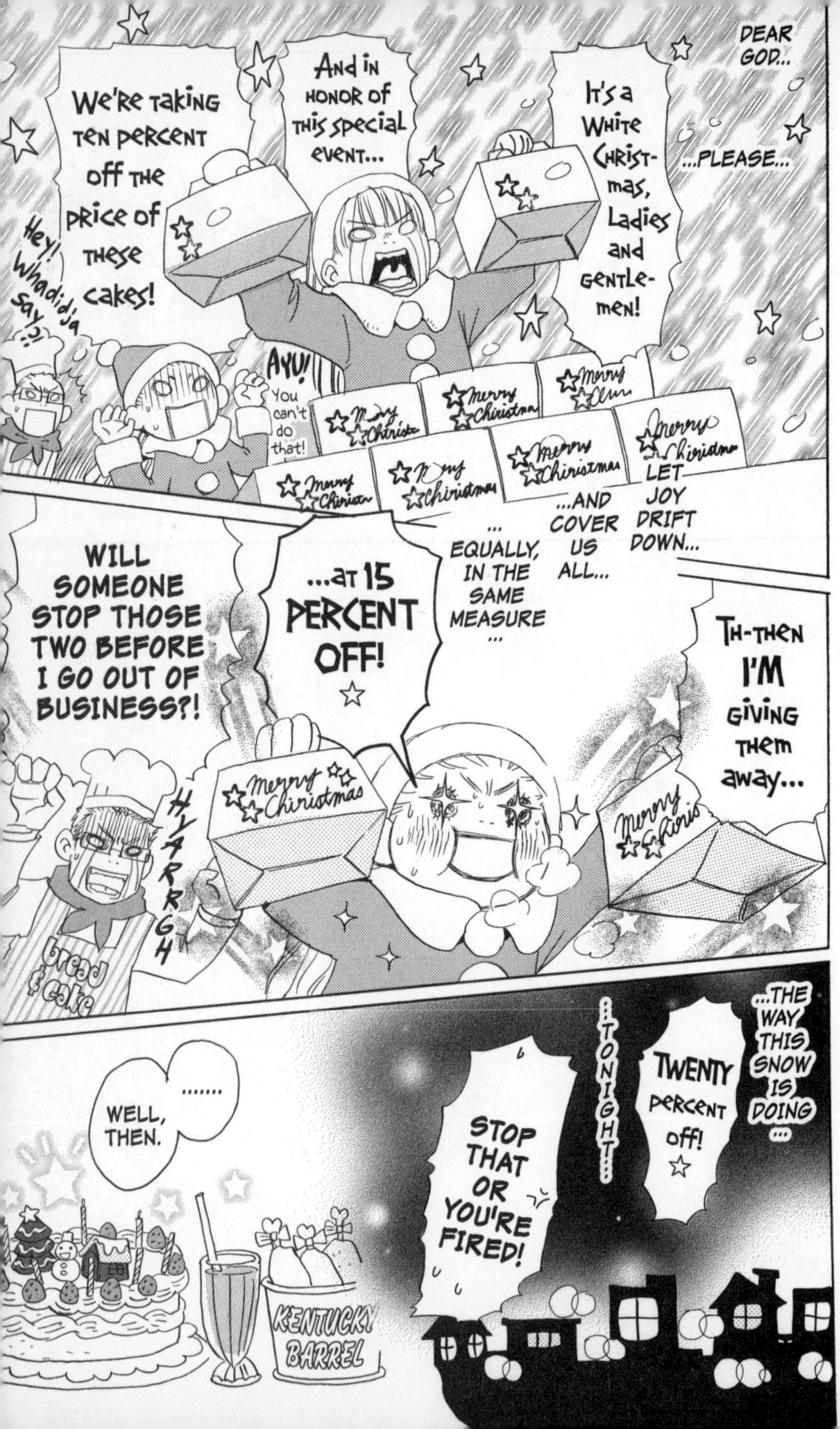
DEAR GOD...
...PLEASE...
It's a White Christmas, Ladies and gentlemen!
And in honor of this special event...
We're taking ten percent off the price of these cakes!
Hey! Whadidja say?!
AYU! You can't do that!
LET JOY DRIFT DOWN...
...AND COVER US ALL...
...EQUALLY, IN THE SAME MEASURE...
TH-THEN I'M GIVING THEM away...
...at 15 PERCENT OFF!
WILL SOMEONE STOP THOSE TWO BEFORE I GO OUT OF BUSINESS?!
Merry Christmas
HYARRGH
bread & cake
...THE WAY THIS SNOW IS DOING...
...TONIGHT...
TWENTY percent off!
STOP THAT OR YOU'RE FIRED!
....
WELL, THEN.
KENTUCKY BARREL

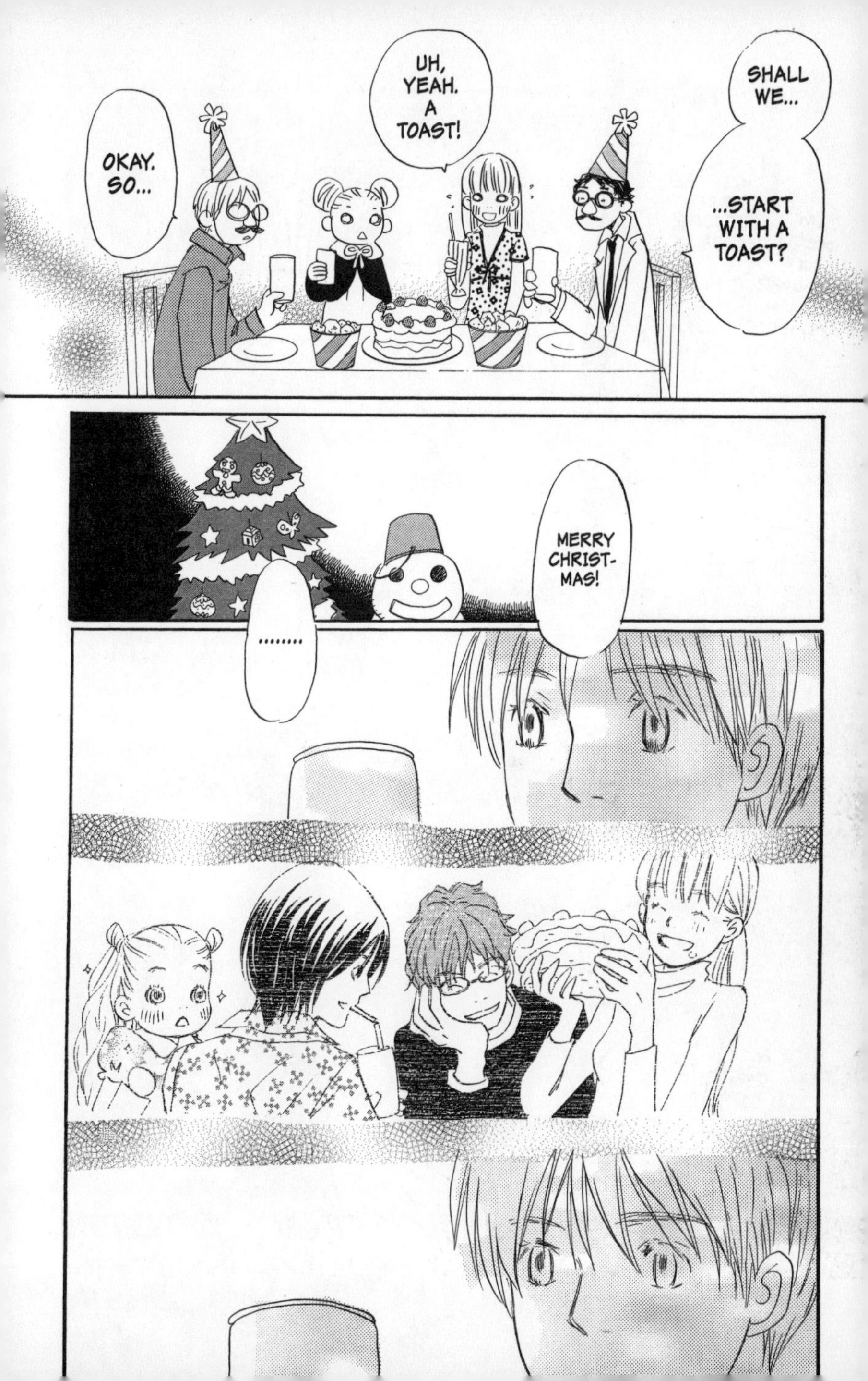
SHALL WE...
...START WITH A TOAST?
UH, YEAH. A TOAST!
OKAY. SO...
MERRY CHRIST-MAS!
....

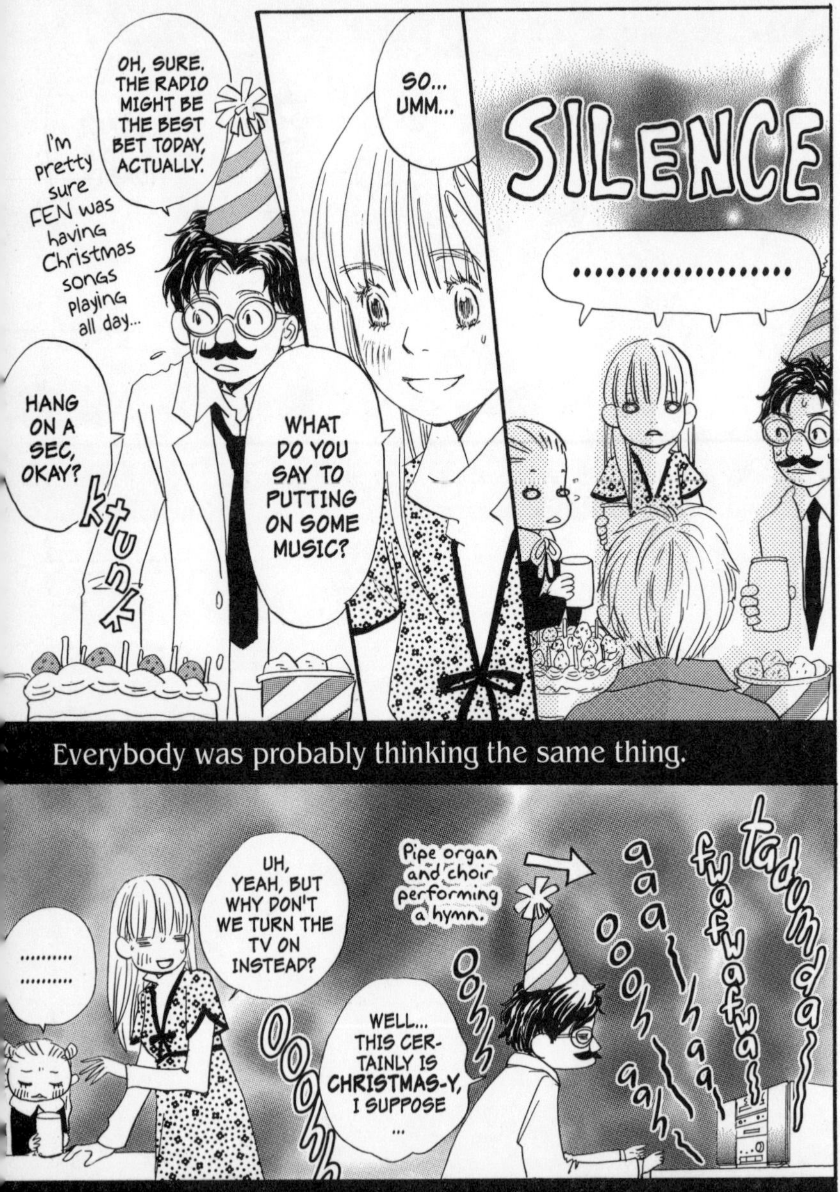
SILENCE
....
SO... UMM...
WHAT DO YOU SAY TO PUTTING ON SOME MUSIC?
OH, SURE. THE RADIO MIGHT BE THE BEST BET TODAY, ACTUALLY.
I'm pretty sure FEN was having Christmas songs playing all day...
HANG ON A SEC, OKAY?
ktunk
Everybody was probably thinking the same thing.
tadumdaa~
fwafwafwa~
aaa~haa~
ooooh~aah~
Pipe organ and choir performing a hymn.
ooohh
ooohh
WELL... THIS CERTAINLY IS CHRISTMAS-Y, I SUPPOSE...
UH, YEAH, BUT WHY DON'T WE TURN THE TV ON INSTEAD?
....
....
But if we said it out loud...

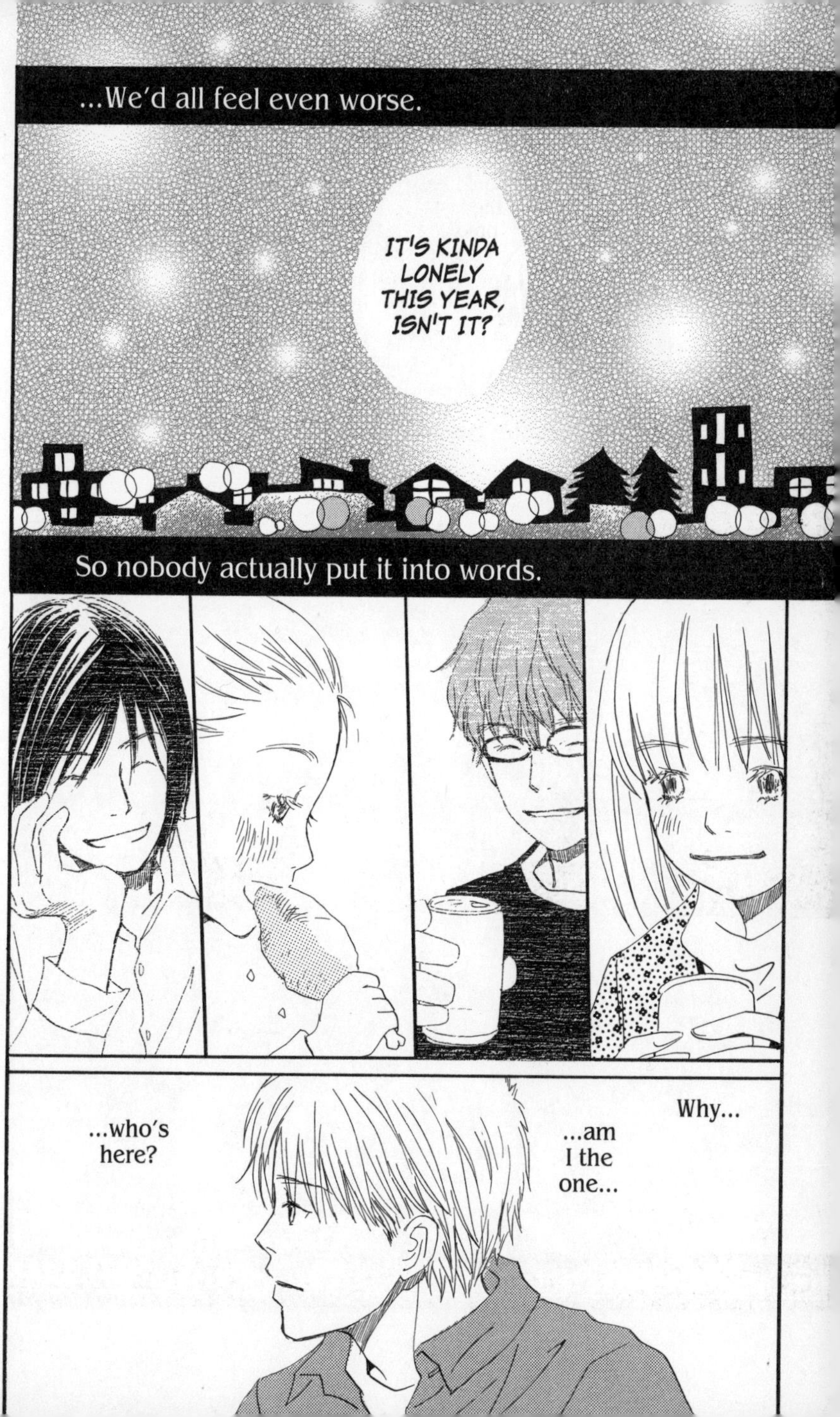
...We'd all feel even worse.
IT'S KINDA LONELY THIS YEAR, ISN'T IT?
So nobody actually put it into words.
Why...
...am I the one...
...who's here?

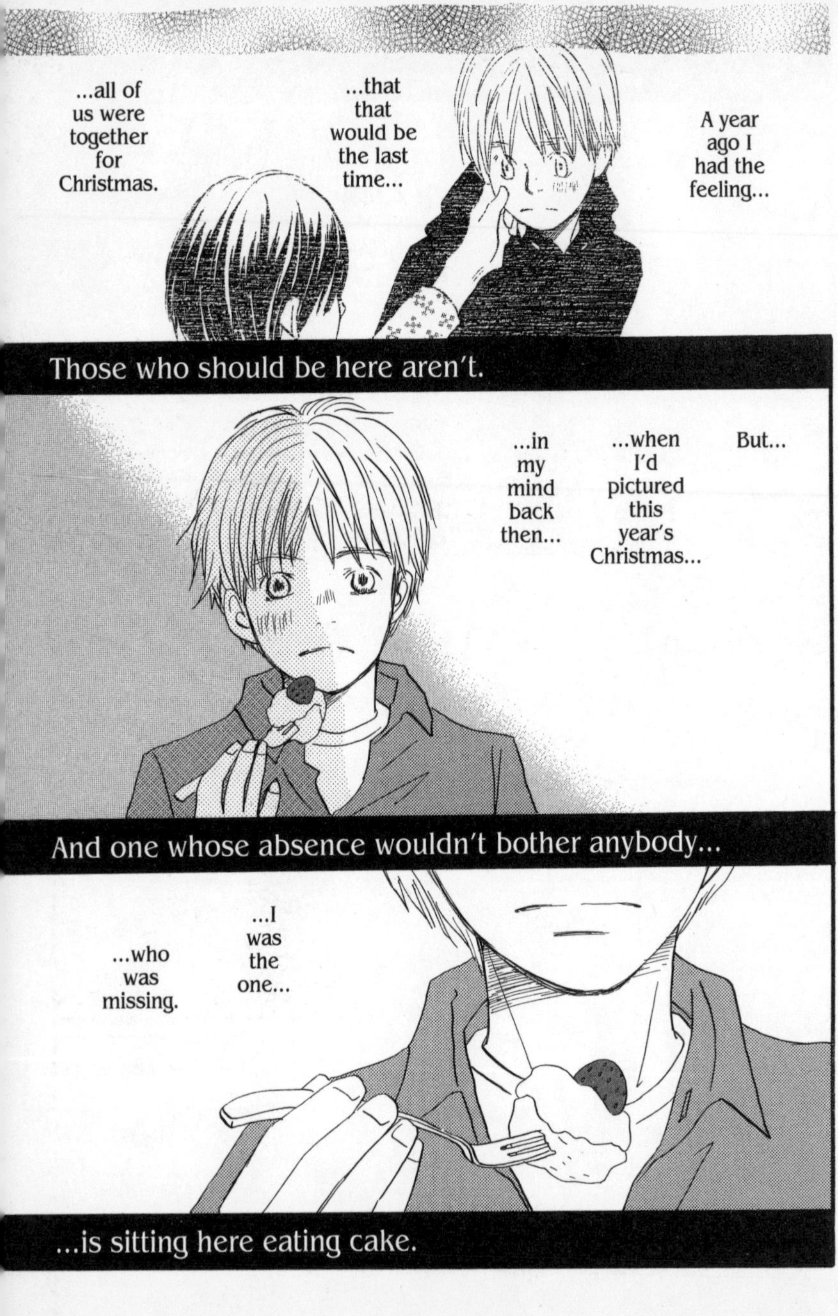
A year ago I had the feeling...
...that that would be the last time...
...all of us were together for Christmas.
Those who should be here aren't.
But...
...when I'd pictured this year's Christmas...
...in my mind back then...
And one whose absence wouldn't bother anybody...
...I was the one...
...who was missing.
...is sitting here eating cake.

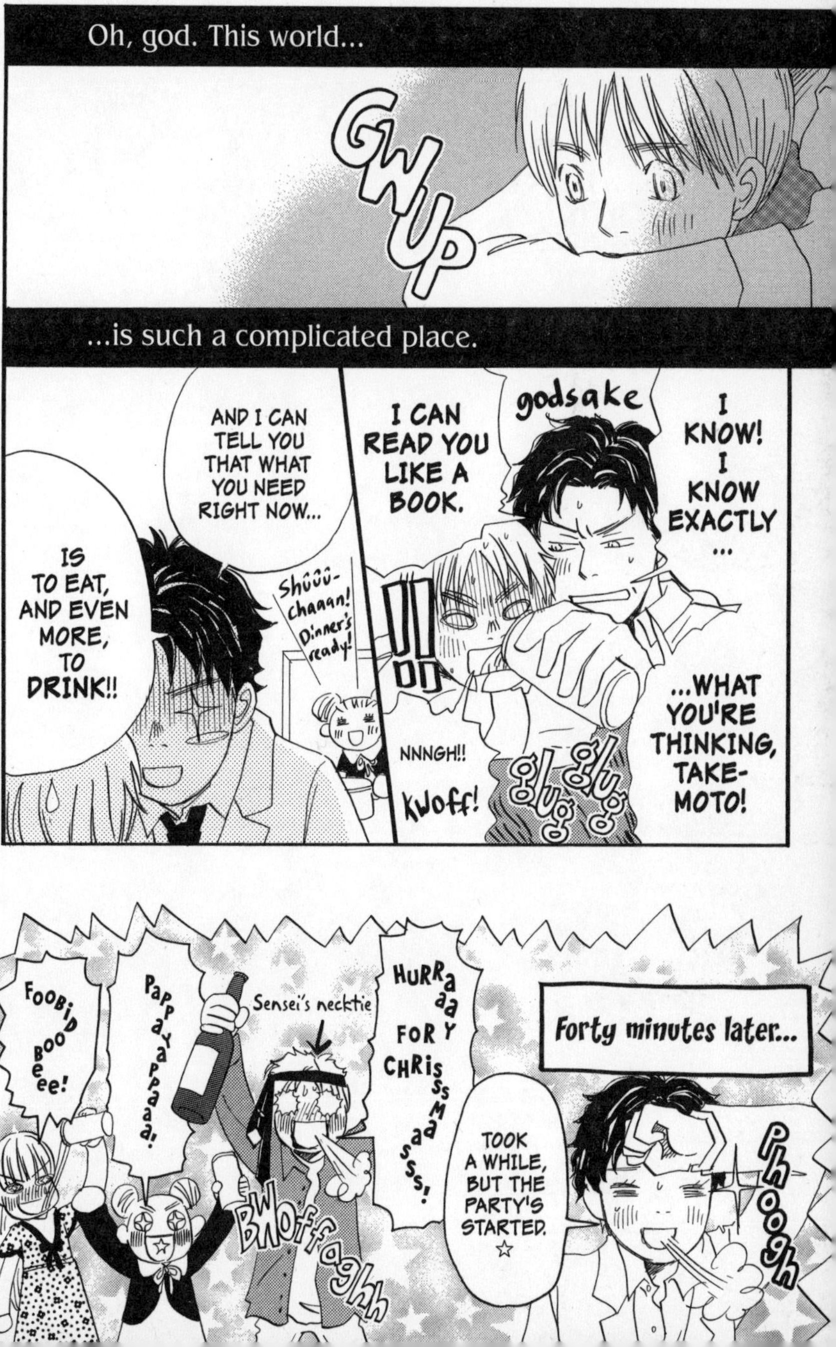
Oh, god. This world...
GWUP
...is such a complicated place.
godsake
I KNOW! I KNOW EXACTLY...
I CAN READ YOU LIKE A BOOK.
...WHAT YOU'RE THINKING, TAKE-MOTO!
!!
glug glug
NNNGH!!
KWOFF!
AND I CAN TELL YOU THAT WHAT YOU NEED RIGHT NOW...
IS TO EAT, AND EVEN MORE, TO DRINK!!
Shûûû-chaaan! Dinner's ready!
Forty minutes later...
Phoogh
TOOK A WHILE, BUT THE PARTY'S STARTED. ☆
HURRaaaY FOR CHRISSSMaaaSSS!
Sensei's necktie
BWOFFaghh
Pappayappaaa!
FOOBIDDOOBeee!

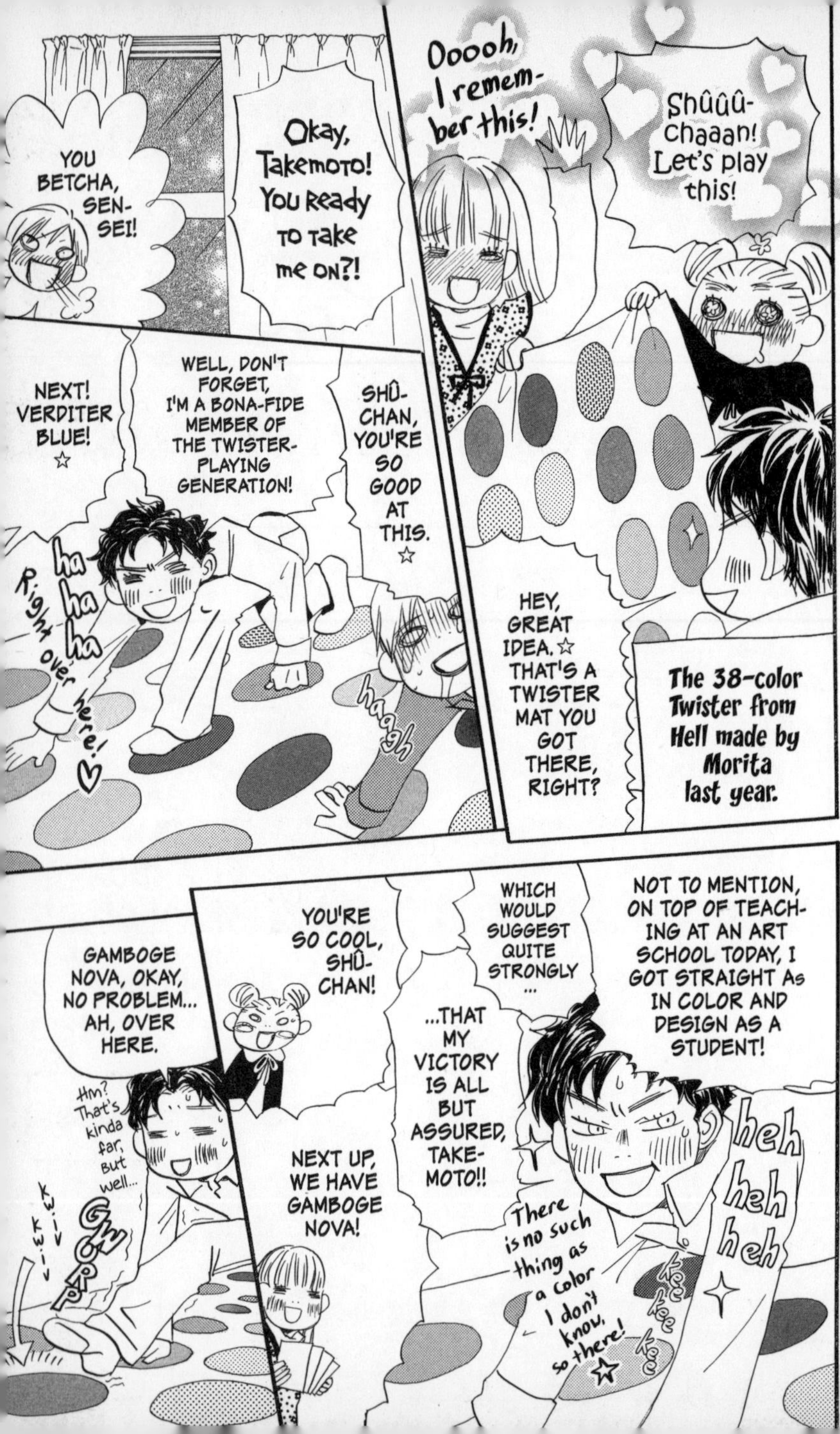

Shûûû-chaaan! Let's play this!
Ooooh, I remember this!
HEY, GREAT IDEA. ☆ THAT'S A TWISTER MAT YOU GOT THERE, RIGHT?
The 38-color Twister from Hell made by Morita last year.
Okay, Takemoto! You ready to take me on?!
YOU BETCHA, SEN-SEI!
SHÛ-CHAN, YOU'RE SO GOOD AT THIS. ☆
haggh
WELL, DON'T FORGET, I'M A BONA-FIDE MEMBER OF THE TWISTER-PLAYING GENERATION!
NEXT! VERDITER BLUE! ☆
ha ha ha
Right over here! ♡
NOT TO MENTION, ON TOP OF TEACHING AT AN ART SCHOOL TODAY, I GOT STRAIGHT As IN COLOR AND DESIGN AS A STUDENT!
heh heh heh
WHICH WOULD SUGGEST QUITE STRONGLY ...
...THAT MY VICTORY IS ALL BUT ASSURED, TAKE-MOTO!!
kee kee kee
There is no such thing as a color I don't know, so there! ☆
YOU'RE SO COOL, SHÛ-CHAN!
NEXT UP, WE HAVE GAMBOGE NOVA!
GAMBOGE NOVA, OKAY, NO PROBLEM... AH, OVER HERE.
Hm? That's kinda far, but well...
GWORP

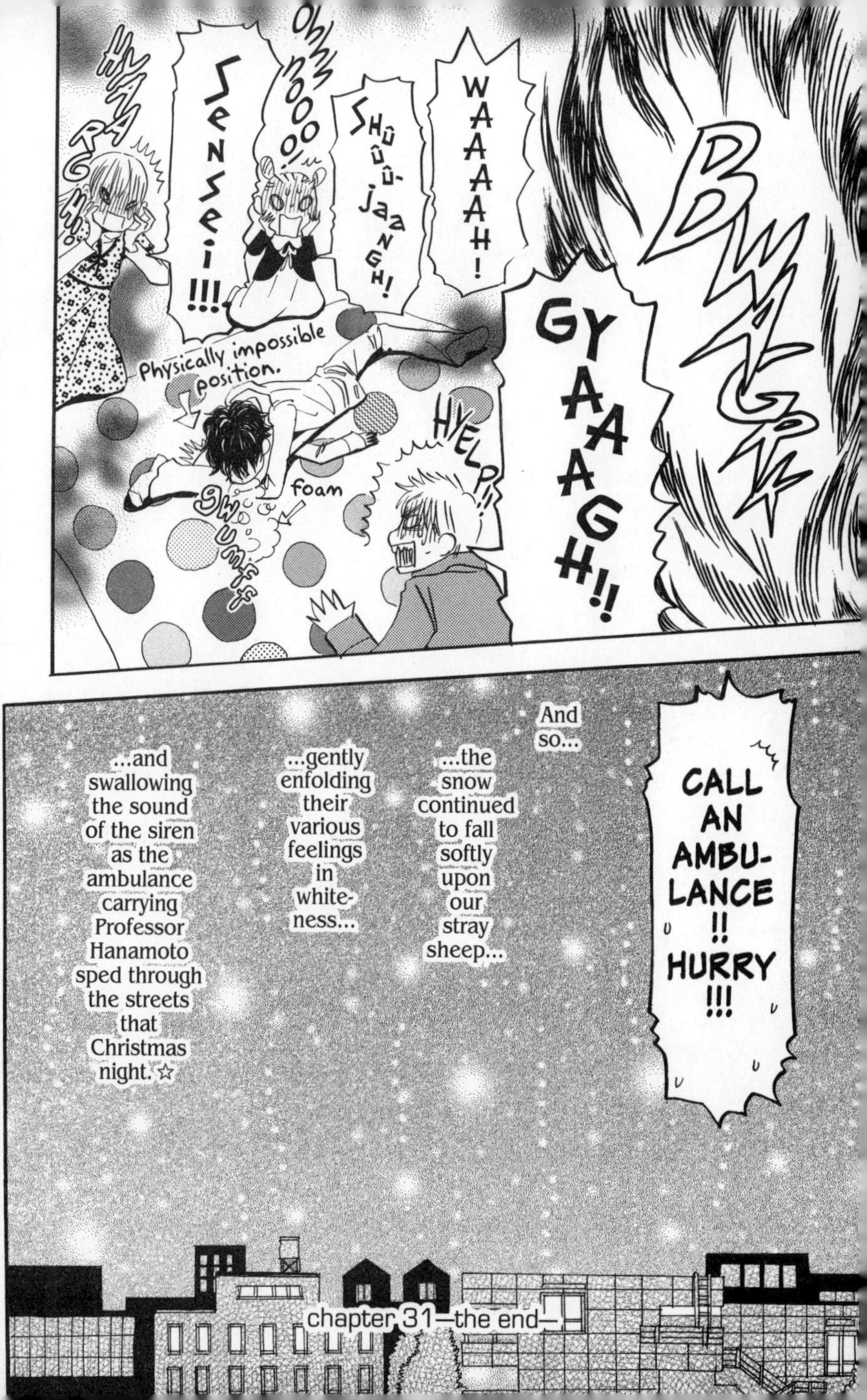
BDWANGK
GYAAAGH!!
HYELP!!
WAAAAAH!
SHÛÛÛ-jaaNGH!
Ohhh noooo!
Sensei!!!
HYAAARAGH!
Physically impossible position.
foam
gwumff
CALL AN AMBULANCE!! HURRY!!!
And so...
...the snow continued to fall softly upon our stray sheep...
...gently enfolding their various feelings in whiteness...
...and swallowing the sound of the siren as the ambulance carrying Professor Hanamoto sped through the streets that Christmas night. ☆
chapter 31—the end—

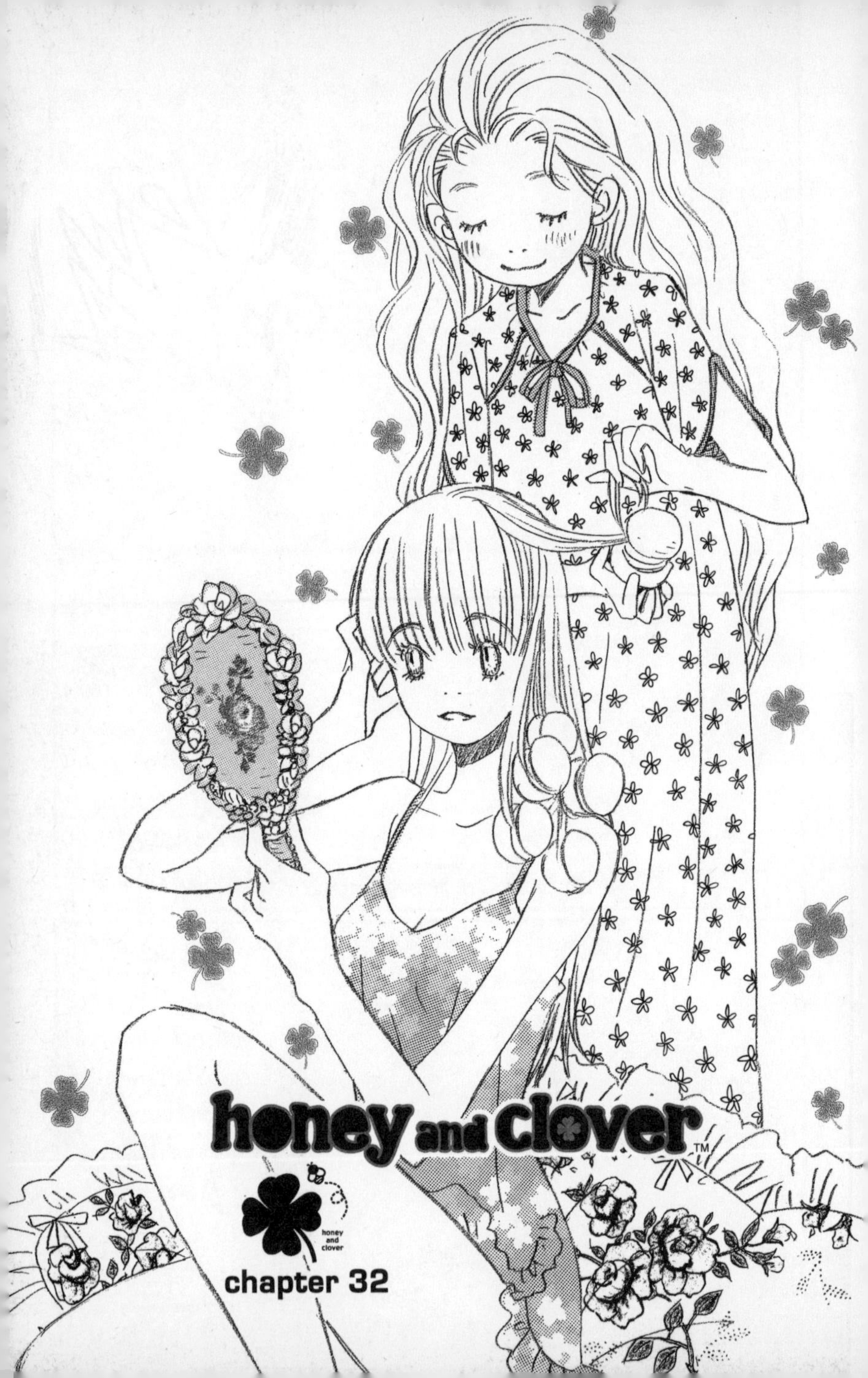
honey and clover™
honey and clover
chapter 32

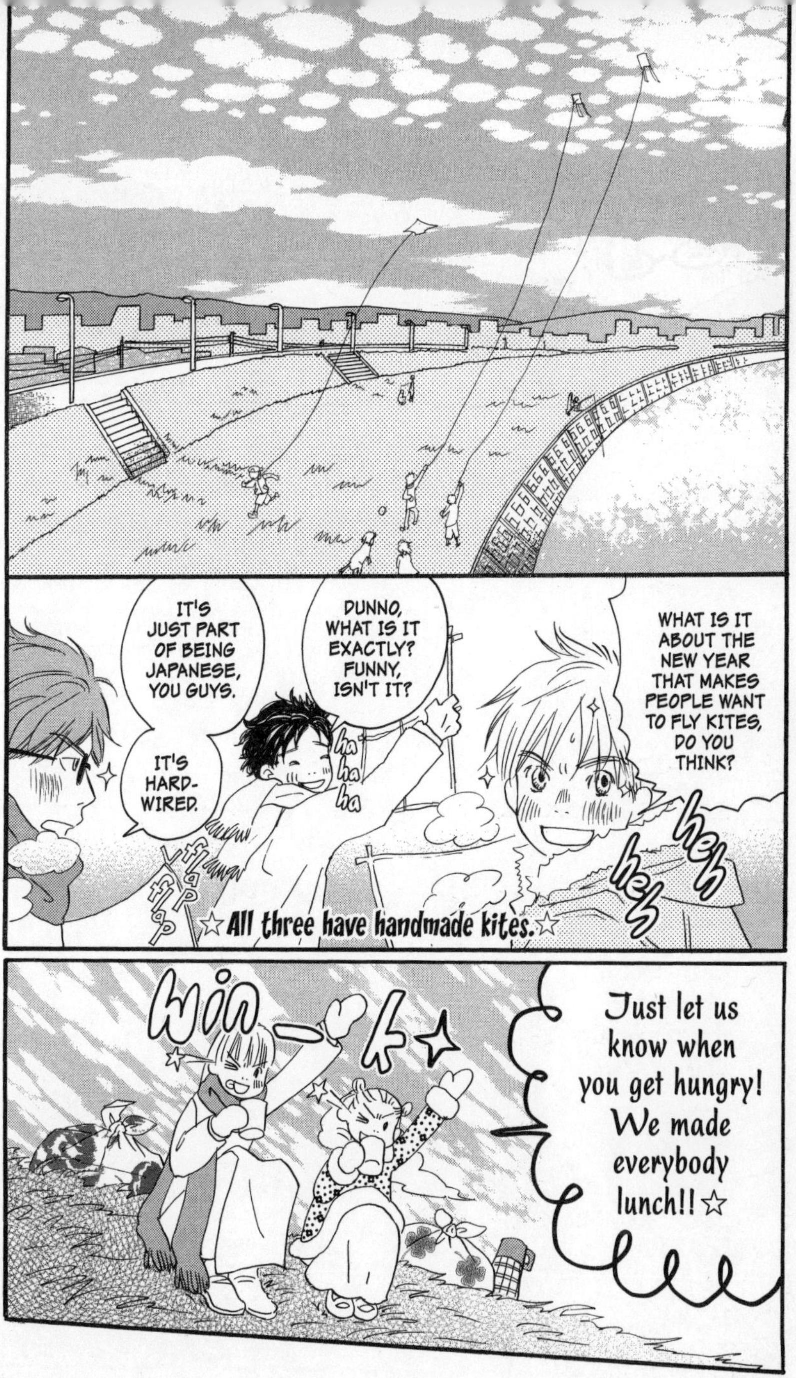
WHAT IS IT ABOUT THE NEW YEAR THAT MAKES PEOPLE WANT TO FLY KITES, DO YOU THINK?
heh heh
DUNNO, WHAT IS IT EXACTLY? FUNNY, ISN'T IT?
ha ha ha
IT'S JUST PART OF BEING JAPANESE, YOU GUYS.
IT'S HARD-WIRED.
flap flap
☆All three have handmade kites.☆
Just let us know when you get hungry! We made everybody lunch!! ☆
Win-k

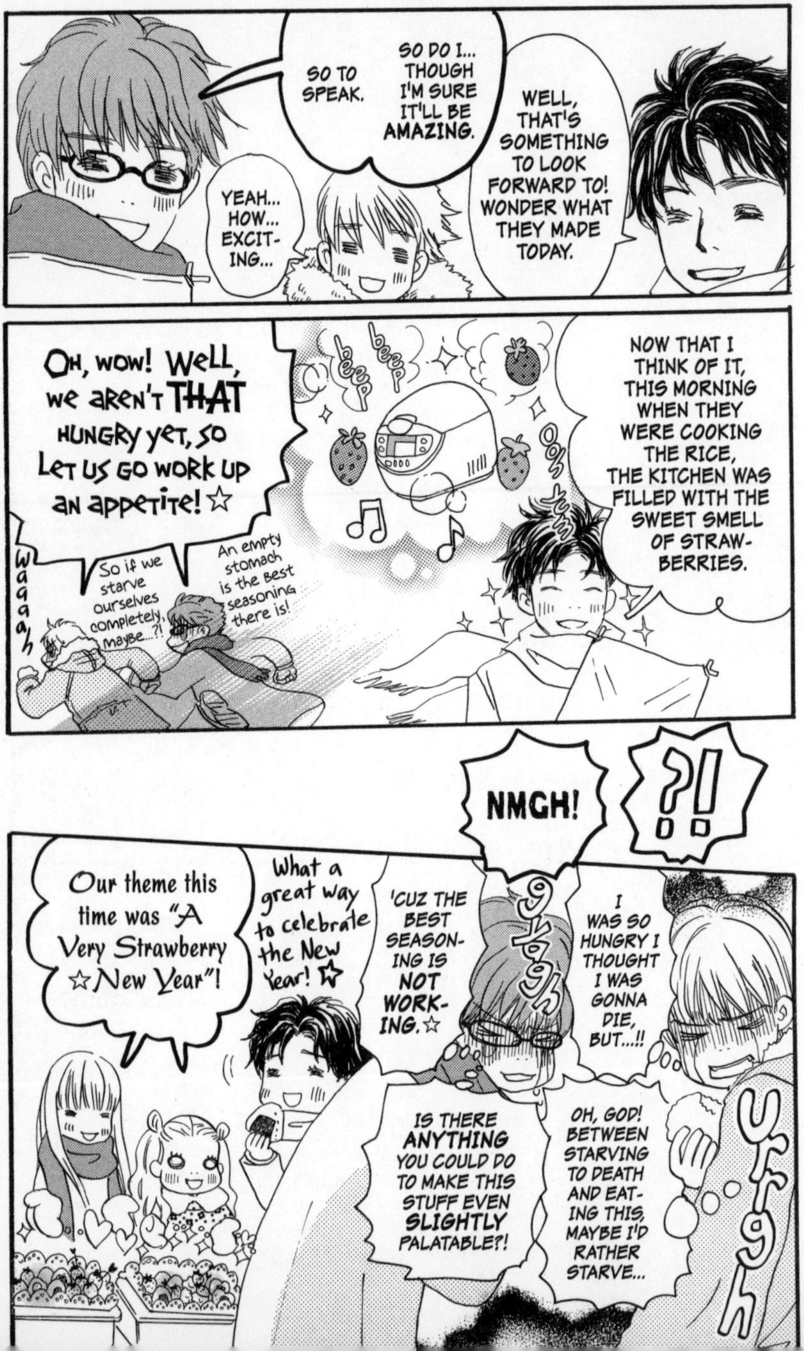
WELL, THAT'S SOMETHING TO LOOK FORWARD TO! WONDER WHAT THEY MADE TODAY.
SO DO I... THOUGH I'M SURE IT'LL BE AMAZING.
SO TO SPEAK.
YEAH... HOW... EXCIT-ING...
NOW THAT I THINK OF IT, THIS MORNING WHEN THEY WERE COOKING THE RICE, THE KITCHEN WAS FILLED WITH THE SWEET SMELL OF STRAW-BERRIES.
ooh yum
beep
beep
OH, WOW! WELL, WE AREN'T THAT HUNGRY YET, SO LET US GO WORK UP AN APPETITE! ☆
An empty stomach is the best seasoning there is!
So if we starve ourselves completely, maybe...?!
Waaaah
?!
NMGH!
I WAS SO HUNGRY I THOUGHT I WAS GONNA DIE, BUT...!!
gyagh
'CUZ THE BEST SEASON-ING IS NOT WORK-ING.☆
What a great way to celebrate the New Year! ☆
Our theme this time was "A Very Strawberry ☆New Year"!
Urgh
OH, GOD! BETWEEN STARVING TO DEATH AND EAT-ING THIS, MAYBE I'D RATHER STARVE...
IS THERE ANYTHING YOU COULD DO TO MAKE THIS STUFF EVEN SLIGHTLY PALATABLE?!

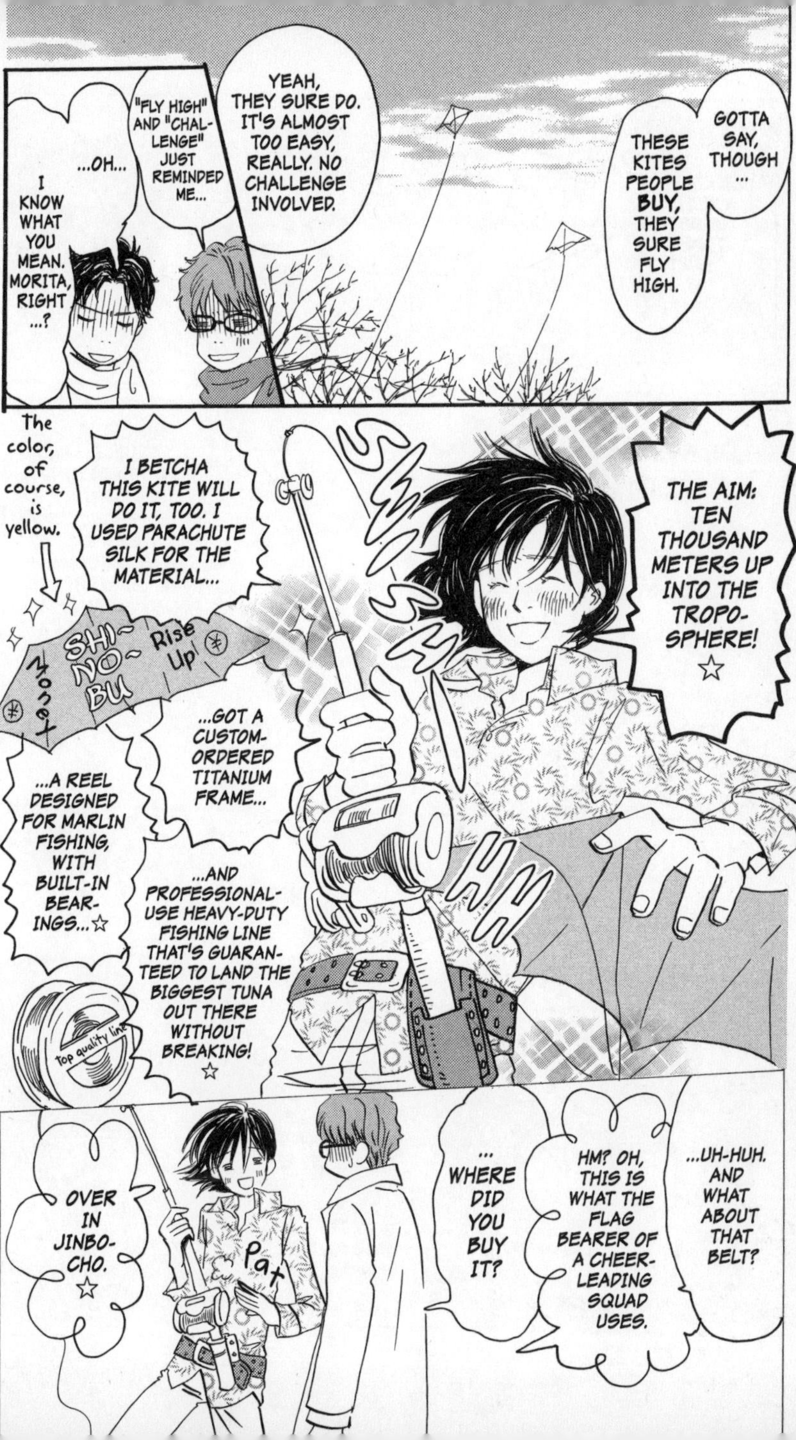
GOTTA SAY, THOUGH ...
THESE KITES PEOPLE BUY, THEY SURE FLY HIGH.
YEAH, THEY SURE DO. IT'S ALMOST TOO EASY, REALLY. NO CHALLENGE INVOLVED.
"FLY HIGH" AND "CHALLENGE" JUST REMINDED ME...
...OH...
I KNOW WHAT YOU MEAN. MORITA, RIGHT ...?
THE AIM: TEN THOUSAND METERS UP INTO THE TROPOSPHERE! ☆
SWISHHH
I BETCHA THIS KITE WILL DO IT, TOO. I USED PARACHUTE SILK FOR THE MATERIAL...
The color, of course, is yellow.
SHI~NO~BU
Rise Up
Money
...GOT A CUSTOM-ORDERED TITANIUM FRAME...
...A REEL DESIGNED FOR MARLIN FISHING, WITH BUILT-IN BEARINGS...☆
...AND PROFESSIONAL-USE HEAVY-DUTY FISHING LINE THAT'S GUARANTEED TO LAND THE BIGGEST TUNA OUT THERE WITHOUT BREAKING! ☆
Top quality line
...UH-HUH. AND WHAT ABOUT THAT BELT?
HM? OH, THIS IS WHAT THE FLAG BEARER OF A CHEERLEADING SQUAD USES.
... WHERE DID YOU BUY IT?
OVER IN JINBO-CHO. ☆
Pat

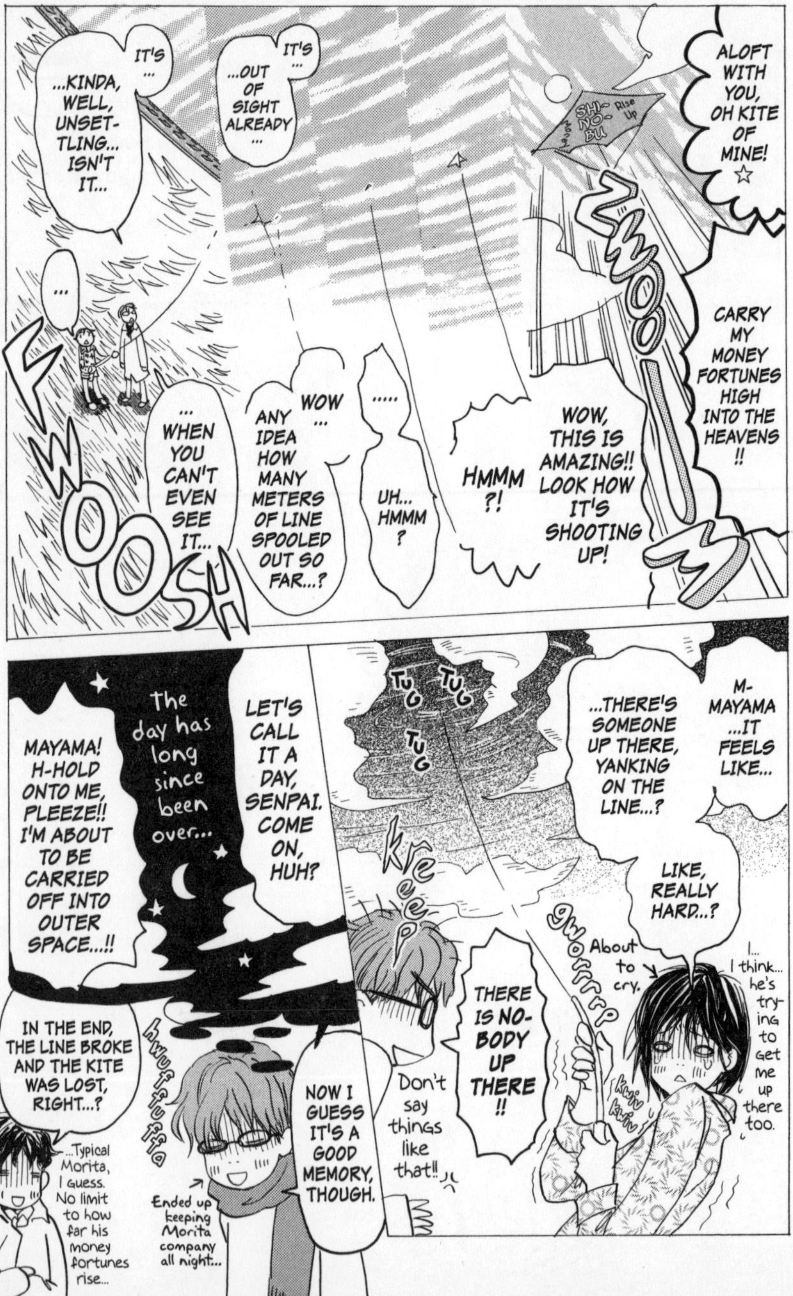
ALOFT WITH YOU, OH KITE OF MINE! ☆
CARRY MY MONEY FORTUNES HIGH INTO THE HEAVENS!!
ZWOOOM
SHI-NO-BU Rise Up Money
WOW, THIS IS AMAZING!! LOOK HOW IT'S SHOOTING UP!
HMMM?!
IT'S ... ...OUT OF SIGHT ALREADY ...
.....
UH... HMMM?
WOW ... ANY IDEA HOW MANY METERS OF LINE SPOOLED OUT SO FAR...?
IT'S ... ...KINDA, WELL, UNSETTLING... ISN'T IT...
... WHEN YOU CAN'T EVEN SEE IT...
...
WOOOSH
M-MAYAMA ...IT FEELS LIKE...
...THERE'S SOMEONE UP THERE, YANKING ON THE LINE...?
TUG TUG TUG
LIKE, REALLY HARD...?
kreeep
gworrrrp
About to cry.
I... I think... he's trying to get me up there too.
kwiv kwiv
THERE IS NOBODY UP THERE!!
Don't say things like that!!
LET'S CALL IT A DAY, SENPAI. COME ON, HUH?
The day has long since been over...
MAYAMA! H-HOLD ONTO ME, PLEEZE!! I'M ABOUT TO BE CARRIED OFF INTO OUTER SPACE...!!
NOW I GUESS IT'S A GOOD MEMORY, THOUGH.
hwufufuffa
Ended up keeping Morita company all night...
IN THE END, THE LINE BROKE AND THE KITE WAS LOST, RIGHT...?
...Typical Morita, I guess. No limit to how far his money fortunes rise...

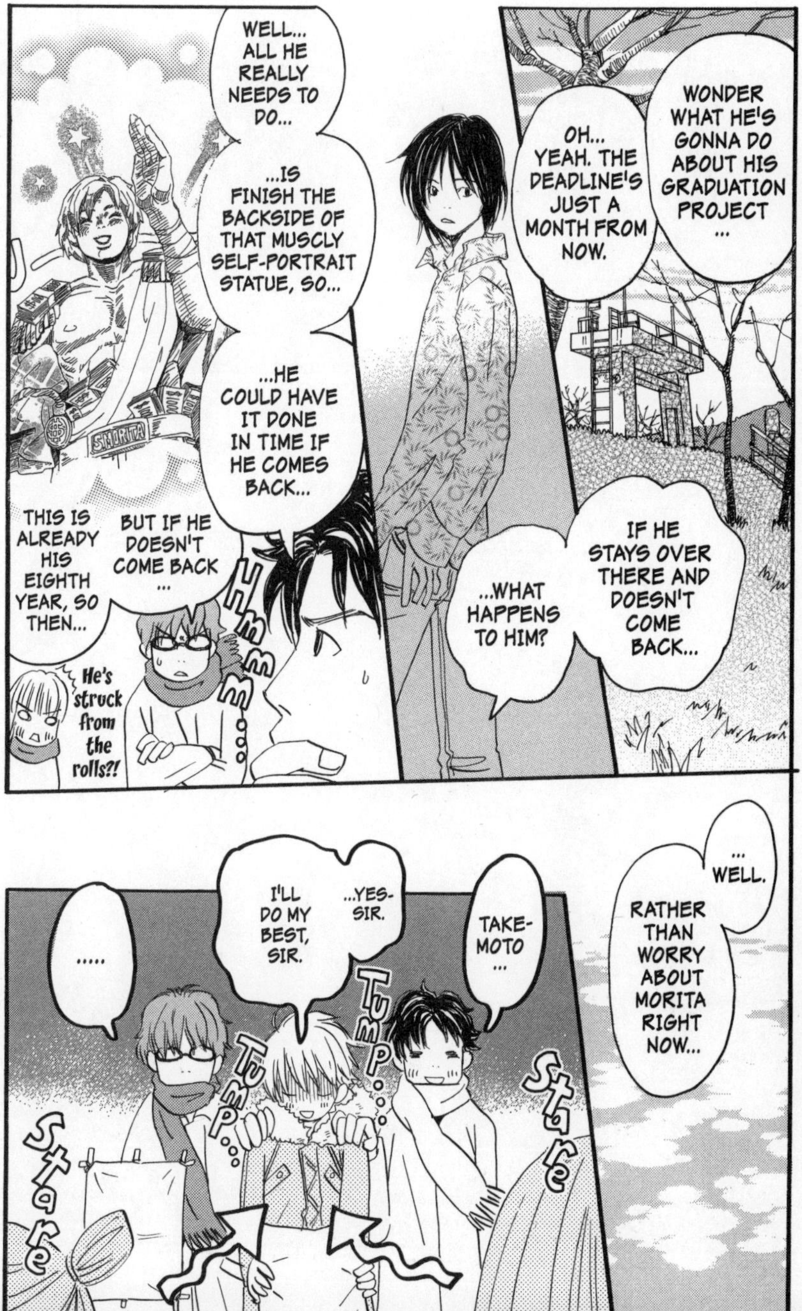
WONDER WHAT HE'S GONNA DO ABOUT HIS GRADUATION PROJECT ...
OH... YEAH. THE DEADLINE'S JUST A MONTH FROM NOW.
IF HE STAYS OVER THERE AND DOESN'T COME BACK...
...WHAT HAPPENS TO HIM?
WELL... ALL HE REALLY NEEDS TO DO...
...IS FINISH THE BACKSIDE OF THAT MUSCLY SELF-PORTRAIT STATUE, SO...
...HE COULD HAVE IT DONE IN TIME IF HE COMES BACK...
BUT IF HE DOESN'T COME BACK ...
THIS IS ALREADY HIS EIGHTH YEAR, SO THEN...
HMMM...
He's struck from the rolls?!
... WELL.
RATHER THAN WORRY ABOUT MORITA RIGHT NOW...
TAKE-MOTO ...
...YES-SIR.
I'LL DO MY BEST, SIR.
.....
TUMP...
TUMP...
Stare
Stare

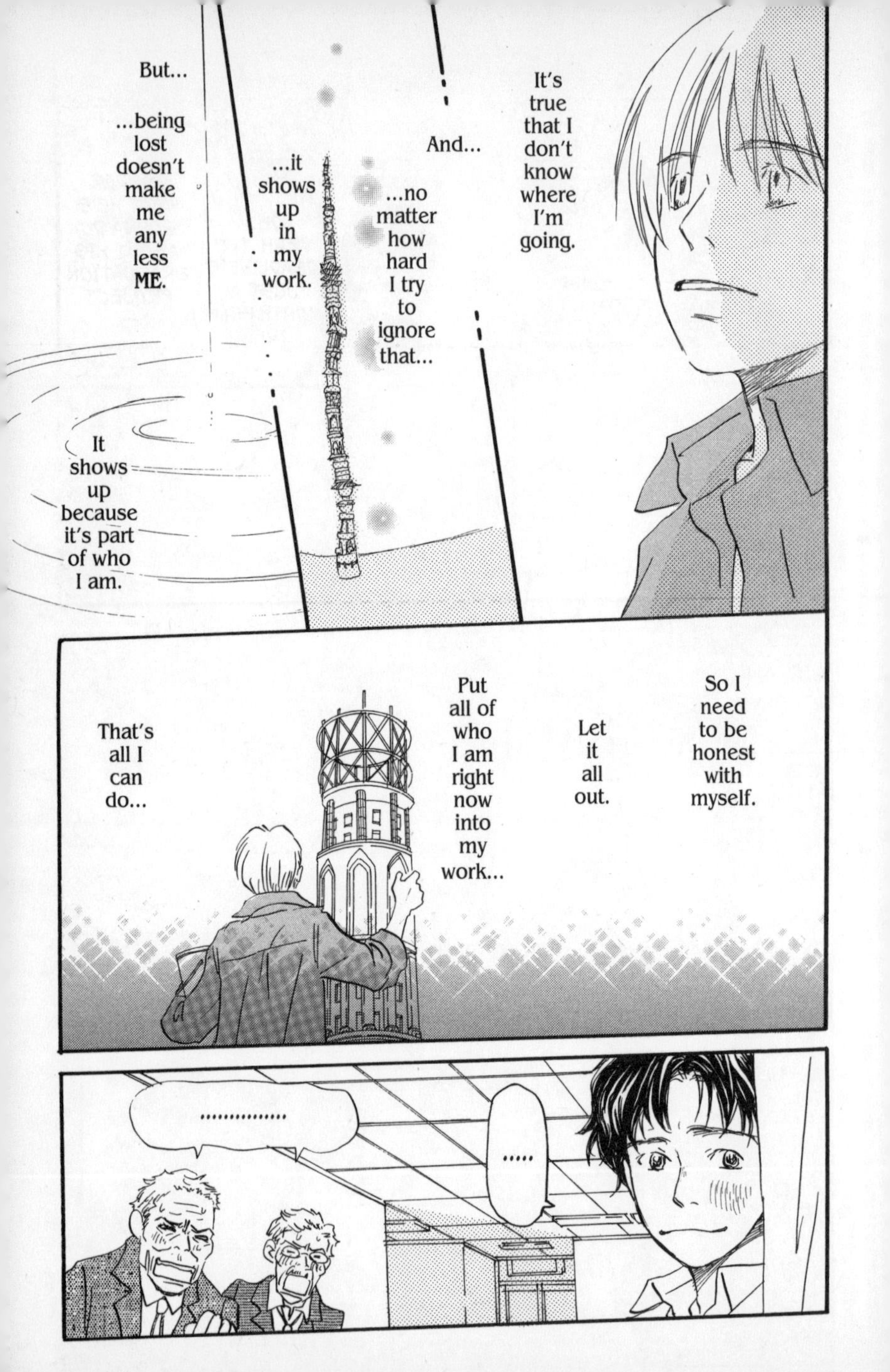
It's true that I don't know where I'm going.
And...
...no matter how hard I try to ignore that...
...it shows up in my work.
But...
...being lost doesn't make me any less **ME**.
It shows up because it's part of who I am.
So I need to be honest with myself.
Let it all out.
Put all of who I am right now into my work...
That's all I can do...
.....
....

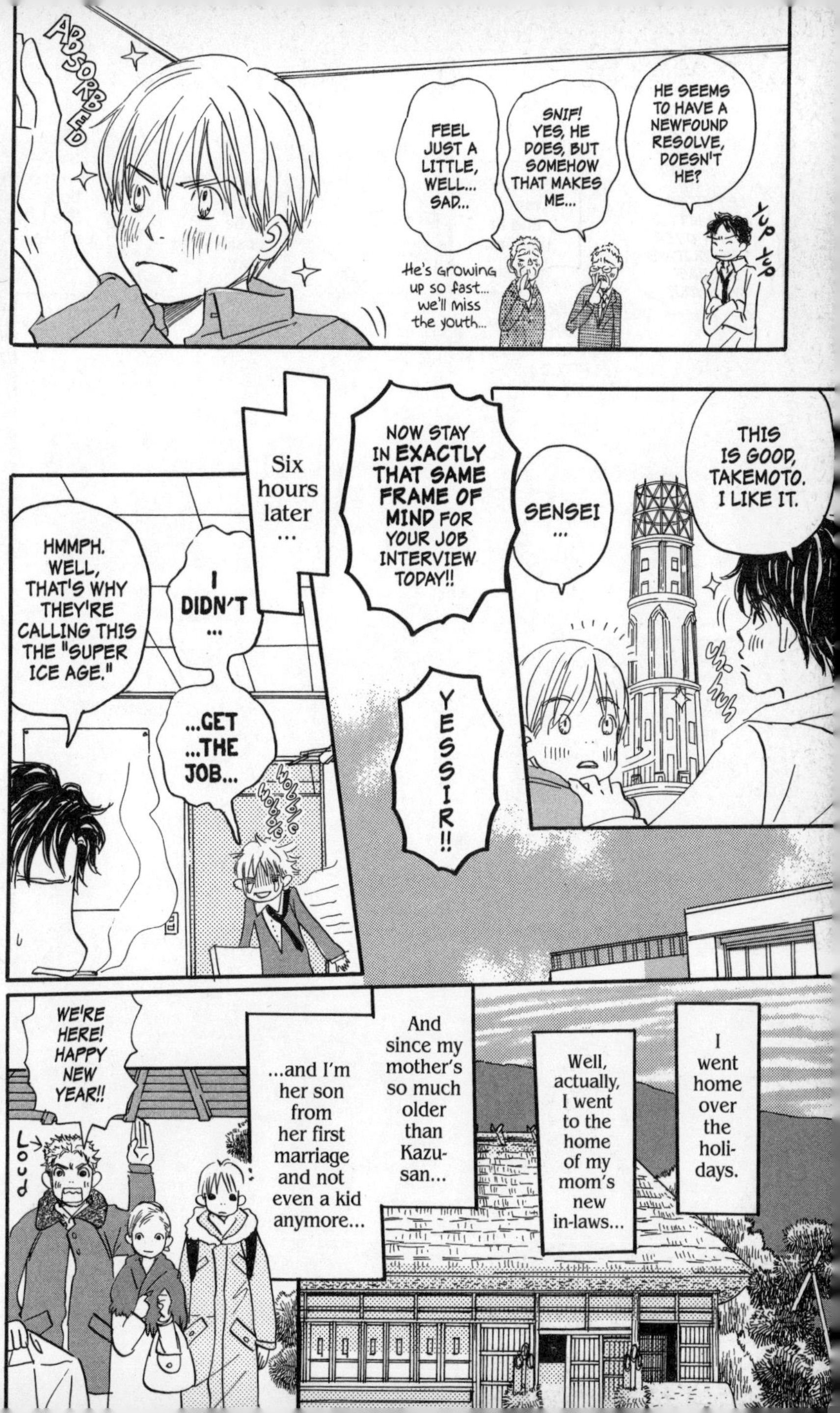
HE SEEMS TO HAVE A NEWFOUND RESOLVE, DOESN'T HE?
YUP YUP
SNIF! YES, HE DOES, BUT SOMEHOW THAT MAKES ME...
FEEL JUST A LITTLE, WELL... SAD...
He's growing up so fast... we'll miss the youth...
ABSORBED
THIS IS GOOD, TAKEMOTO. I LIKE IT.
SENSEI ...
uh-huh
NOW STAY IN EXACTLY THAT SAME FRAME OF MIND FOR YOUR JOB INTERVIEW TODAY!!
YESSIR!!
Six hours later ...
I DIDN'T ...
...GET ...THE JOB...
wobble wobble
HMMPH. WELL, THAT'S WHY THEY'RE CALLING THIS THE "SUPER ICE AGE."
I went home over the holi- days.
Well, actually, I went to the home of my mom's new in-laws...
And since my mother's so much older than Kazu-san...
...and I'm her son from her first marriage and not even a kid anymore...
WE'RE HERE! HAPPY NEW YEAR!!
Loud

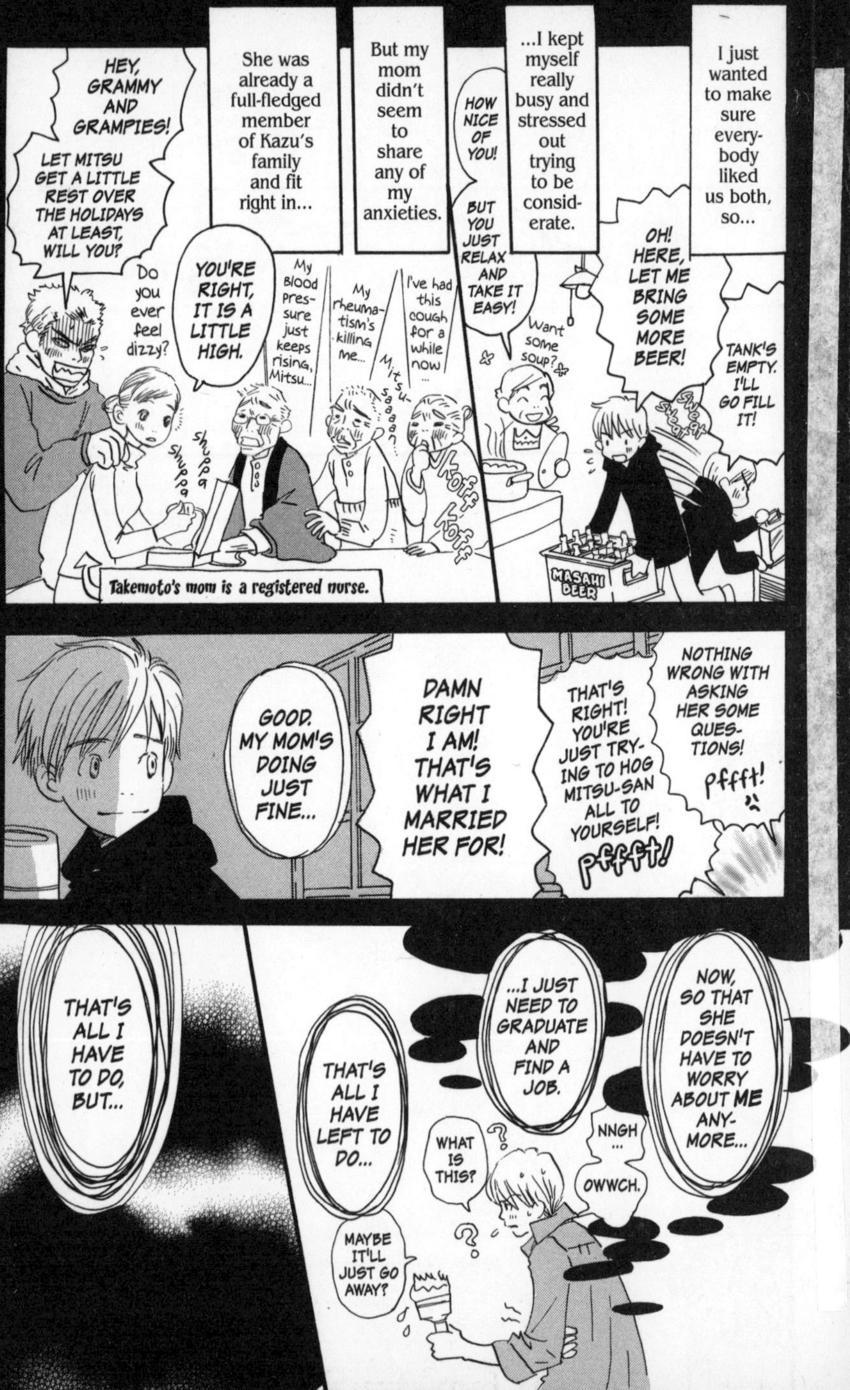
I just wanted to make sure every-body liked us both, so...
...I kept myself really busy and stressed out trying to be consid-erate.
But my mom didn't seem to share any of my anxieties.
She was already a full-fledged member of Kazu's family and fit right in...
TANK'S EMPTY. I'LL GO FILL IT!
Sweat sweat
OH! HERE, LET ME BRING SOME MORE BEER!
HOW NICE OF YOU!
BUT YOU JUST RELAX AND TAKE IT EASY!
Want some soup?
MASAHI BEER
HEY, GRAMMY AND GRAMPIES!
LET MITSU GET A LITTLE REST OVER THE HOLIDAYS AT LEAST, WILL YOU?
Do you ever feel dizzy?
YOU'RE RIGHT, IT IS A LITTLE HIGH.
My blood pres-sure just keeps rising, Mitsu...
My rheuma-tism's killing me...
I've had this cough for a while now...
Mitsu-saaaan...
koff koff
shuppa shuppa
Takemoto's mom is a registered nurse.
NOTHING WRONG WITH ASKING HER SOME QUES-TIONS!
pffft!
THAT'S RIGHT! YOU'RE JUST TRY-ING TO HOG MITSU-SAN ALL TO YOURSELF!
pffft!
DAMN RIGHT I AM! THAT'S WHAT I MARRIED HER FOR!
GOOD. MY MOM'S DOING JUST FINE...
NOW, SO THAT SHE DOESN'T HAVE TO WORRY ABOUT ME ANY-MORE...
...I JUST NEED TO GRADUATE AND FIND A JOB.
NNGH...
OWWCH.
WHAT IS THIS?
MAYBE IT'LL JUST GO AWAY?
THAT'S ALL I HAVE LEFT TO DO...
THAT'S ALL I HAVE TO DO, BUT...

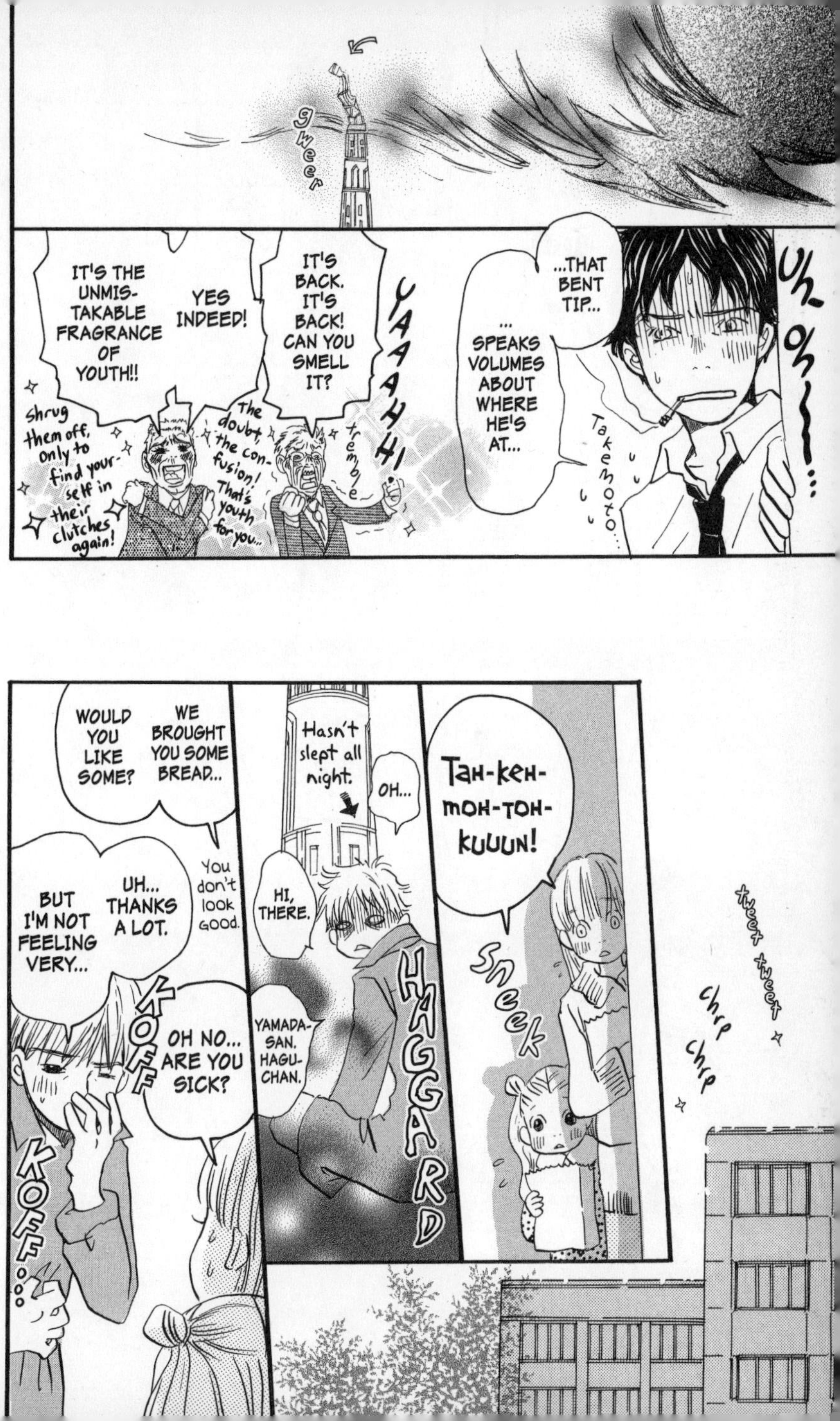
gweer
Uh-oh!...
...THAT BENT TIP...
...SPEAKS VOLUMES ABOUT WHERE HE'S AT...
Takemoto...
YAAAAHH!
tremble
IT'S BACK. IT'S BACK! CAN YOU SMELL IT?
The doubt, the confusion! That's youth for you...
YES INDEED!
IT'S THE UNMISTAKABLE FRAGRANCE OF YOUTH!!
shrug them off, only to find yourself in their clutches again!
tweet tweet
chrp chrp
TAH-KEH-MOH-TOH-KUUUN!
Sneek
OH...
Hasn't slept all night.
HI, THERE.
HAGGARD
YAMADA-SAN. HAGU-CHAN.
WE BROUGHT YOU SOME BREAD...
WOULD YOU LIKE SOME?
You don't look good.
UH... THANKS A LOT.
BUT I'M NOT FEELING VERY...
KOFF
OH NO... ARE YOU SICK?
KOFF KOFF...

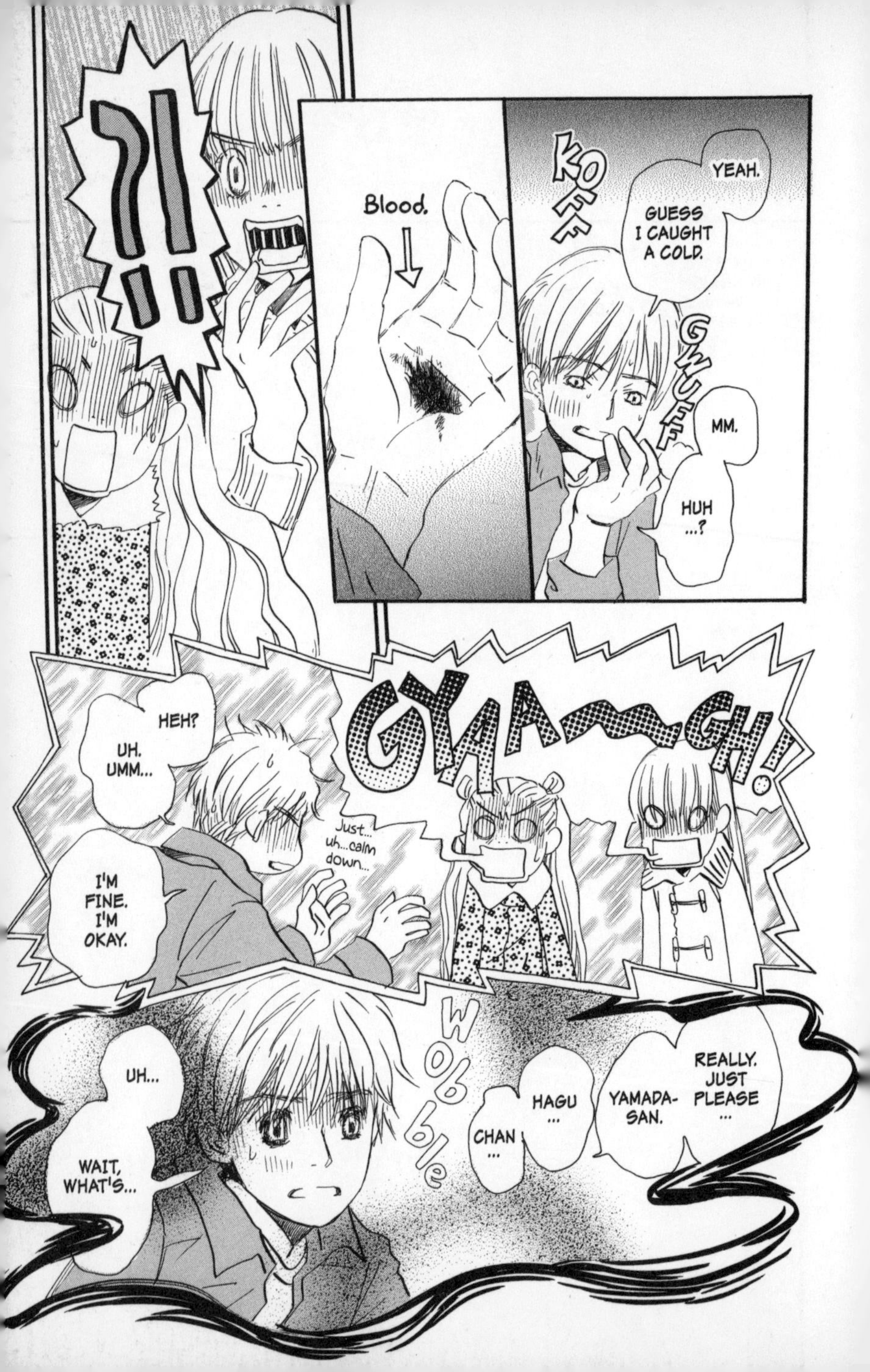
YEAH.
GUESS I CAUGHT A COLD.
KOFF
GWUFF
MM.
HUH ...?
Blood.
?!!!
GYAAAGH!
Just... uh...calm down...
HEH?
UH. UMM...
I'M FINE. I'M OKAY.
REALLY. JUST PLEASE ...
YAMADA-SAN.
HAGU ...
CHAN ...
wobble
UH...
WAIT, WHAT'S...

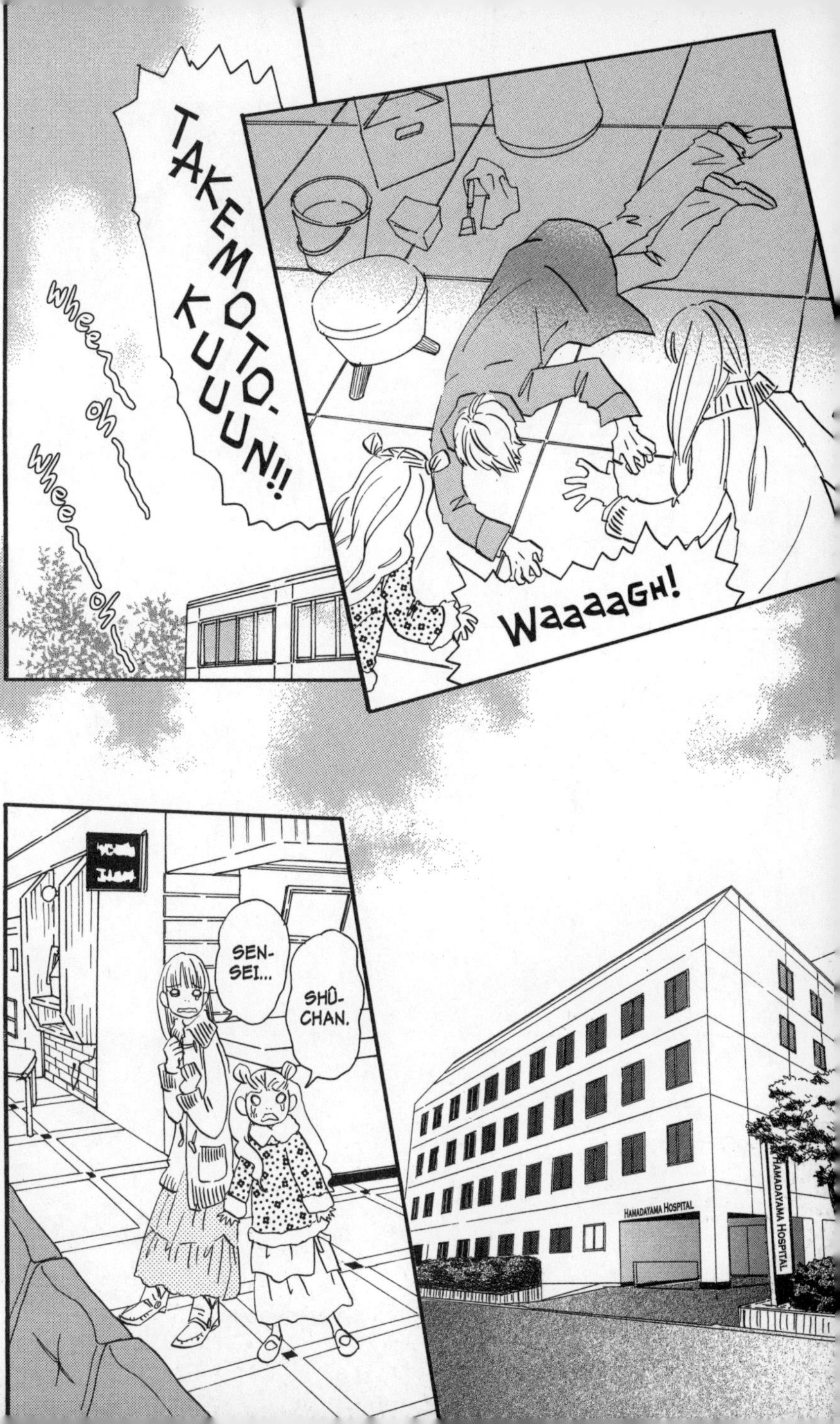
WAAAAGH!
TAKEMOTO-KUUUN!!
whee~oh~whee~oh~
HAMADAYAMA HOSPITAL
HAMADAYAMA HOSPITAL
SEN-SEI...
SHÛ-CHAN.

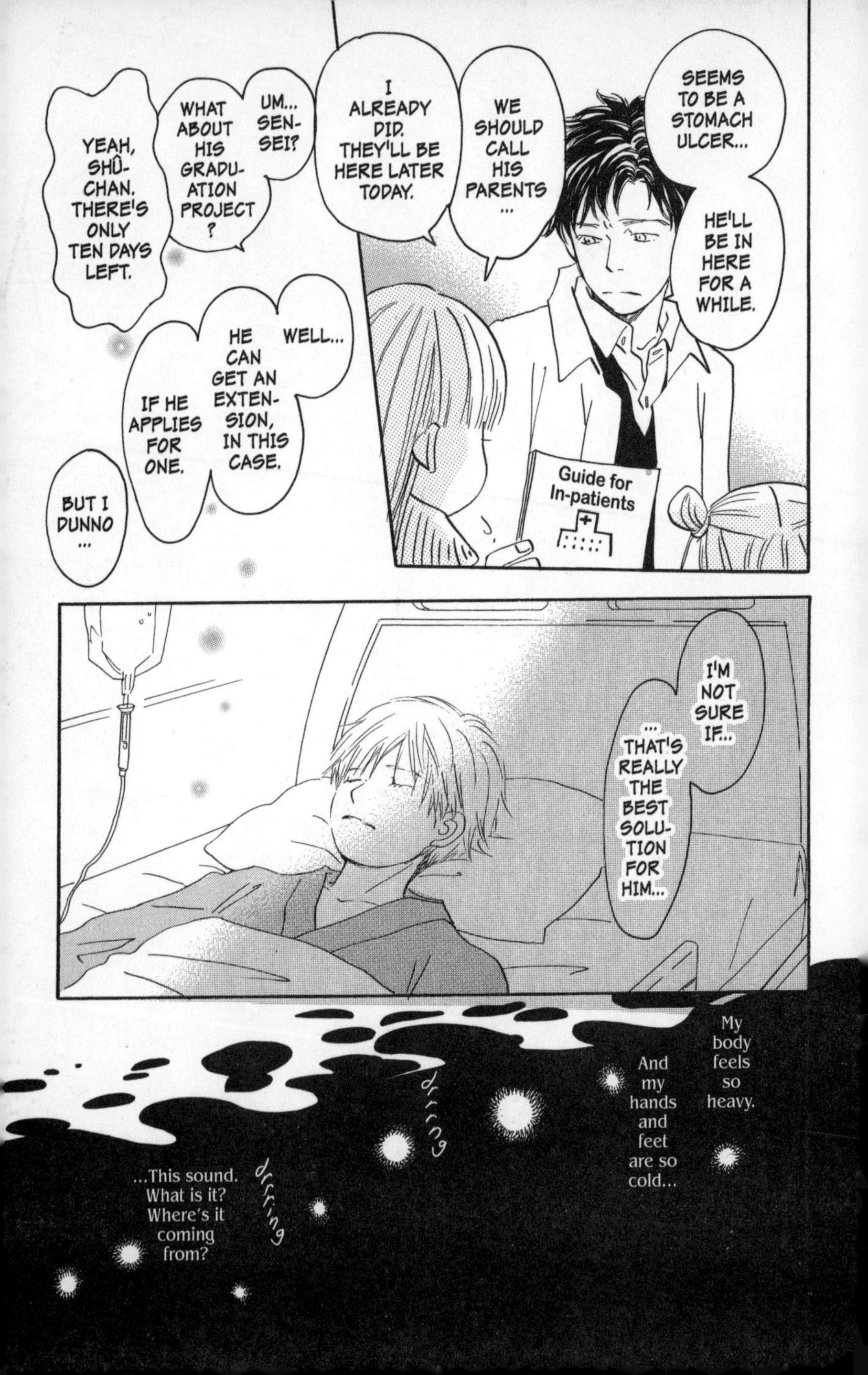
SEEMS TO BE A STOMACH ULCER...
HE'LL BE IN HERE FOR A WHILE.
WE SHOULD CALL HIS PARENTS ...
I ALREADY DID. THEY'LL BE HERE LATER TODAY.
Guide for In-patients
UM... SEN-SEI?
WHAT ABOUT HIS GRADUATION PROJECT?
YEAH, SHÛ-CHAN. THERE'S ONLY TEN DAYS LEFT.
WELL...
HE CAN GET AN EXTENSION, IN THIS CASE.
IF HE APPLIES FOR ONE.
BUT I DUNNO ...
I'M NOT SURE IF...
... THAT'S REALLY THE BEST SOLUTION FOR HIM...
My body feels so heavy.
And my hands and feet are so cold...
drrrng
drrring
...This sound. What is it? Where's it coming from?

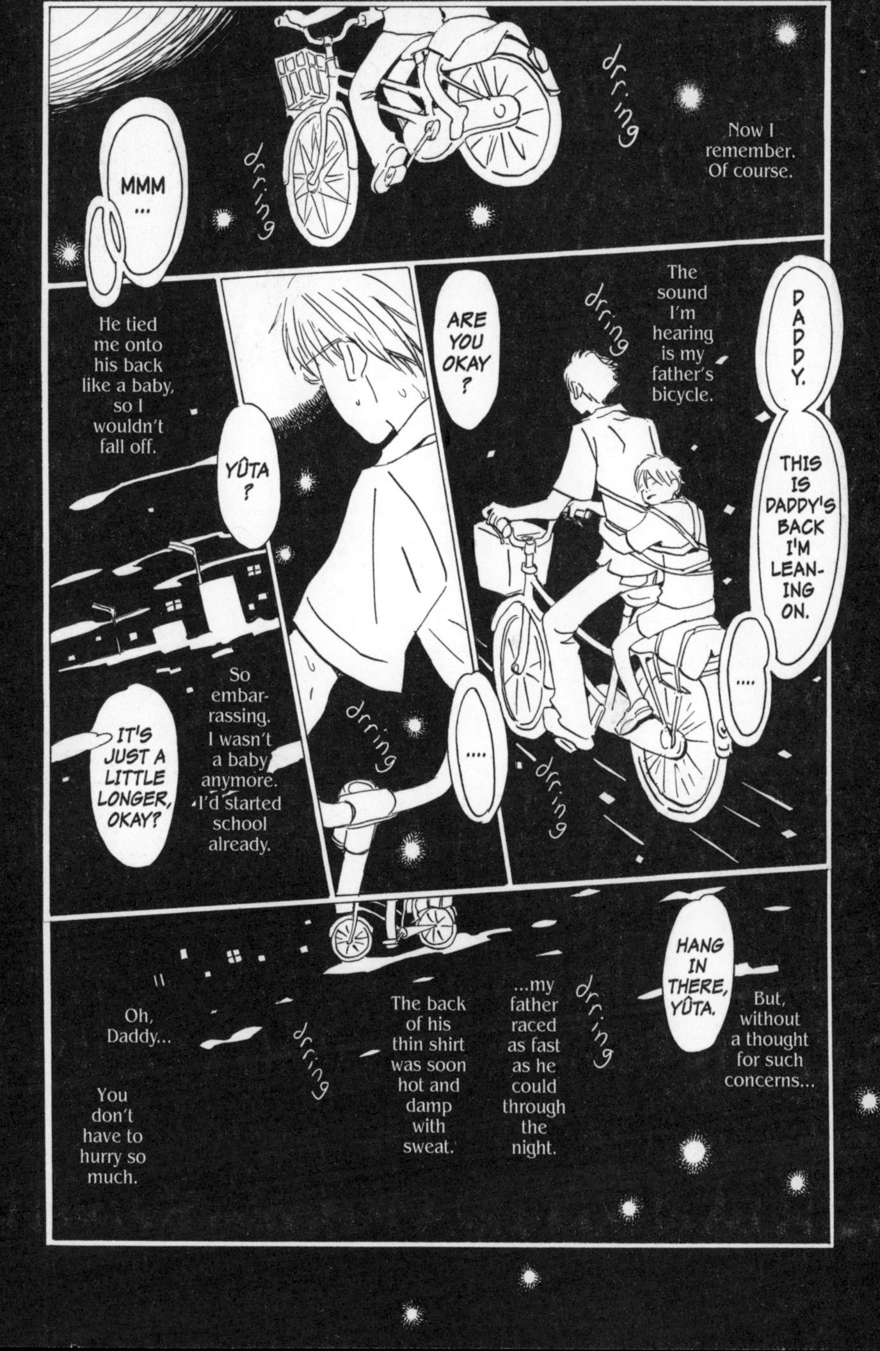
Now I remember. Of course.
drring
drring
MMM ...
DADDY.
THIS IS DADDY'S BACK I'M LEANING ON.
The sound I'm hearing is my father's bicycle.
drring
....
drring
ARE YOU OKAY ?
YÛTA ?
....
drring
He tied me onto his back like a baby, so I wouldn't fall off.
So embarrassing. I wasn't a baby anymore. I'd started school already.
IT'S JUST A LITTLE LONGER, OKAY?
HANG IN THERE, YÛTA.
But, without a thought for such concerns...
drring
...my father raced as fast as he could through the night.
The back of his thin shirt was soon hot and damp with sweat.
drring
Oh, Daddy...
You don't have to hurry so much.

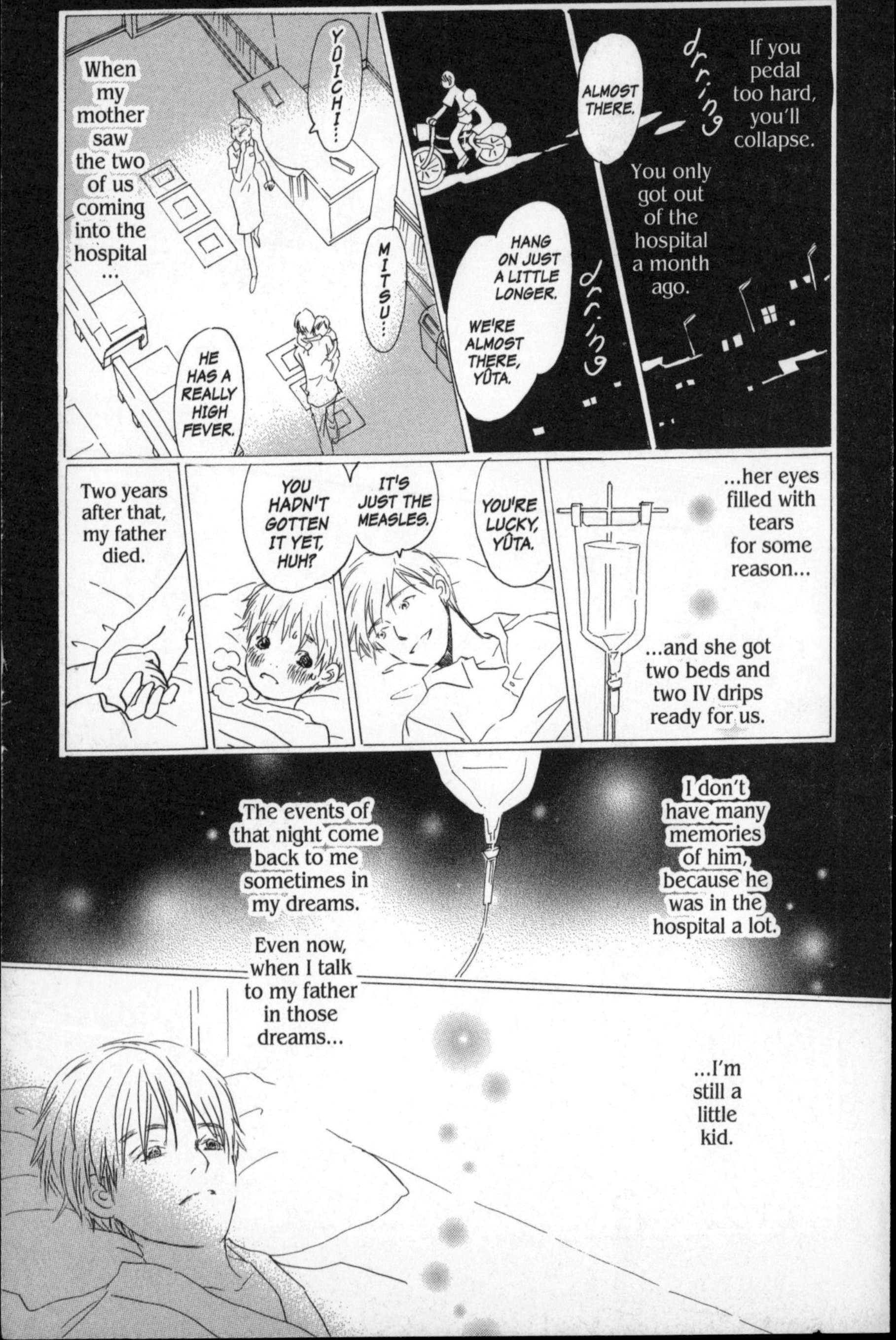
If you pedal too hard, you'll collapse.
drring
You only got out of the hospital a month ago.
drring
ALMOST THERE.
HANG ON JUST A LITTLE LONGER.
WE'RE ALMOST THERE, YŪTA.
YOICHI...
When my mother saw the two of us coming into the hospital...
MITSU...
HE HAS A REALLY HIGH FEVER.
...her eyes filled with tears for some reason...
...and she got two beds and two IV drips ready for us.
YOU'RE LUCKY, YŪTA.
IT'S JUST THE MEASLES.
YOU HADN'T GOTTEN IT YET, HUH?
Two years after that, my father died.
I don't have many memories of him, because he was in the hospital a lot.
The events of that night come back to me sometimes in my dreams.
Even now, when I talk to my father in those dreams...
...I'm still a little kid.

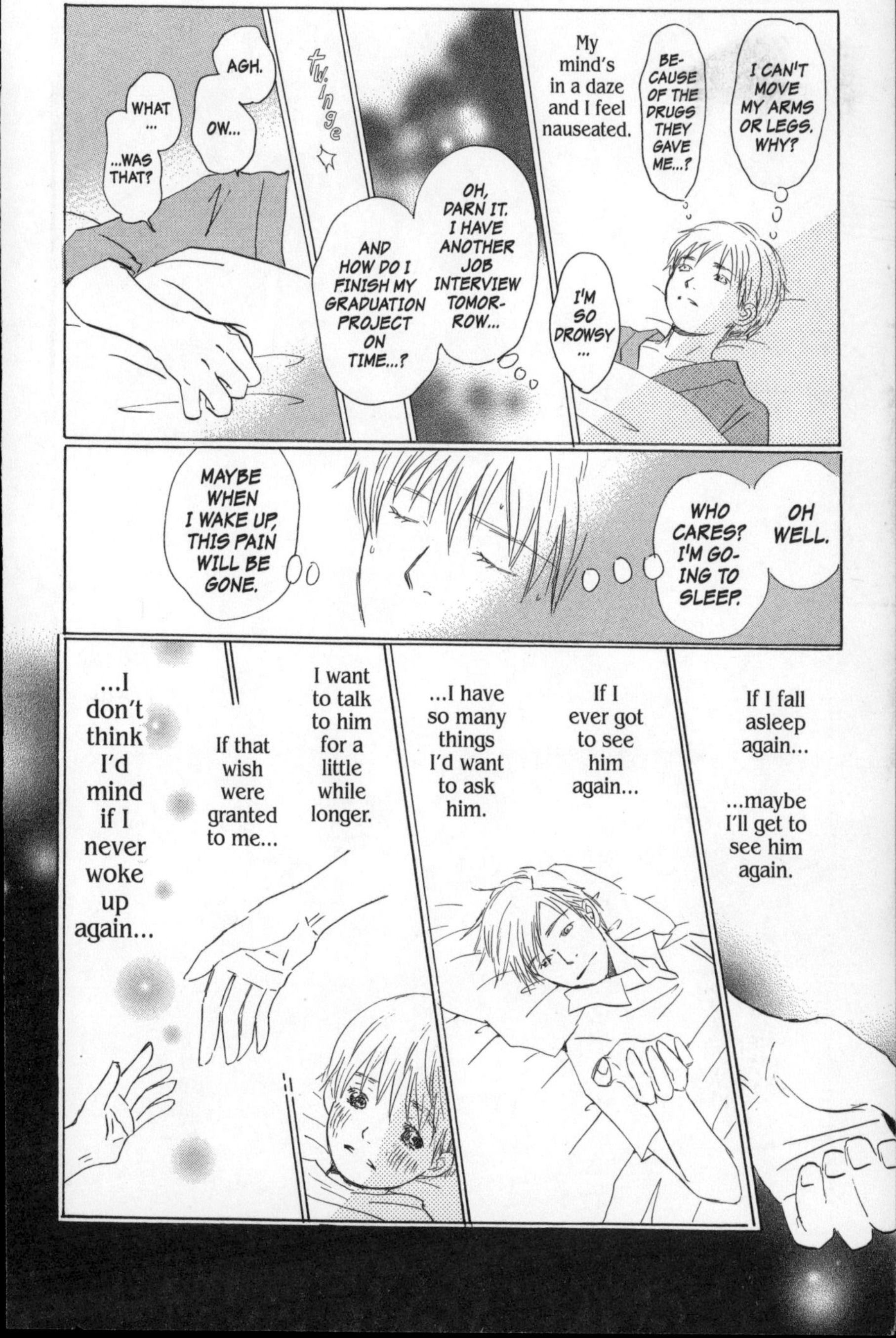
I CAN'T MOVE MY ARMS OR LEGS. WHY?
BECAUSE OF THE DRUGS THEY GAVE ME...?
My mind's in a daze and I feel nauseated.
I'M SO DROWSY...
OH, DARN IT. I HAVE ANOTHER JOB INTERVIEW TOMORROW...
AND HOW DO I FINISH MY GRADUATION PROJECT ON TIME...?
twinge
AGH.
OW...
WHAT... ...WAS THAT?
OH WELL.
WHO CARES? I'M GOING TO SLEEP.
MAYBE WHEN I WAKE UP, THIS PAIN WILL BE GONE.
If I fall asleep again...
...maybe I'll get to see him again.
If I ever got to see him again...
...I have so many things I'd want to ask him.
I want to talk to him for a little while longer.
If that wish were granted to me...
...I don't think I'd mind if I never woke up again...

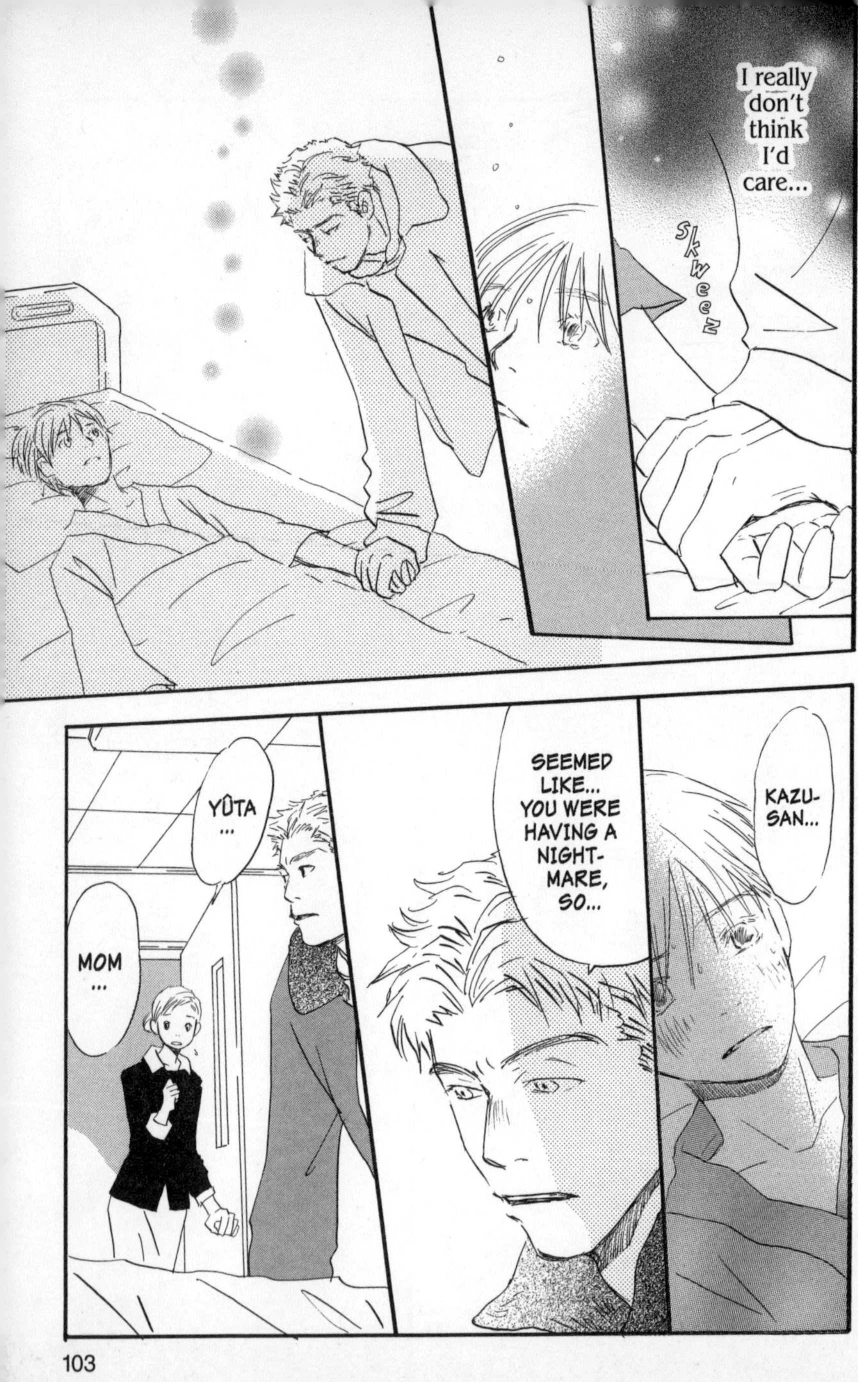
I really don't think I'd care...
SKWEEZ
KAZU-SAN...
SEEMED LIKE... YOU WERE HAVING A NIGHTMARE, SO...
YÛTA ...
MOM ...

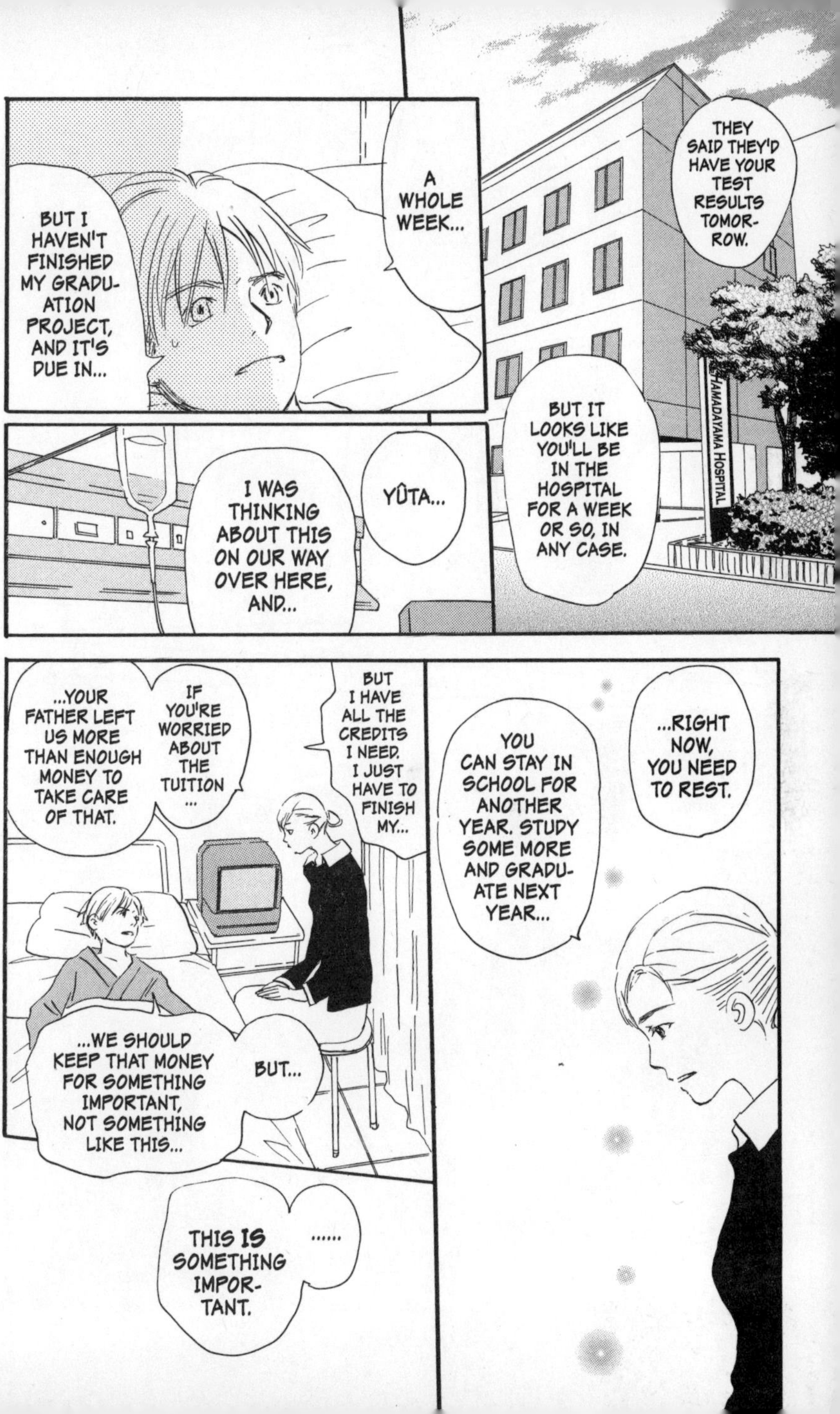
THEY SAID THEY'D HAVE YOUR TEST RESULTS TOMOR-ROW.
HAMADAYAMA HOSPITAL
BUT IT LOOKS LIKE YOU'LL BE IN THE HOSPITAL FOR A WEEK OR SO, IN ANY CASE.
A WHOLE WEEK...
BUT I HAVEN'T FINISHED MY GRADU-ATION PROJECT, AND IT'S DUE IN...
YÛTA...
I WAS THINKING ABOUT THIS ON OUR WAY OVER HERE, AND...
...RIGHT NOW, YOU NEED TO REST.
YOU CAN STAY IN SCHOOL FOR ANOTHER YEAR. STUDY SOME MORE AND GRADU-ATE NEXT YEAR...
BUT I HAVE ALL THE CREDITS I NEED. I JUST HAVE TO FINISH MY...
IF YOU'RE WORRIED ABOUT THE TUITION ...
...YOUR FATHER LEFT US MORE THAN ENOUGH MONEY TO TAKE CARE OF THAT.
BUT...
...WE SHOULD KEEP THAT MONEY FOR SOMETHING IMPORTANT, NOT SOMETHING LIKE THIS...
......
THIS IS SOMETHING IMPOR-TANT.

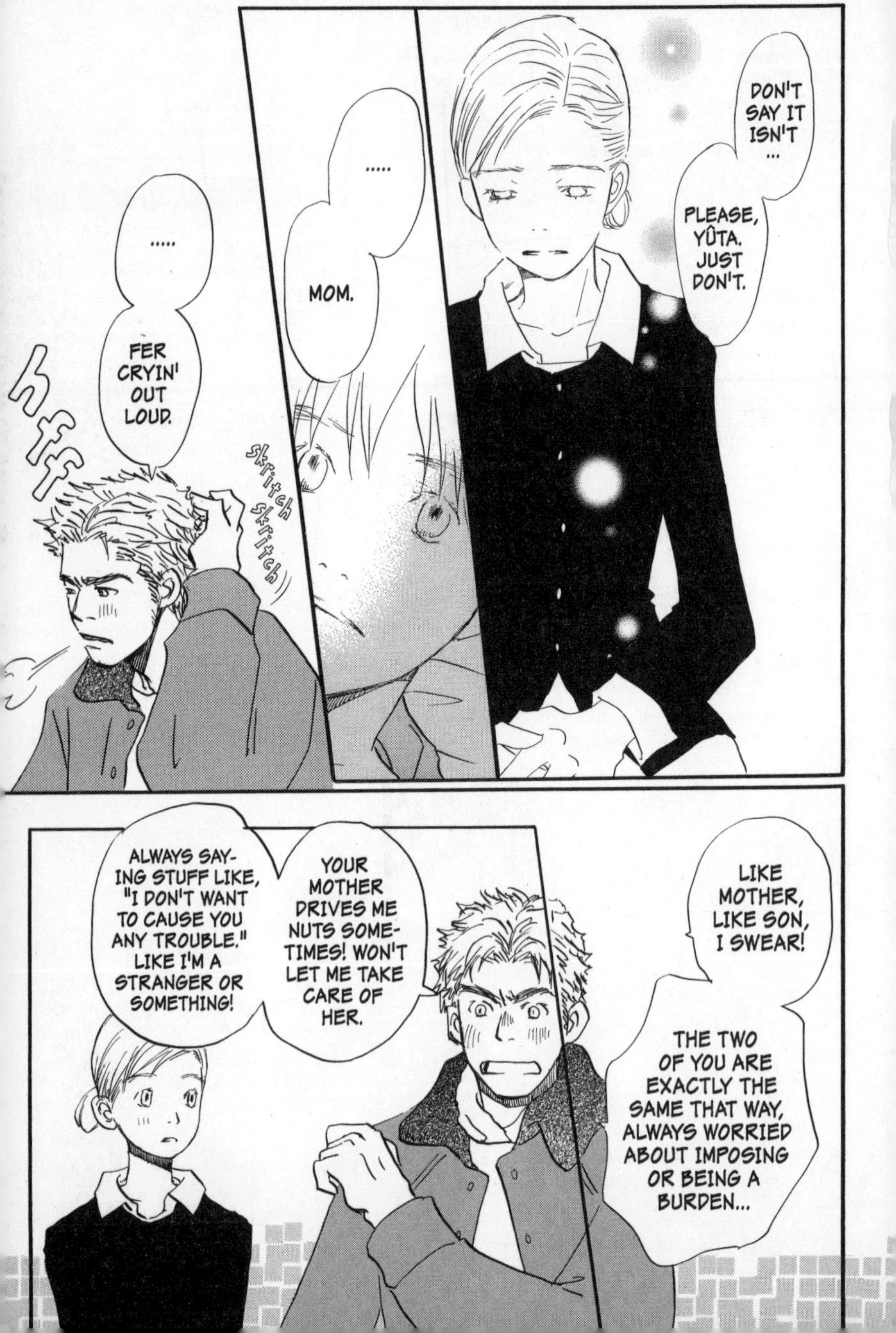
DON'T SAY IT ISN'T ...
PLEASE, YÛTA. JUST DON'T.
.....
MOM.
.....
FER CRYIN' OUT LOUD.
skritch skritch
hff
LIKE MOTHER, LIKE SON, I SWEAR!
THE TWO OF YOU ARE EXACTLY THE SAME THAT WAY, ALWAYS WORRIED ABOUT IMPOSING OR BEING A BURDEN...
YOUR MOTHER DRIVES ME NUTS SOME-TIMES! WON'T LET ME TAKE CARE OF HER.
ALWAYS SAY-ING STUFF LIKE, "I DON'T WANT TO CAUSE YOU ANY TROUBLE." LIKE I'M A STRANGER OR SOMETHING!

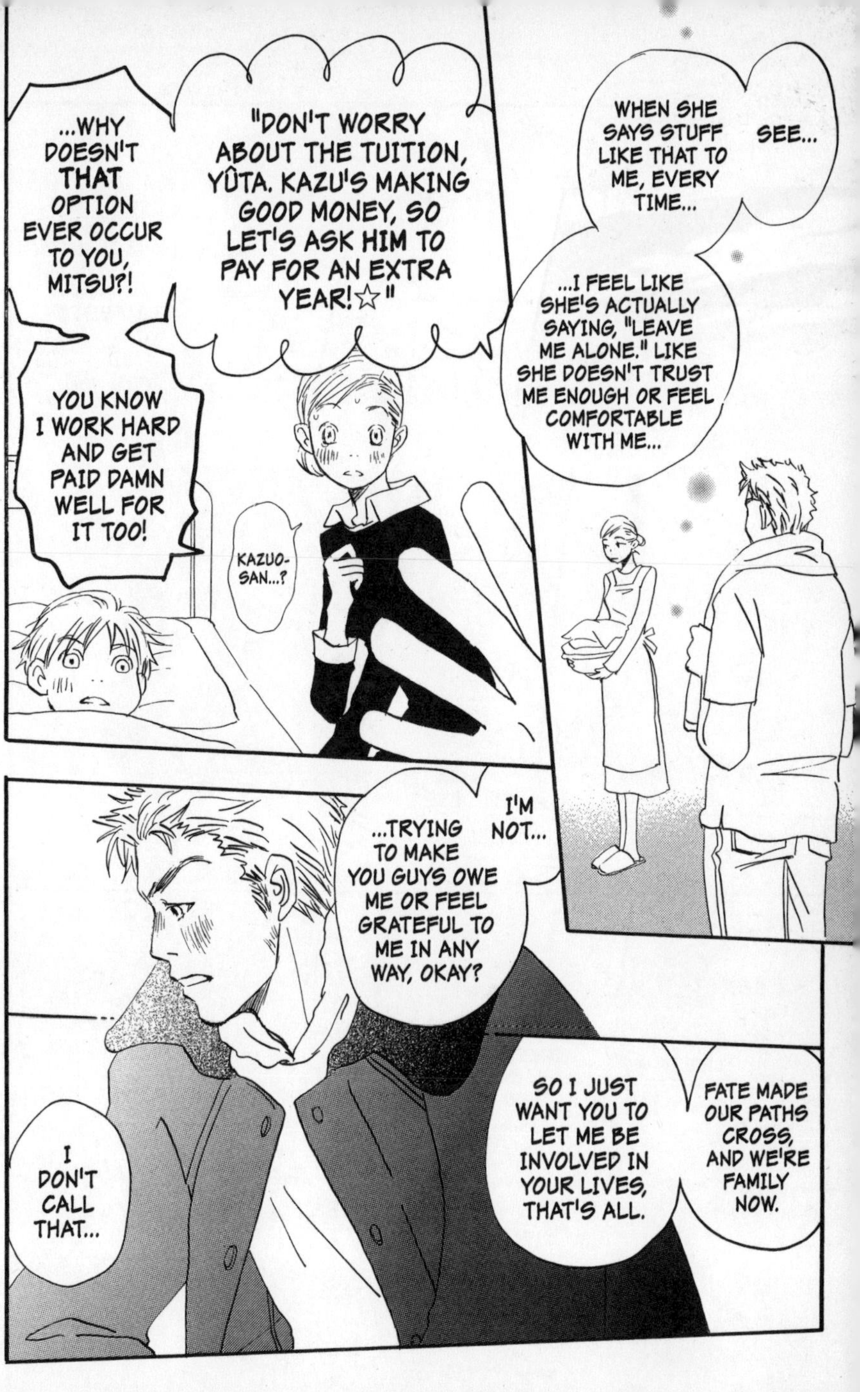

SEE...
WHEN SHE SAYS STUFF LIKE THAT TO ME, EVERY TIME...
...I FEEL LIKE SHE'S ACTUALLY SAYING, "LEAVE ME ALONE." LIKE SHE DOESN'T TRUST ME ENOUGH OR FEEL COMFORTABLE WITH ME...
"DON'T WORRY ABOUT THE TUITION, YÛTA. KAZU'S MAKING GOOD MONEY, SO LET'S ASK HIM TO PAY FOR AN EXTRA YEAR!☆"
...WHY DOESN'T THAT OPTION EVER OCCUR TO YOU, MITSU?!
YOU KNOW I WORK HARD AND GET PAID DAMN WELL FOR IT TOO!
KAZUO-SAN...?
I'M NOT...
...TRYING TO MAKE YOU GUYS OWE ME OR FEEL GRATEFUL TO ME IN ANY WAY, OKAY?
FATE MADE OUR PATHS CROSS, AND WE'RE FAMILY NOW.
SO I JUST WANT YOU TO LET ME BE INVOLVED IN YOUR LIVES, THAT'S ALL.
I DON'T CALL THAT...

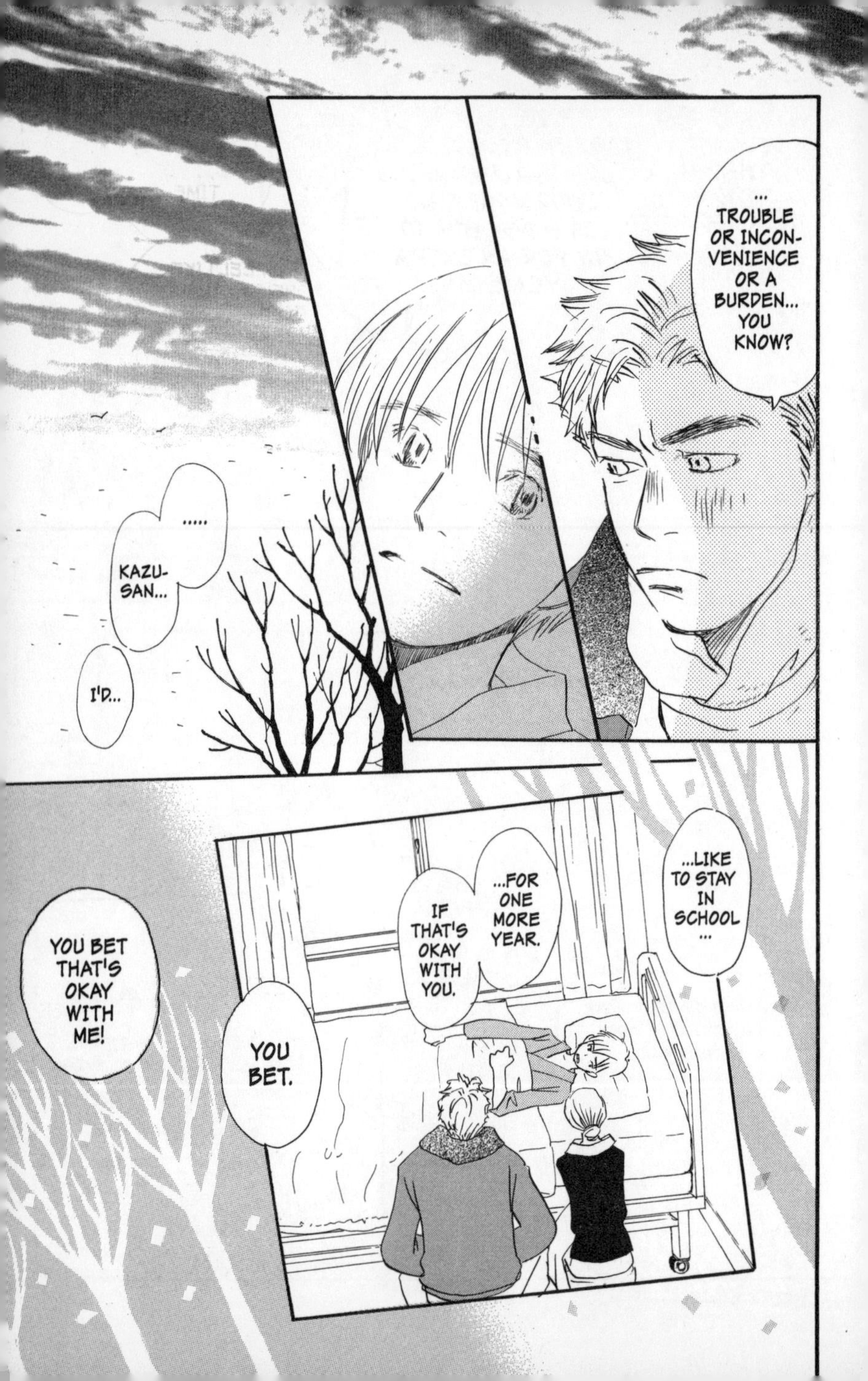
... TROUBLE OR INCON-VENIENCE OR A BURDEN... YOU KNOW?
.....
KAZU-SAN...
I'D...
...LIKE TO STAY IN SCHOOL ...
...FOR ONE MORE YEAR.
IF THAT'S OKAY WITH YOU.
YOU BET.
YOU BET THAT'S OKAY WITH ME!

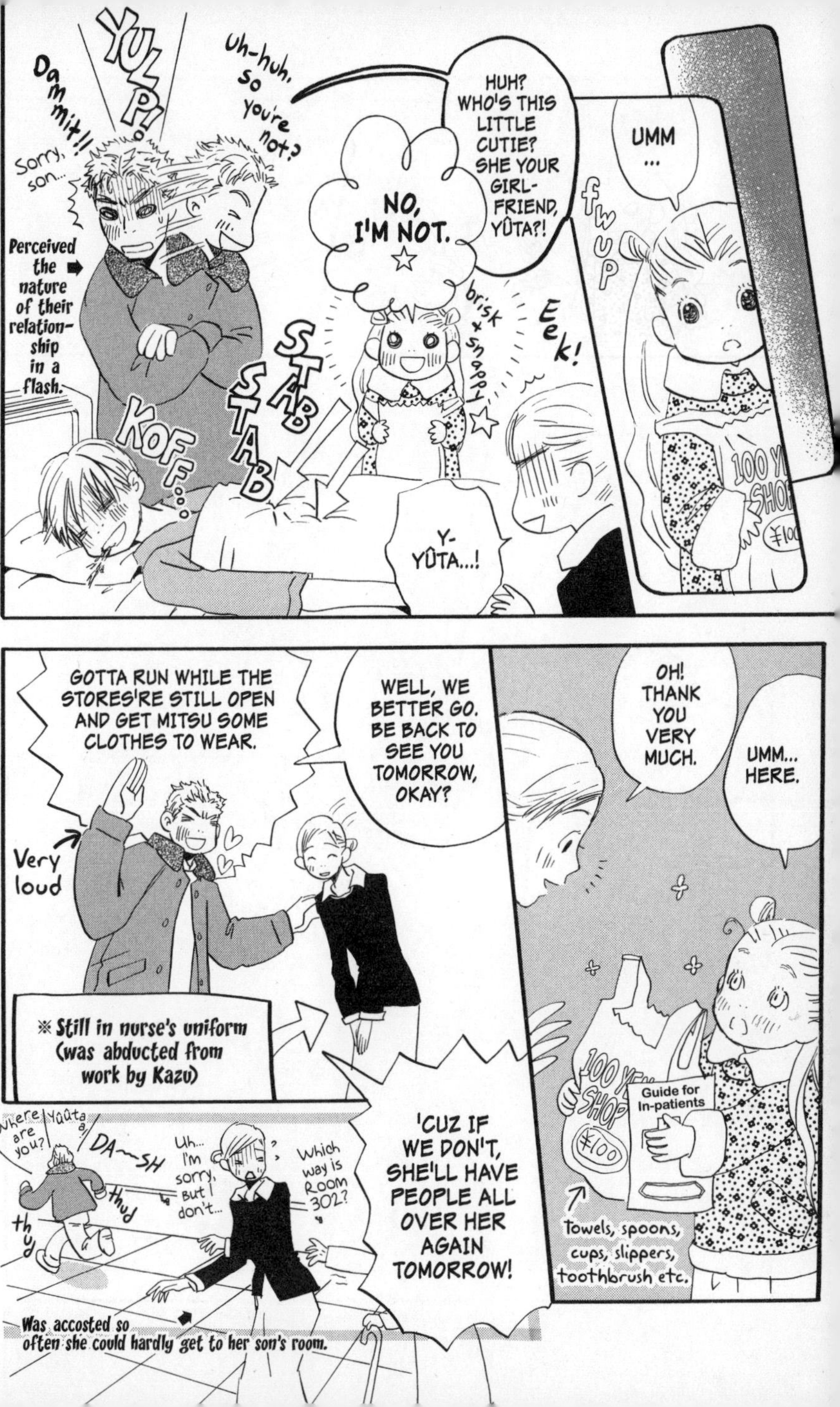
UMM ...
fwup
HUH? WHO'S THIS LITTLE CUTIE? SHE YOUR GIRLFRIEND, YÛTA?!
NO, I'M NOT. ☆
Uh-huh, so you're not?
YULP!
Dammit!!
Sorry, son...
Perceived the nature of their relationship in a flash.
brisk + snappy
Eek!
STAB STAB
KOFF...
Y-YÛTA...!
UMM... HERE.
OH! THANK YOU VERY MUCH.
Guide for In-patients
100 YEN SHOP
¥100
Towels, spoons, cups, slippers, toothbrush etc.
WELL, WE BETTER GO. BE BACK TO SEE YOU TOMORROW, OKAY?
GOTTA RUN WHILE THE STORES'RE STILL OPEN AND GET MITSU SOME CLOTHES TO WEAR.
Very loud
※ Still in nurse's uniform (was abducted from work by Kazu)
'CUZ IF WE DON'T, SHE'LL HAVE PEOPLE ALL OVER HER AGAIN TOMORROW!
Which way is Room 302?
Uh... I'm sorry, but I don't...
DA~SH
Yûta
Where are you?
thud
thud
Was accosted so often she could hardly get to her son's room.

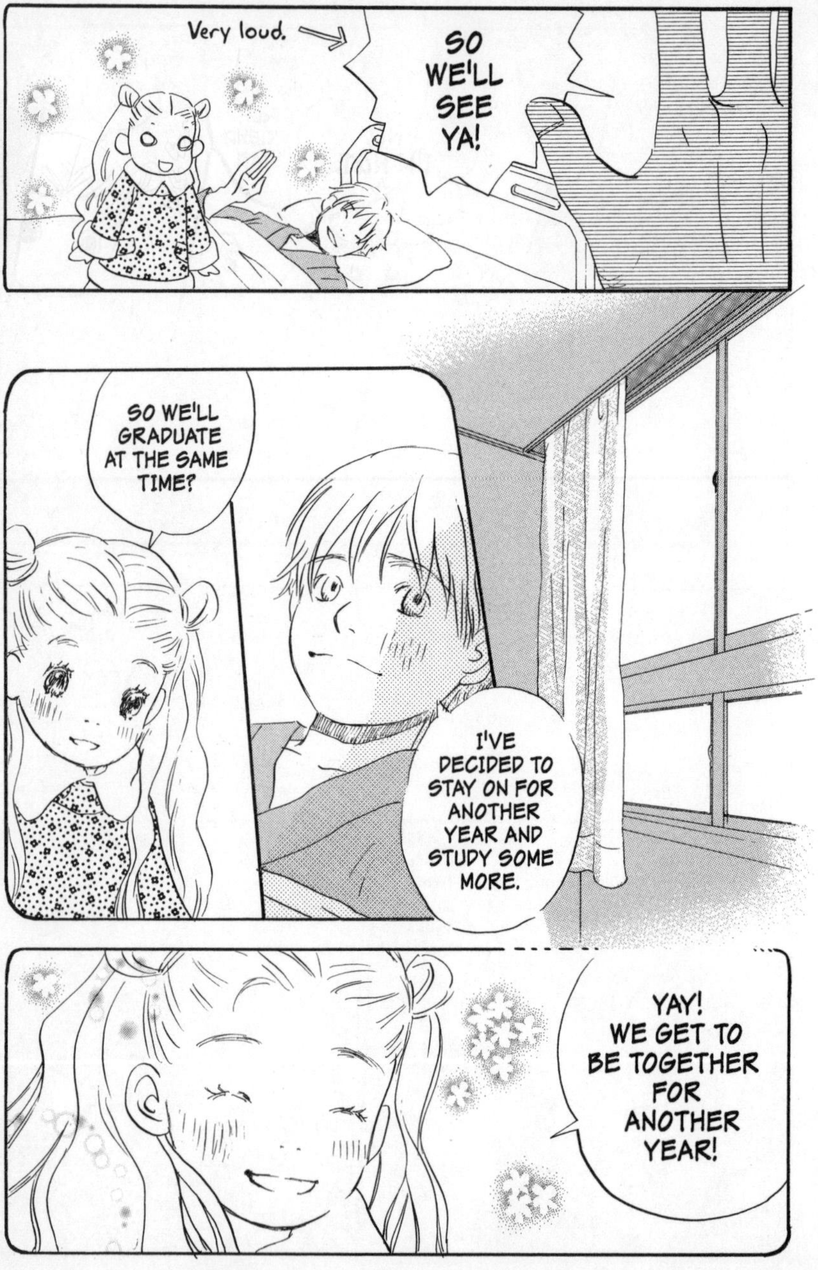
SO WE'LL SEE YA!
Very loud.
SO WE'LL GRADUATE AT THE SAME TIME?
I'VE DECIDED TO STAY ON FOR ANOTHER YEAR AND STUDY SOME MORE.
YAY! WE GET TO BE TOGETHER FOR ANOTHER YEAR!

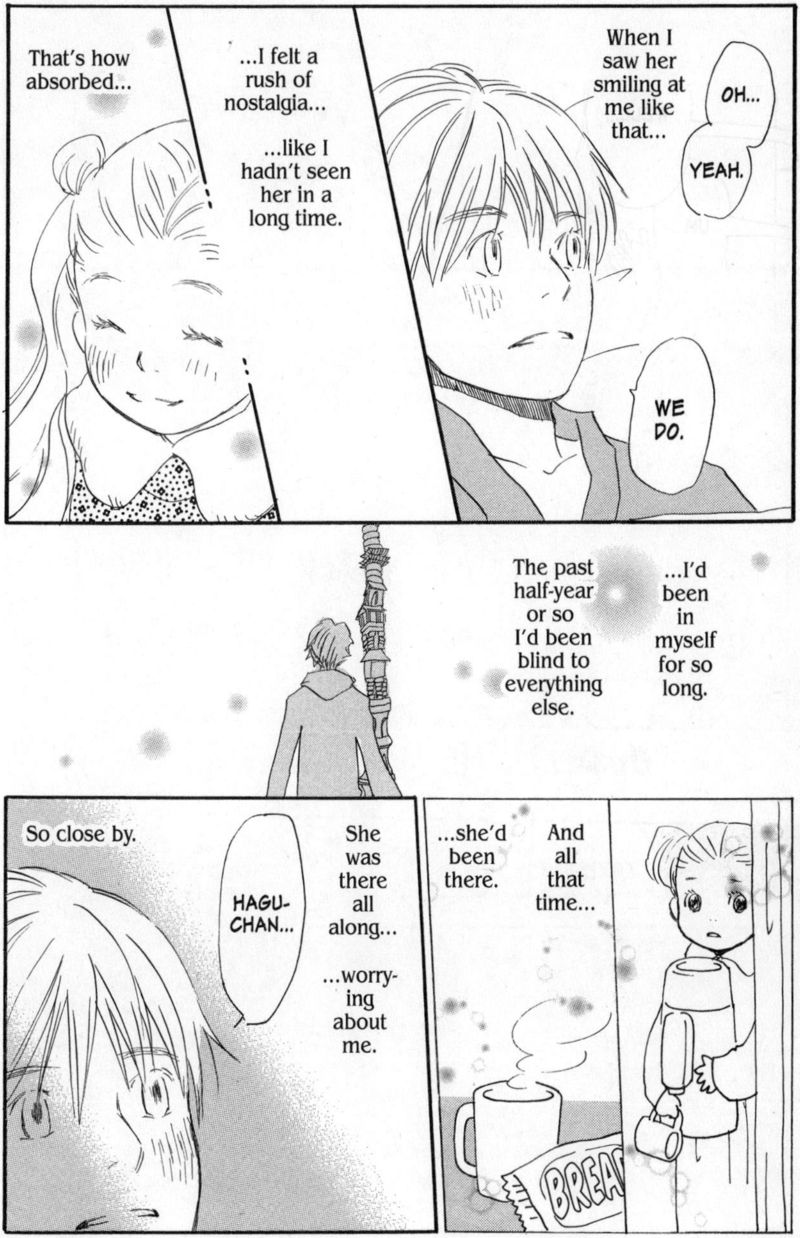
When I saw her smiling at me like that...
OH... YEAH.
WE DO.
...I felt a rush of nostalgia...
...like I hadn't seen her in a long time.
That's how absorbed...
...I'd been in myself for so long.
The past half-year or so I'd been blind to everything else.
And all that time...
...she'd been there.
BREA
She was there all along...
...worrying about me.
HAGU-CHAN...
So close by.

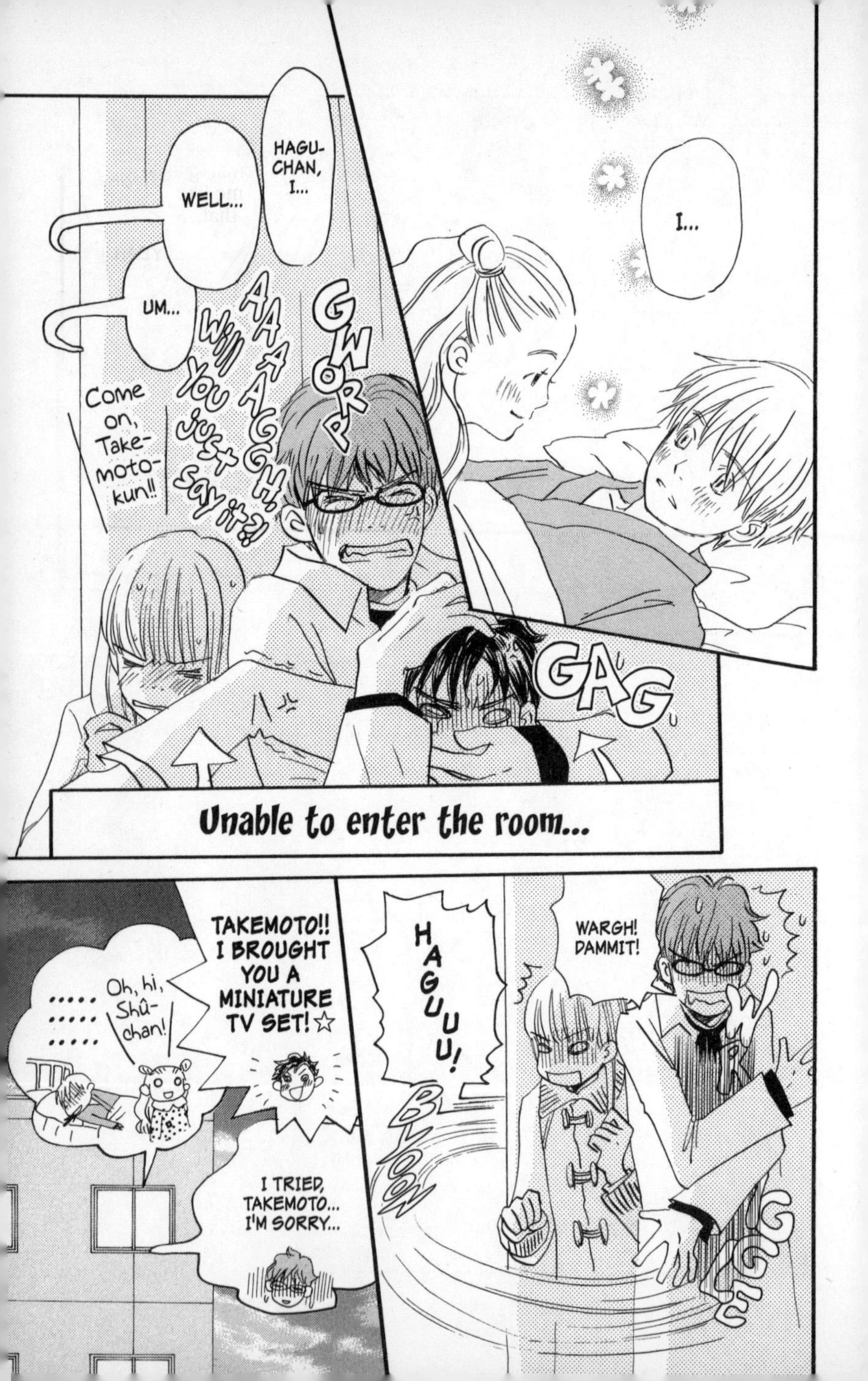
I...
HAGU-CHAN, I...
WELL...
UM...
GWORP
AAAAGH, Will you just say it?!
Come on, Take-moto-kun!!
GAG
Unable to enter the room...
WARGH! DAMMIT!
HAGUUU!
TAKEMOTO!! I BROUGHT YOU A MINIATURE TV SET! ☆
Oh, hi, Shû-chan!
....
I TRIED, TAKEMOTO... I'M SORRY...

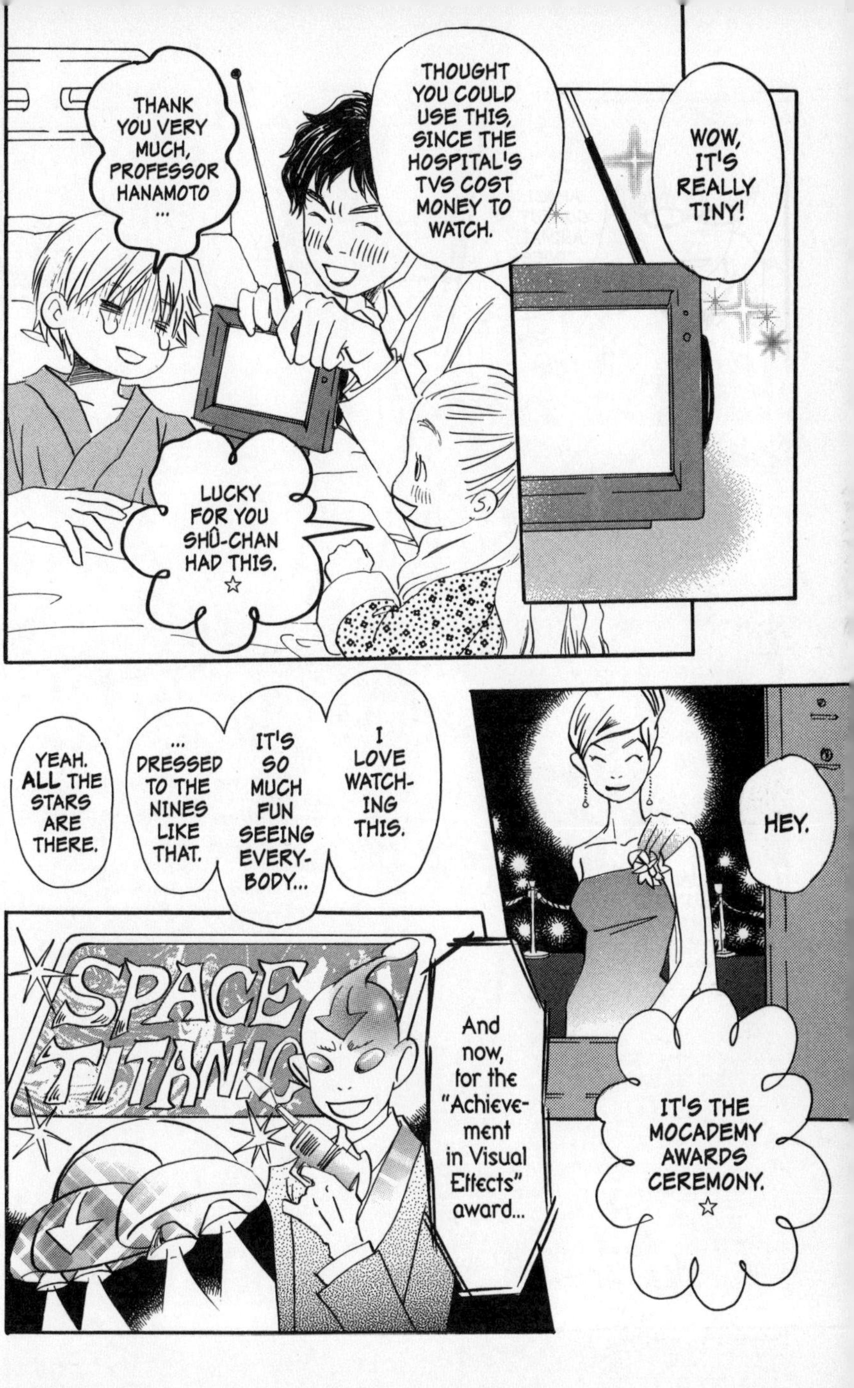
WOW, IT'S REALLY TINY!
THOUGHT YOU COULD USE THIS, SINCE THE HOSPITAL'S TVS COST MONEY TO WATCH.
THANK YOU VERY MUCH, PROFESSOR HANAMOTO ...
LUCKY FOR YOU SHÛ-CHAN HAD THIS. ☆
HEY.
IT'S THE MOCADEMY AWARDS CEREMONY. ☆
I LOVE WATCHING THIS.
IT'S SO MUCH FUN SEEING EVERYBODY...
... DRESSED TO THE NINES LIKE THAT.
YEAH. **ALL** THE STARS ARE THERE.
SPACE TITANIC
And now, for the "Achievement in Visual Effects" award...

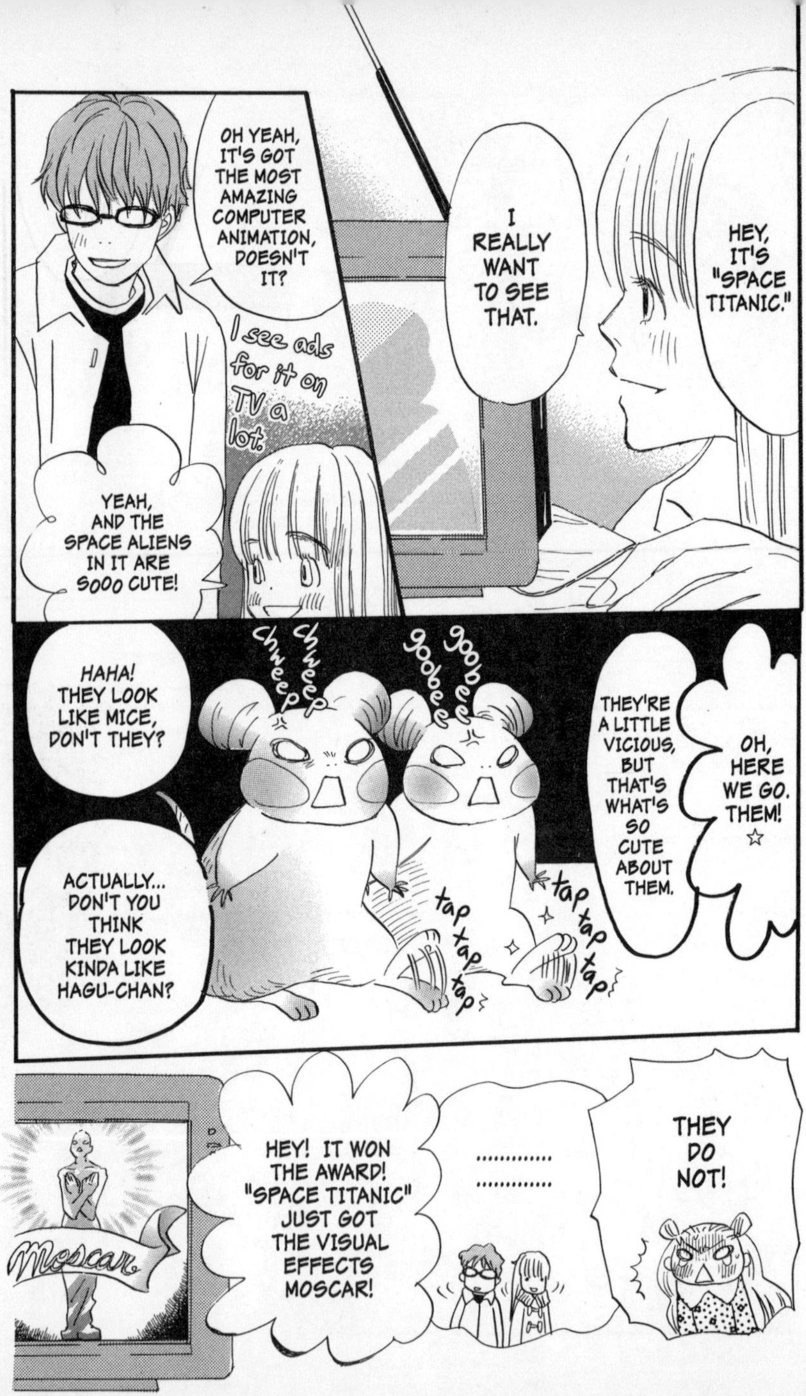

HEY, IT'S "SPACE TITANIC."
I REALLY WANT TO SEE THAT.
OH YEAH, IT'S GOT THE MOST AMAZING COMPUTER ANIMATION, DOESN'T IT?
I see ads for it on TV a lot.
YEAH, AND THE SPACE ALIENS IN IT ARE SOOO CUTE!
OH, HERE WE GO. THEM! ☆
THEY'RE A LITTLE VICIOUS, BUT THAT'S WHAT'S SO CUTE ABOUT THEM.
goobee goobee
tap tap tap
chweep chweep
HAHA! THEY LOOK LIKE MICE, DON'T THEY?
ACTUALLY... DON'T YOU THINK THEY LOOK KINDA LIKE HAGU-CHAN?
tap tap tap
THEY DO NOT!
....
....
HEY! IT WON THE AWARD! "SPACE TITANIC" JUST GOT THE VISUAL EFFECTS MOSCAR!
Moscar

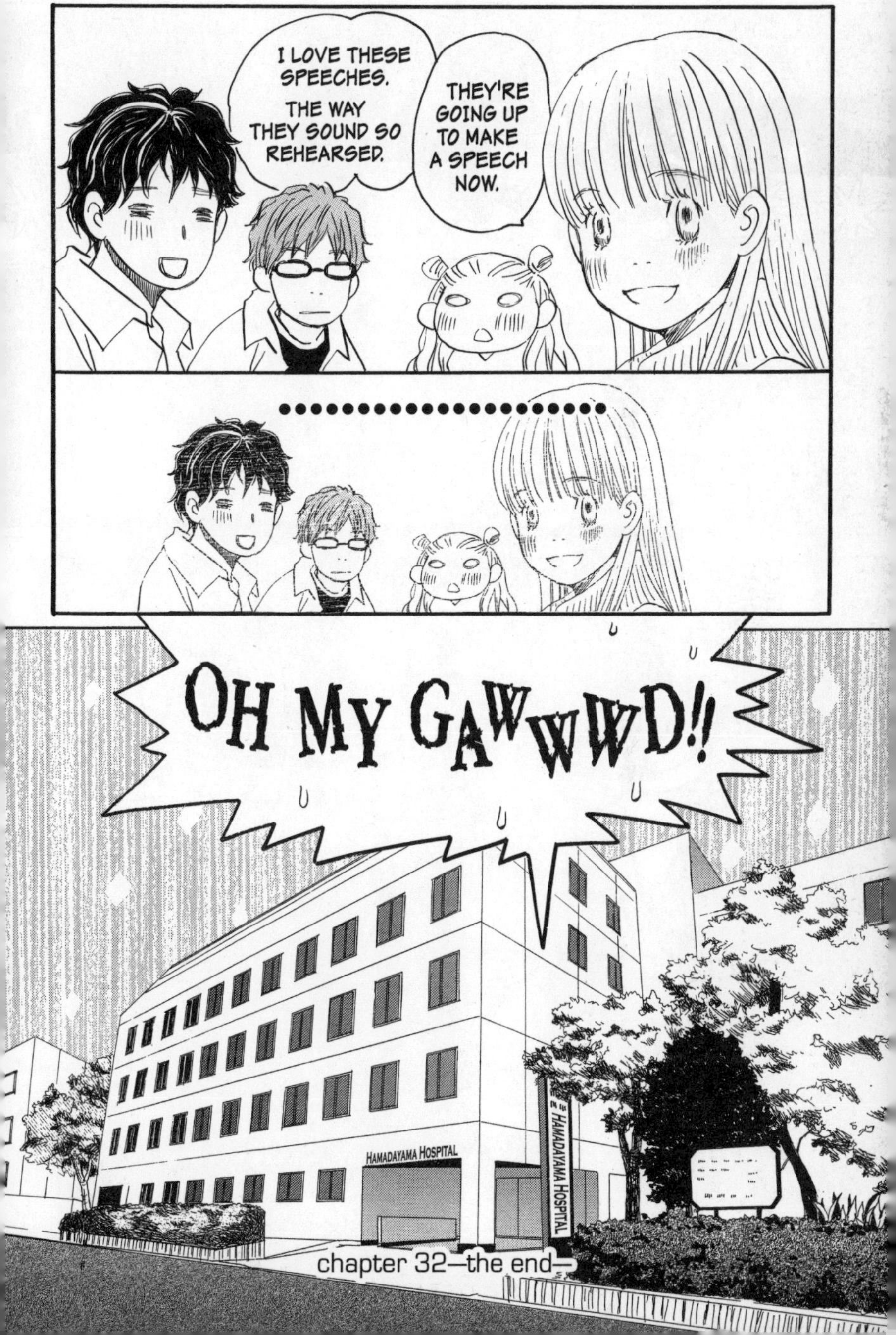
THEY'RE GOING UP TO MAKE A SPEECH NOW.
I LOVE THESE SPEECHES.
THE WAY THEY SOUND SO REHEARSED.
……………………
OH MY GAWWWD!!
HAMADAYAMA HOSPITAL
HAMADAYAMA HOSPITAL
chapter 32—the end—

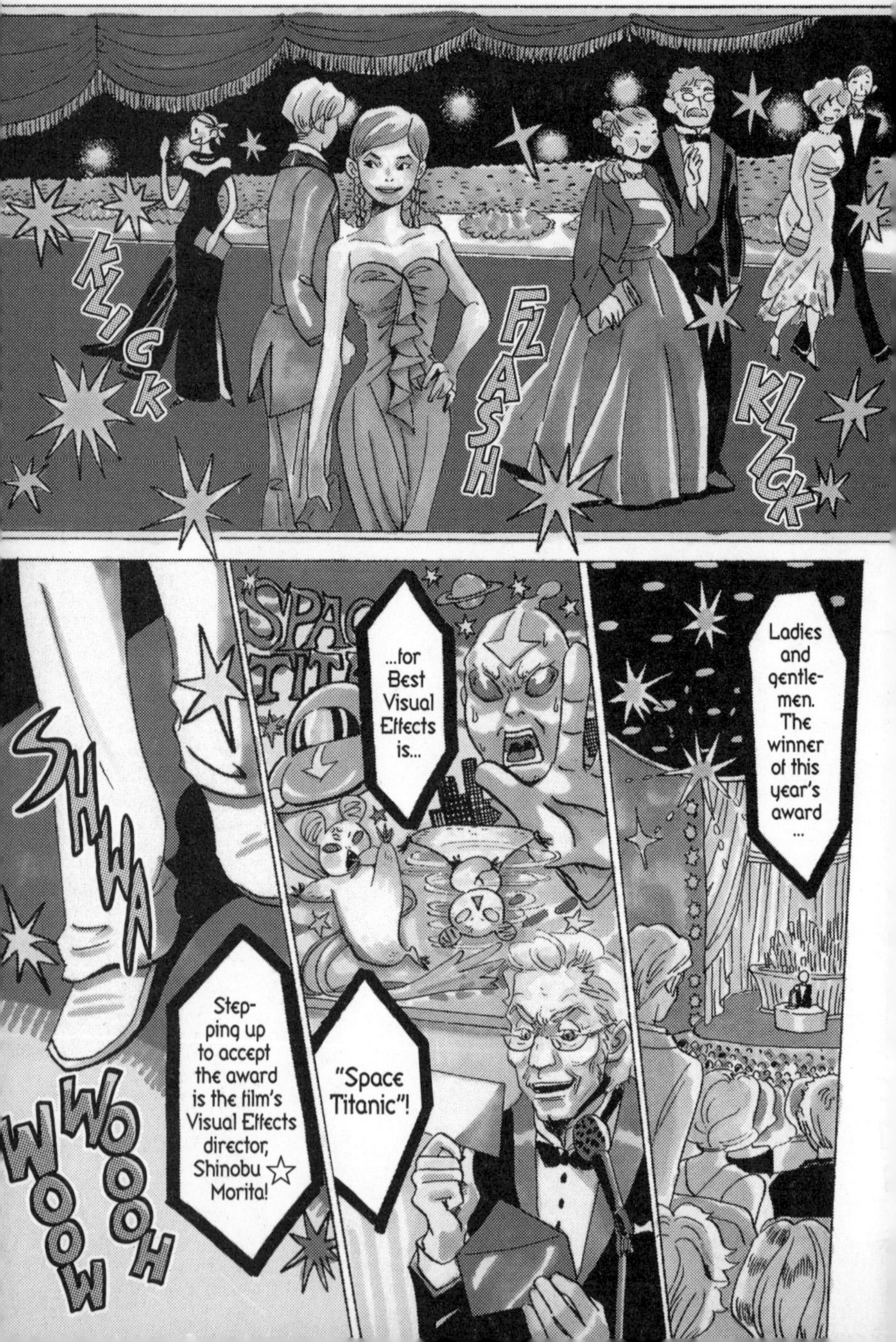
KLICK
FLASH
KLICK
Ladies and gentlemen. The winner of this year's award ...
...for Best Visual Effects is...
"Space Titanic"!
Stepping up to accept the award is the film's Visual Effects director, Shinobu☆Morita!
SHWA
WOOOH
WOOOW

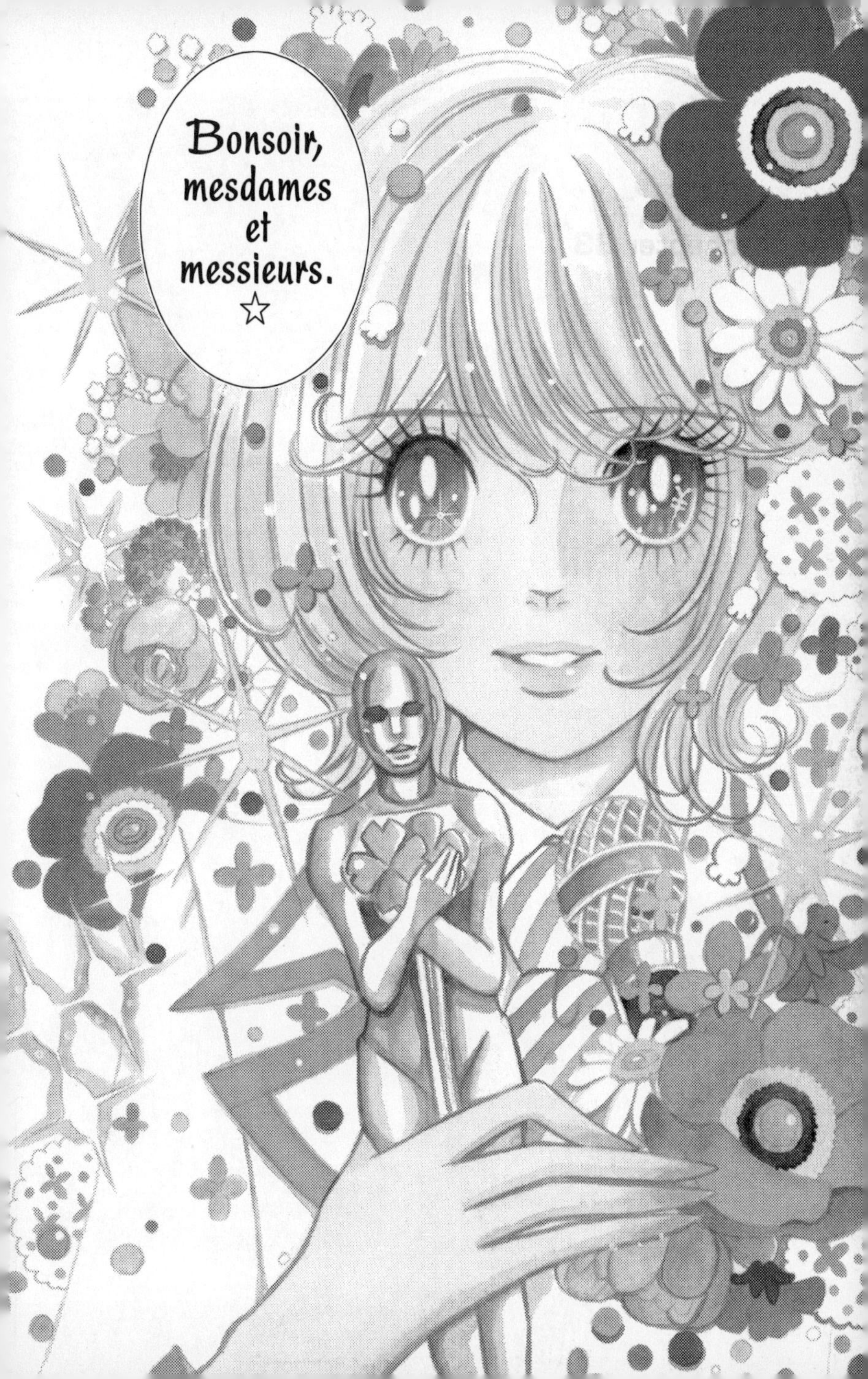
Bonsoir, mesdames et messieurs. ☆

honey and clover™

chapter 33

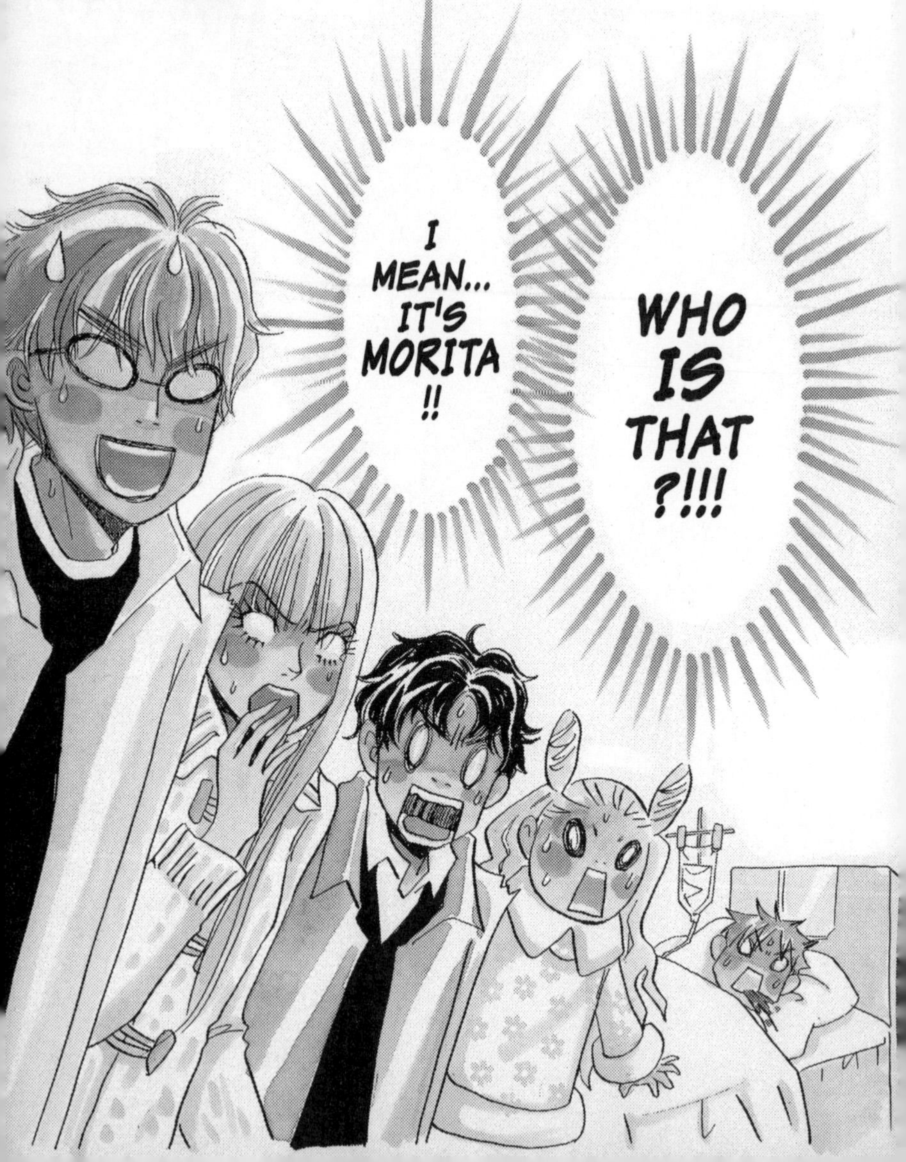
WHO IS THAT ?!!!
I MEAN... IT'S MORITA !!

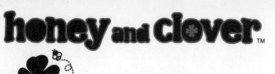

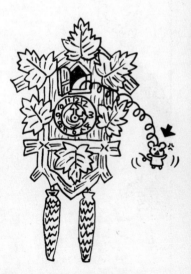

Hagu Clock (made by Morita)
Country-style Kamakura carving
Material: Sandalwood (because it smells good)

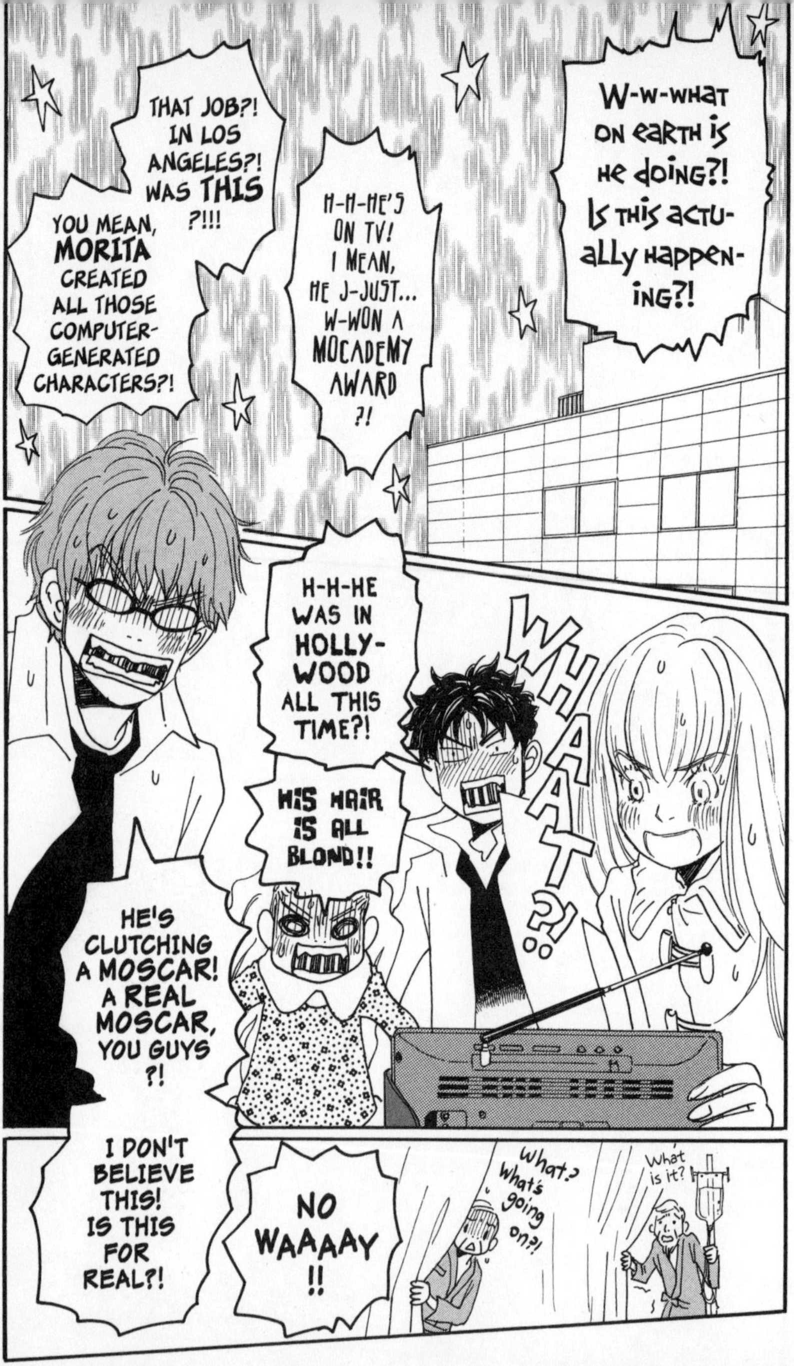
W-w-what on earth is he doing?! Is this actually happening?!
H-H-he's on TV! I mean, he j-just... w-won a Mocademy Award?!
That job?! In Los Angeles?! Was THIS?!!!
You mean, MORITA created all those computer-generated characters?!
WHAAAT?!
H-H-he was in HOLLYWOOD all this time?!
His hair is all blond!!
He's clutching a MOSCAR! A REAL MOSCAR, you guys?!
What is it?
What? What's going on?!
NO WAAAAY!!
I don't believe this! Is this for real?!

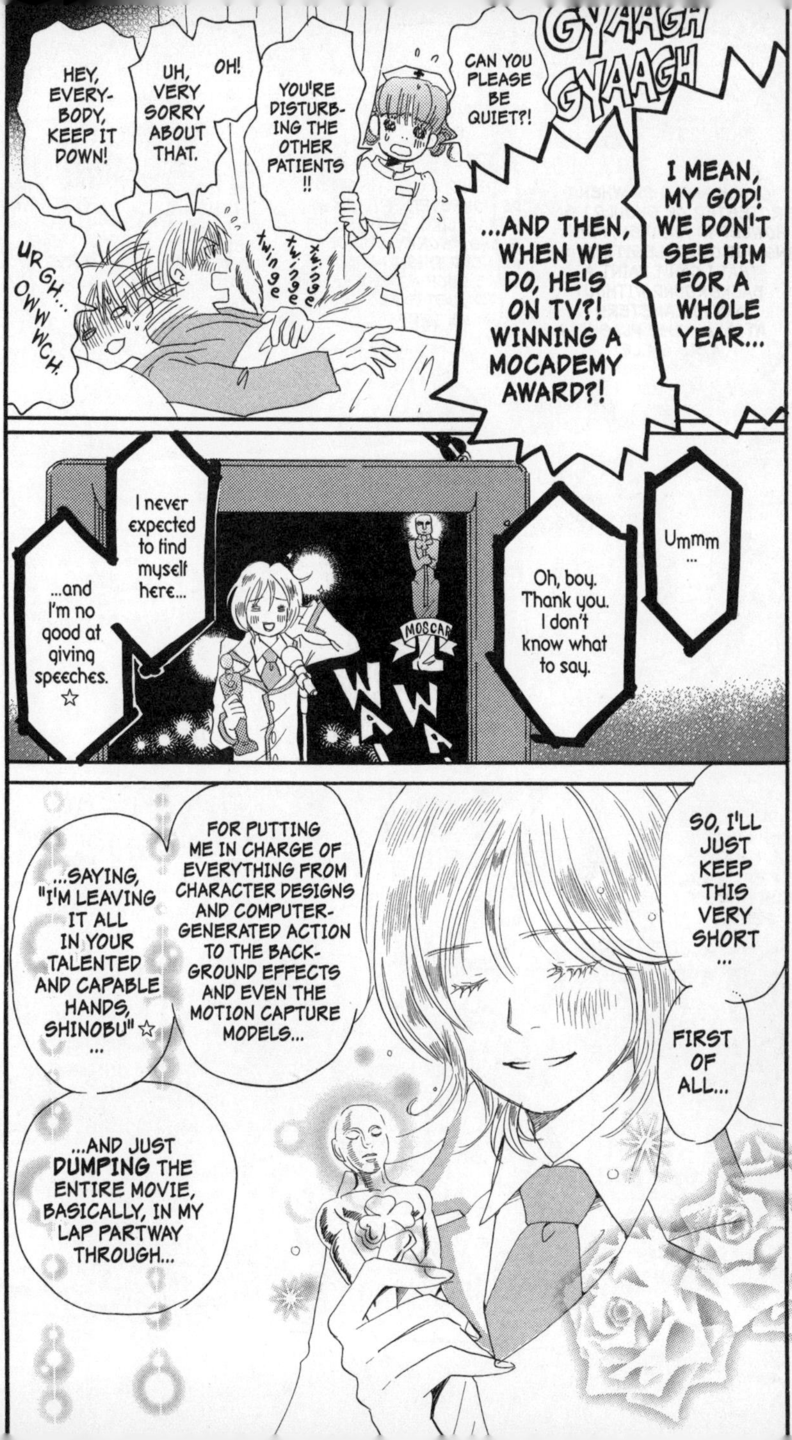
GYAAGH
GYAAGH
I MEAN, MY GOD! WE DON'T SEE HIM FOR A WHOLE YEAR...
...AND THEN, WHEN WE DO, HE'S ON TV?! WINNING A MOCADEMY AWARD?!
CAN YOU PLEASE BE QUIET?!
YOU'RE DISTURBING THE OTHER PATIENTS!!
OH!
UH, VERY SORRY ABOUT THAT.
HEY, EVERYBODY, KEEP IT DOWN!
twinge twinge twinge
URGH... OWWWCH.
Ummm ...
Oh, boy. Thank you. I don't know what to say.
MOSCAR
WAWA
I never expected to find myself here...
...and I'm no good at giving speeches. ☆
SO, I'LL JUST KEEP THIS VERY SHORT ...
FIRST OF ALL...
FOR PUTTING ME IN CHARGE OF EVERYTHING FROM CHARACTER DESIGNS AND COMPUTER-GENERATED ACTION TO THE BACKGROUND EFFECTS AND EVEN THE MOTION CAPTURE MODELS...
...SAYING, "I'M LEAVING IT ALL IN YOUR TALENTED AND CAPABLE HANDS, SHINOBU" ☆ ...
...AND JUST **DUMPING** THE ENTIRE MOVIE, BASICALLY, IN MY LAP PARTWAY THROUGH...

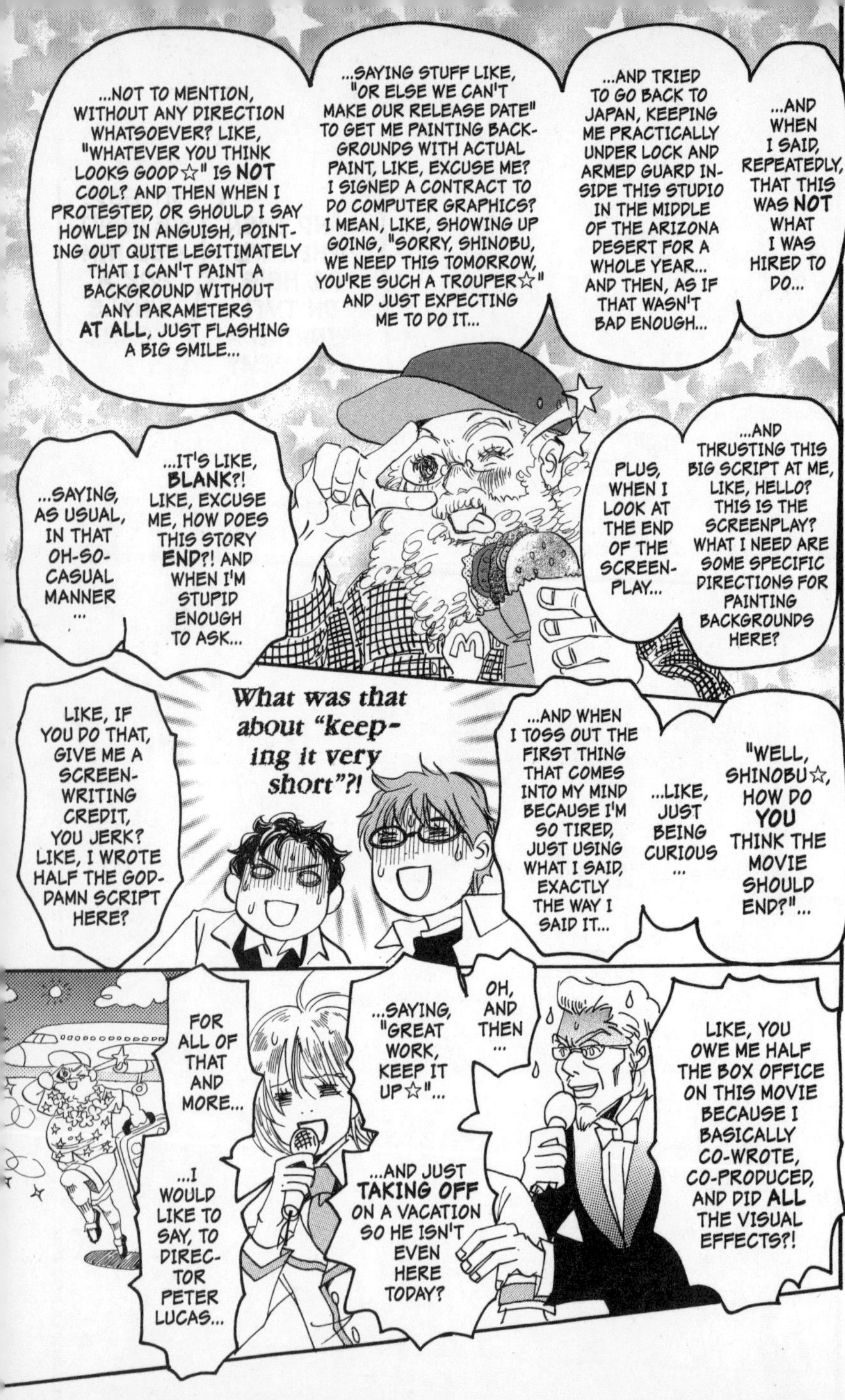
...AND WHEN I SAID, REPEATEDLY, THAT THIS WAS **NOT** WHAT I WAS HIRED TO DO...
...AND TRIED TO GO BACK TO JAPAN, KEEPING ME PRACTICALLY UNDER LOCK AND ARMED GUARD INSIDE THIS STUDIO IN THE MIDDLE OF THE ARIZONA DESERT FOR A WHOLE YEAR... AND THEN, AS IF THAT WASN'T BAD ENOUGH...
...SAYING STUFF LIKE, "OR ELSE WE CAN'T MAKE OUR RELEASE DATE" TO GET ME PAINTING BACKGROUNDS WITH ACTUAL PAINT, LIKE, EXCUSE ME? I SIGNED A CONTRACT TO DO COMPUTER GRAPHICS? I MEAN, LIKE, SHOWING UP GOING, "SORRY, SHINOBU, WE NEED THIS TOMORROW, YOU'RE SUCH A TROUPER☆" AND JUST EXPECTING ME TO DO IT...
...NOT TO MENTION, WITHOUT ANY DIRECTION WHATSOEVER? LIKE, "WHATEVER YOU THINK LOOKS GOOD☆" IS **NOT** COOL? AND THEN WHEN I PROTESTED, OR SHOULD I SAY HOWLED IN ANGUISH, POINTING OUT QUITE LEGITIMATELY THAT I CAN'T PAINT A BACKGROUND WITHOUT ANY PARAMETERS **AT ALL**, JUST FLASHING A BIG SMILE...
...AND THRUSTING THIS BIG SCRIPT AT ME, LIKE, HELLO? THIS IS THE SCREENPLAY? WHAT I NEED ARE SOME SPECIFIC DIRECTIONS FOR PAINTING BACKGROUNDS HERE?
PLUS, WHEN I LOOK AT THE END OF THE SCREENPLAY...
...IT'S LIKE, **BLANK**?! LIKE, EXCUSE ME, HOW DOES THIS STORY **END**?! AND WHEN I'M STUPID ENOUGH TO ASK...
...SAYING, AS USUAL, IN THAT OH-SO-CASUAL MANNER ...
"WELL, SHINOBU☆, HOW DO **YOU** THINK THE MOVIE SHOULD END?"...
...LIKE, JUST BEING CURIOUS ...
...AND WHEN I TOSS OUT THE FIRST THING THAT COMES INTO MY MIND BECAUSE I'M SO TIRED, JUST USING WHAT I SAID, EXACTLY THE WAY I SAID IT...
What was that about "keeping it very short"?!
LIKE, IF YOU DO THAT, GIVE ME A SCREENWRITING CREDIT, YOU JERK? LIKE, I WROTE HALF THE GODDAMN SCRIPT HERE?
LIKE, YOU OWE ME HALF THE BOX OFFICE ON THIS MOVIE BECAUSE I BASICALLY CO-WROTE, CO-PRODUCED, AND DID **ALL** THE VISUAL EFFECTS?!
OH, AND THEN ...
...SAYING, "GREAT WORK, KEEP IT UP☆"...
FOR ALL OF THAT AND MORE...
...AND JUST **TAKING OFF** ON A VACATION SO HE ISN'T EVEN HERE TODAY?
...I WOULD LIKE TO SAY, TO DIRECTOR PETER LUCAS...

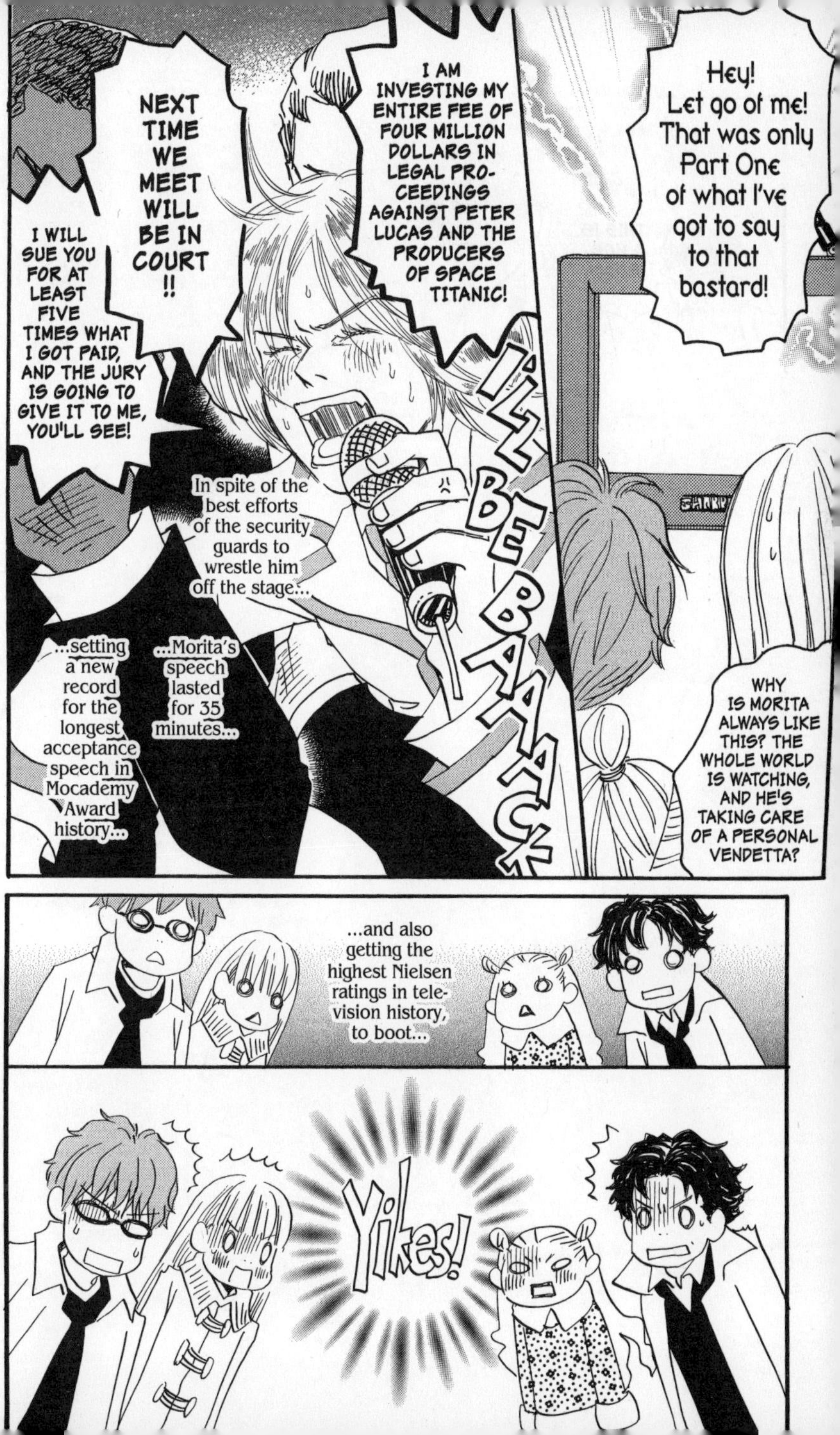
Hey! Let go of me! That was only Part One of what I've got to say to that bastard!
WHY IS MORITA ALWAYS LIKE THIS? THE WHOLE WORLD IS WATCHING, AND HE'S TAKING CARE OF A PERSONAL VENDETTA?
I AM INVESTING MY ENTIRE FEE OF FOUR MILLION DOLLARS IN LEGAL PRO-CEEDINGS AGAINST PETER LUCAS AND THE PRODUCERS OF SPACE TITANIC!
NEXT TIME WE MEET WILL BE IN COURT !!
I WILL SUE YOU FOR AT LEAST FIVE TIMES WHAT I GOT PAID, AND THE JURY IS GOING TO GIVE IT TO ME, YOU'LL SEE!
I'LL BE BAAACK
In spite of the best efforts of the security guards to wrestle him off the stage...
...Morita's speech lasted for 35 minutes...
...setting a new record for the longest acceptance speech in Mocademy Award history...
...and also getting the highest Nielsen ratings in tele-vision history, to boot...
Yikes!

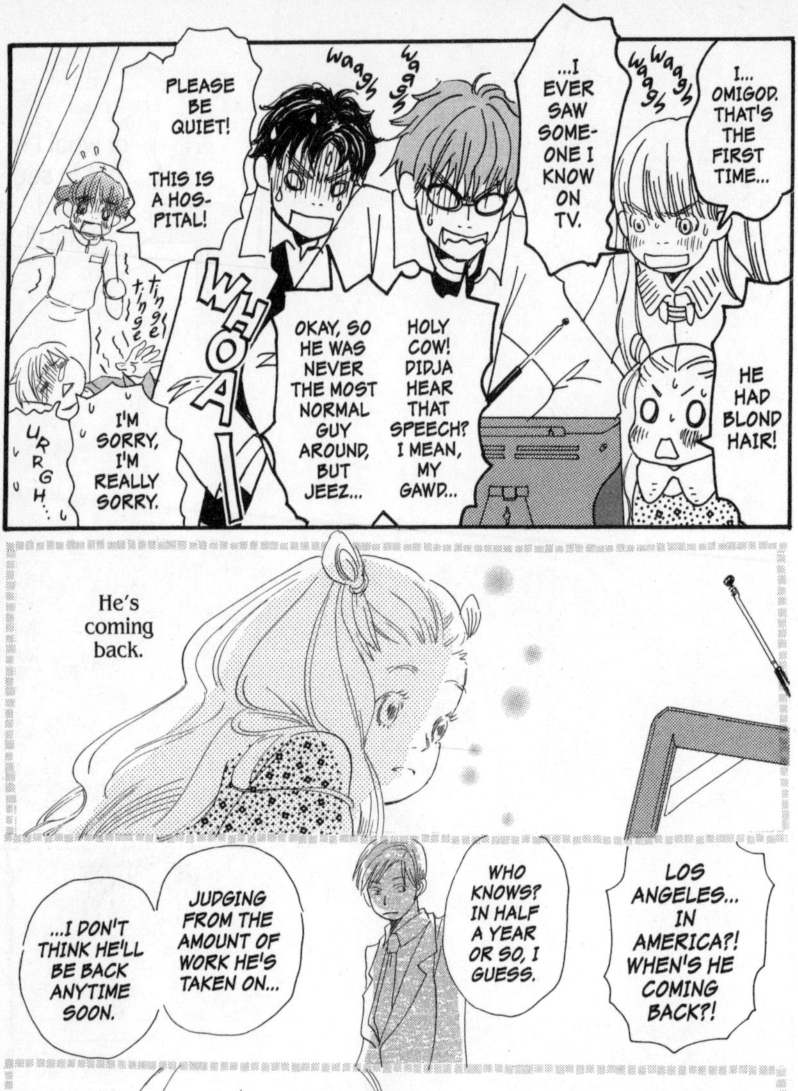
waagh
waagh
I... OMIGOD. THAT'S THE FIRST TIME...
...I EVER SAW SOME-ONE I KNOW ON TV.
HE HAD BLOND HAIR!
waagh
HOLY COW! DIDJA HEAR THAT SPEECH? I MEAN, MY GAWD...
waagh
OKAY, SO HE WAS NEVER THE MOST NORMAL GUY AROUND, BUT JEEZ...
WHOA!
PLEASE BE QUIET!
THIS IS A HOS-PITAL!
I'M SORRY, I'M REALLY SORRY.
He's coming back.
LOS ANGELES... IN AMERICA?! WHEN'S HE COMING BACK?!
WHO KNOWS? IN HALF A YEAR OR SO, I GUESS.
JUDGING FROM THE AMOUNT OF WORK HE'S TAKEN ON...
...I DON'T THINK HE'LL BE BACK ANYTIME SOON.
Morita's coming back.

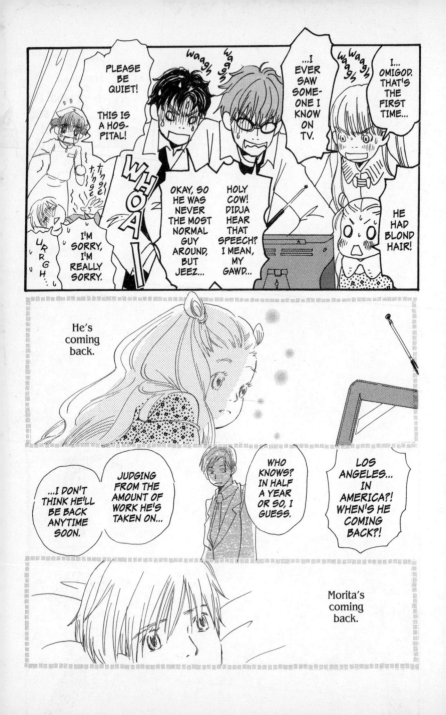

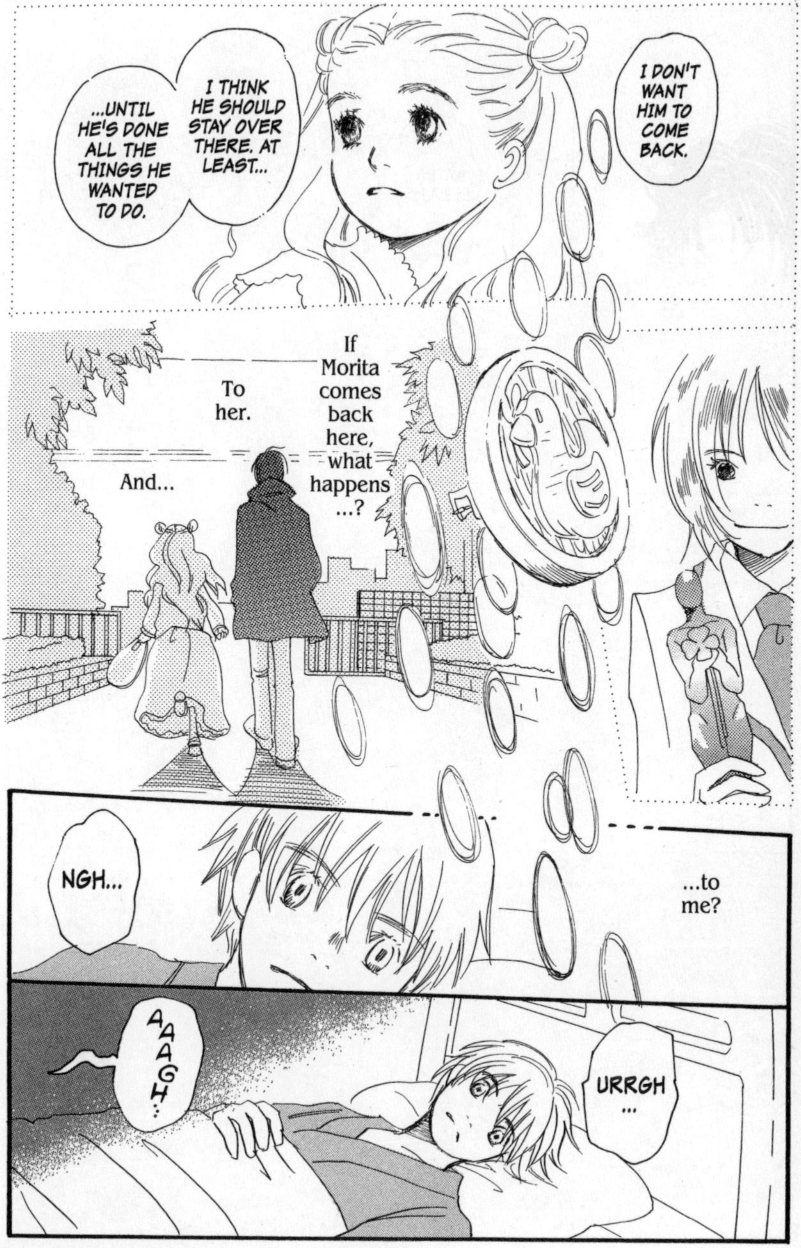
I DON'T WANT HIM TO COME BACK.
I THINK HE SHOULD STAY OVER THERE. AT LEAST...
...UNTIL HE'S DONE ALL THE THINGS HE WANTED TO DO.
If Morita comes back here, what happens ...?
To her.
And...
...to me?
NGH...
URRGH ...
AAAGH...

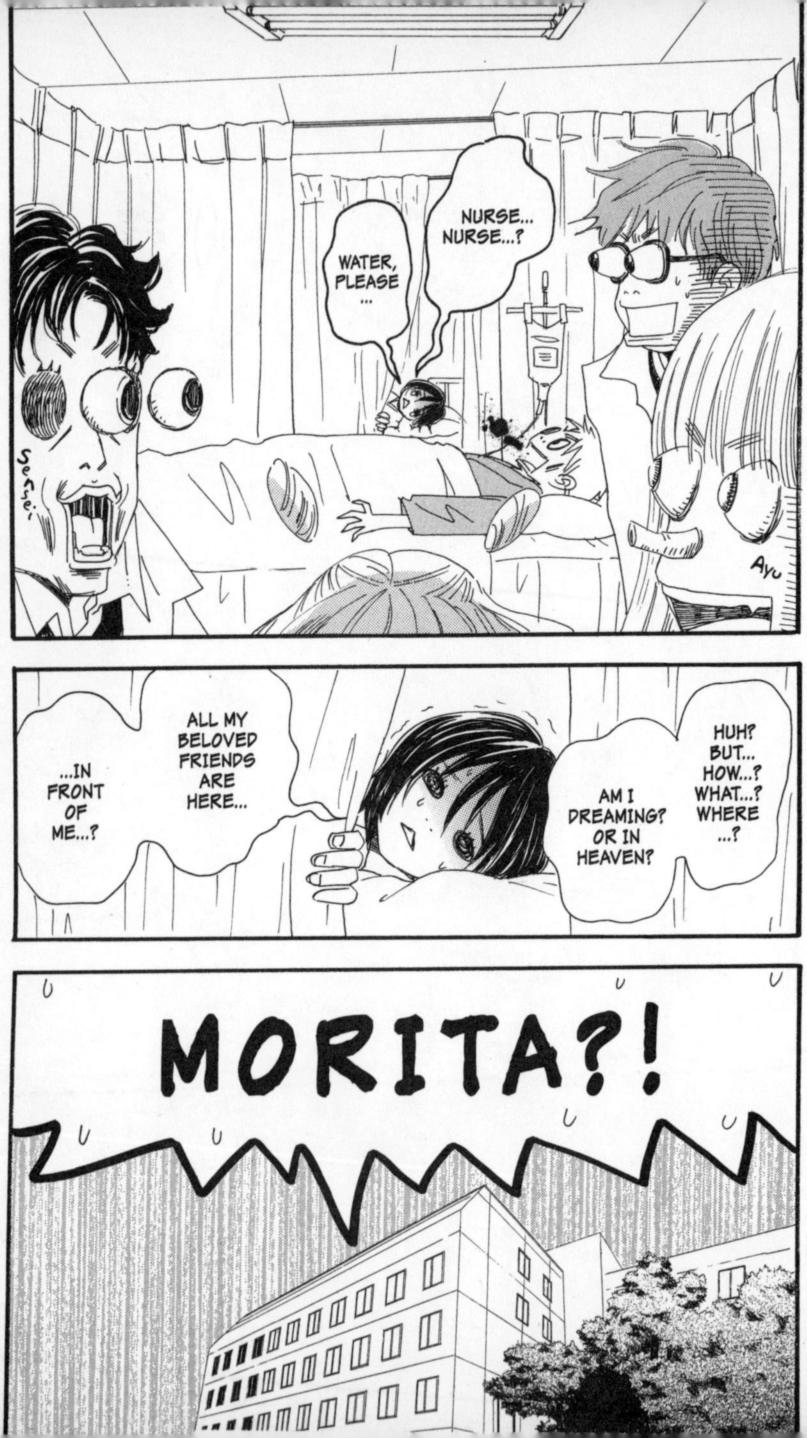
NURSE... NURSE...?
WATER, PLEASE ...
Ayu
Sensei
HUH? BUT... HOW...? WHAT...? WHERE ...?
AM I DREAMING? OR IN HEAVEN?
ALL MY BELOVED FRIENDS ARE HERE...
...IN FRONT OF ME...?
MORITA?!

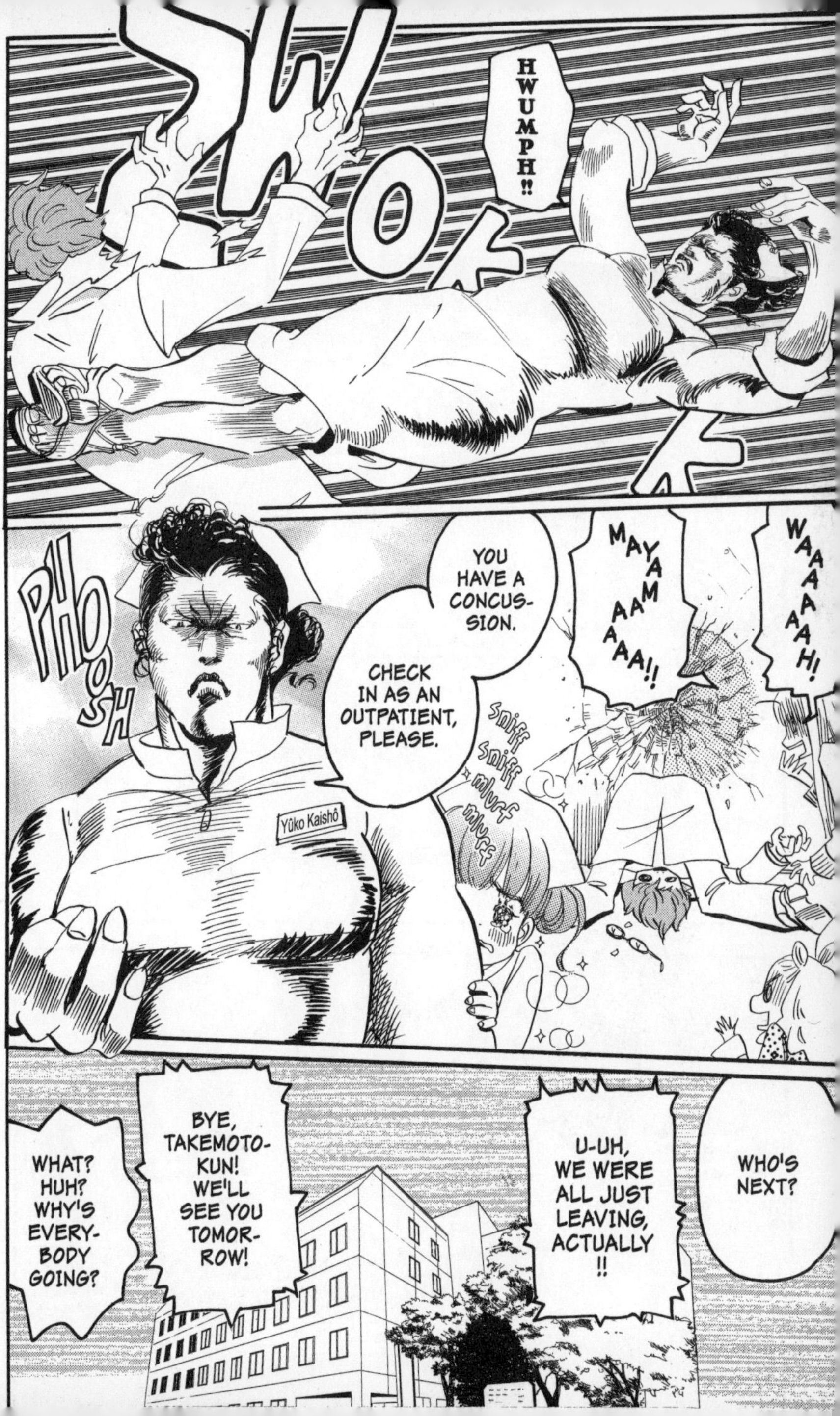
HWUMPH!!
WAAAAAAH!
MAYAMAAAAAA!!
YOU HAVE A CONCUS-SION.
CHECK IN AS AN OUTPATIENT, PLEASE.
PHOOSH
Sniff sniff mlurf mlurf
Yûko Kaishô
WHO'S NEXT?
U-UH, WE WERE ALL JUST LEAVING, ACTUALLY!!
BYE, TAKEMOTO-KUN! WE'LL SEE YOU TOMOR-ROW!
WHAT? HUH? WHY'S EVERY-BODY GOING?

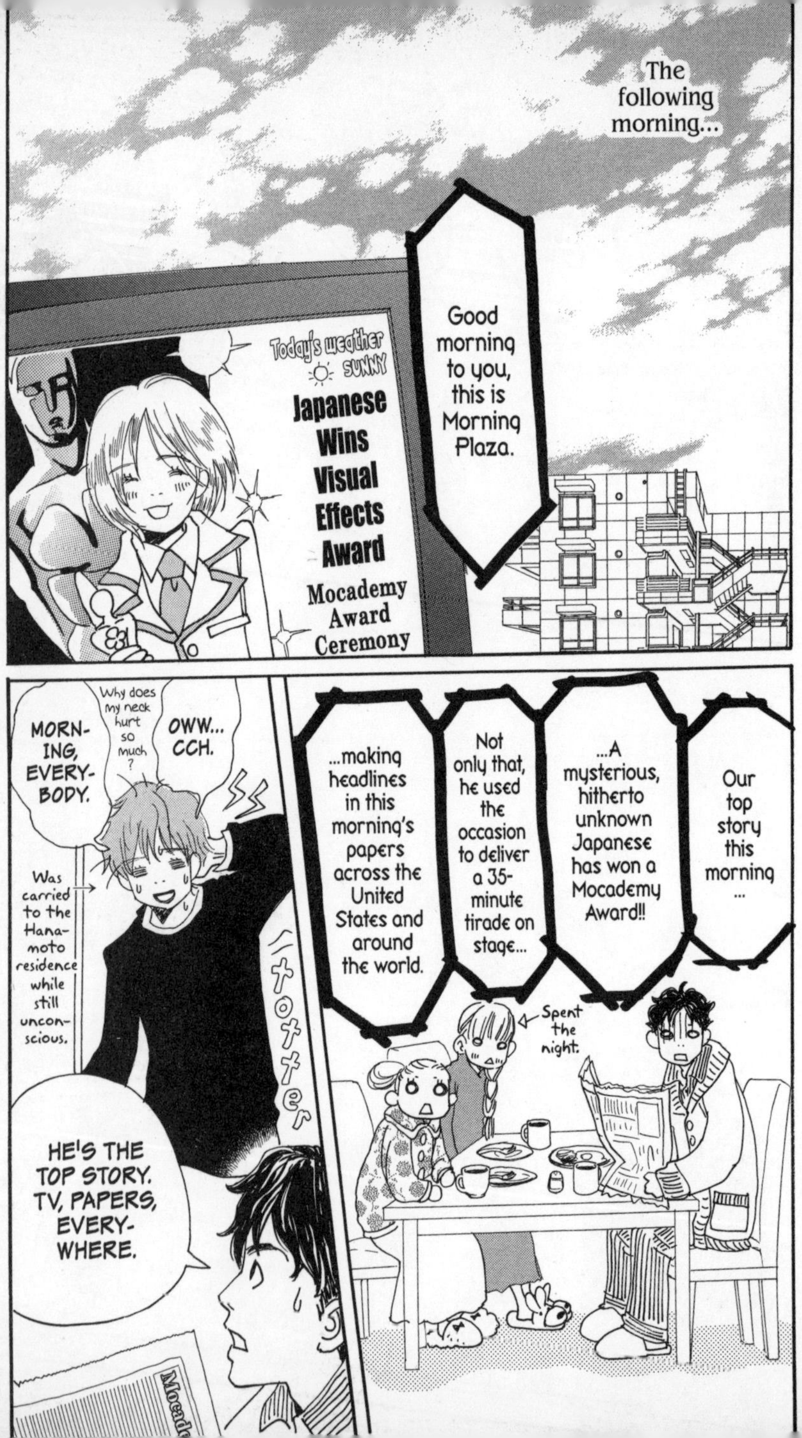

The following morning...
Good morning to you, this is Morning Plaza.
Today's weather SUNNY
Japanese Wins Visual Effects Award
Mocademy Award Ceremony
Our top story this morning ...
...A mysterious, hitherto unknown Japanese has won a Mocademy Award!!
Not only that, he used the occasion to deliver a 35-minute tirade on stage...
...making headlines in this morning's papers across the United States and around the world.
Spent the night.
OWW... CCH.
Why does my neck hurt so much?
MORNING, EVERYBODY.
Was carried to the Hanamoto residence while still unconscious.
totter
HE'S THE TOP STORY. TV, PAPERS, EVERYWHERE.

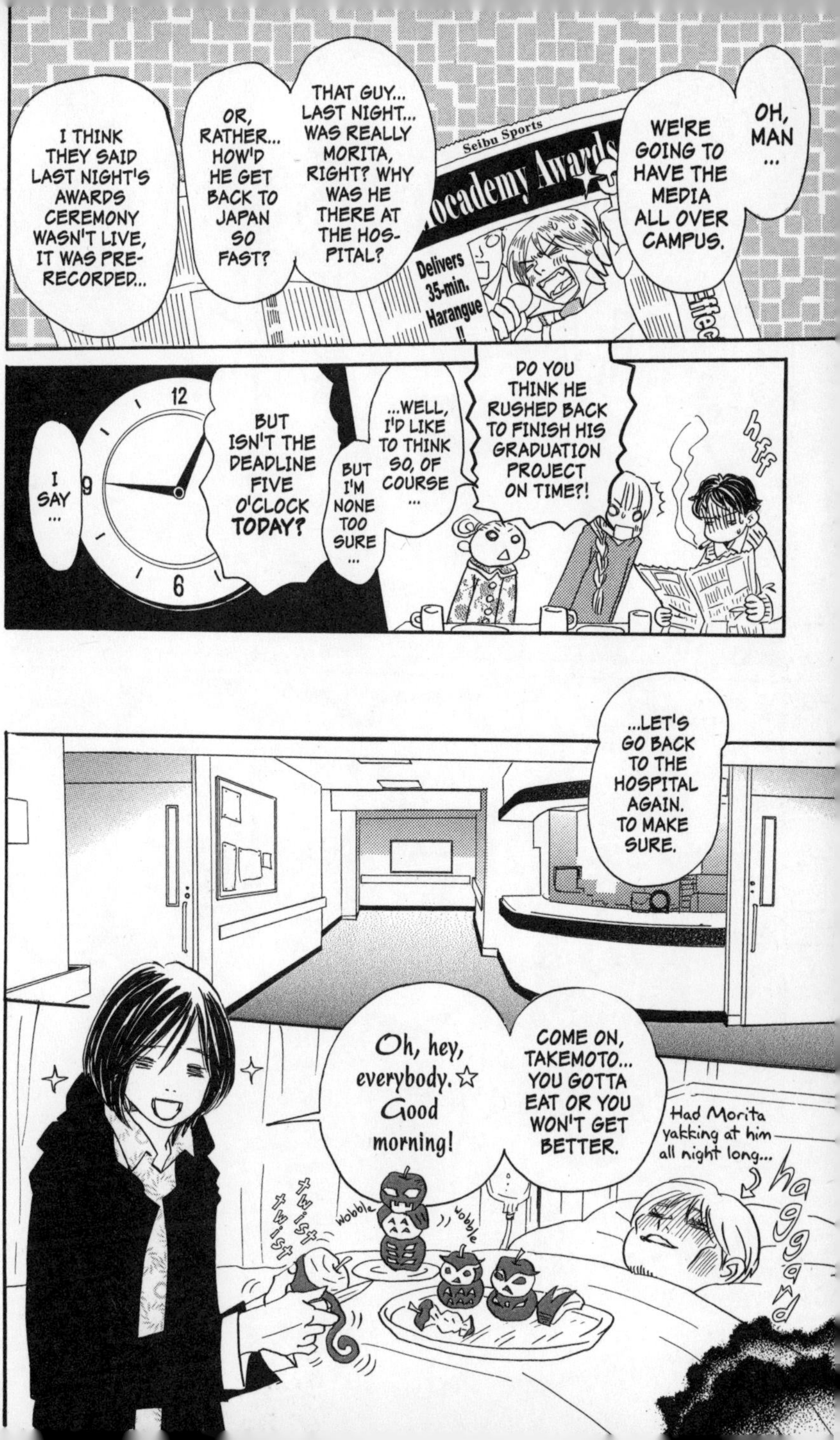
OH, MAN ...
WE'RE GOING TO HAVE THE MEDIA ALL OVER CAMPUS.
Seibu Sports
Delivers 35-min. Harangue !!
THAT GUY... LAST NIGHT... WAS REALLY MORITA, RIGHT? WHY WAS HE THERE AT THE HOSPITAL?
OR, RATHER... HOW'D HE GET BACK TO JAPAN SO FAST?
I THINK THEY SAID LAST NIGHT'S AWARDS CEREMONY WASN'T LIVE, IT WAS PRE-RECORDED...
hff
DO YOU THINK HE RUSHED BACK TO FINISH HIS GRADUATION PROJECT ON TIME?!
...WELL, I'D LIKE TO THINK SO, OF COURSE ...
BUT I'M NONE TOO SURE ...
BUT ISN'T THE DEADLINE FIVE O'CLOCK **TODAY?**
I SAY ...
...LET'S GO BACK TO THE HOSPITAL AGAIN. TO MAKE SURE.
haggard
Had Morita yakking at him all night long...
COME ON, TAKEMOTO... YOU GOTTA EAT OR YOU WON'T GET BETTER.
Oh, hey, everybody.☆ Good morning!
wobble
wobble
twist twist

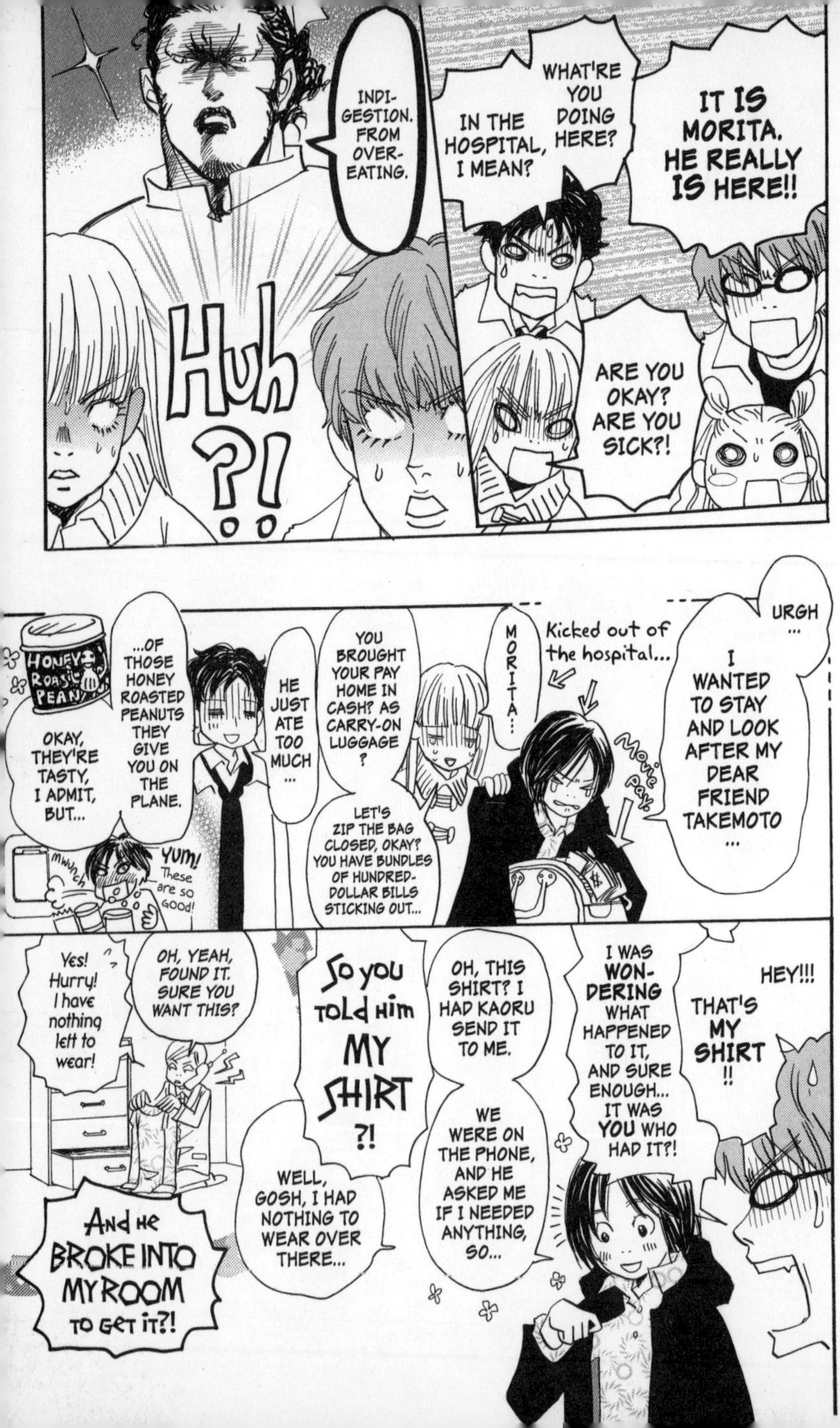
IT IS MORITA. HE REALLY IS HERE!!
WHAT'RE YOU DOING HERE?
IN THE HOSPITAL, I MEAN?
ARE YOU OKAY? ARE YOU SICK?!
INDI-GESTION. FROM OVER-EATING.
Huh?!
URGH...
I WANTED TO STAY AND LOOK AFTER MY DEAR FRIEND TAKEMOTO...
Kicked out of the hospital...
MORITA...
Movie pay.
YOU BROUGHT YOUR PAY HOME IN CASH? AS CARRY-ON LUGGAGE?
LET'S ZIP THE BAG CLOSED, OKAY? YOU HAVE BUNDLES OF HUNDRED-DOLLAR BILLS STICKING OUT...
HE JUST ATE TOO MUCH...
...OF THOSE HONEY ROASTED PEANUTS THEY GIVE YOU ON THE PLANE.
HONEY ROASTED PEAN
OKAY, THEY'RE TASTY, I ADMIT, BUT...
YUM! These are so good!
mwunch
HEY!!! THAT'S MY SHIRT!!
I WAS WONDERING WHAT HAPPENED TO IT, AND SURE ENOUGH... IT WAS YOU WHO HAD IT?!
OH, THIS SHIRT? I HAD KAORU SEND IT TO ME.
WE WERE ON THE PHONE, AND HE ASKED ME IF I NEEDED ANYTHING, SO...
SO YOU TOLD HIM MY SHIRT?!
WELL, GOSH, I HAD NOTHING TO WEAR OVER THERE...
OH, YEAH, FOUND IT. SURE YOU WANT THIS?
Yes! Hurry! I have nothing left to wear!
And he BROKE INTO MY ROOM to get it?!

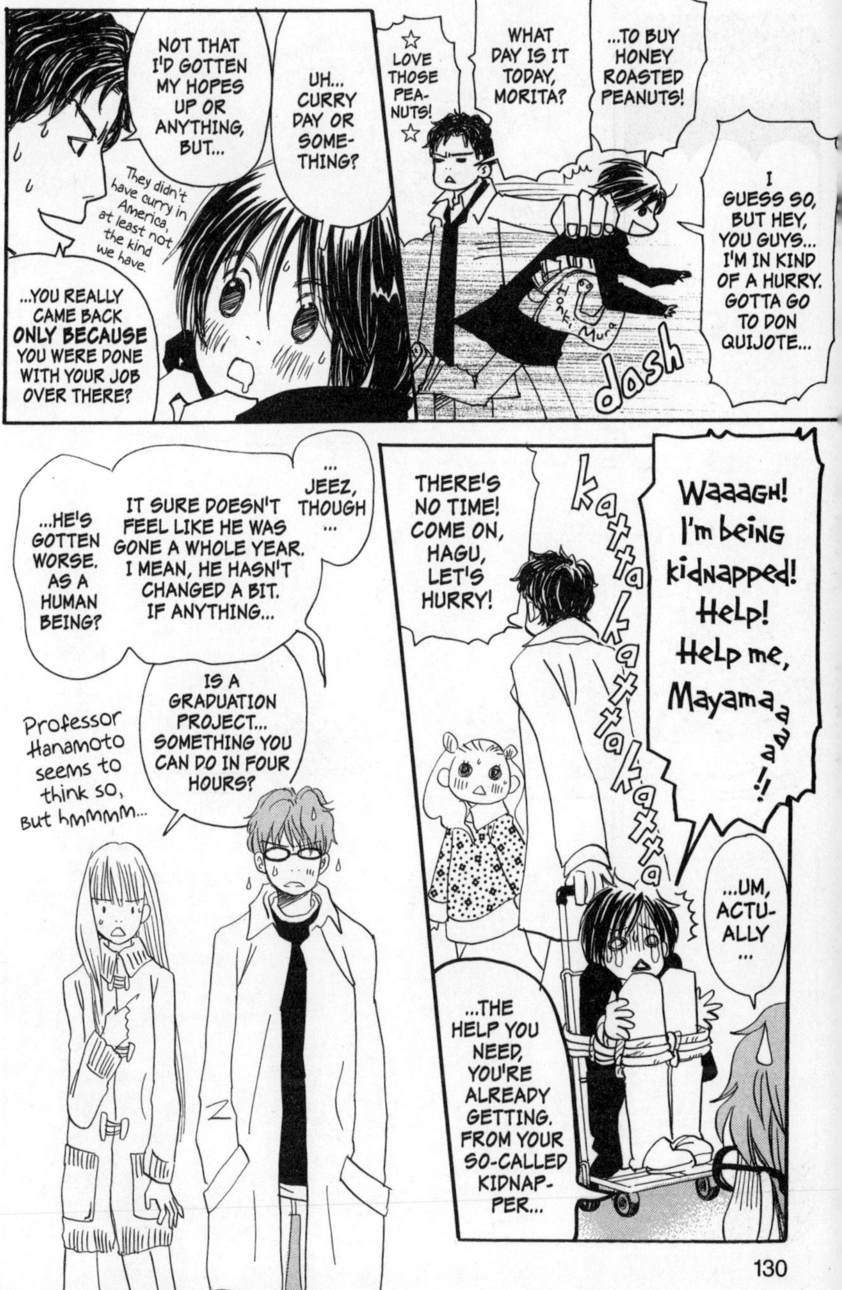
I GUESS SO, BUT HEY, YOU GUYS... I'M IN KIND OF A HURRY. GOTTA GO TO DON QUIJOTE...
...TO BUY HONEY ROASTED PEANUTS!
Honki Mura
dash
WHAT DAY IS IT TODAY, MORITA?
☆ LOVE THOSE PEA-NUTS! ☆
UH... CURRY DAY OR SOME-THING?
They didn't have curry in America, at least not the kind we have.
NOT THAT I'D GOTTEN MY HOPES UP OR ANYTHING, BUT...
...YOU REALLY CAME BACK **ONLY BECAUSE** YOU WERE DONE WITH YOUR JOB OVER THERE?
Waaagh! I'm being kidnapped! Help! Help me, Mayamaaaa!!
kattakattakattakatta
THERE'S NO TIME! COME ON, HAGU, LET'S HURRY!
...UM, ACTU-ALLY...
...THE HELP YOU NEED, YOU'RE ALREADY GETTING. FROM YOUR SO-CALLED KIDNAP-PER...
...JEEZ, THOUGH...
IT SURE DOESN'T FEEL LIKE HE WAS GONE A WHOLE YEAR. I MEAN, HE HASN'T CHANGED A BIT. IF ANYTHING...
...HE'S GOTTEN WORSE. AS A HUMAN BEING?
IS A GRADUATION PROJECT... SOMETHING YOU CAN DO IN FOUR HOURS?
Professor Hanamoto seems to think so, but hmmmm...

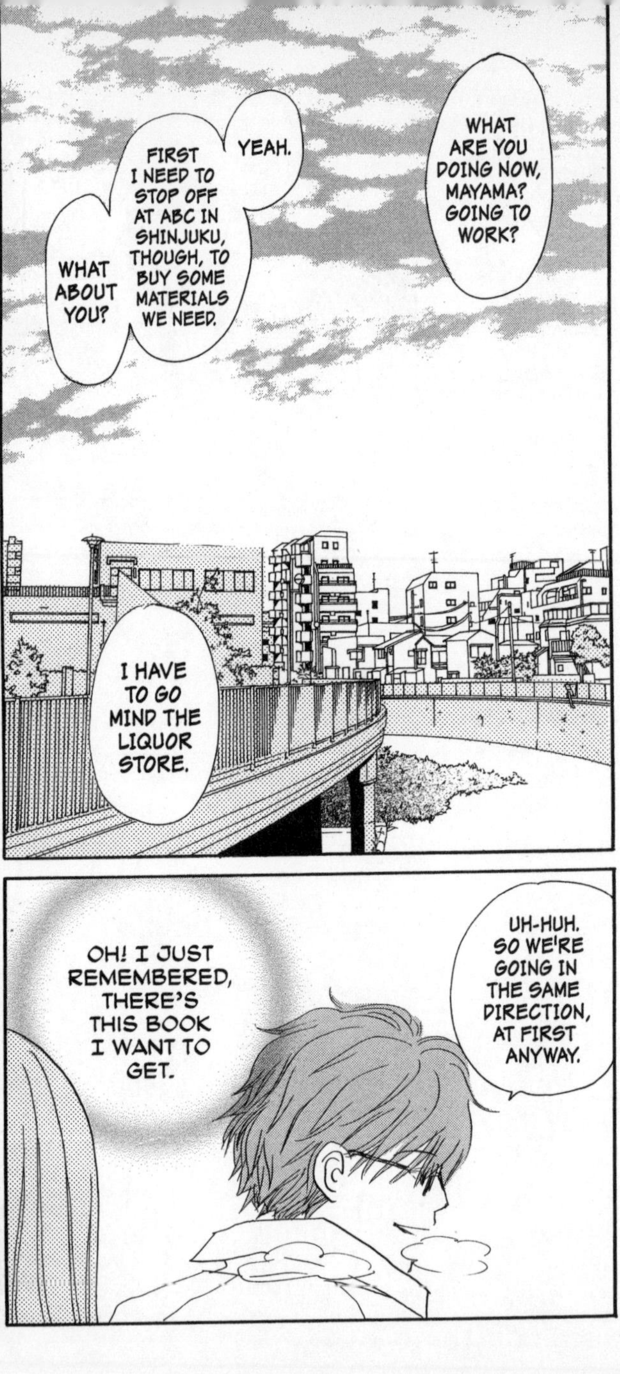
WHAT ARE YOU DOING NOW, MAYAMA? GOING TO WORK?
YEAH.
FIRST I NEED TO STOP OFF AT ABC IN SHINJUKU, THOUGH, TO BUY SOME MATERIALS WE NEED.
WHAT ABOUT YOU?
I HAVE TO GO MIND THE LIQUOR STORE.
UH-HUH. SO WE'RE GOING IN THE SAME DIRECTION, AT FIRST ANYWAY.
OH! I JUST REMEMBERED, THERE'S THIS BOOK I WANT TO GET.

I love jello!

Jello is an edible jewel.

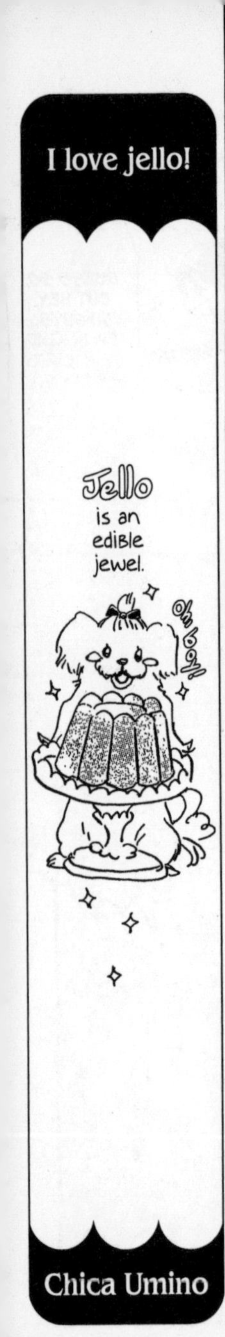
oh boy!

Chica Umino

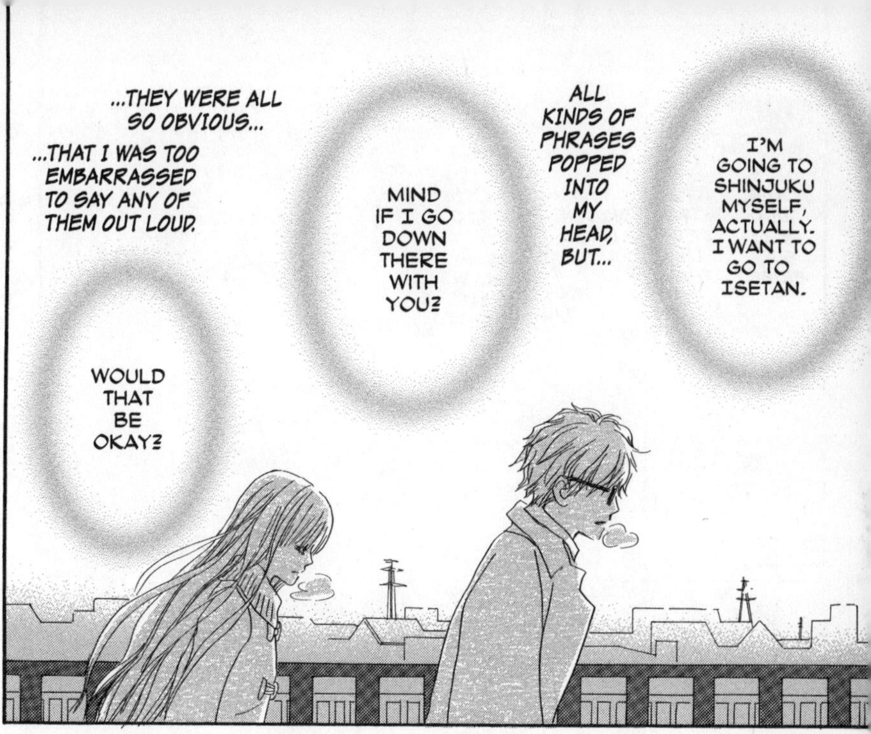
I'M GOING TO SHINJUKU MYSELF, ACTUALLY. I WANT TO GO TO ISETAN.
ALL KINDS OF PHRASES POPPED INTO MY HEAD, BUT...
MIND IF I GO DOWN THERE WITH YOU?
WOULD THAT BE OKAY?
...THEY WERE ALL SO OBVIOUS...
...THAT I WAS TOO EMBARRASSED TO SAY ANY OF THEM OUT LOUD.

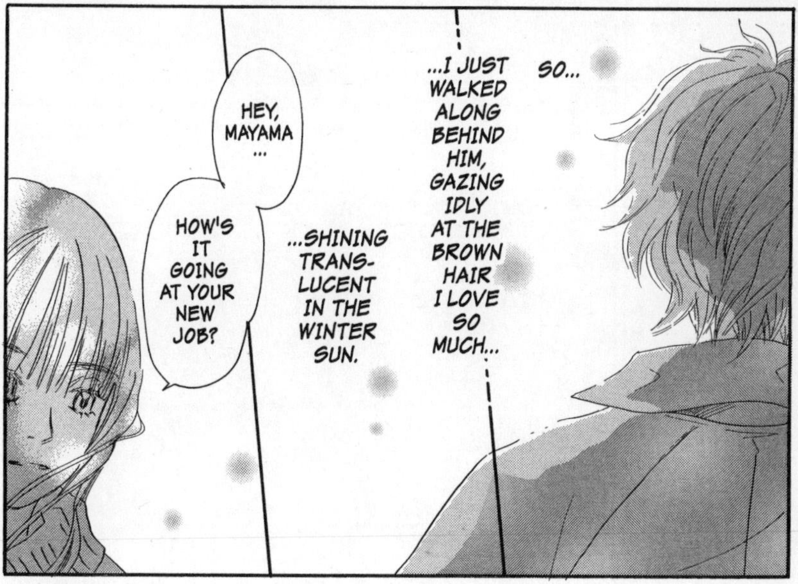
SO...
...I JUST WALKED ALONG BEHIND HIM, GAZING IDLY AT THE BROWN HAIR I LOVE SO MUCH...
...SHINING TRANS-LUCENT IN THE WINTER SUN.
HEY, MAYAMA...
HOW'S IT GOING AT YOUR NEW JOB?

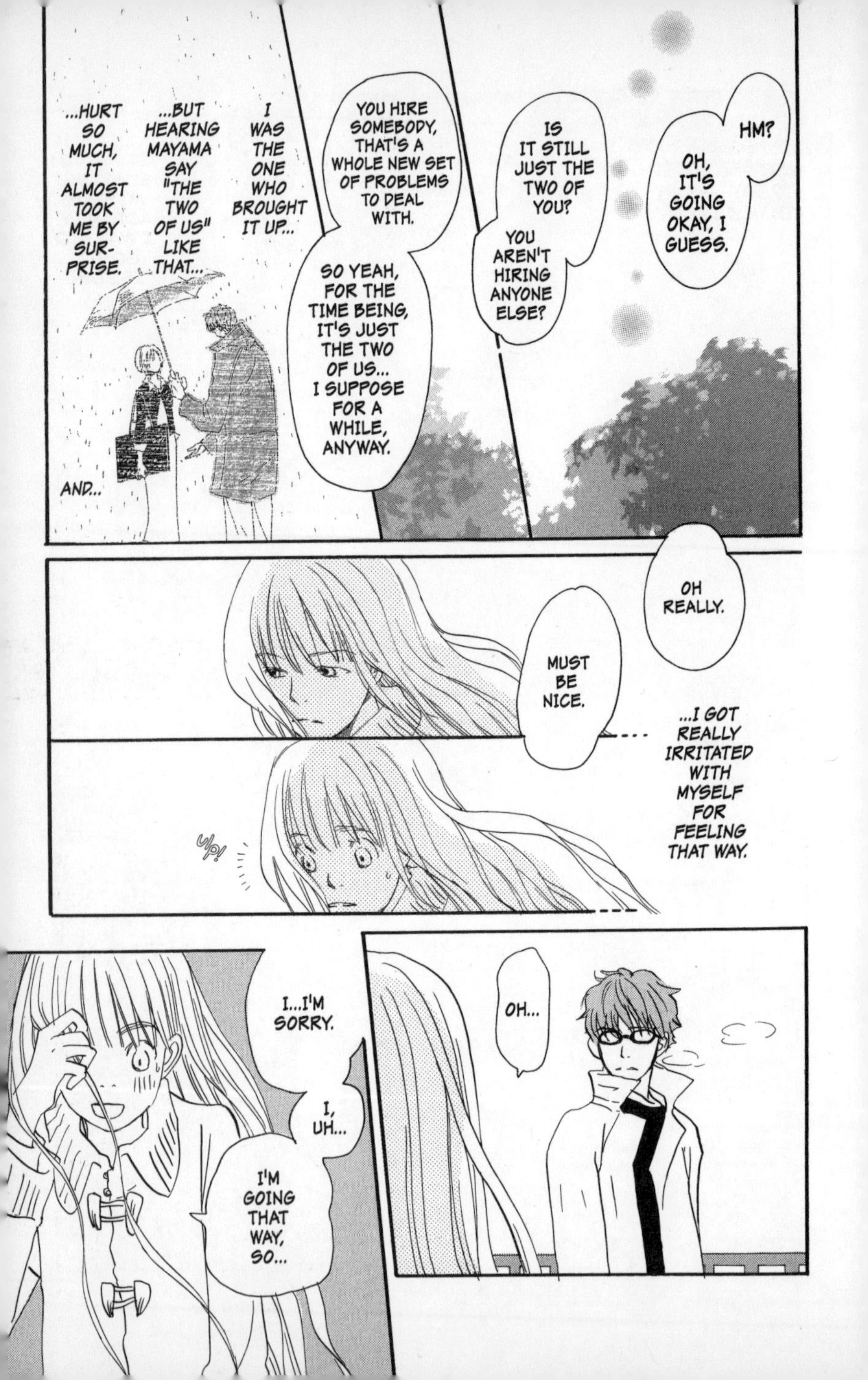
HM?
OH, IT'S GOING OKAY, I GUESS.
IS IT STILL JUST THE TWO OF YOU?
YOU AREN'T HIRING ANYONE ELSE?
YOU HIRE SOMEBODY, THAT'S A WHOLE NEW SET OF PROBLEMS TO DEAL WITH.
SO YEAH, FOR THE TIME BEING, IT'S JUST THE TWO OF US... I SUPPOSE FOR A WHILE, ANYWAY.
I WAS THE ONE WHO BROUGHT IT UP...
...BUT HEARING MAYAMA SAY "THE TWO OF US" LIKE THAT...
...HURT SO MUCH, IT ALMOST TOOK ME BY SUR-PRISE.
AND...
OH REALLY.
MUST BE NICE.
...I GOT REALLY IRRITATED WITH MYSELF FOR FEELING THAT WAY.
ULP!
OH...
I...I'M SORRY.
I, UH...
I'M GOING THAT WAY, SO...

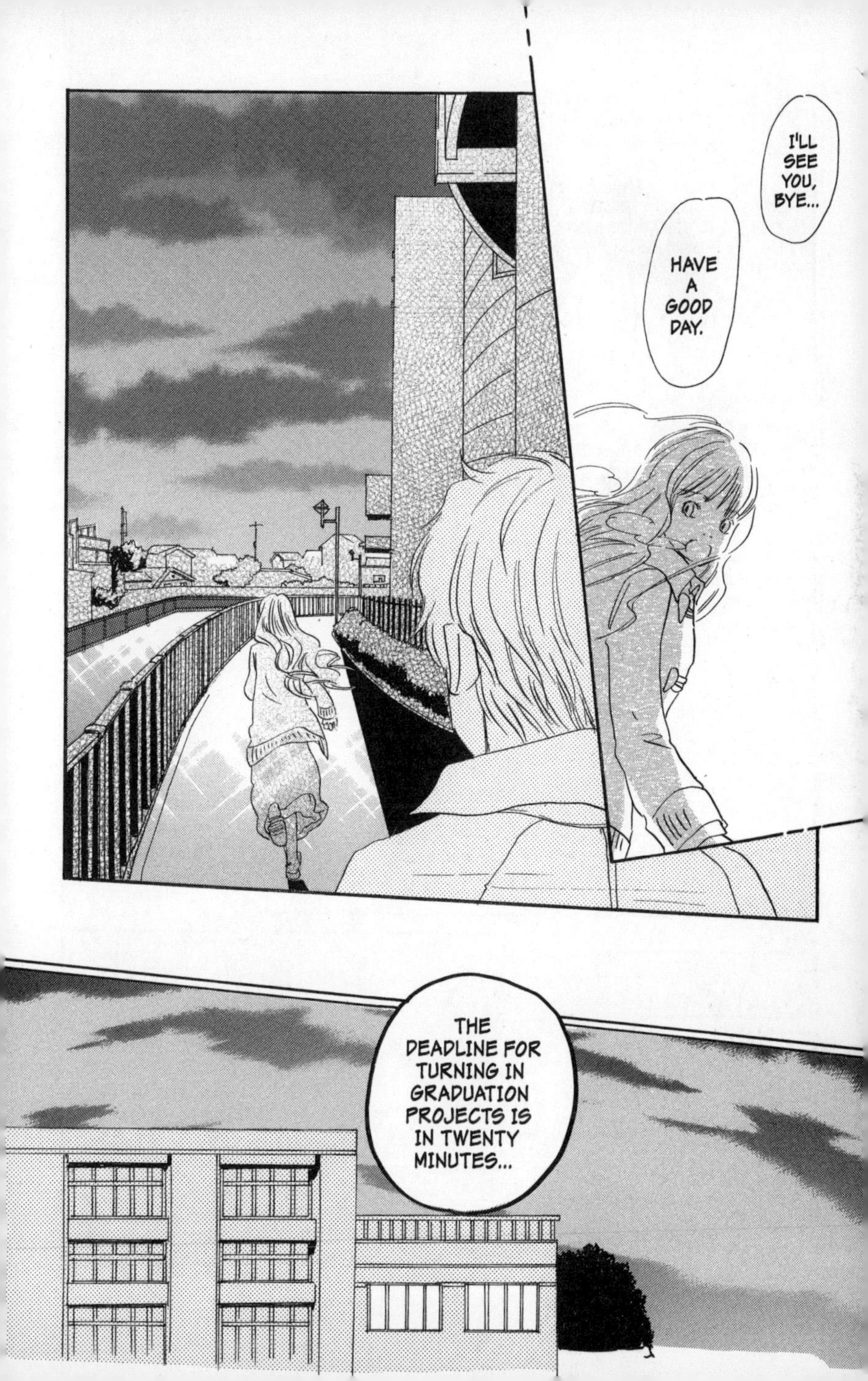
I'LL SEE YOU, BYE...
HAVE A GOOD DAY.
THE DEADLINE FOR TURNING IN GRADUATION PROJECTS IS IN TWENTY MINUTES...

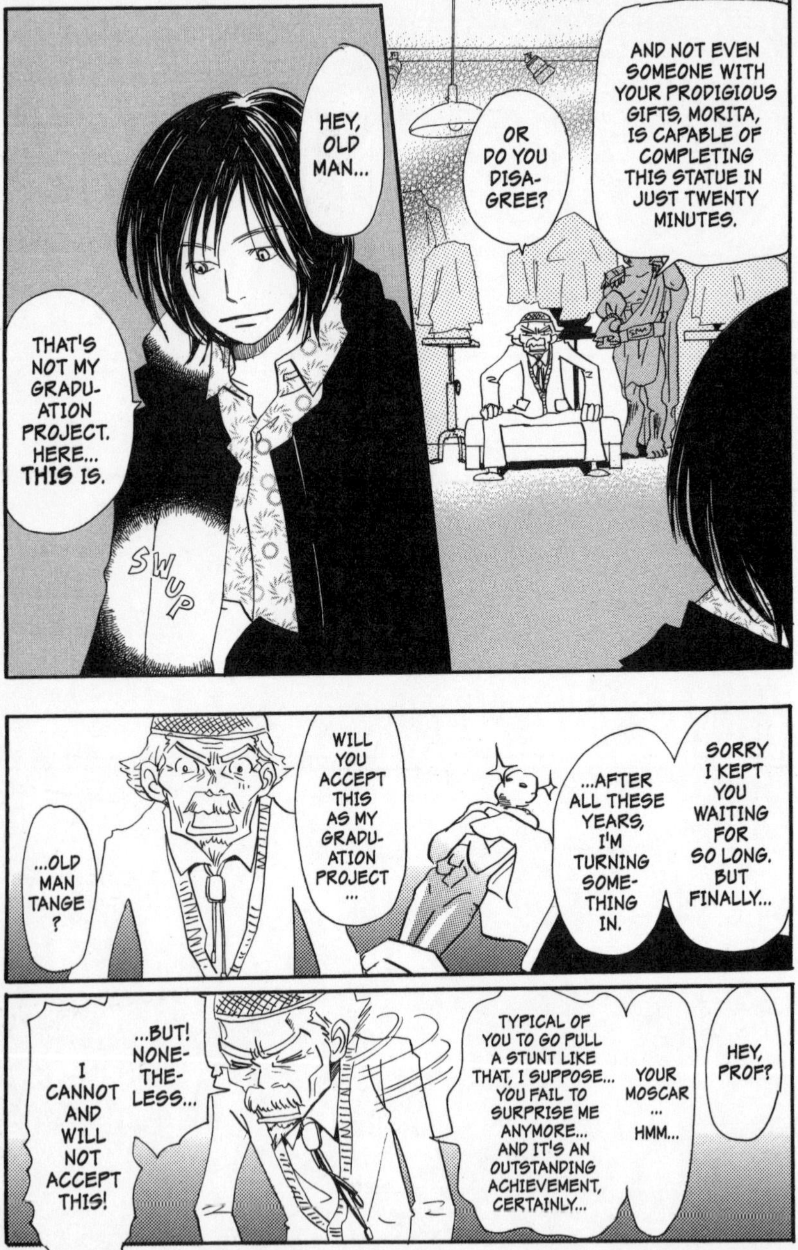
AND NOT EVEN SOMEONE WITH YOUR PRODIGIOUS GIFTS, MORITA, IS CAPABLE OF COMPLETING THIS STATUE IN JUST TWENTY MINUTES.
OR DO YOU DISA-GREE?
HEY, OLD MAN...
THAT'S NOT MY GRADU-ATION PROJECT. HERE... THIS IS.
SWUP
SORRY I KEPT YOU WAITING FOR SO LONG. BUT FINALLY...
...AFTER ALL THESE YEARS, I'M TURNING SOME-THING IN.
WILL YOU ACCEPT THIS AS MY GRADU-ATION PROJECT...
...OLD MAN TANGE?
HEY, PROF?
YOUR MOSCAR... HMM...
TYPICAL OF YOU TO GO PULL A STUNT LIKE THAT, I SUPPOSE... YOU FAIL TO SURPRISE ME ANYMORE... AND IT'S AN OUTSTANDING ACHIEVEMENT, CERTAINLY...
...BUT! NONE-THE-LESS...
I CANNOT AND WILL NOT ACCEPT THIS!

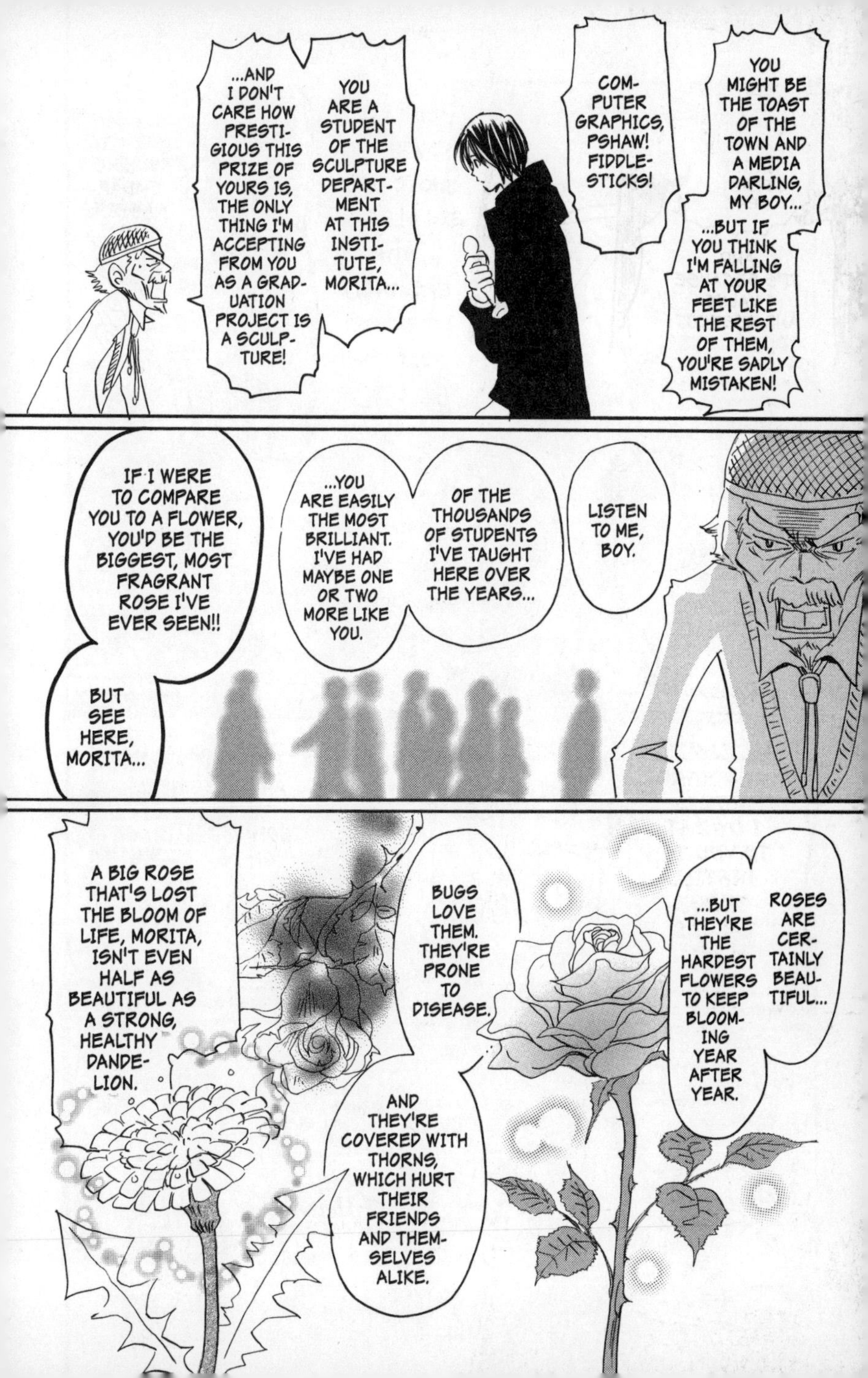
YOU MIGHT BE THE TOAST OF THE TOWN AND A MEDIA DARLING, MY BOY...
...BUT IF YOU THINK I'M FALLING AT YOUR FEET LIKE THE REST OF THEM, YOU'RE SADLY MISTAKEN!
COMPUTER GRAPHICS, PSHAW! FIDDLESTICKS!
YOU ARE A STUDENT OF THE SCULPTURE DEPARTMENT AT THIS INSTITUTE, MORITA...
...AND I DON'T CARE HOW PRESTIGIOUS THIS PRIZE OF YOURS IS, THE ONLY THING I'M ACCEPTING FROM YOU AS A GRADUATION PROJECT IS A SCULPTURE!
LISTEN TO ME, BOY.
OF THE THOUSANDS OF STUDENTS I'VE TAUGHT HERE OVER THE YEARS...
...YOU ARE EASILY THE MOST BRILLIANT. I'VE HAD MAYBE ONE OR TWO MORE LIKE YOU.
IF I WERE TO COMPARE YOU TO A FLOWER, YOU'D BE THE BIGGEST, MOST FRAGRANT ROSE I'VE EVER SEEN!!
BUT SEE HERE, MORITA...
ROSES ARE CERTAINLY BEAUTIFUL...
...BUT THEY'RE THE HARDEST FLOWERS TO KEEP BLOOMING YEAR AFTER YEAR.
BUGS LOVE THEM. THEY'RE PRONE TO DISEASE.
AND THEY'RE COVERED WITH THORNS, WHICH HURT THEIR FRIENDS AND THEMSELVES ALIKE.
A BIG ROSE THAT'S LOST THE BLOOM OF LIFE, MORITA, ISN'T EVEN HALF AS BEAUTIFUL AS A STRONG, HEALTHY DANDELION.

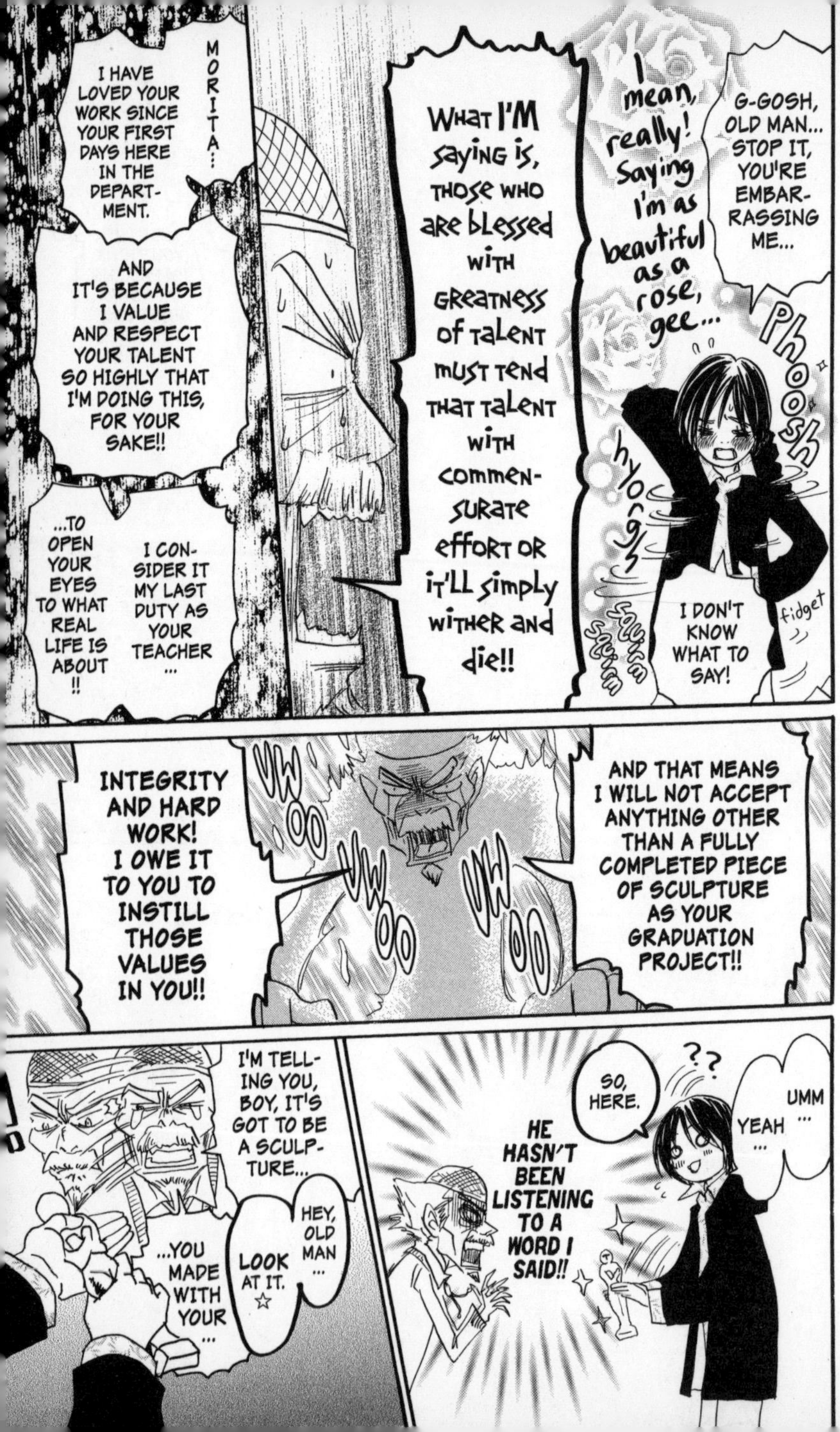
G-GOSH, OLD MAN... STOP IT, YOU'RE EMBARRASSING ME...
I mean, really! Saying I'm as beautiful as a rose, gee...
Phoosh
hyorgh
I DON'T KNOW WHAT TO SAY!
fidget
squirm squirm
WHAT I'M saying is, THOSE WHO are blessed with greatness of talent must tend that talent with commensurate effort or it'll simply wither and die!!
MORITA...
I HAVE LOVED YOUR WORK SINCE YOUR FIRST DAYS HERE IN THE DEPARTMENT.
AND IT'S BECAUSE I VALUE AND RESPECT YOUR TALENT SO HIGHLY THAT I'M DOING THIS, FOR YOUR SAKE!!
I CONSIDER IT MY LAST DUTY AS YOUR TEACHER...
...TO OPEN YOUR EYES TO WHAT REAL LIFE IS ABOUT!!
AND THAT MEANS I WILL NOT ACCEPT ANYTHING OTHER THAN A FULLY COMPLETED PIECE OF SCULPTURE AS YOUR GRADUATION PROJECT!!
WOO
WOO
WOO
INTEGRITY AND HARD WORK! I OWE IT TO YOU TO INSTILL THOSE VALUES IN YOU!!
UMM...
YEAH...
??
SO, HERE.
HE HASN'T BEEN LISTENING TO A WORD I SAID!!
I'M TELLING YOU, BOY, IT'S GOT TO BE A SCULPTURE...
HEY, OLD MAN...
LOOK AT IT. ☆
...YOU MADE WITH YOUR...

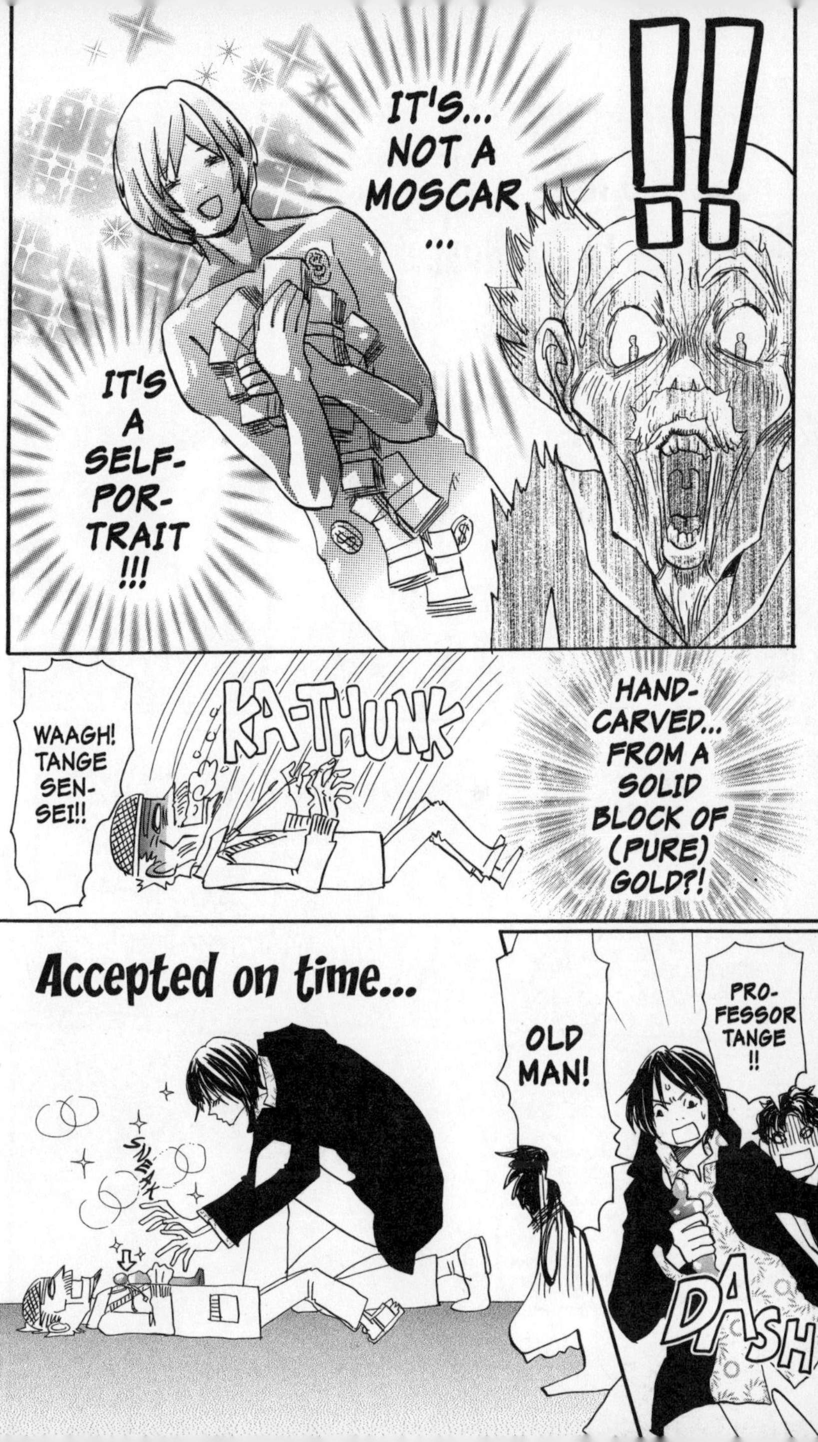
!!
IT'S... NOT A MOSCAR ...
IT'S A SELF-PORTRAIT !!!
HAND-CARVED... FROM A SOLID BLOCK OF (PURE) GOLD?!
KA-THUNK
WAAGH! TANGE SEN-SEI!!
PRO-FESSOR TANGE !!
OLD MAN!
DASH
Accepted on time...
SNEAK

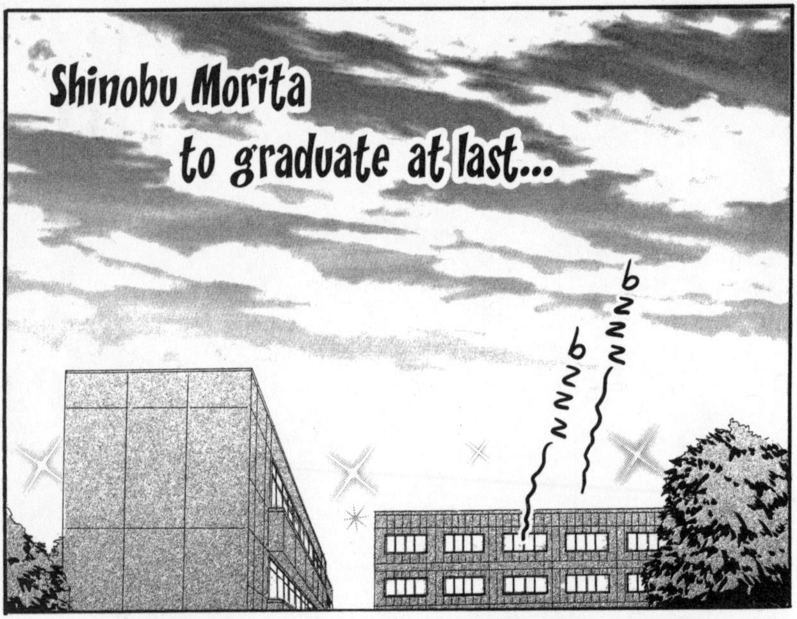
Shinobu Morita to graduate at last...
bzzz
bzzz

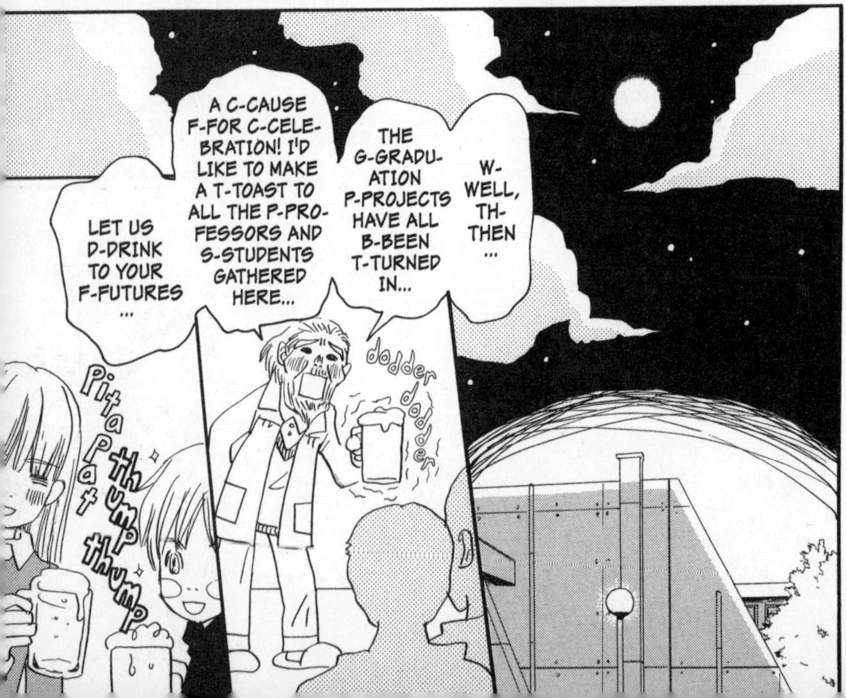
W-WELL, TH-THEN...
THE G-GRADUATION P-PROJECTS HAVE ALL B-BEEN T-TURNED IN...
A C-CAUSE F-FOR C-CELEBRATION! I'D LIKE TO MAKE A T-TOAST TO ALL THE P-PROFESSORS AND S-STUDENTS GATHERED HERE...
LET US D-DRINK TO YOUR F-FUTURES...
dodder dodder
Pita pat
thump thump

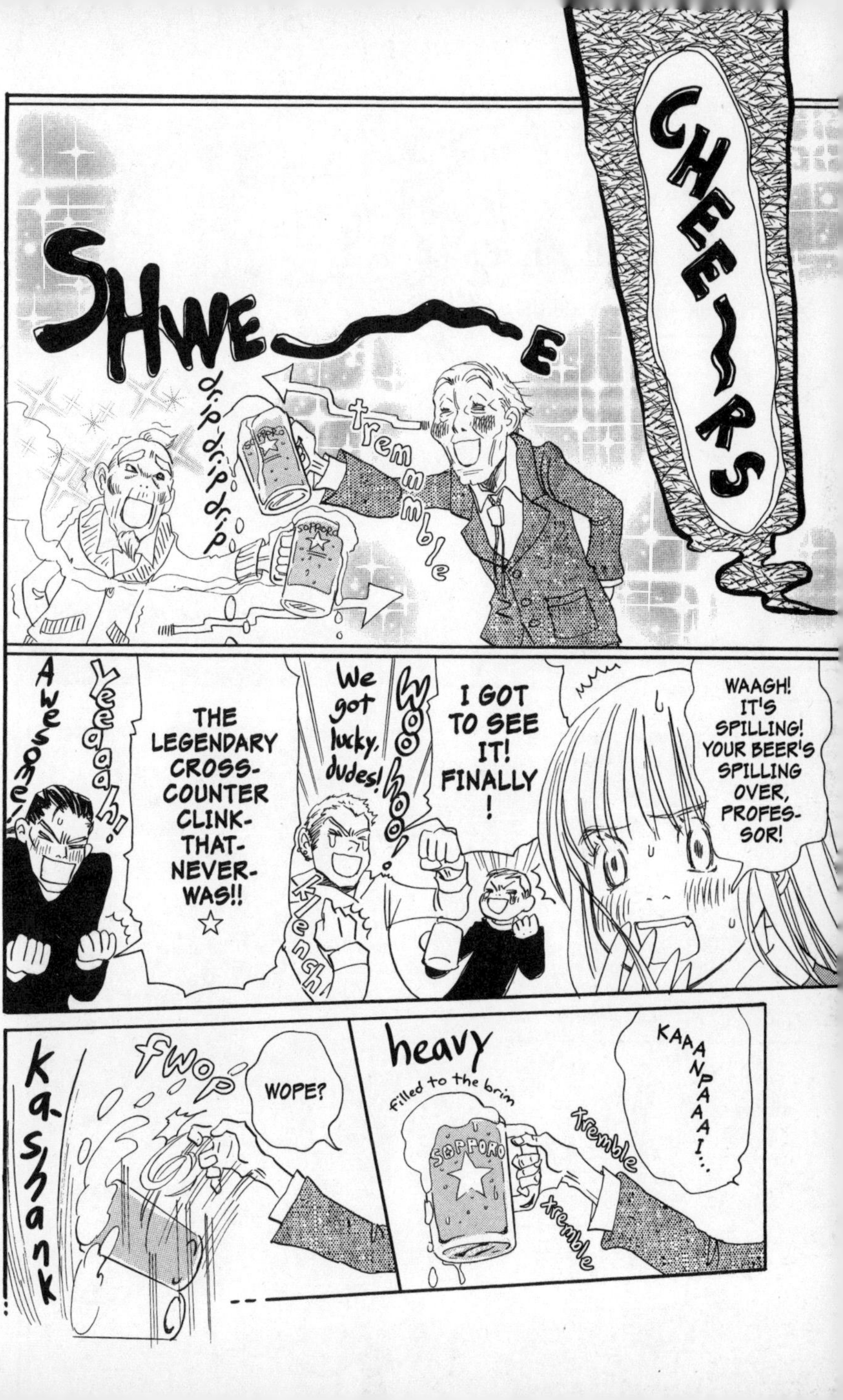
CHEE~RS
SHWE——E
tremmemble
drip drip drip drip
WAAGH! IT'S SPILLING! YOUR BEER'S SPILLING OVER, PROFES-SOR!
I GOT TO SEE IT! FINALLY!
Woohoo!
We got lucky, dudes!
klench
THE LEGENDARY CROSS-COUNTER CLINK-THAT-NEVER-WAS!! ☆
Yeeaaah!
Awesome!
KAAANPAAAI...
tremble
tremble
heavy
filled to the brim
WOPE?
fwop
ka-shank

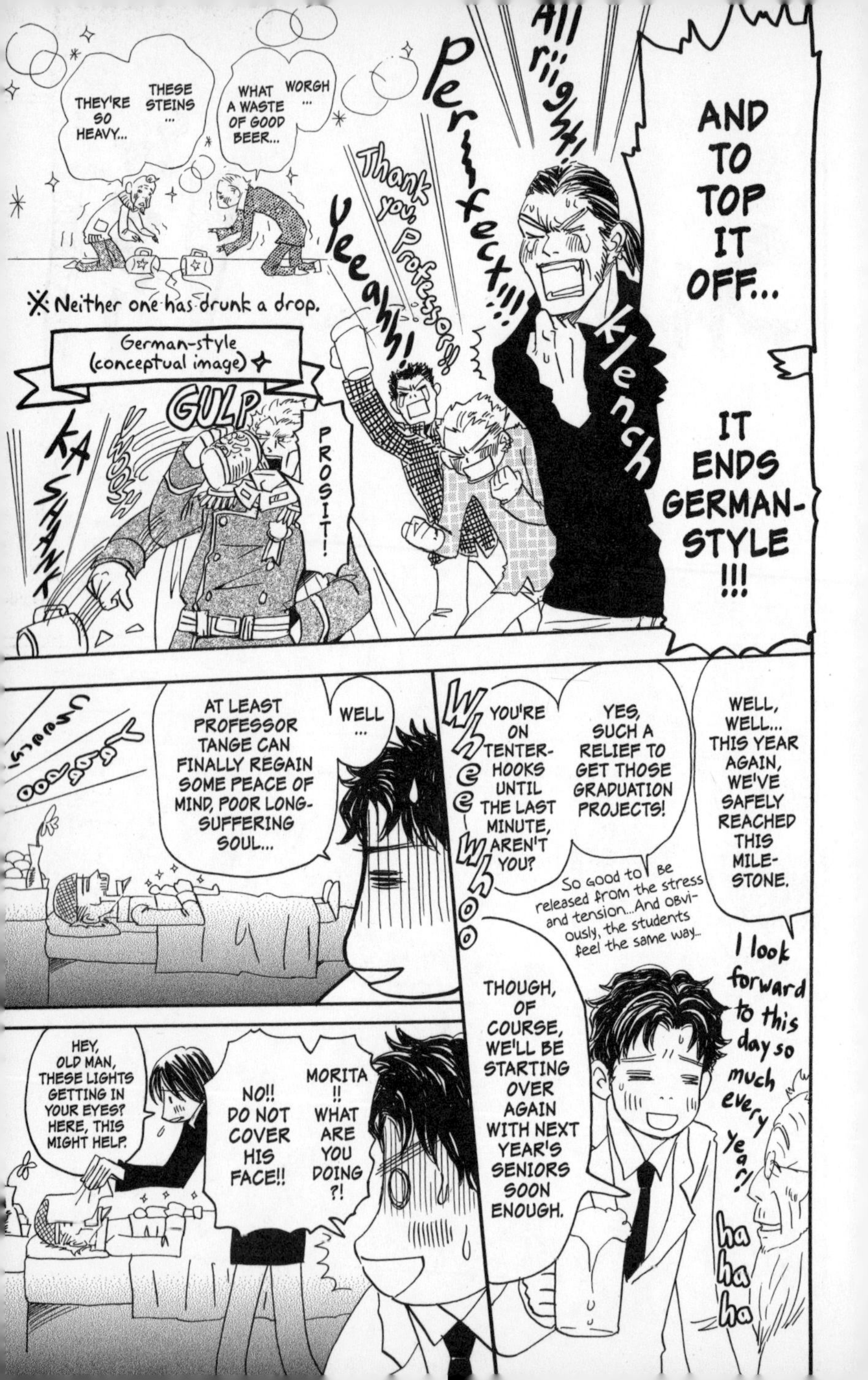
AND TO TOP IT OFF...
IT ENDS GERMAN-STYLE!!!
All riiiight!
Per~fect!!!
Klench
Thank you, Professor!!
Yeeahh!
WORGH ...
WHAT A WASTE OF GOOD BEER...
THESE STEINS ...
THEY'RE SO HEAVY...
※Neither one has drunk a drop.
German-style (conceptual image)
PROSIT!
GULP
WOOSH
KA SHANK
WELL, WELL... THIS YEAR AGAIN, WE'VE SAFELY REACHED THIS MILESTONE.
YES, SUCH A RELIEF TO GET THOSE GRADUATION PROJECTS!
YOU'RE ON TENTERHOOKS UNTIL THE LAST MINUTE, AREN'T YOU?
Wheee whooo
So good to be released from the stress and tension...And obviously, the students feel the same way...
I look forward to this day so much every year!
ha ha ha
THOUGH, OF COURSE, WE'LL BE STARTING OVER AGAIN WITH NEXT YEAR'S SENIORS SOON ENOUGH.
WELL ...
AT LEAST PROFESSOR TANGE CAN FINALLY REGAIN SOME PEACE OF MIND, POOR LONG-SUFFERING SOUL...
MORITA!! WHAT ARE YOU DOING?!
NO!! DO NOT COVER HIS FACE!!
HEY, OLD MAN, THESE LIGHTS GETTING IN YOUR EYES? HERE, THIS MIGHT HELP.

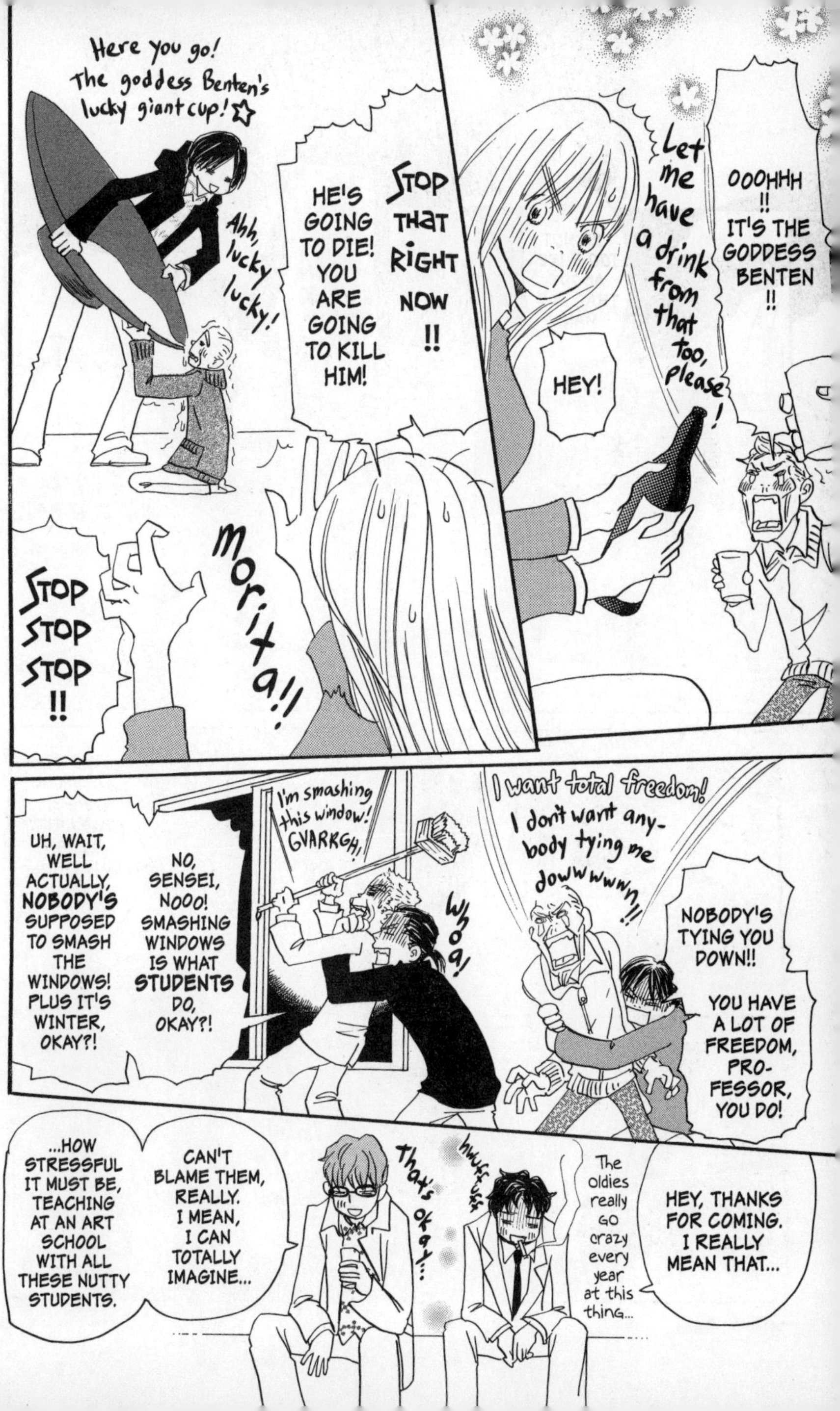
OOOHHH!! IT'S THE GODDESS BENTEN!!
Let me have a drink from that too, please!
HEY!
STOP THAT RIGHT NOW!!
HE'S GOING TO DIE! YOU ARE GOING TO KILL HIM!
Here you go! The goddess Benten's lucky giant cup!
Ahh, lucky lucky!
Morita!!
STOP STOP STOP!!
I want total freedom!
I don't want anybody tying me dowwwwwn!!
NOBODY'S TYING YOU DOWN!!
YOU HAVE A LOT OF FREEDOM, PROFESSOR, YOU DO!
I'm smashing this window! GVARRGH,
Whoa!
NO, SENSEI, NOOO! SMASHING WINDOWS IS WHAT STUDENTS DO, OKAY?!
UH, WAIT, WELL ACTUALLY, NOBODY'S SUPPOSED TO SMASH THE WINDOWS! PLUS IT'S WINTER, OKAY?!
HEY, THANKS FOR COMING. I REALLY MEAN THAT...
The oldies really go crazy every year at this thing...
hwuffuff
That's okay...
CAN'T BLAME THEM, REALLY. I MEAN, I CAN TOTALLY IMAGINE...
...HOW STRESSFUL IT MUST BE, TEACHING AT AN ART SCHOOL WITH ALL THESE NUTTY STUDENTS.

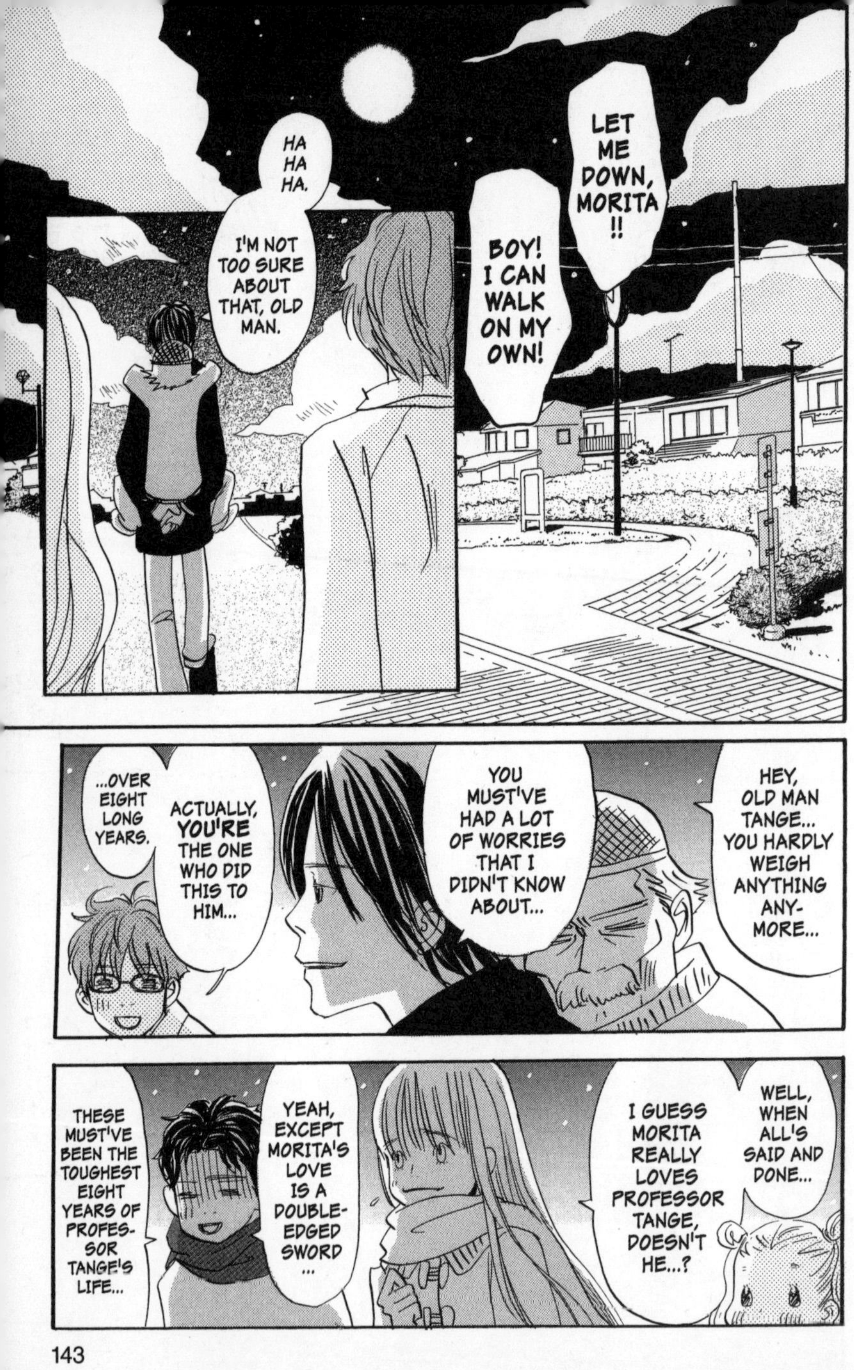
LET ME DOWN, MORITA!!
BOY! I CAN WALK ON MY OWN!
HA HA HA.
I'M NOT TOO SURE ABOUT THAT, OLD MAN.
HEY, OLD MAN TANGE... YOU HARDLY WEIGH ANYTHING ANY-MORE...
YOU MUST'VE HAD A LOT OF WORRIES THAT I DIDN'T KNOW ABOUT...
ACTUALLY, **YOU'RE** THE ONE WHO DID THIS TO HIM...
...OVER EIGHT LONG YEARS.
WELL, WHEN ALL'S SAID AND DONE...
I GUESS MORITA REALLY LOVES PROFESSOR TANGE, DOESN'T HE...?
YEAH, EXCEPT MORITA'S LOVE IS A DOUBLE-EDGED SWORD...
THESE MUST'VE BEEN THE TOUGHEST EIGHT YEARS OF PROFES-SOR TANGE'S LIFE...

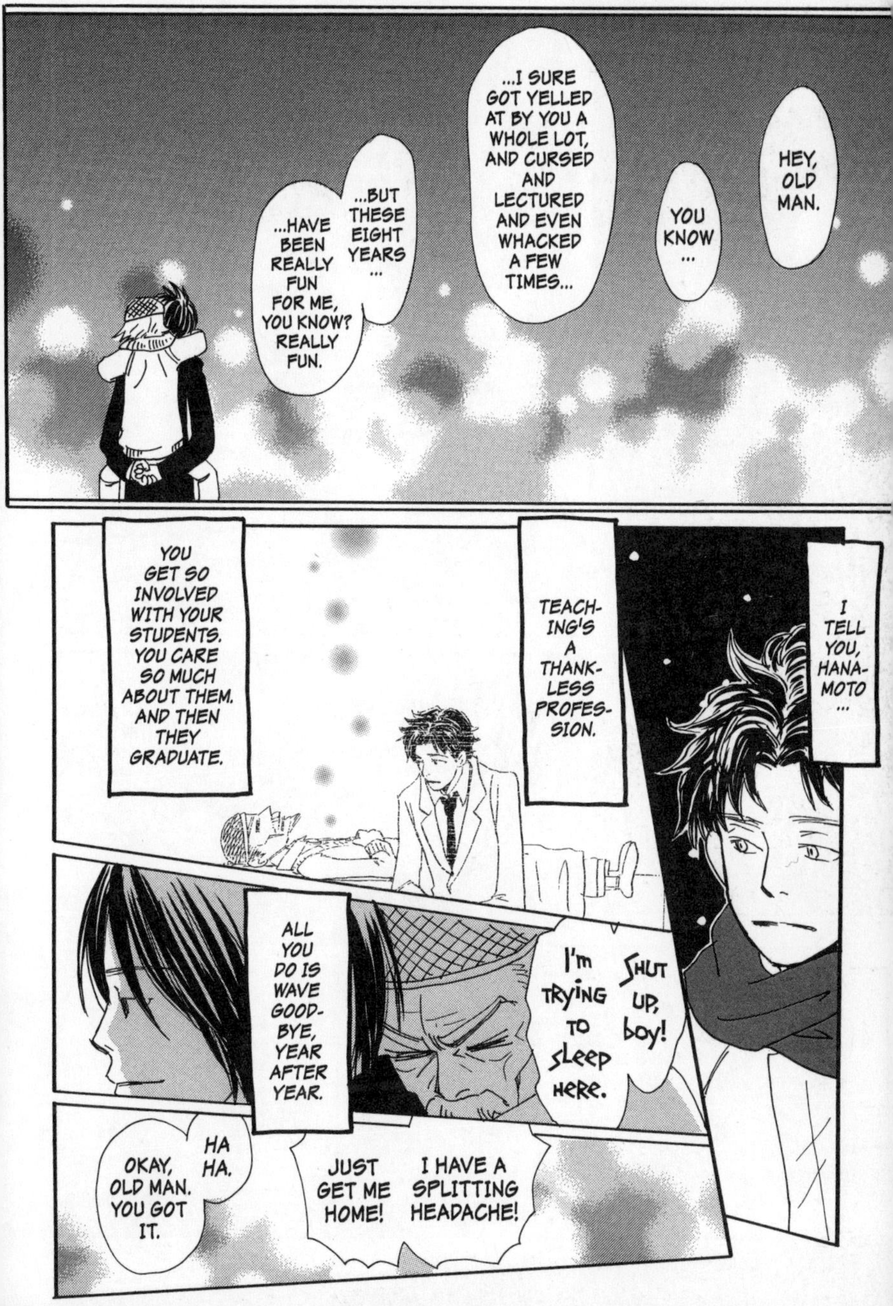
HEY, OLD MAN.
YOU KNOW...
...I SURE GOT YELLED AT BY YOU A WHOLE LOT, AND CURSED AND LECTURED AND EVEN WHACKED A FEW TIMES...
...BUT THESE EIGHT YEARS...
...HAVE BEEN REALLY FUN FOR ME, YOU KNOW? REALLY FUN.
I TELL YOU, HANAMOTO...
TEACHING'S A THANKLESS PROFESSION.
YOU GET SO INVOLVED WITH YOUR STUDENTS. YOU CARE SO MUCH ABOUT THEM. AND THEN THEY GRADUATE.
ALL YOU DO IS WAVE GOOD-BYE, YEAR AFTER YEAR.
SHUT UP, BOY!
I'M TRYING TO SLEEP HERE.
I HAVE A SPLITTING HEADACHE!
JUST GET ME HOME!
HA HA.
OKAY, OLD MAN. YOU GOT IT.

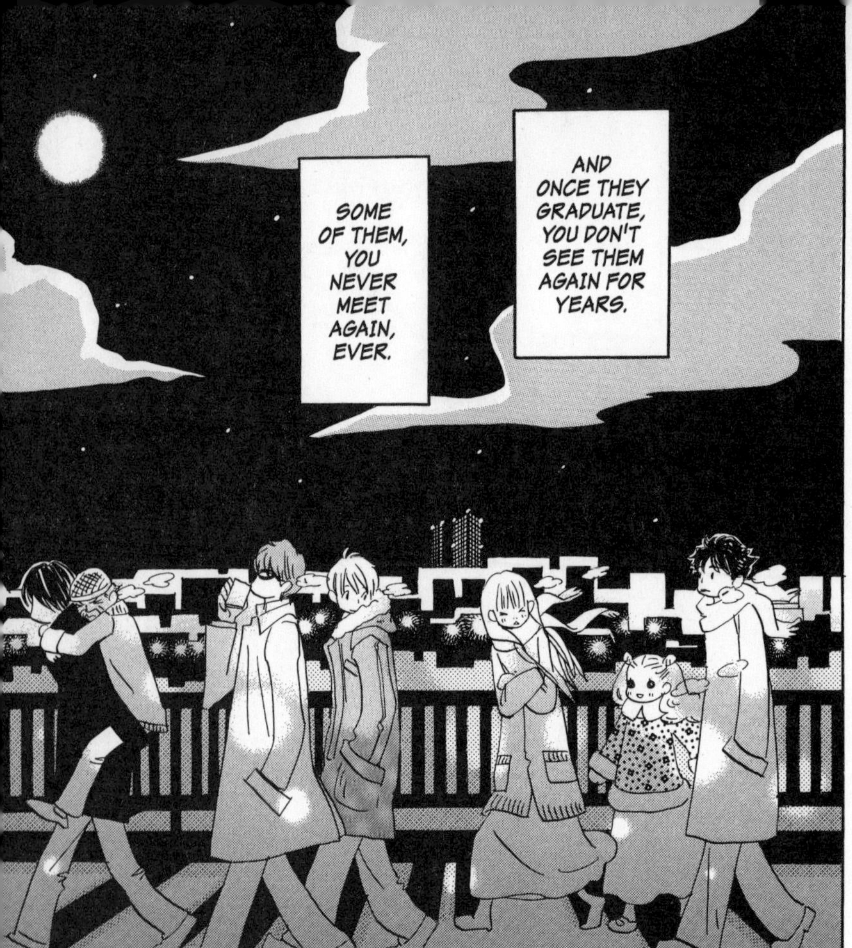
AND ONCE THEY GRADUATE, YOU DON'T SEE THEM AGAIN FOR YEARS.
SOME OF THEM, YOU NEVER MEET AGAIN, EVER.
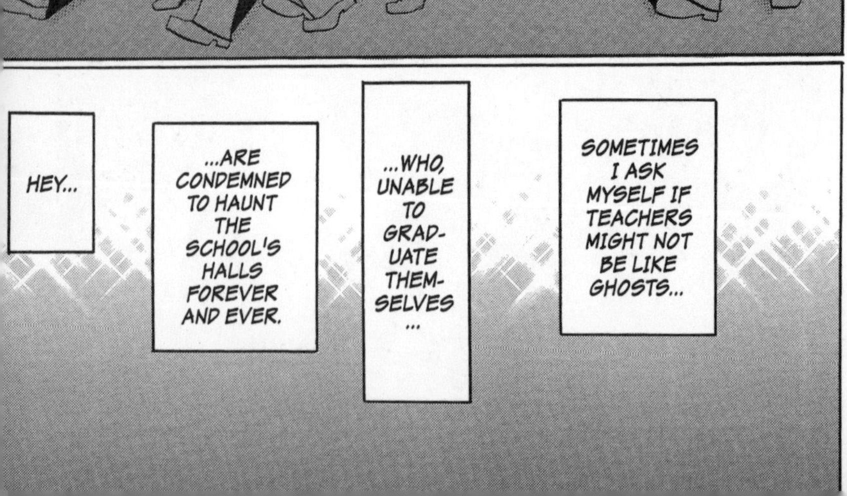
SOMETIMES I ASK MYSELF IF TEACHERS MIGHT NOT BE LIKE GHOSTS...
...WHO, UNABLE TO GRAD-UATE THEM-SELVES ...
...ARE CONDEMNED TO HAUNT THE SCHOOL'S HALLS FOREVER AND EVER.
HEY...

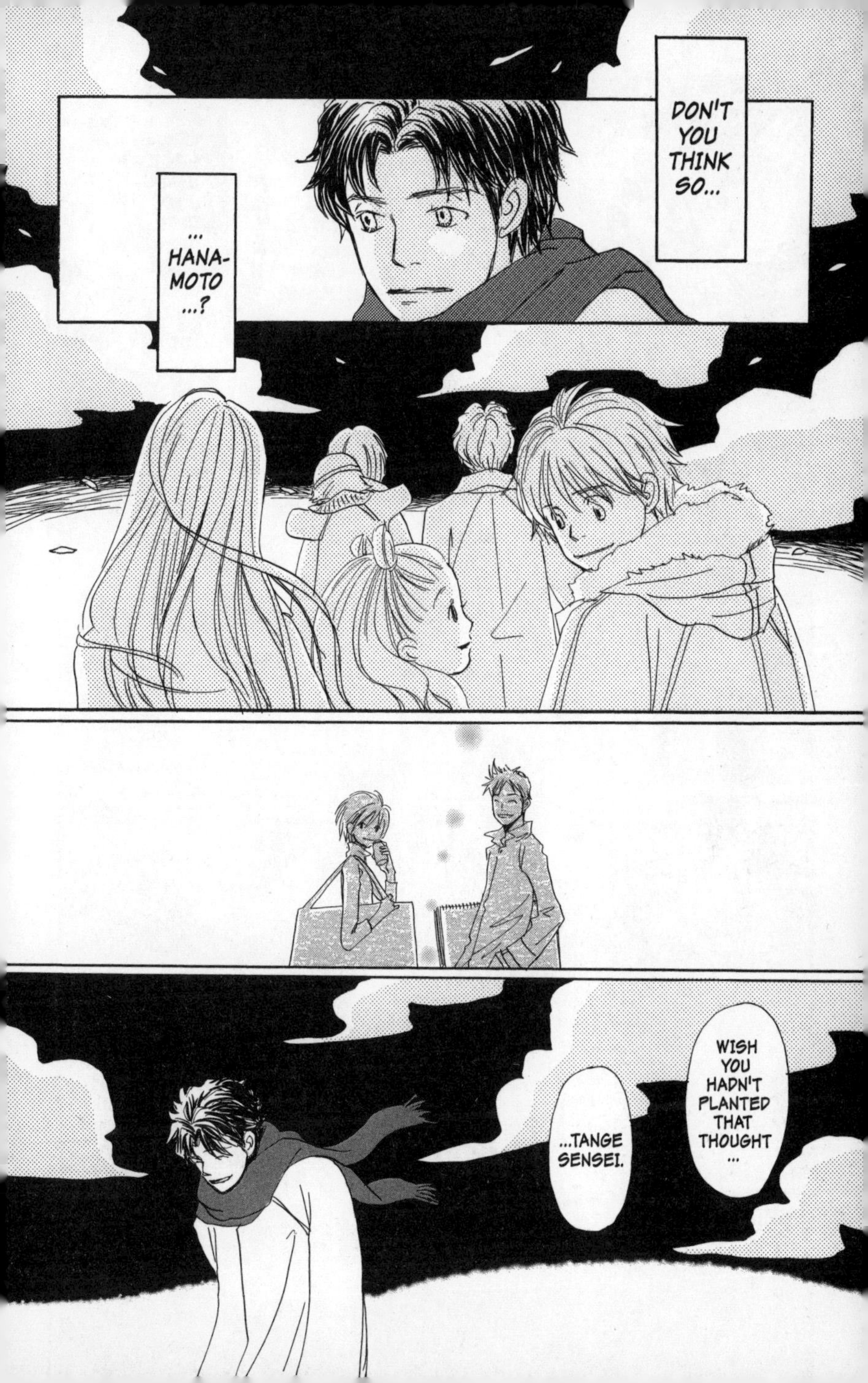
DON'T YOU THINK SO...
... HANA-MOTO ...?
WISH YOU HADN'T PLANTED THAT THOUGHT ...
...TANGE SENSEI.

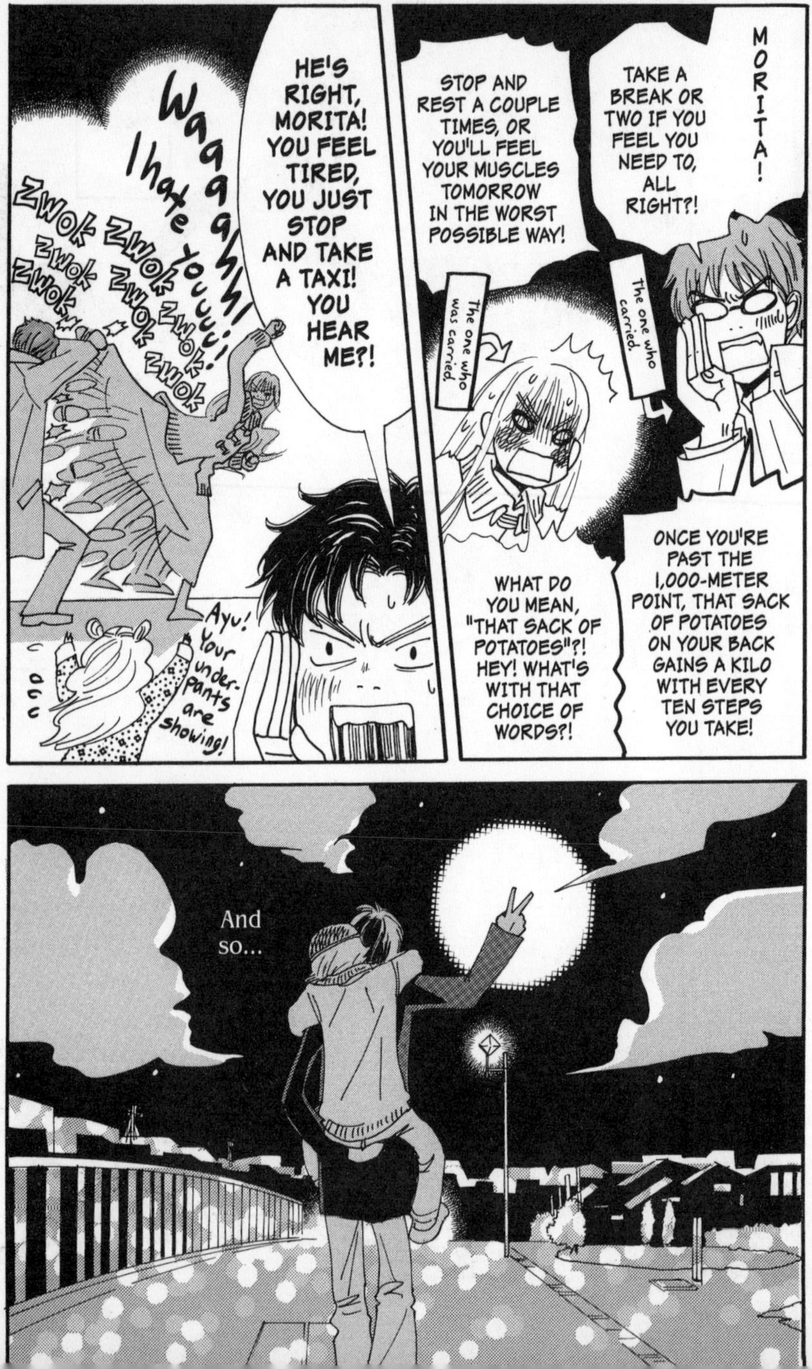
MORITA!
TAKE A BREAK OR TWO IF YOU FEEL YOU NEED TO, ALL RIGHT?!
STOP AND REST A COUPLE TIMES, OR YOU'LL FEEL YOUR MUSCLES TOMORROW IN THE WORST POSSIBLE WAY!
The one who carried.
The one who was carried.
ONCE YOU'RE PAST THE 1,000-METER POINT, THAT SACK OF POTATOES ON YOUR BACK GAINS A KILO WITH EVERY TEN STEPS YOU TAKE!
WHAT DO YOU MEAN, "THAT SACK OF POTATOES"?! HEY! WHAT'S WITH THAT CHOICE OF WORDS?!
HE'S RIGHT, MORITA! YOU FEEL TIRED, YOU JUST STOP AND TAKE A TAXI! YOU HEAR ME?!
Waaaaahh! I hate youuuu!
Zwok Zwok Zwok Zwok Zwok Zwok Zwok Zwok Zwok
Ayu! Your under-pants are showing!
And so...

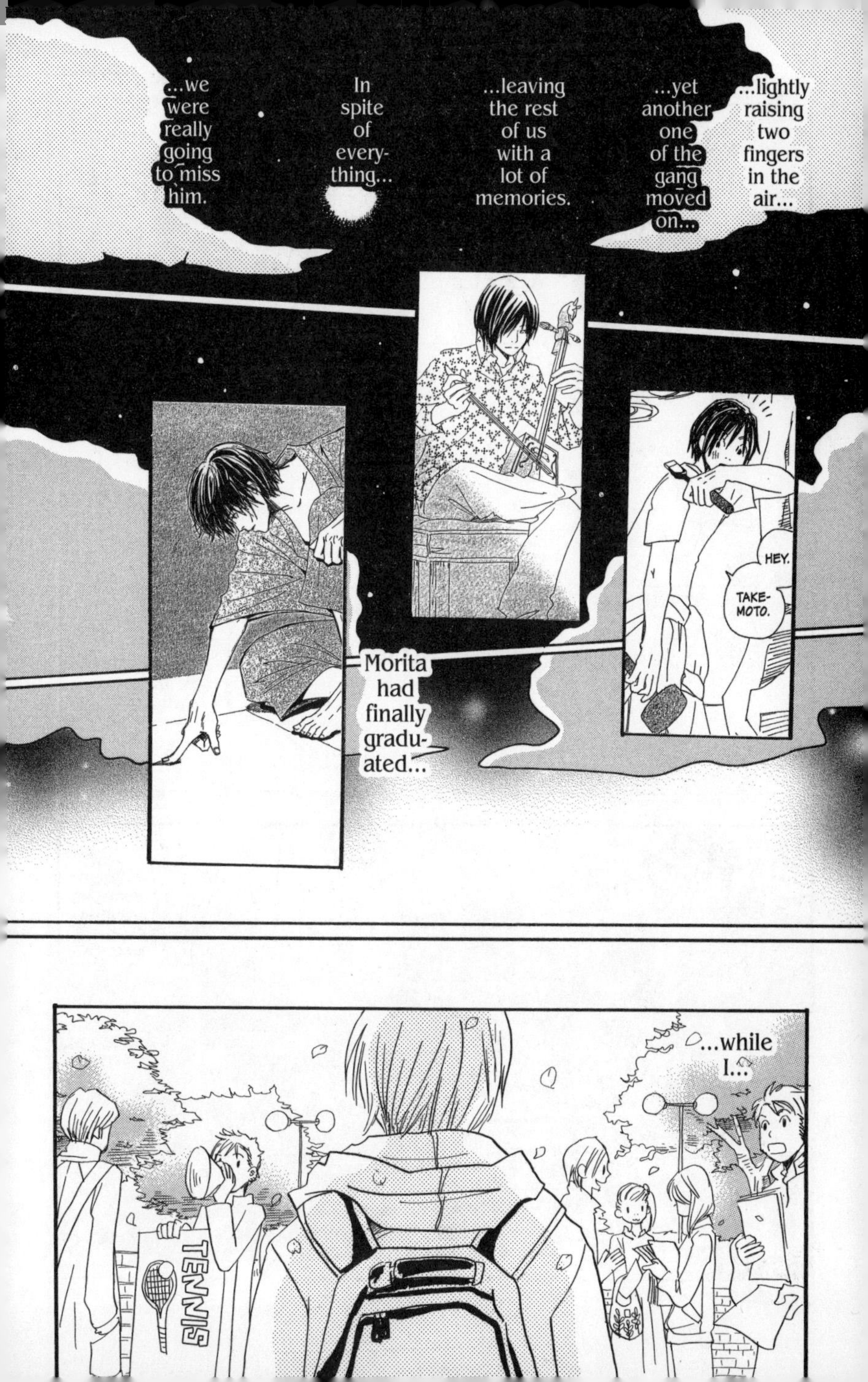
...lightly raising two fingers in the air...
...yet another one of the gang moved on...
...leaving the rest of us with a lot of memories.
In spite of every-thing...
...we were really going to miss him.
HEY.
TAKE-MOTO.
Morita had finally gradu-ated...
...while I...
TENNIS

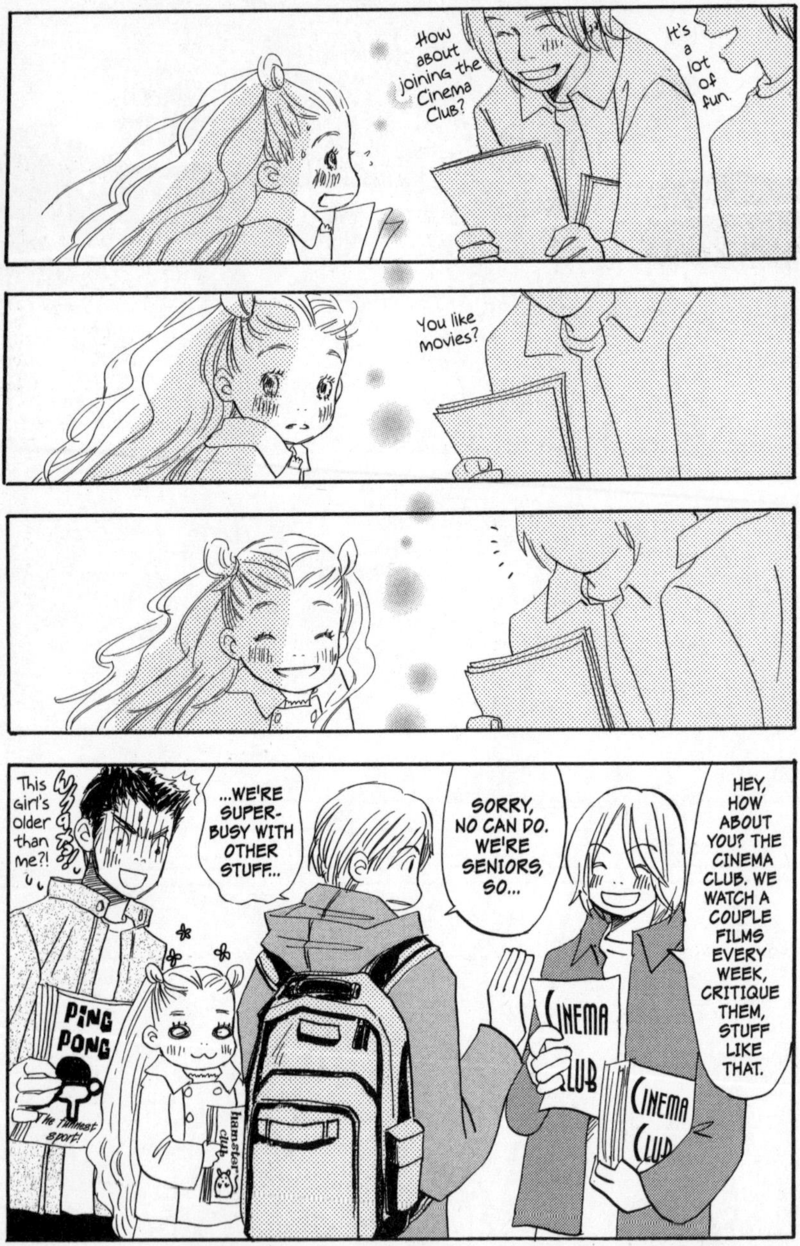
It's a lot of fun.
How about joining the Cinema Club?
You like movies?
HEY, HOW ABOUT YOU? THE CINEMA CLUB. WE WATCH A COUPLE FILMS EVERY WEEK, CRITIQUE THEM, STUFF LIKE THAT.
CINEMA CLUB
CINEMA CLUB
SORRY, NO CAN DO. WE'RE SENIORS, SO...
...WE'RE SUPER-BUSY WITH OTHER STUFF...
This Girl's older than me?!
hamster club
PING PONG
The funnest sport!

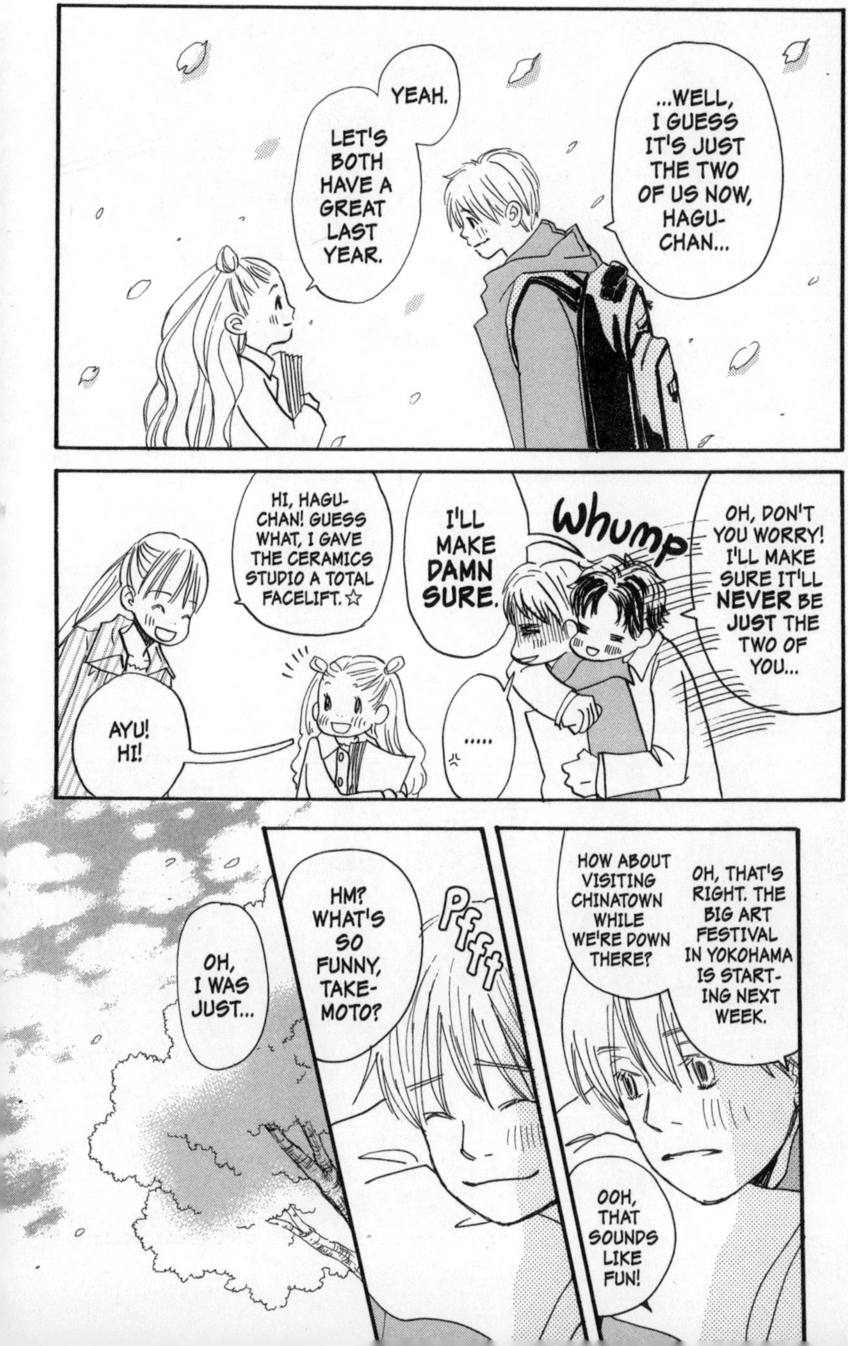
...WELL, I GUESS IT'S JUST THE TWO OF US NOW, HAGU-CHAN...
YEAH. LET'S BOTH HAVE A GREAT LAST YEAR.
Whump
OH, DON'T YOU WORRY! I'LL MAKE SURE IT'LL NEVER BE JUST THE TWO OF YOU...
I'LL MAKE DAMN SURE.
HI, HAGU-CHAN! GUESS WHAT, I GAVE THE CERAMICS STUDIO A TOTAL FACELIFT.☆
.....
AYU! HI!
OH, THAT'S RIGHT. THE BIG ART FESTIVAL IN YOKOHAMA IS START-ING NEXT WEEK.
HOW ABOUT VISITING CHINATOWN WHILE WE'RE DOWN THERE?
OOH, THAT SOUNDS LIKE FUN!
Pffft
HM? WHAT'S SO FUNNY, TAKE-MOTO?
OH, I WAS JUST...

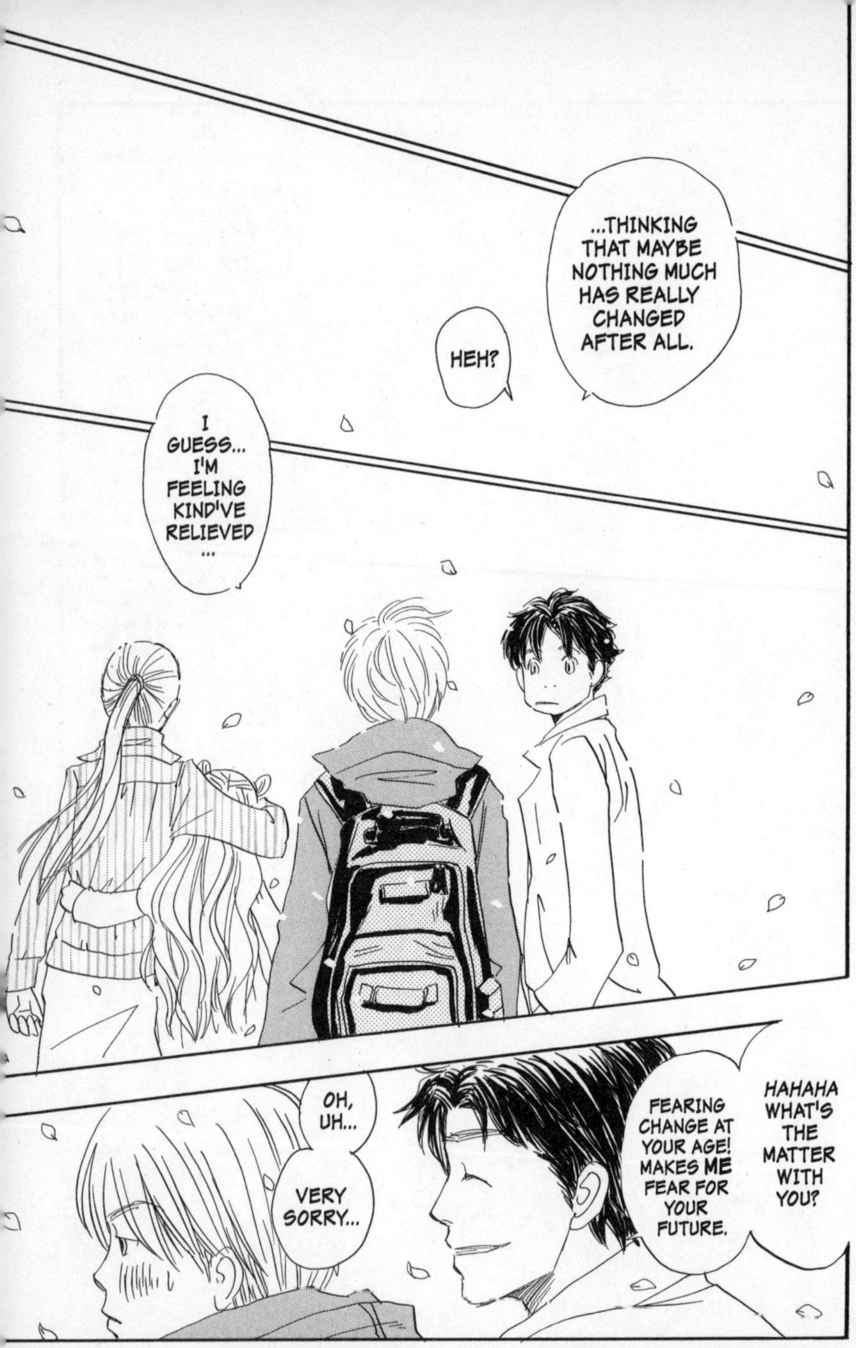
...THINKING THAT MAYBE NOTHING MUCH HAS REALLY CHANGED AFTER ALL.
HEH?
I GUESS... I'M FEELING KIND'VE RELIEVED...
HAHAHA WHAT'S THE MATTER WITH YOU?
FEARING CHANGE AT YOUR AGE! MAKES ME FEAR FOR YOUR FUTURE.
OH, UH...
VERY SORRY...

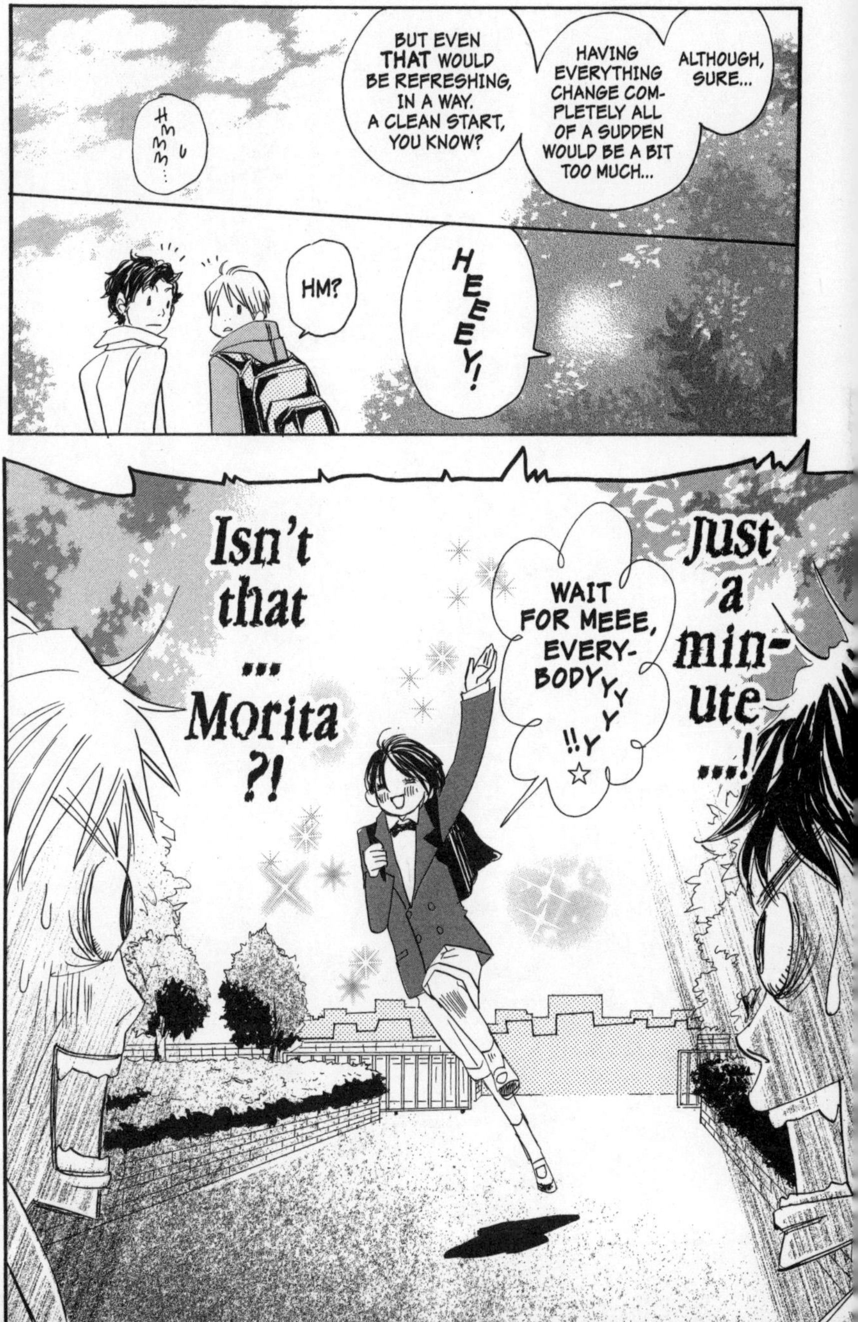
ALTHOUGH, SURE...
HAVING EVERYTHING CHANGE COMPLETELY ALL OF A SUDDEN WOULD BE A BIT TOO MUCH...
BUT EVEN THAT WOULD BE REFRESHING, IN A WAY. A CLEAN START, YOU KNOW?
HMMM...
HEEEY!
HM?
Just a minute...!
WAIT FOR MEEE, EVERYBODYYYY!!☆
Isn't that... Morita?!

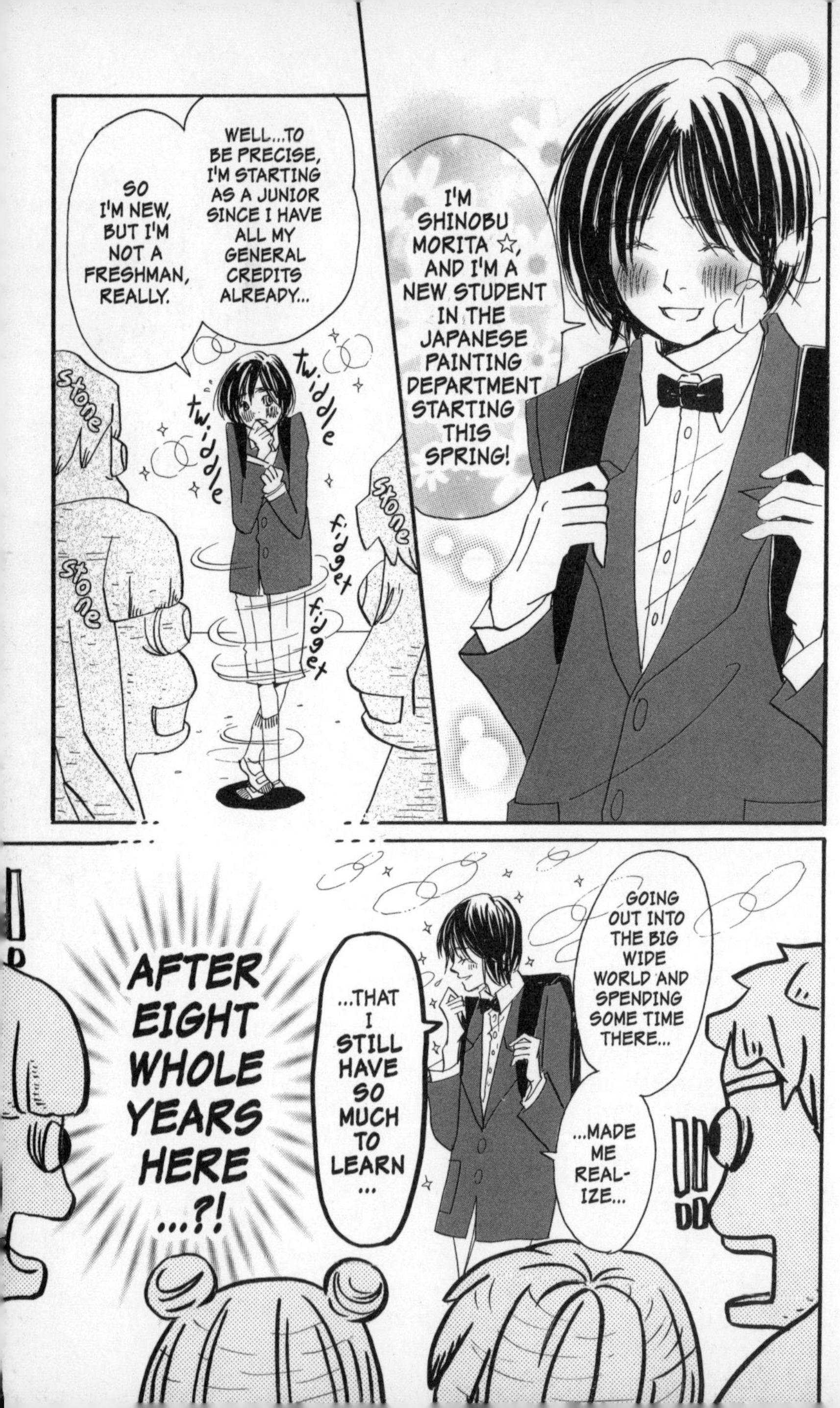
I'M SHINOBU MORITA ☆, AND I'M A NEW STUDENT IN THE JAPANESE PAINTING DEPARTMENT STARTING THIS SPRING!
WELL...TO BE PRECISE, I'M STARTING AS A JUNIOR SINCE I HAVE ALL MY GENERAL CREDITS ALREADY...
SO I'M NEW, BUT I'M NOT A FRESHMAN, REALLY.
twiddle twiddle
fidget fidget
stone
stone
stone
GOING OUT INTO THE BIG WIDE WORLD AND SPENDING SOME TIME THERE...
...MADE ME REALIZE...
...THAT I STILL HAVE SO MUCH TO LEARN...
AFTER EIGHT WHOLE YEARS HERE...?!

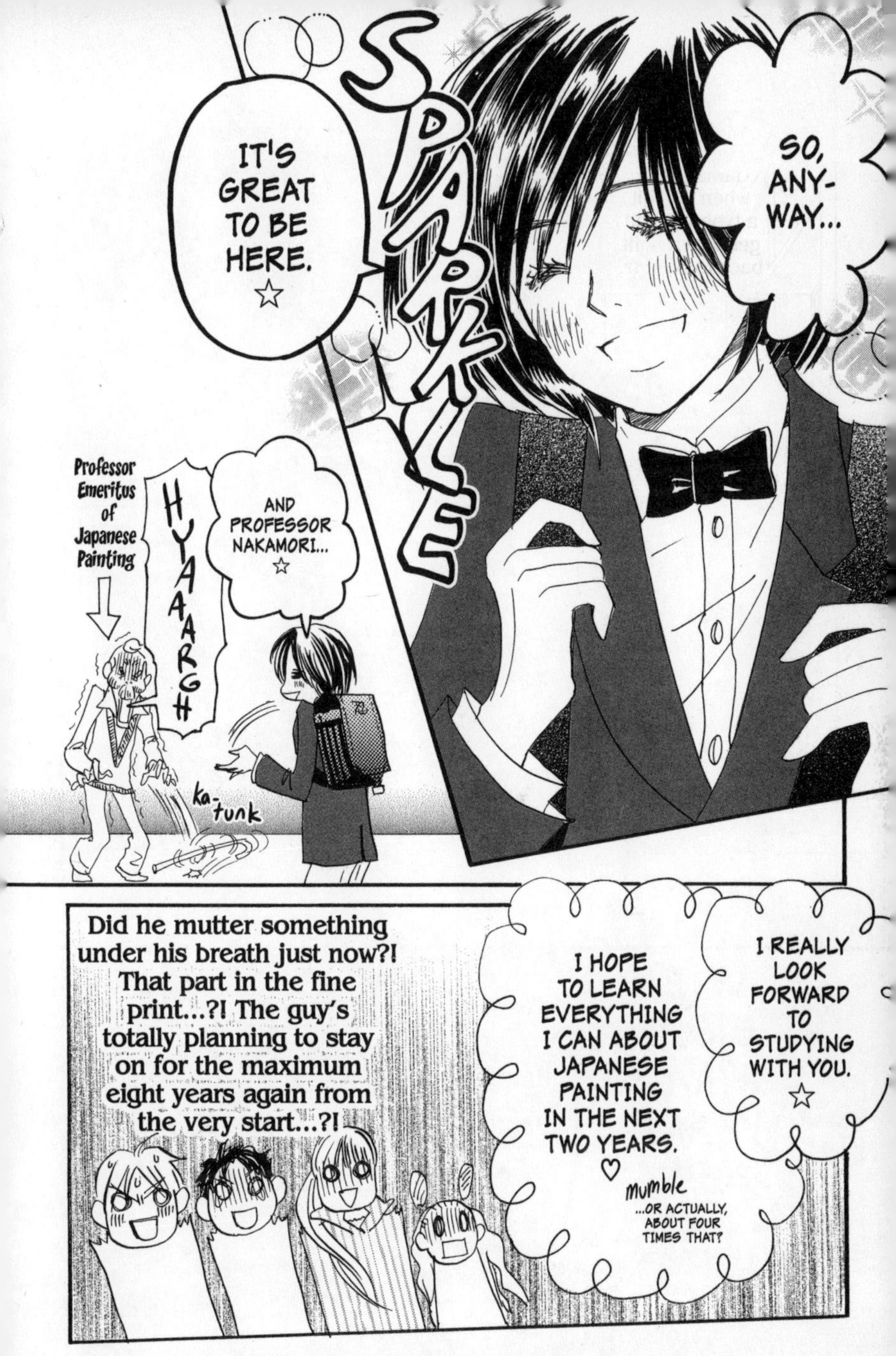
SO, ANY-WAY...
SPARKLE
IT'S GREAT TO BE HERE. ☆
AND PROFESSOR NAKAMORI... ☆
HYAAARGH
Professor Emeritus of Japanese Painting
ka-tunk
I REALLY LOOK FORWARD TO STUDYING WITH YOU. ☆
I HOPE TO LEARN EVERYTHING I CAN ABOUT JAPANESE PAINTING IN THE NEXT TWO YEARS. ♡
mumble
...OR ACTUALLY, ABOUT FOUR TIMES THAT?
Did he mutter something under his breath just now?! That part in the fine print...?! The guy's totally planning to stay on for the maximum eight years again from the very start...?!

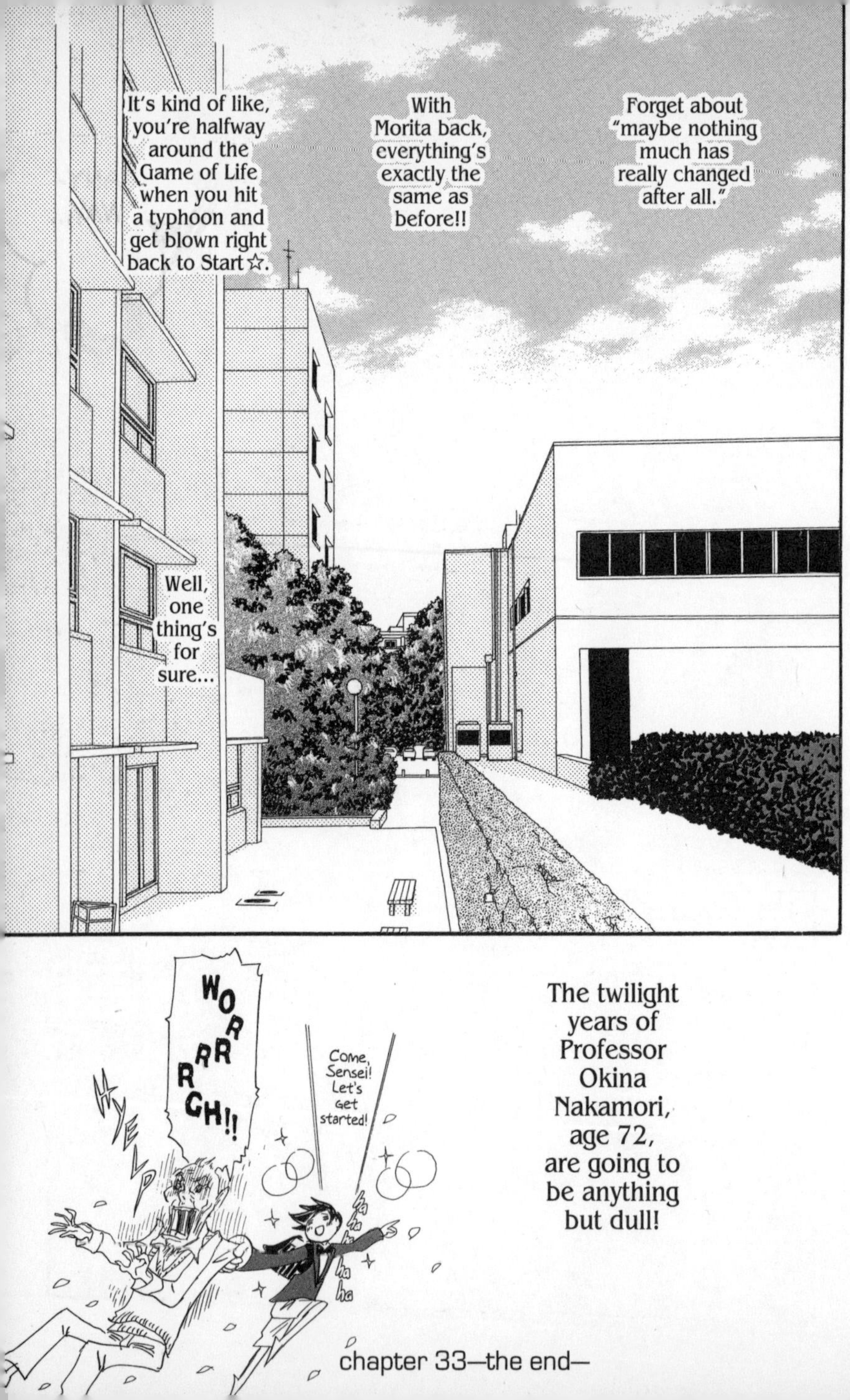
Forget about "maybe nothing much has really changed after all."
With Morita back, everything's exactly the same as before!!
It's kind of like, you're halfway around the Game of Life when you hit a typhoon and get blown right back to Start☆.
Well, one thing's for sure...
The twilight years of Professor Okina Nakamori, age 72, are going to be anything but dull!
Come, Sensei! Let's get started!
WORRRRRGH!!
HYELP
ha ha ha ha ha
chapter 33—the end—

HAGU PEZ
HONEY and CLOVER......
Hagu PEZ by Shinobu Morita

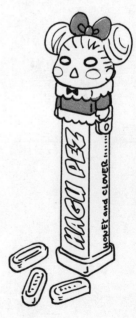

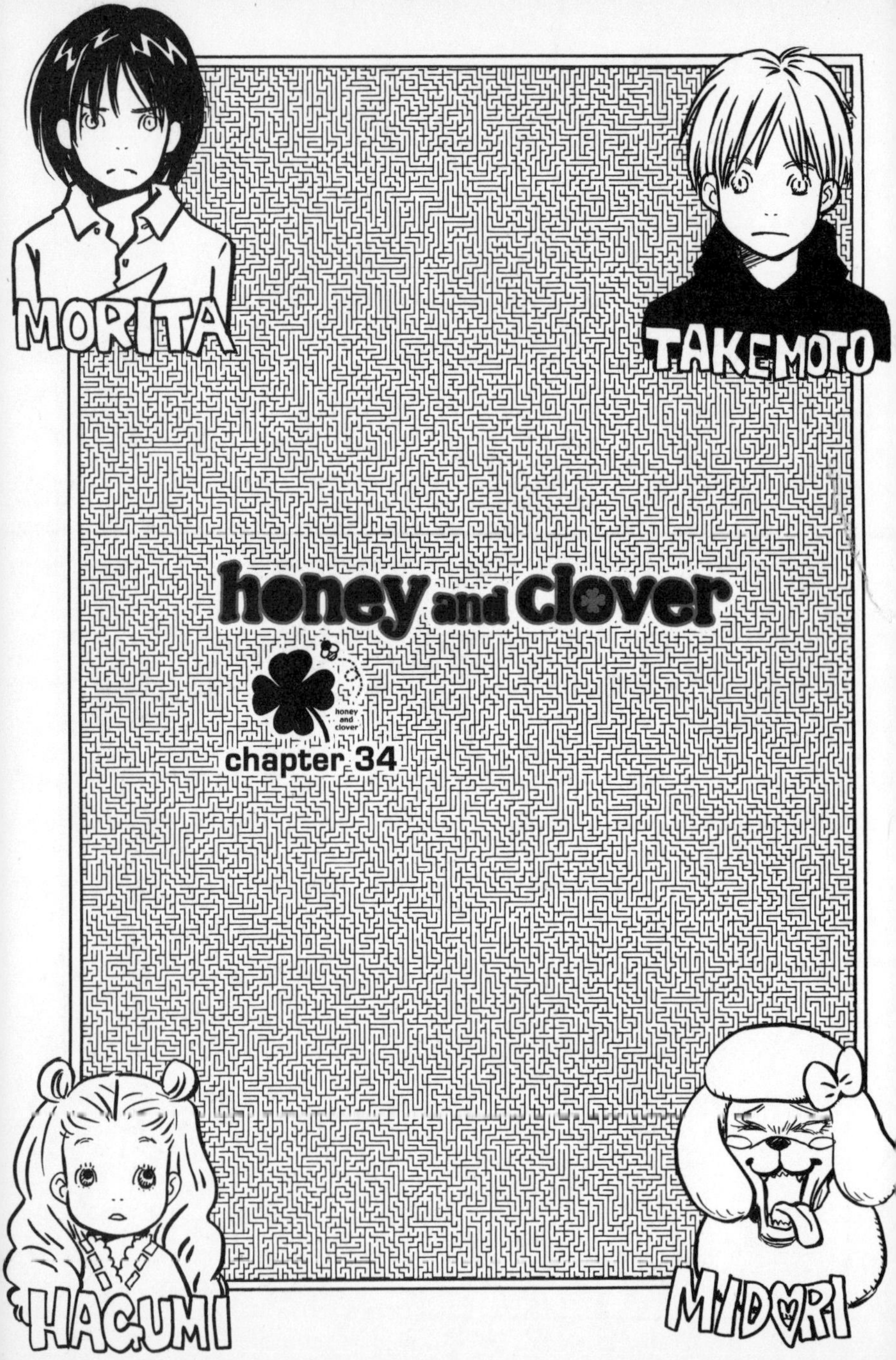
MORITA
TAKEMOTO
honey and clover
honey and clover
chapter 34
HAGUMI
MIDORI

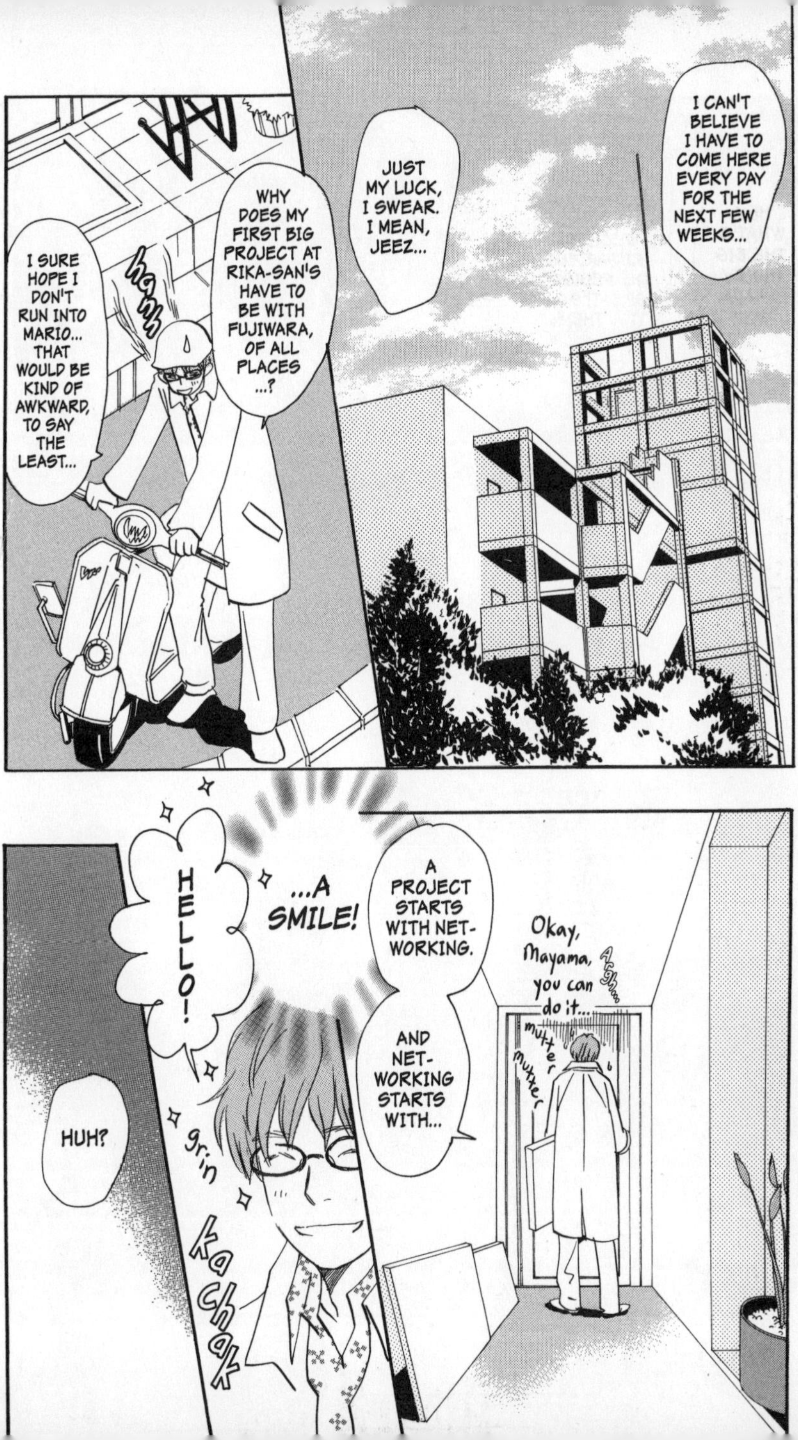
I CAN'T BELIEVE I HAVE TO COME HERE EVERY DAY FOR THE NEXT FEW WEEKS...
JUST MY LUCK, I SWEAR. I MEAN, JEEZ...
WHY DOES MY FIRST BIG PROJECT AT RIKA-SAN'S HAVE TO BE WITH FUJIWARA, OF ALL PLACES ...?
I SURE HOPE I DON'T RUN INTO MARIO... THAT WOULD BE KIND OF AWKWARD, TO SAY THE LEAST...
Okay, Mayama, you can do it...
Agh...
mutter
mutter
A PROJECT STARTS WITH NET-WORKING.
AND NET-WORKING STARTS WITH...
...A SMILE!
HELLO!
grin
ka chak
HUH?

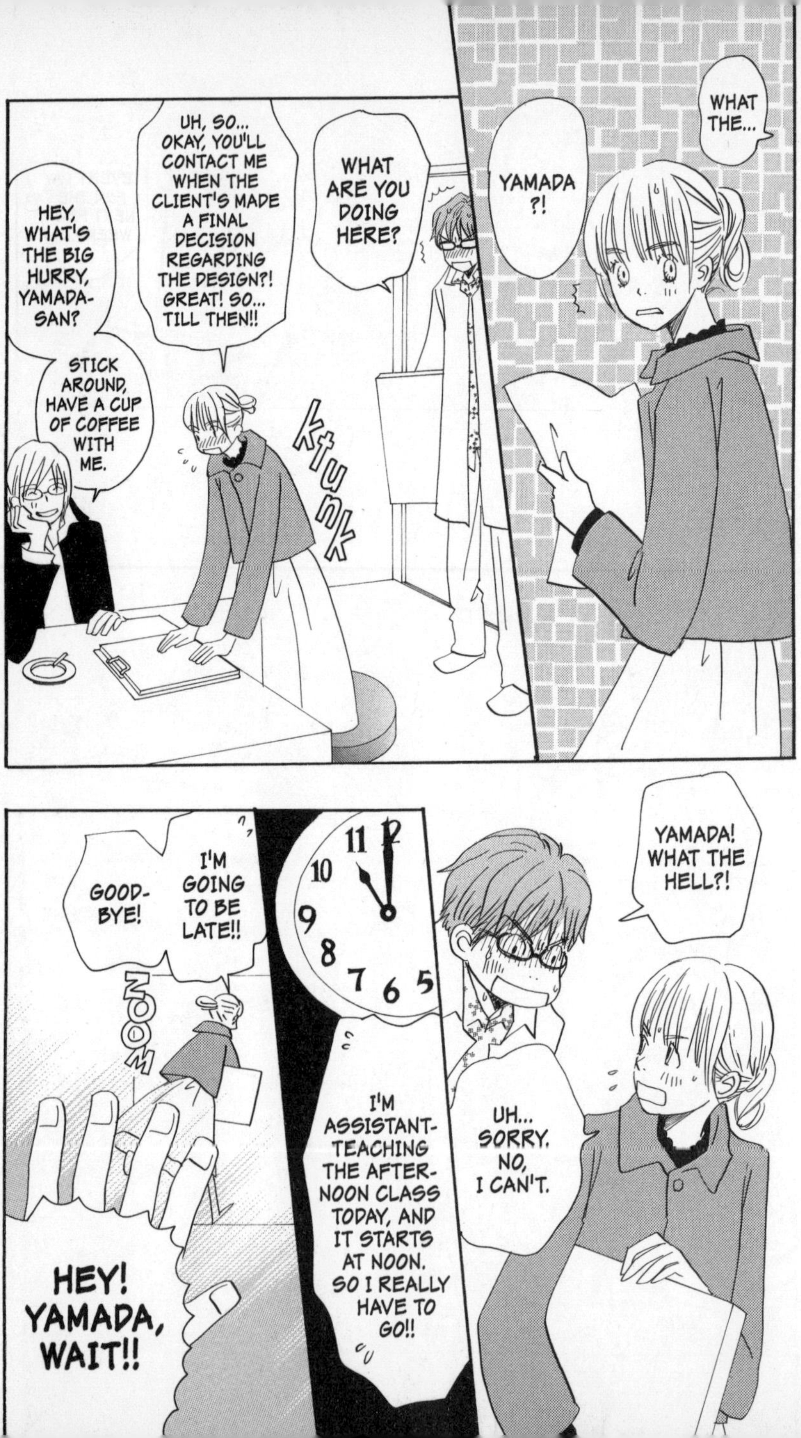
WHAT THE...
YAMADA ?!
WHAT ARE YOU DOING HERE?
UH, SO... OKAY, YOU'LL CONTACT ME WHEN THE CLIENT'S MADE A FINAL DECISION REGARDING THE DESIGN?! GREAT! SO... TILL THEN!!
HEY, WHAT'S THE BIG HURRY, YAMADA-SAN?
STICK AROUND, HAVE A CUP OF COFFEE WITH ME.
ktunk
YAMADA! WHAT THE HELL?!
UH... SORRY. NO, I CAN'T.
I'M ASSISTANT-TEACHING THE AFTER-NOON CLASS TODAY, AND IT STARTS AT NOON. SO I REALLY HAVE TO GO!!
I'M GOING TO BE LATE!!
GOOD-BYE!
ZOOM
HEY! YAMADA, WAIT!!

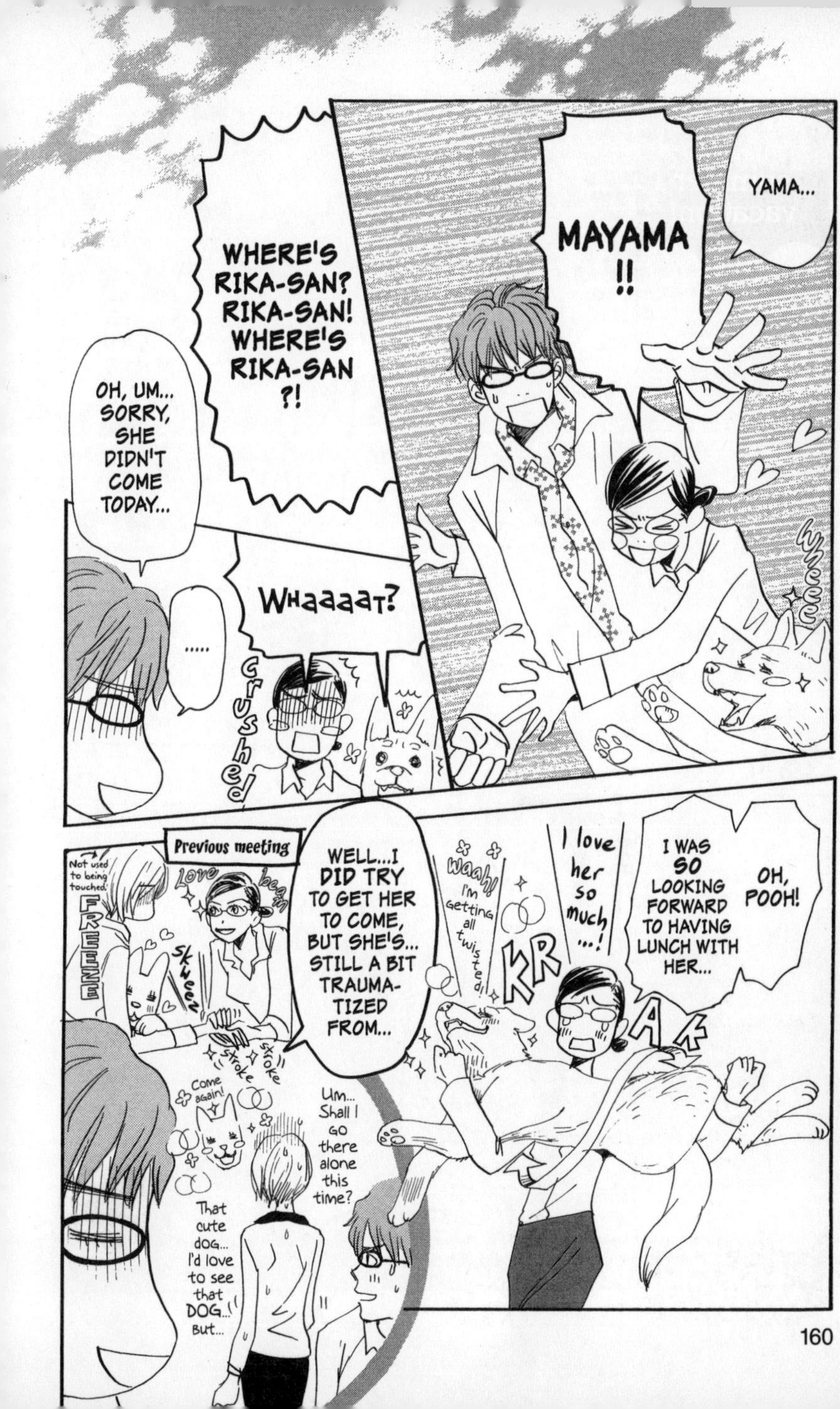
YAMA...
MAYAMA !!
wheee
WHERE'S RIKA-SAN? RIKA-SAN! WHERE'S RIKA-SAN ?!
OH, UM... SORRY, SHE DIDN'T COME TODAY...
WHaaaaT?
crushed
......
OH, POOH!
I WAS SO LOOKING FORWARD TO HAVING LUNCH WITH HER...
I love her so much...!
KRAK
waah! I'm getting all twisted!
WELL...I DID TRY TO GET HER TO COME, BUT SHE'S... STILL A BIT TRAUMATIZED FROM...
Previous meeting
Love beam
Not used to being touched.
FREEZE
skweez
stroke stroke
Come again!
Um... Shall I go there alone this time?
That cute dog... I'd love to see that DOG..! But...

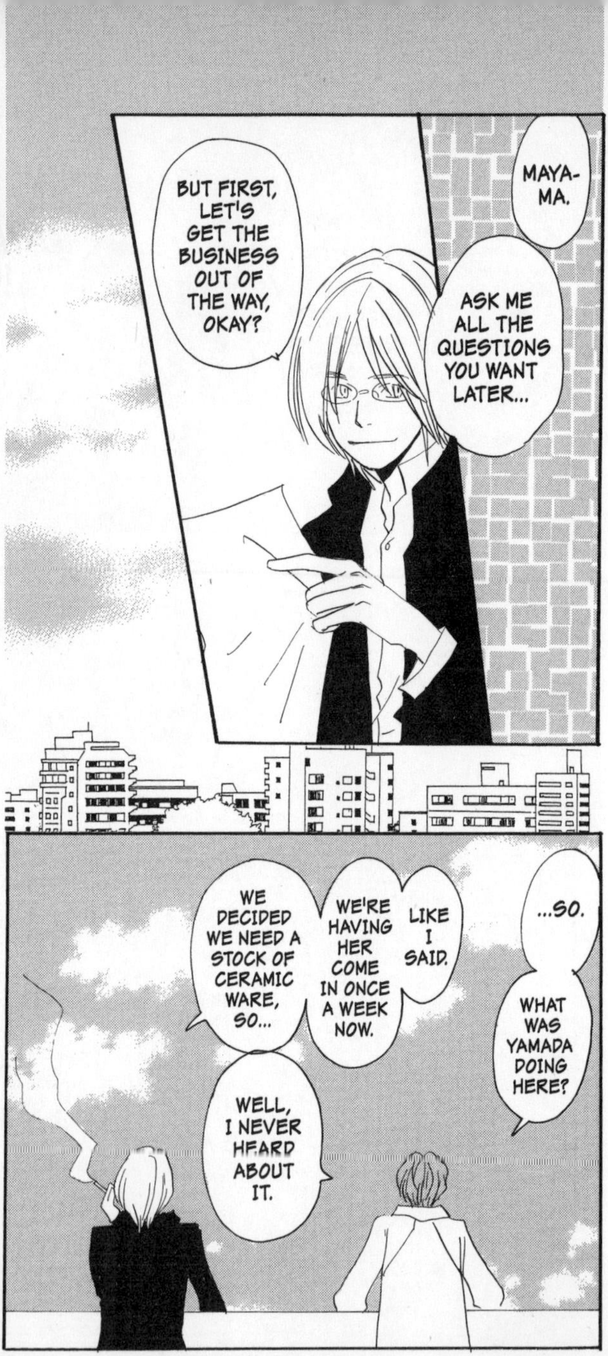
MAYA-MA.
ASK ME ALL THE QUESTIONS YOU WANT LATER...
BUT FIRST, LET'S GET THE BUSINESS OUT OF THE WAY, OKAY?
...SO.
WHAT WAS YAMADA DOING HERE?
LIKE I SAID.
WE'RE HAVING HER COME IN ONCE A WEEK NOW.
WE DECIDED WE NEED A STOCK OF CERAMIC WARE, SO...
WELL, I NEVER HEARD ABOUT IT.

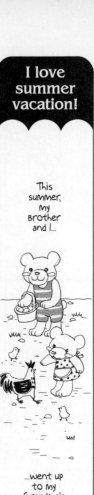

I love summer vacation!

This summer, my brother and I...

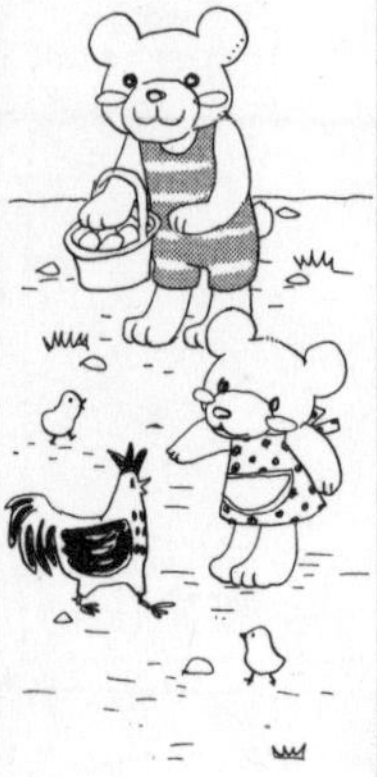

...went up to my Grandma's house in Yamagata, where we did battle with her chickens and vegetable patch.

Chica Umino

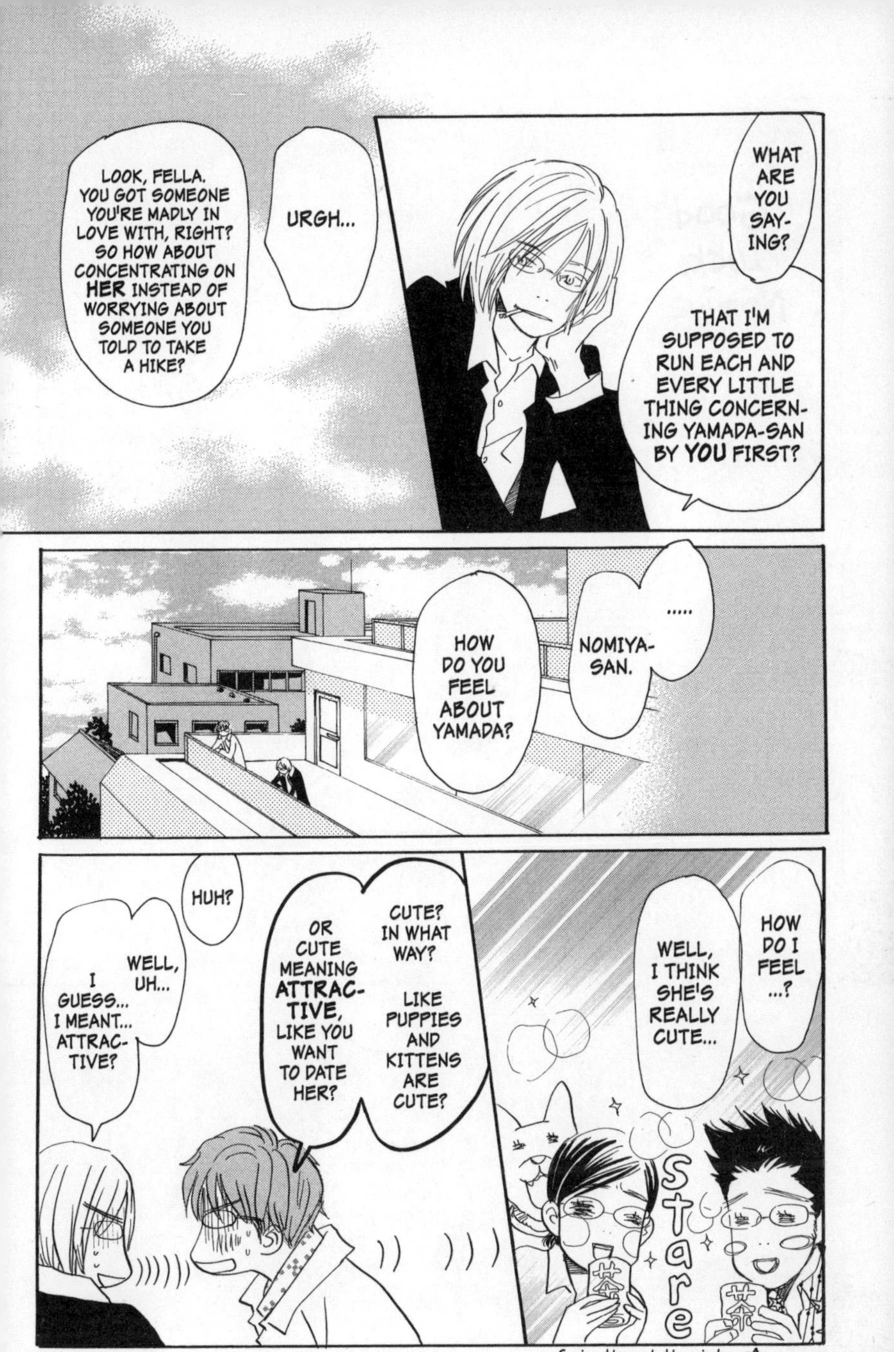
WHAT ARE YOU SAYING?
THAT I'M SUPPOSED TO RUN EACH AND EVERY LITTLE THING CONCERNING YAMADA-SAN BY YOU FIRST?
URGH...
LOOK, FELLA. YOU GOT SOMEONE YOU'RE MADLY IN LOVE WITH, RIGHT? SO HOW ABOUT CONCENTRATING ON HER INSTEAD OF WORRYING ABOUT SOMEONE YOU TOLD TO TAKE A HIKE?
.....
NOMIYA-SAN.
HOW DO YOU FEEL ABOUT YAMADA?
HOW DO I FEEL ...?
WELL, I THINK SHE'S REALLY CUTE...
Stare
CUTE? IN WHAT WAY? LIKE PUPPIES AND KITTENS ARE CUTE?
OR CUTE MEANING ATTRACTIVE, LIKE YOU WANT TO DATE HER?
HUH?
WELL, UH...
I GUESS... I MEANT... ATTRACTIVE?

Spying through the window. ☆

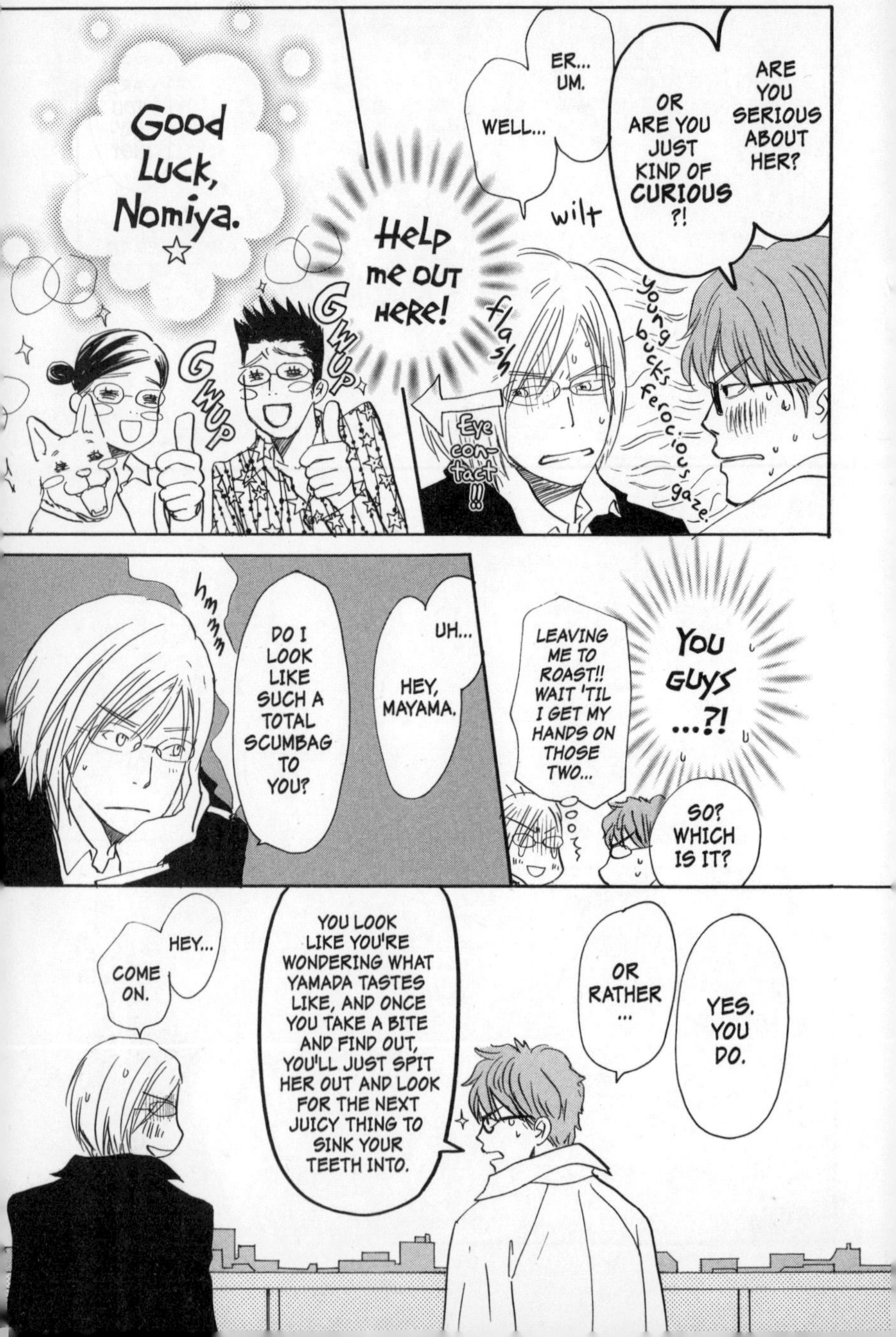
ARE YOU SERIOUS ABOUT HER?
OR ARE YOU JUST KIND OF CURIOUS ?!
young buck's ferocious gaze
ER... UM.
WELL...
wilt
flash
Eye con-tact !!
Help me out here!
GWUP
GWUP
GWUP
Good Luck, Nomiya. ☆
YOU GUYS ...?!
LEAVING ME TO ROAST!! WAIT 'TIL I GET MY HANDS ON THOSE TWO...
SO? WHICH IS IT?
UH...
HEY, MAYAMA.
DO I LOOK LIKE SUCH A TOTAL SCUMBAG TO YOU?
hmmm
YES. YOU DO.
OR RATHER ...
YOU LOOK LIKE YOU'RE WONDERING WHAT YAMADA TASTES LIKE, AND ONCE YOU TAKE A BITE AND FIND OUT, YOU'LL JUST SPIT HER OUT AND LOOK FOR THE NEXT JUICY THING TO SINK YOUR TEETH INTO.
HEY...
COME ON.

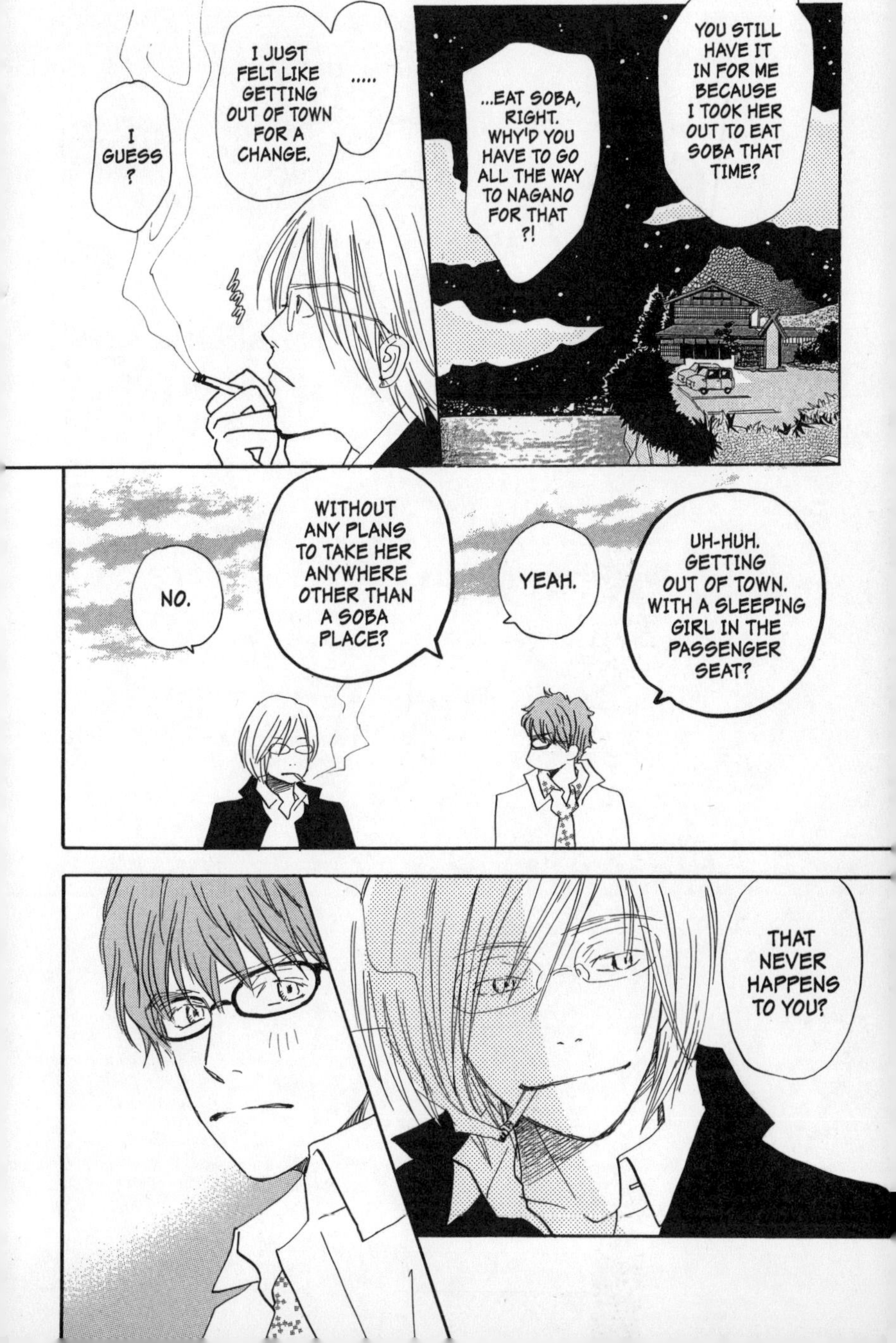
YOU STILL HAVE IT IN FOR ME BECAUSE I TOOK HER OUT TO EAT SOBA THAT TIME?
...EAT SOBA, RIGHT. WHY'D YOU HAVE TO GO ALL THE WAY TO NAGANO FOR THAT ?!
.....
I JUST FELT LIKE GETTING OUT OF TOWN FOR A CHANGE.
I GUESS ?
UH-HUH. GETTING OUT OF TOWN. WITH A SLEEPING GIRL IN THE PASSENGER SEAT?
YEAH.
WITHOUT ANY PLANS TO TAKE HER ANYWHERE OTHER THAN A SOBA PLACE?
NO.
THAT NEVER HAPPENS TO YOU?

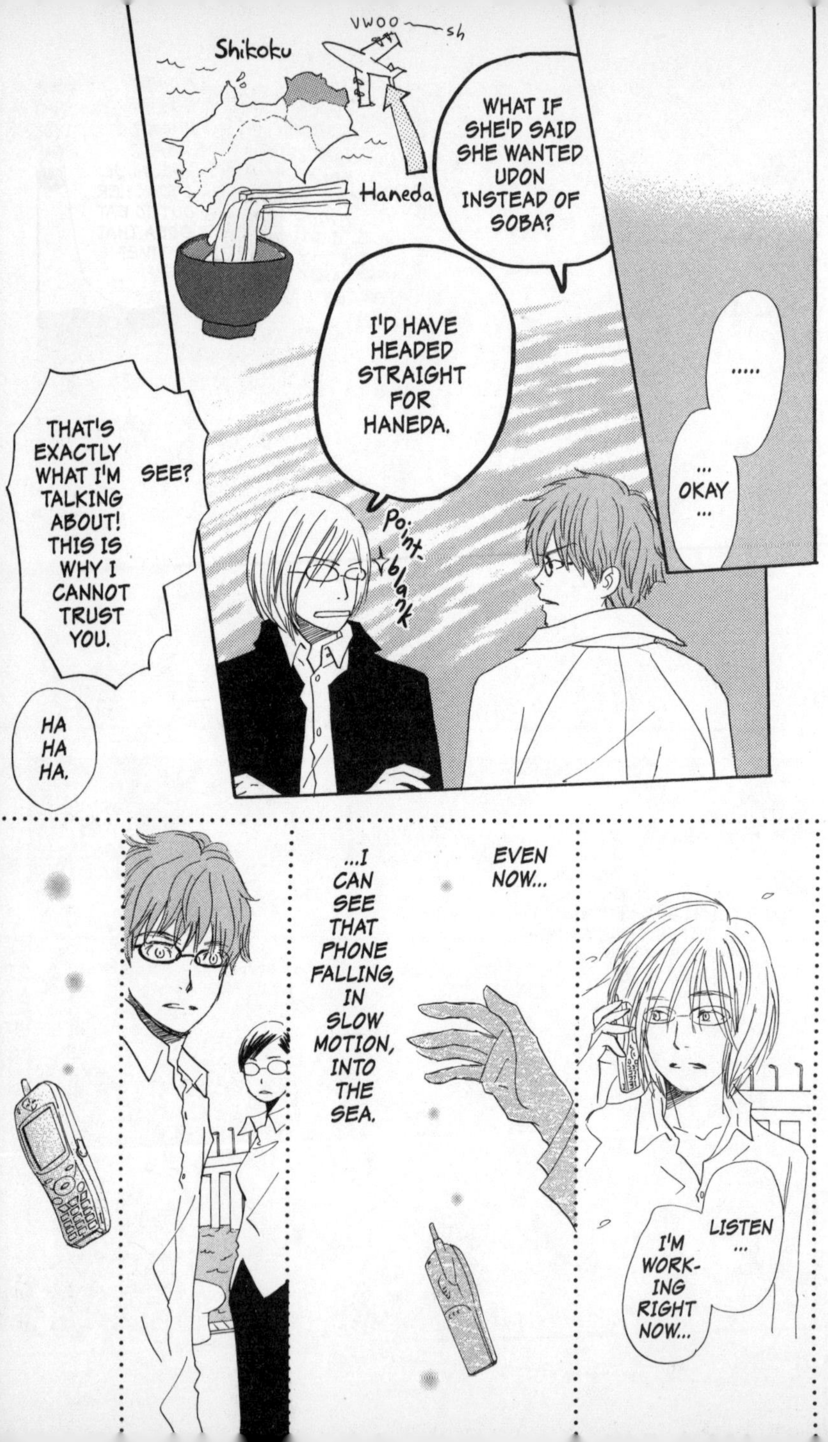
VWOO—sh
Shikoku
Haneda
WHAT IF SHE'D SAID SHE WANTED UDON INSTEAD OF SOBA?
.....
I'D HAVE HEADED STRAIGHT FOR HANEDA.
...OKAY...
Point-blank
SEE?
THAT'S EXACTLY WHAT I'M TALKING ABOUT! THIS IS WHY I CANNOT TRUST YOU.
HA HA HA.
LISTEN...
I'M WORKING RIGHT NOW...
EVEN NOW...
...I CAN SEE THAT PHONE FALLING, IN SLOW MOTION, INTO THE SEA.

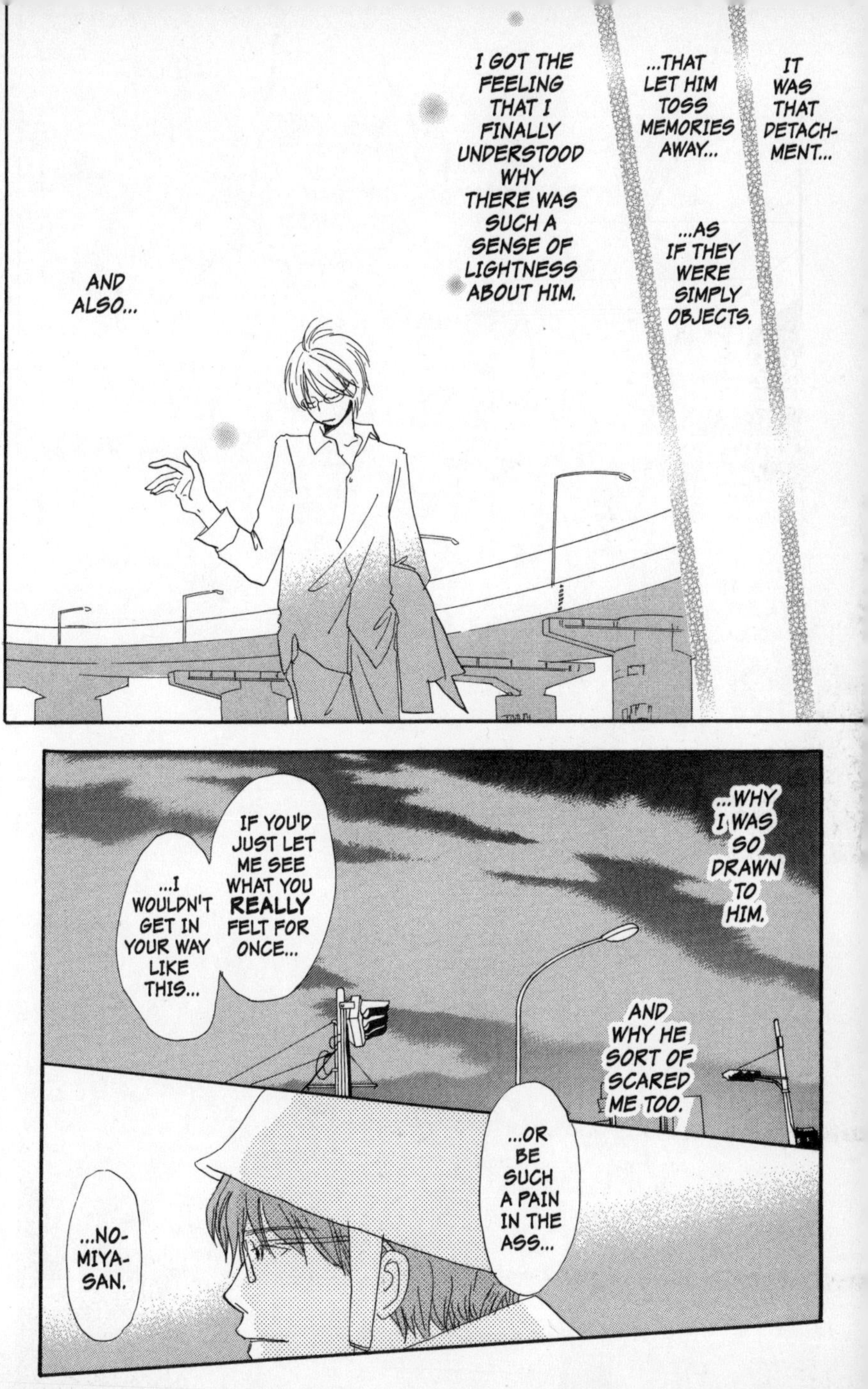
IT WAS THAT DETACHMENT...
...THAT LET HIM TOSS MEMORIES AWAY...
...AS IF THEY WERE SIMPLY OBJECTS.
I GOT THE FEELING THAT I FINALLY UNDERSTOOD WHY THERE WAS SUCH A SENSE OF LIGHTNESS ABOUT HIM.
AND ALSO...
...WHY I WAS SO DRAWN TO HIM.
AND WHY HE SORT OF SCARED ME TOO.
IF YOU'D JUST LET ME SEE WHAT YOU **REALLY** FELT FOR ONCE...
...I WOULDN'T GET IN YOUR WAY LIKE THIS...
...OR BE SUCH A PAIN IN THE ASS...
...NO-MIYA-SAN.

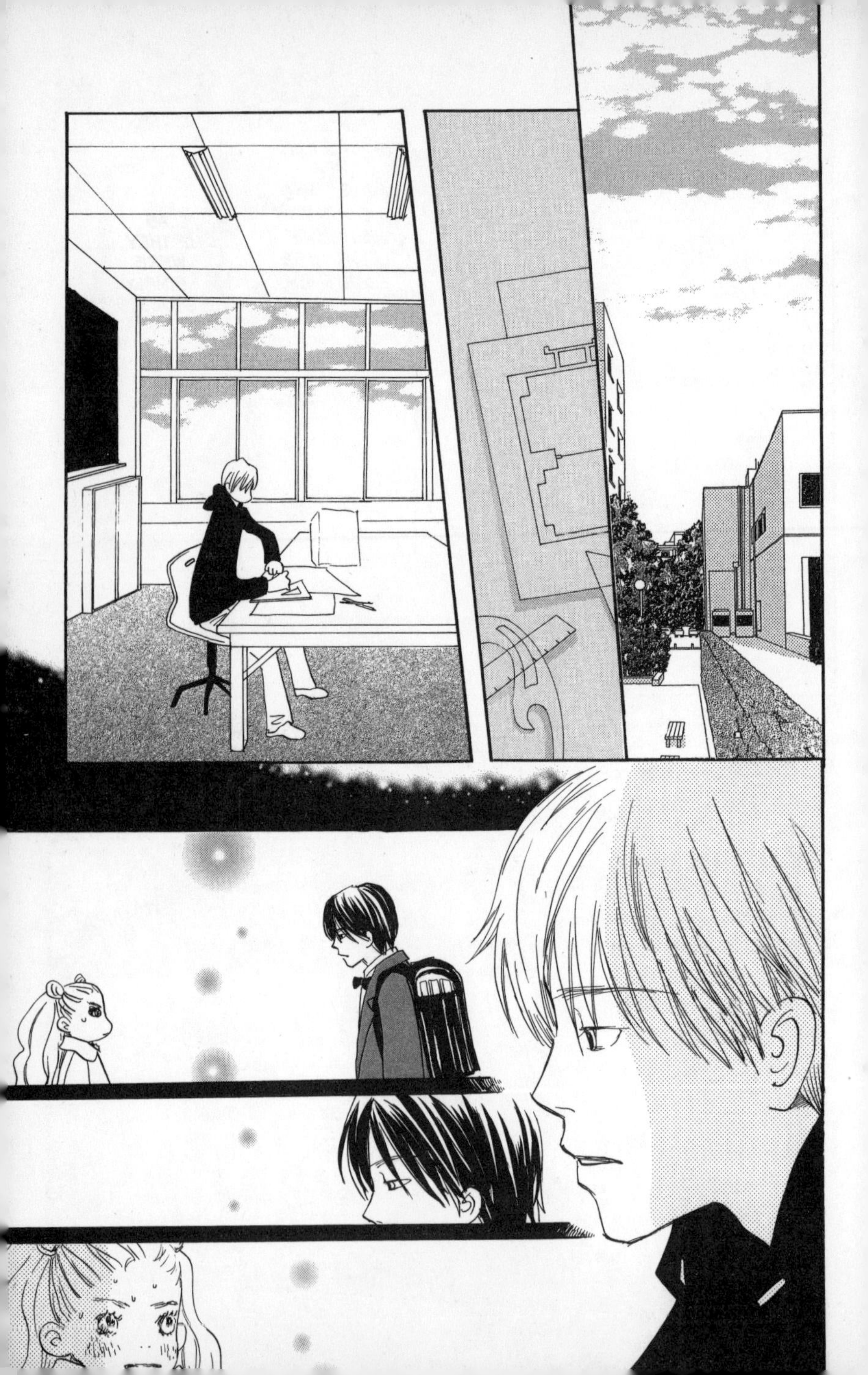

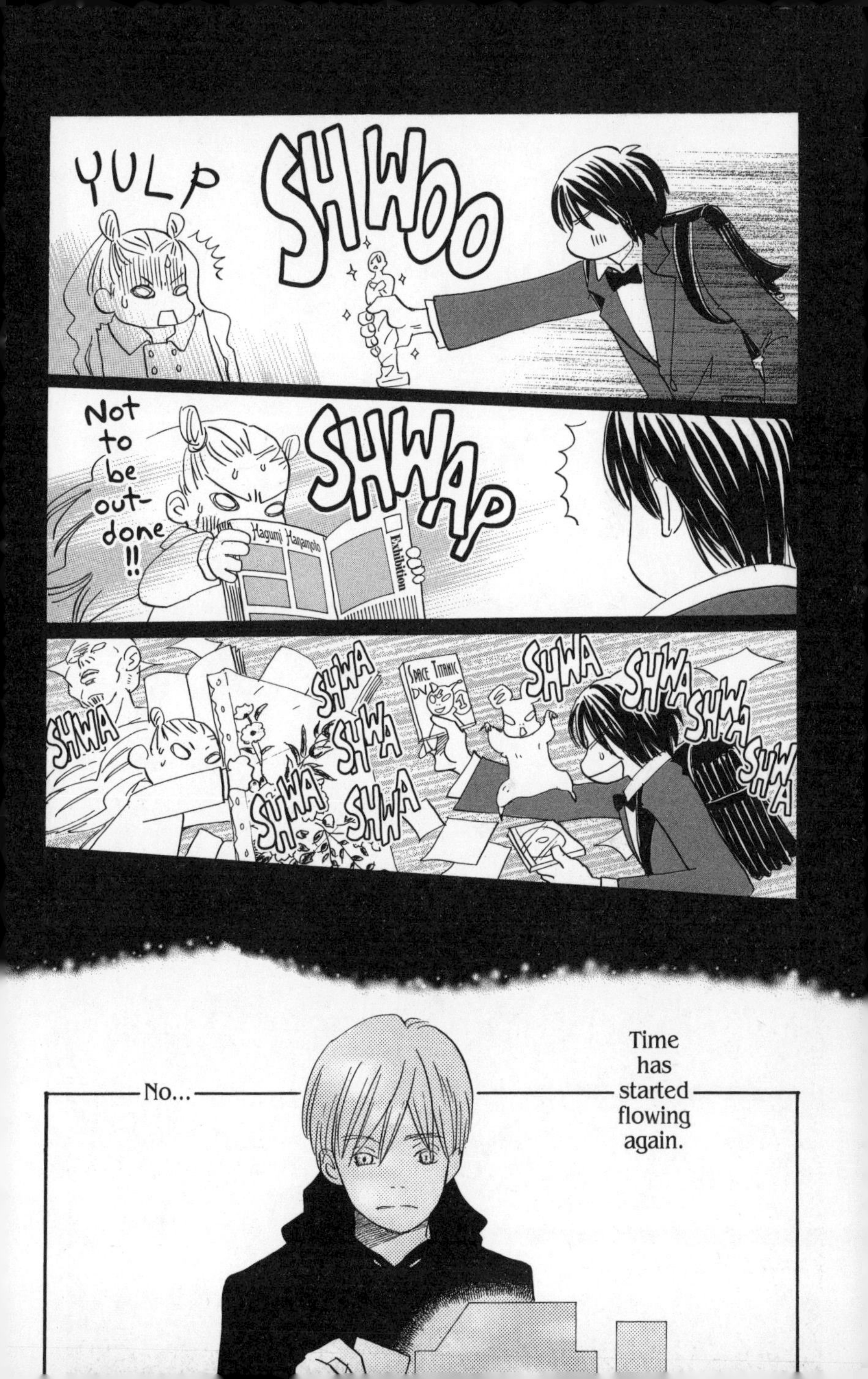
SHWOO
YULP
SHWAP
Not to be out-done!!
Hagumi Hanamoto
Exhibition
SHWA SHWA SHWA SHWA
SPACE TITANIC DVD 1
SHWA SHWA SHWA SHWA SHWA
SHWA
Time has started flowing again.
No...

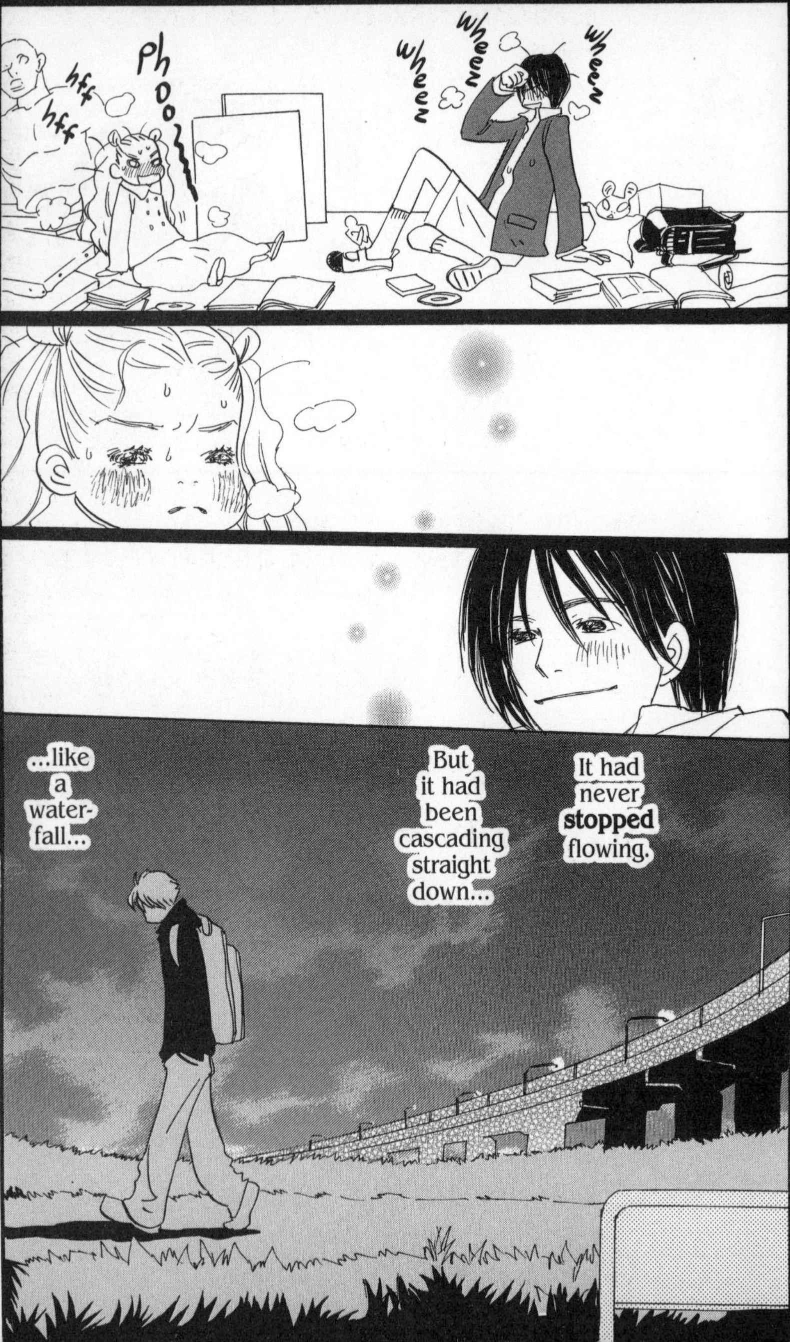
wheez
wheez
wheez
Phoo~~
hff
hff
It had never **stopped** flowing.
But it had been cascading straight down...
...like a water-fall...

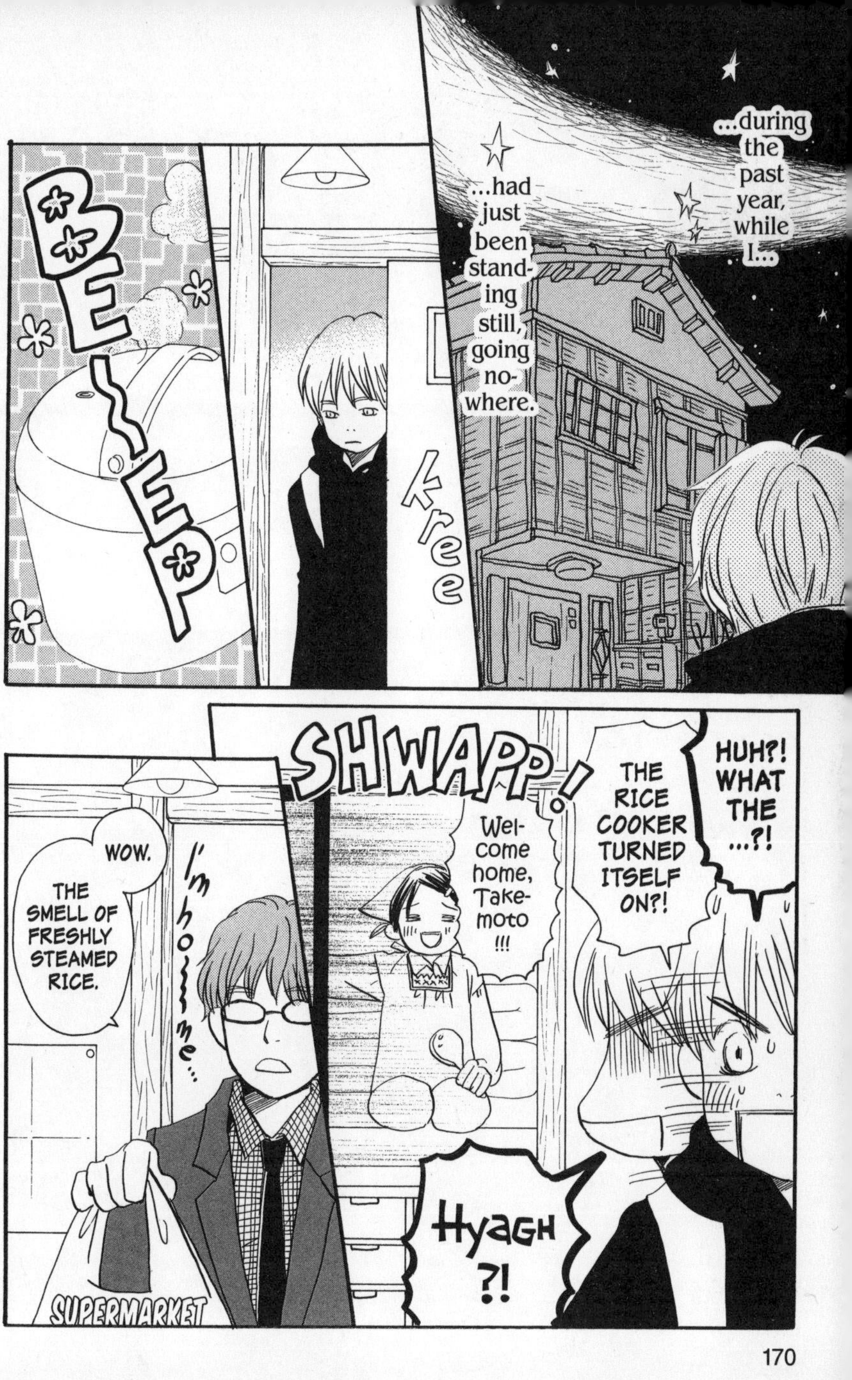
...during the past year, while I...
...had just been standing still, going nowhere.
kree
BE~EP
HUH?! WHAT THE ...?!
THE RICE COOKER TURNED ITSELF ON?!
SHWAPP!
Hyagh ?!
Welcome home, Takemoto !!!
I'm home...
WOW.
THE SMELL OF FRESHLY STEAMED RICE.
SUPERMARKET

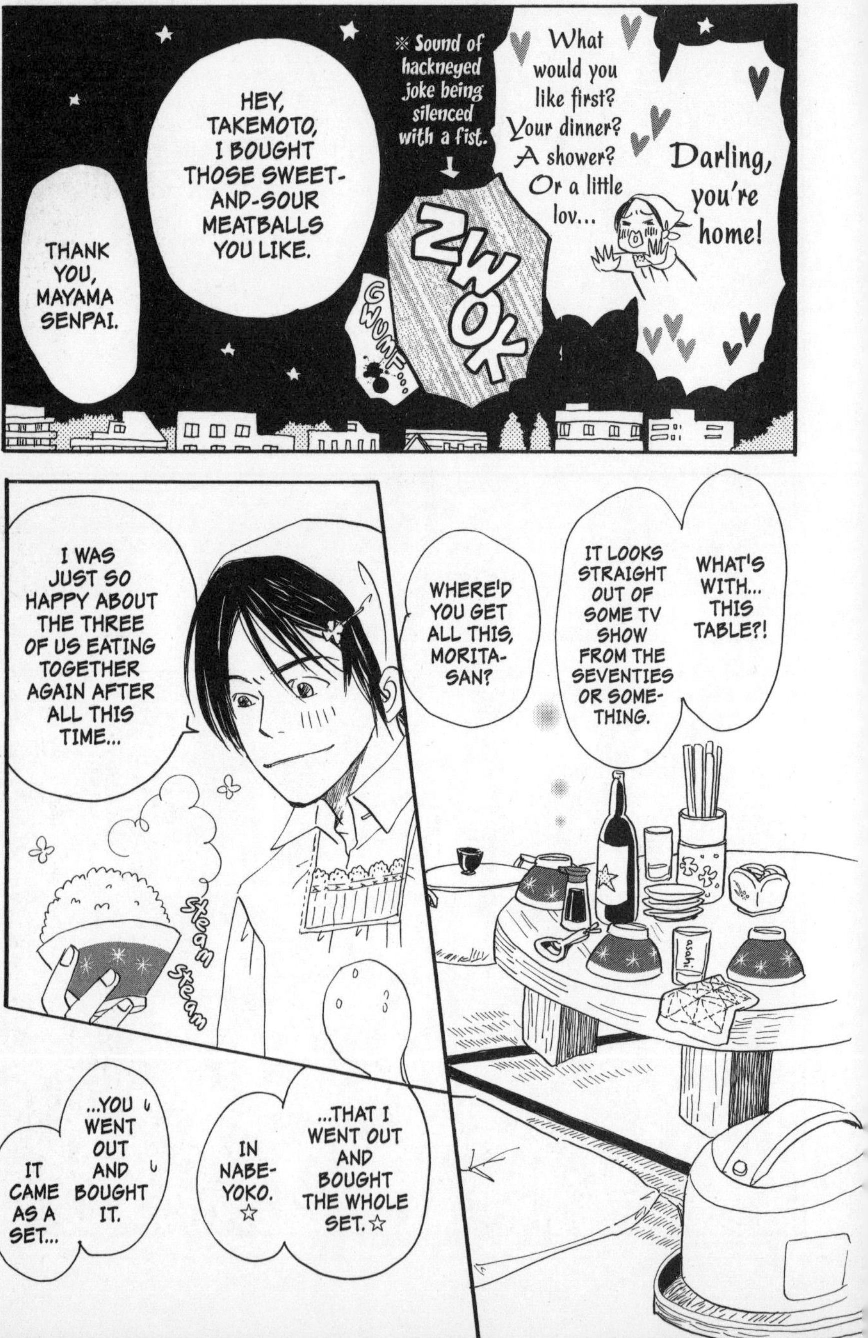
Darling, you're home!
What would you like first? Your dinner? A shower? Or a little lov...
※ Sound of hackneyed joke being silenced with a fist.
ZWOK
GWUMF...
HEY, TAKEMOTO, I BOUGHT THOSE SWEET-AND-SOUR MEATBALLS YOU LIKE.
THANK YOU, MAYAMA SENPAI.
WHAT'S WITH... THIS TABLE?!
IT LOOKS STRAIGHT OUT OF SOME TV SHOW FROM THE SEVENTIES OR SOME-THING.
WHERE'D YOU GET ALL THIS, MORITA-SAN?
I WAS JUST SO HAPPY ABOUT THE THREE OF US EATING TOGETHER AGAIN AFTER ALL THIS TIME...
steam steam
asahi
...THAT I WENT OUT AND BOUGHT THE WHOLE SET.☆
IN NABE-YOKO.☆
...YOU WENT OUT AND BOUGHT IT.
IT CAME AS A SET...

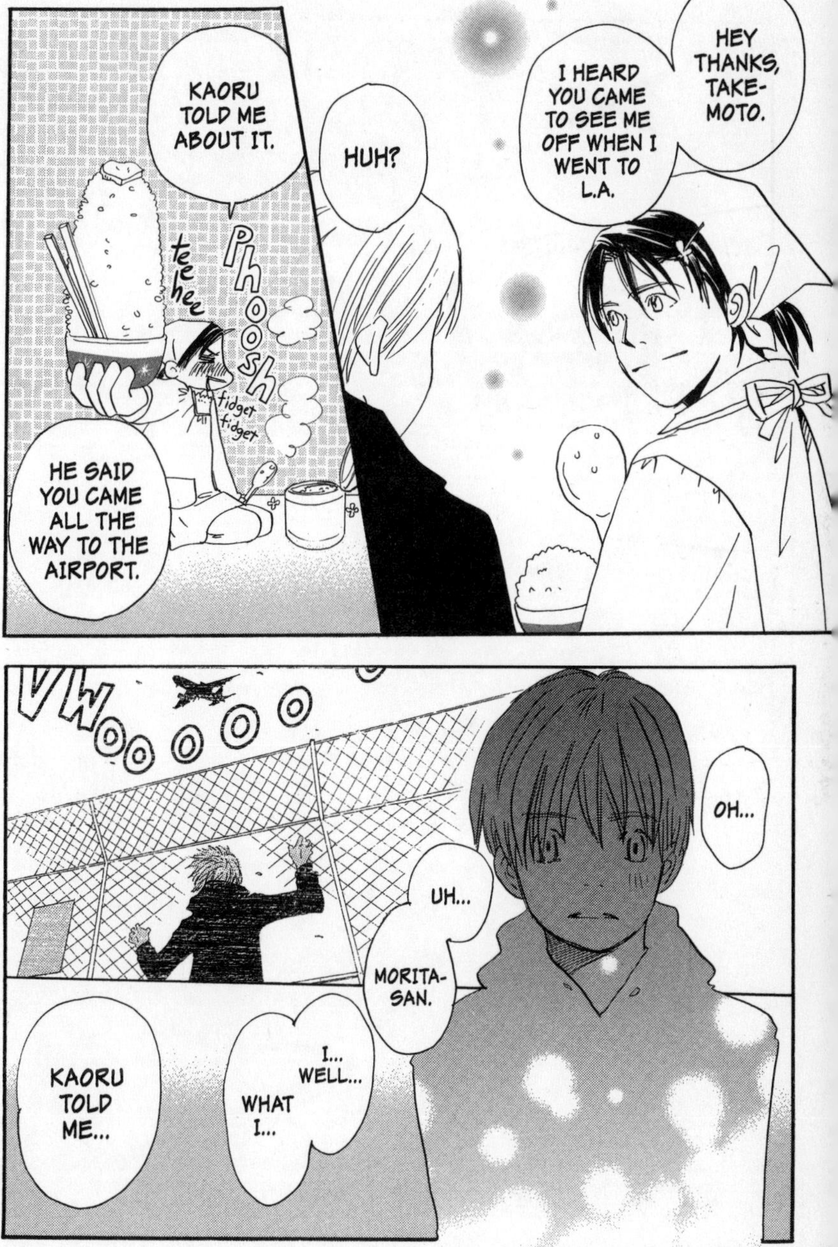
HEY THANKS, TAKE-MOTO.
I HEARD YOU CAME TO SEE ME OFF WHEN I WENT TO L.A.
HUH?
KAORU TOLD ME ABOUT IT.
Phooosh
tee hee
fidget fidget
HE SAID YOU CAME ALL THE WAY TO THE AIRPORT.
OH...
UH...
MORITA-SAN.
VWOOOOOO
I... WELL...
WHAT I...
KAORU TOLD ME...

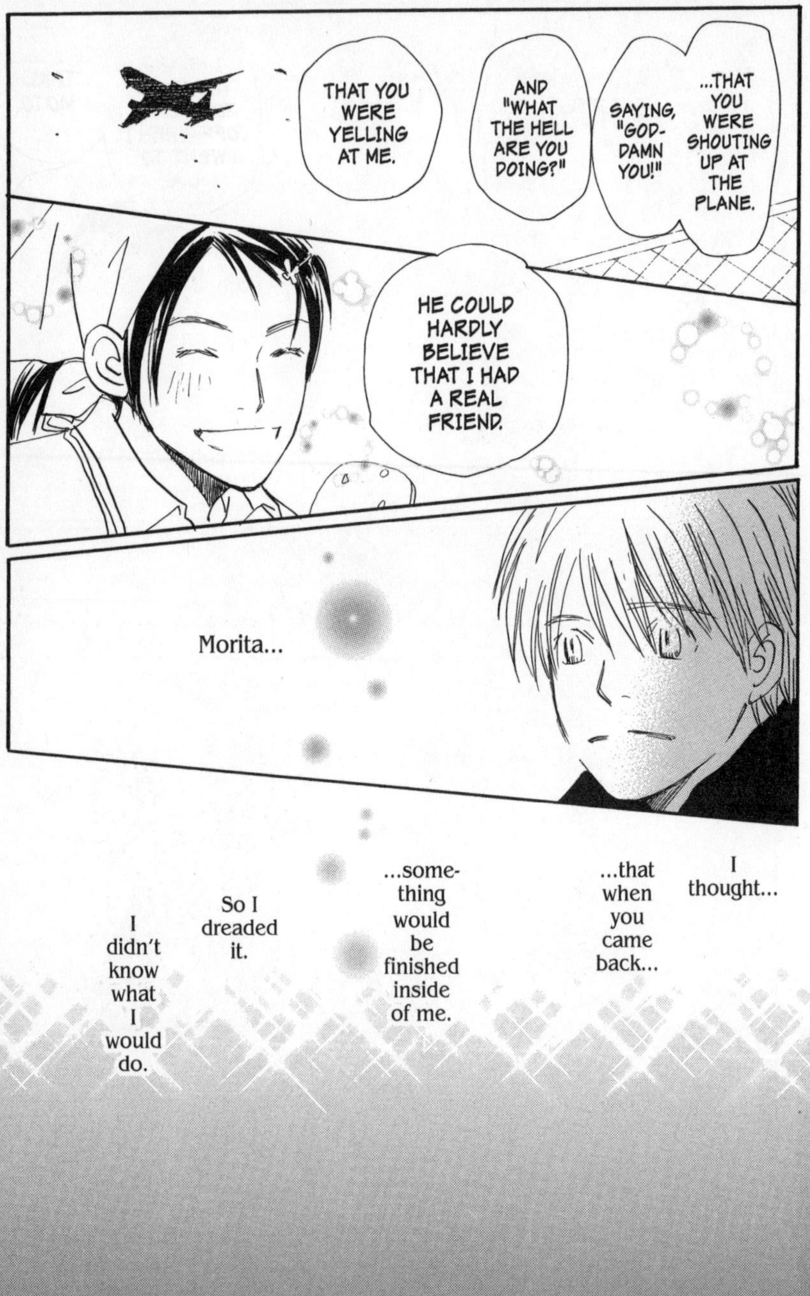
...THAT YOU WERE SHOUTING UP AT THE PLANE.
SAYING, "GOD-DAMN YOU!"
AND "WHAT THE HELL ARE YOU DOING?"
THAT YOU WERE YELLING AT ME.
HE COULD HARDLY BELIEVE THAT I HAD A REAL FRIEND.
Morita...
I thought...
...that when you came back...
...something would be finished inside of me.
So I dreaded it.
I didn't know what I would do.

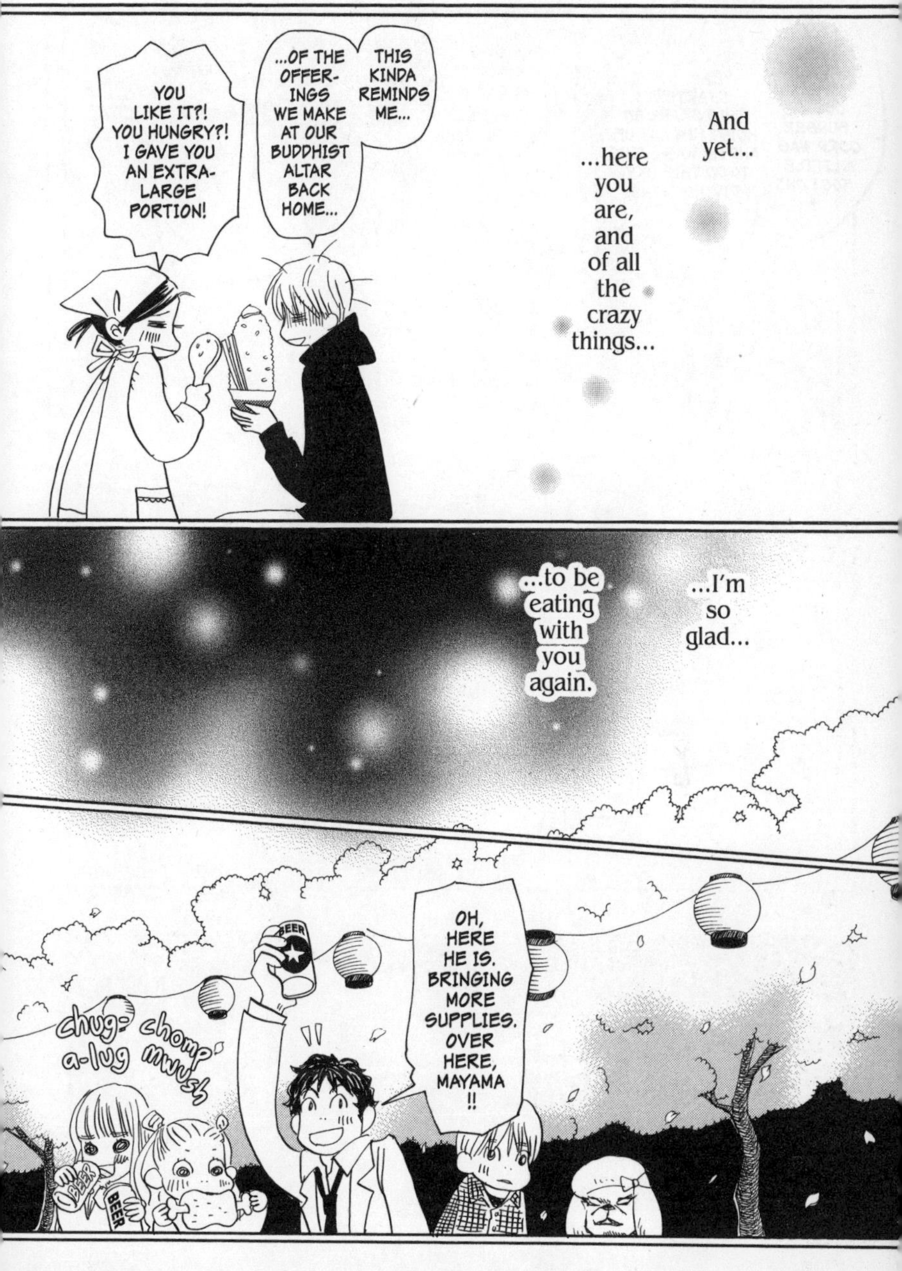
And yet...
...here you are, and of all the crazy things...
THIS KINDA REMINDS ME...
...OF THE OFFERINGS WE MAKE AT OUR BUDDHIST ALTAR BACK HOME...
YOU LIKE IT?! YOU HUNGRY?! I GAVE YOU AN EXTRA-LARGE PORTION!
...I'm so glad...
...to be eating with you again.
OH, HERE HE IS. BRINGING MORE SUPPLIES. OVER HERE, MAYAMA!!
!!
chomp mwush
chug-a-lug
BEER
BEER
BEER

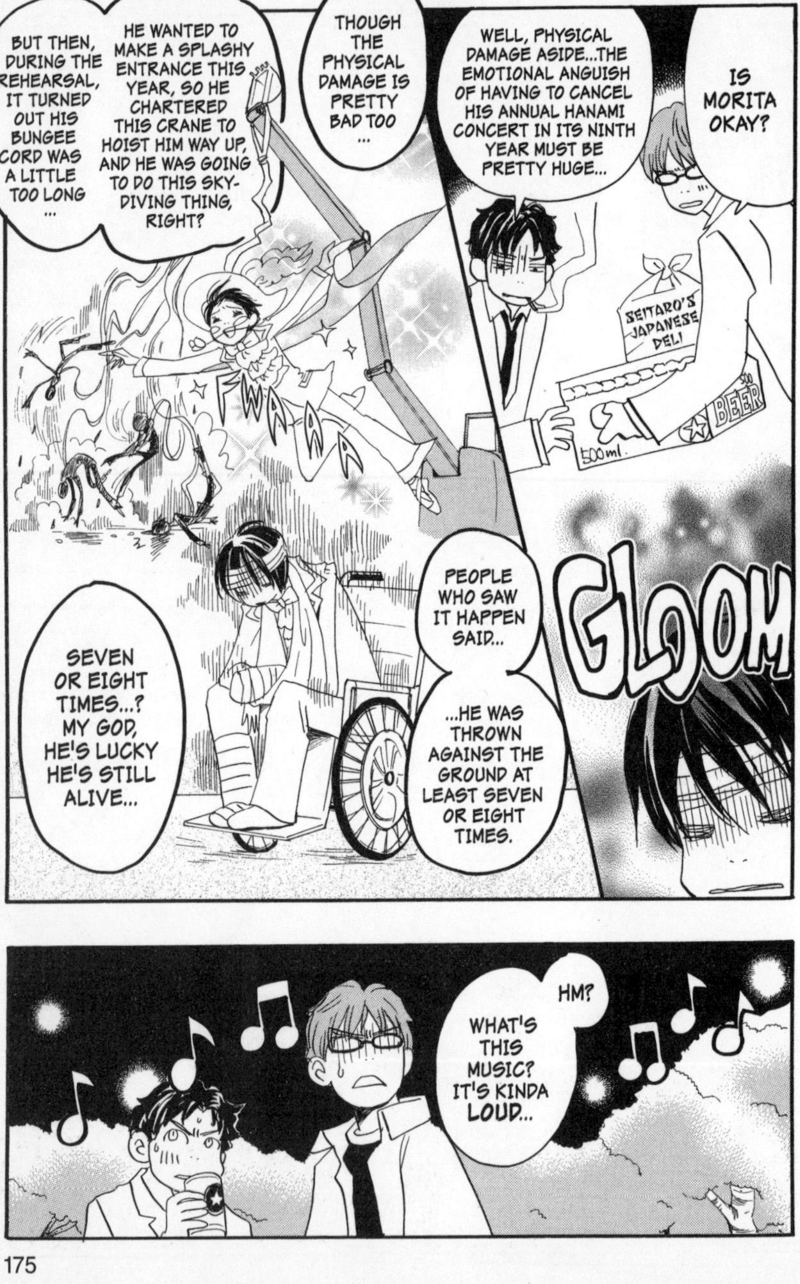
IS MORITA OKAY?
WELL, PHYSICAL DAMAGE ASIDE...THE EMOTIONAL ANGUISH OF HAVING TO CANCEL HIS ANNUAL HANAMI CONCERT IN ITS NINTH YEAR MUST BE PRETTY HUGE...
SEITARO'S JAPANESE DELI
BEER
500ml
GLOOM
THOUGH THE PHYSICAL DAMAGE IS PRETTY BAD TOO ...
HE WANTED TO MAKE A SPLASHY ENTRANCE THIS YEAR, SO HE CHARTERED THIS CRANE TO HOIST HIM WAY UP, AND HE WAS GOING TO DO THIS SKY-DIVING THING, RIGHT?
BUT THEN, DURING THE REHEARSAL, IT TURNED OUT HIS BUNGEE CORD WAS A LITTLE TOO LONG ...
FWAAA
PEOPLE WHO SAW IT HAPPEN SAID...
...HE WAS THROWN AGAINST THE GROUND AT LEAST SEVEN OR EIGHT TIMES.
SEVEN OR EIGHT TIMES...? MY GOD, HE'S LUCKY HE'S STILL ALIVE...
HM?
WHAT'S THIS MUSIC? IT'S KINDA LOUD...

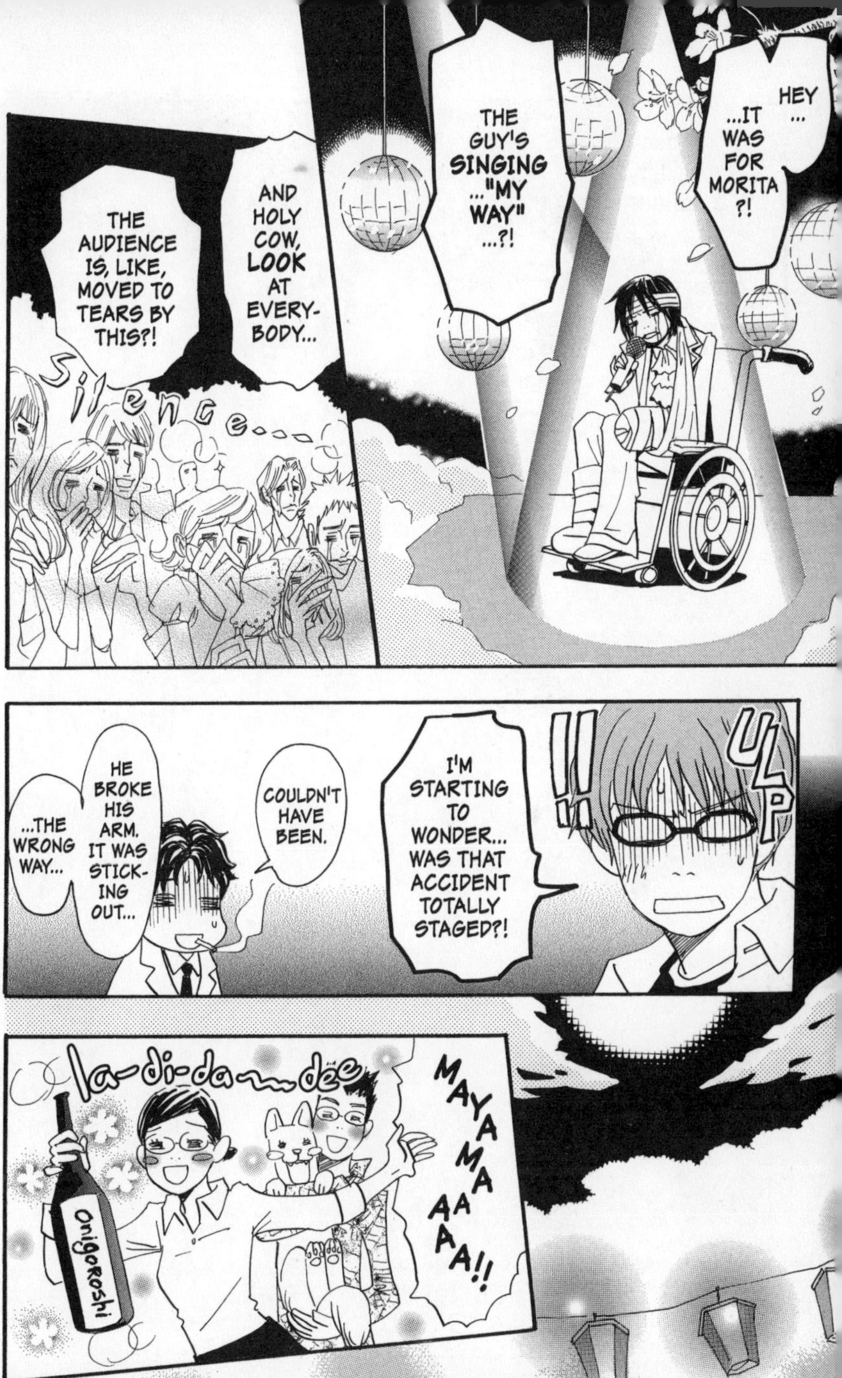
HEY ... ...IT WAS FOR MORITA ?!
THE GUY'S SINGING ..."MY WAY" ...?!
AND HOLY COW, LOOK AT EVERY-BODY...
THE AUDIENCE IS, LIKE, MOVED TO TEARS BY THIS?!
silence...
ULP
!!
I'M STARTING TO WONDER... WAS THAT ACCIDENT TOTALLY STAGED?!
COULDN'T HAVE BEEN.
HE BROKE HIS ARM. IT WAS STICK-ING OUT...
...THE WRONG WAY...
MAYAMAMAAAAAA!!
la-di-da~dee
Onigoroshi

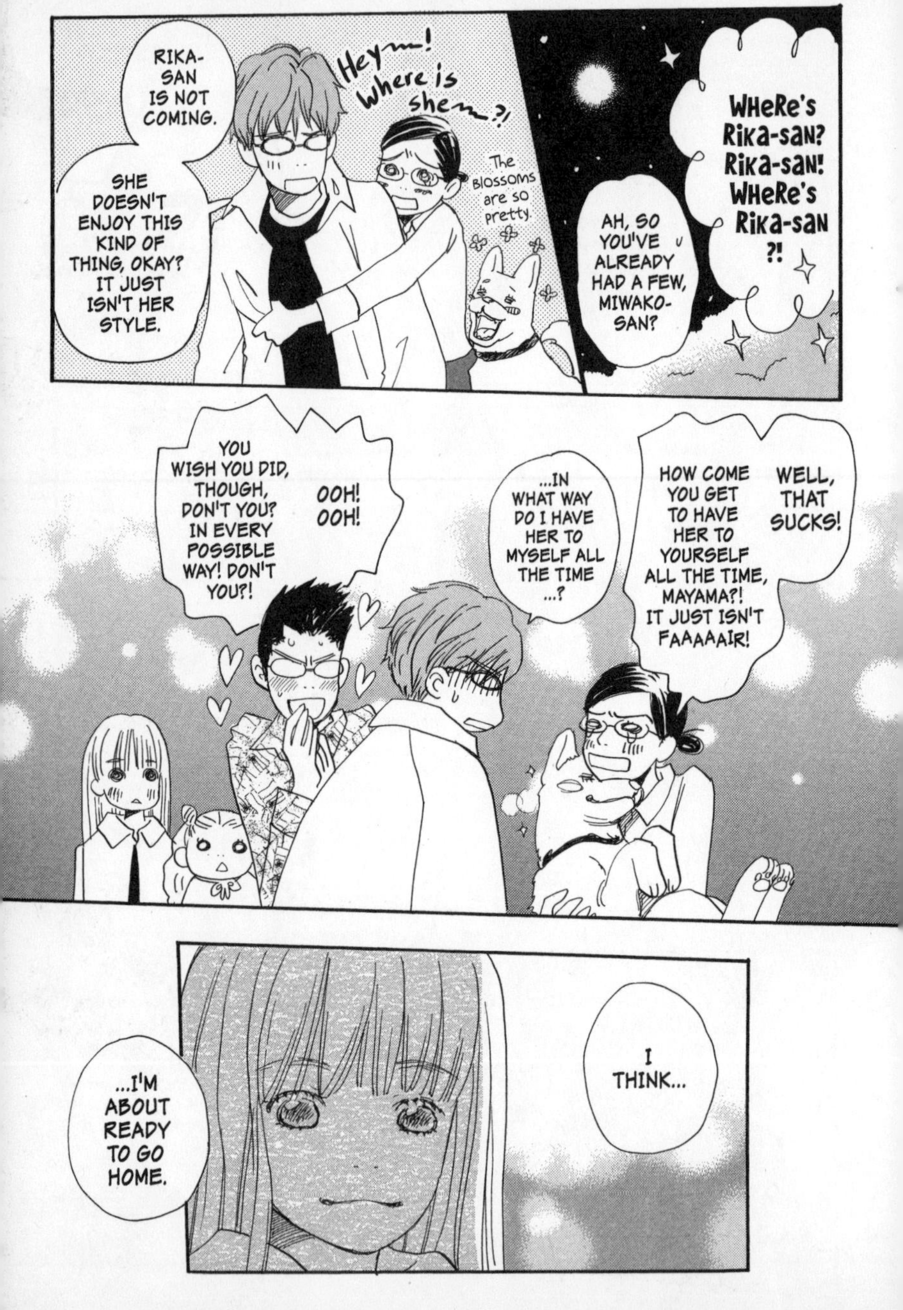
WHERE's Rika-san? Rika-san! WHERE's Rika-san ?!
AH, SO YOU'VE ALREADY HAD A FEW, MIWAKO-SAN?
Hey~! Where is she~?!
The blossoms are so pretty.
RIKA-SAN IS NOT COMING.
SHE DOESN'T ENJOY THIS KIND OF THING, OKAY? IT JUST ISN'T HER STYLE.
WELL, THAT SUCKS!
HOW COME YOU GET TO HAVE HER TO YOURSELF ALL THE TIME, MAYAMA?! IT JUST ISN'T FAAAAAIR!
...IN WHAT WAY DO I HAVE HER TO MYSELF ALL THE TIME ...?
OOH! OOH!
YOU WISH YOU DID, THOUGH, DON'T YOU? IN EVERY POSSIBLE WAY! DON'T YOU?!
I THINK...
...I'M ABOUT READY TO GO HOME.

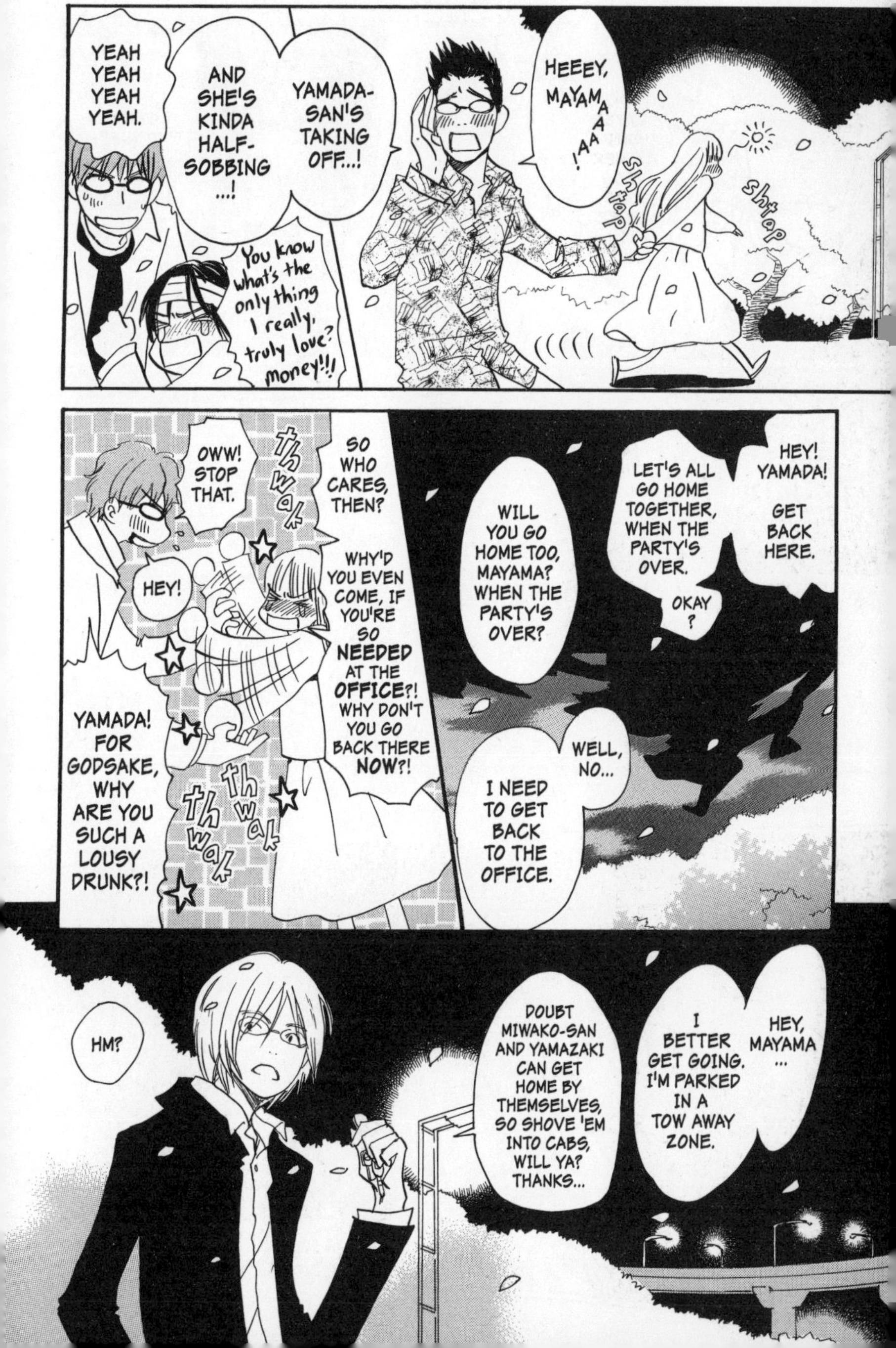
HEEEY, MAYAMAAAA!
shtap
shtap
YAMADA-SAN'S TAKING OFF...!
AND SHE'S KINDA HALF-SOBBING...!
YEAH YEAH YEAH YEAH.
You know what's the only thing I really, truly love? money!!!
HEY! YAMADA!
GET BACK HERE.
LET'S ALL GO HOME TOGETHER, WHEN THE PARTY'S OVER.
OKAY?
WILL YOU GO HOME TOO, MAYAMA? WHEN THE PARTY'S OVER?
WELL, NO...
I NEED TO GET BACK TO THE OFFICE.
SO WHO CARES, THEN?
WHY'D YOU EVEN COME, IF YOU'RE SO NEEDED AT THE OFFICE?! WHY DON'T YOU GO BACK THERE NOW?!
thwak
OWW! STOP THAT.
HEY!
thwak
thwak
YAMADA! FOR GODSAKE, WHY ARE YOU SUCH A LOUSY DRUNK?!
HEY, MAYAMA...
I BETTER GET GOING. I'M PARKED IN A TOW AWAY ZONE.
DOUBT MIWAKO-SAN AND YAMAZAKI CAN GET HOME BY THEMSELVES, SO SHOVE 'EM INTO CABS, WILL YA? THANKS...
HM?

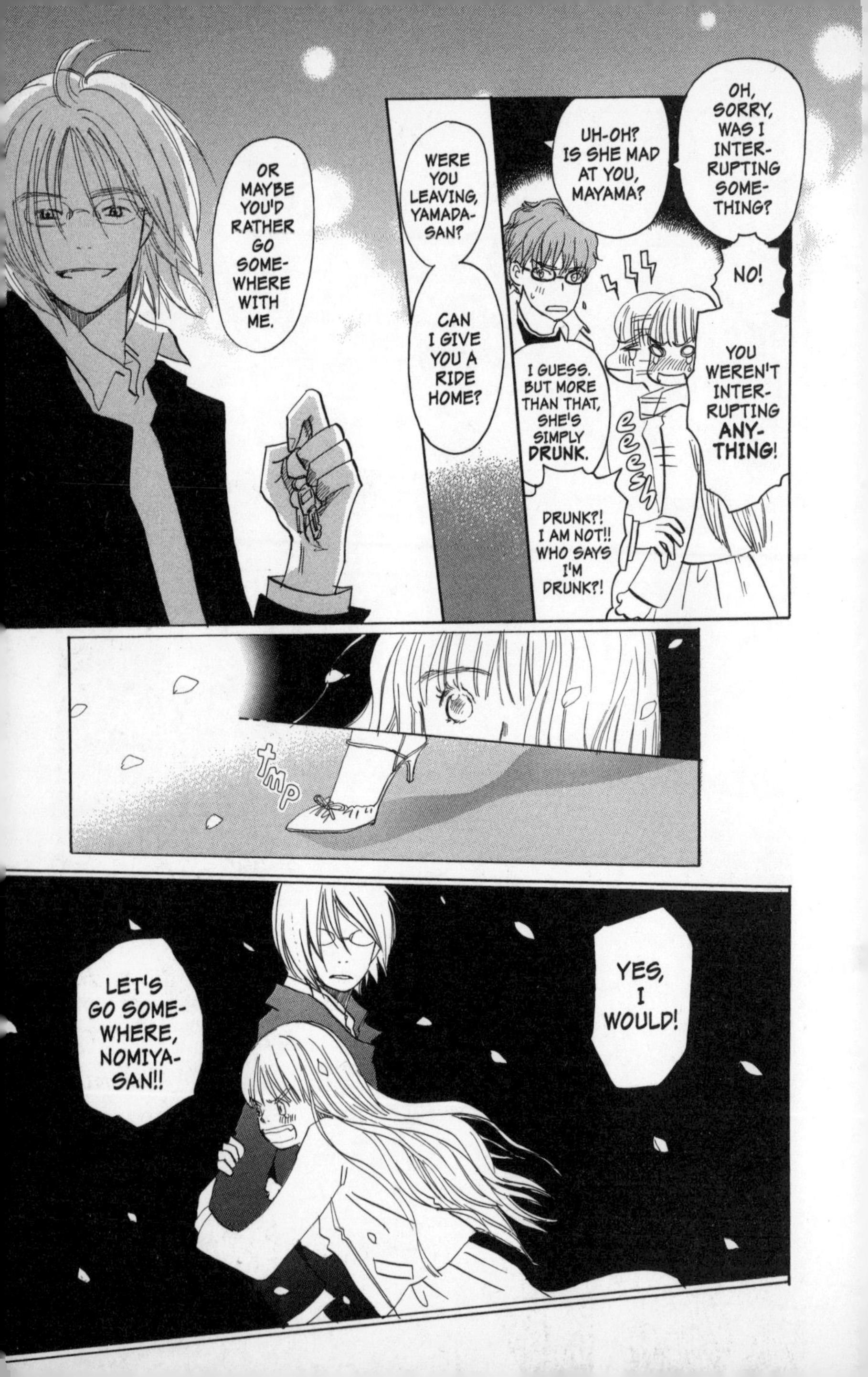

OH, SORRY, WAS I INTER-RUPTING SOME-THING?
UH-OH? IS SHE MAD AT YOU, MAYAMA?
NO!
YOU WEREN'T INTER-RUPTING ANY-THING!
I GUESS. BUT MORE THAN THAT, SHE'S SIMPLY DRUNK.
eeeew
DRUNK?! I AM NOT!! WHO SAYS I'M DRUNK?!
WERE YOU LEAVING, YAMADA-SAN?
CAN I GIVE YOU A RIDE HOME?
OR MAYBE YOU'D RATHER GO SOME-WHERE WITH ME.
tmp
YES, I WOULD!
LET'S GO SOME-WHERE, NOMIYA-SAN!!

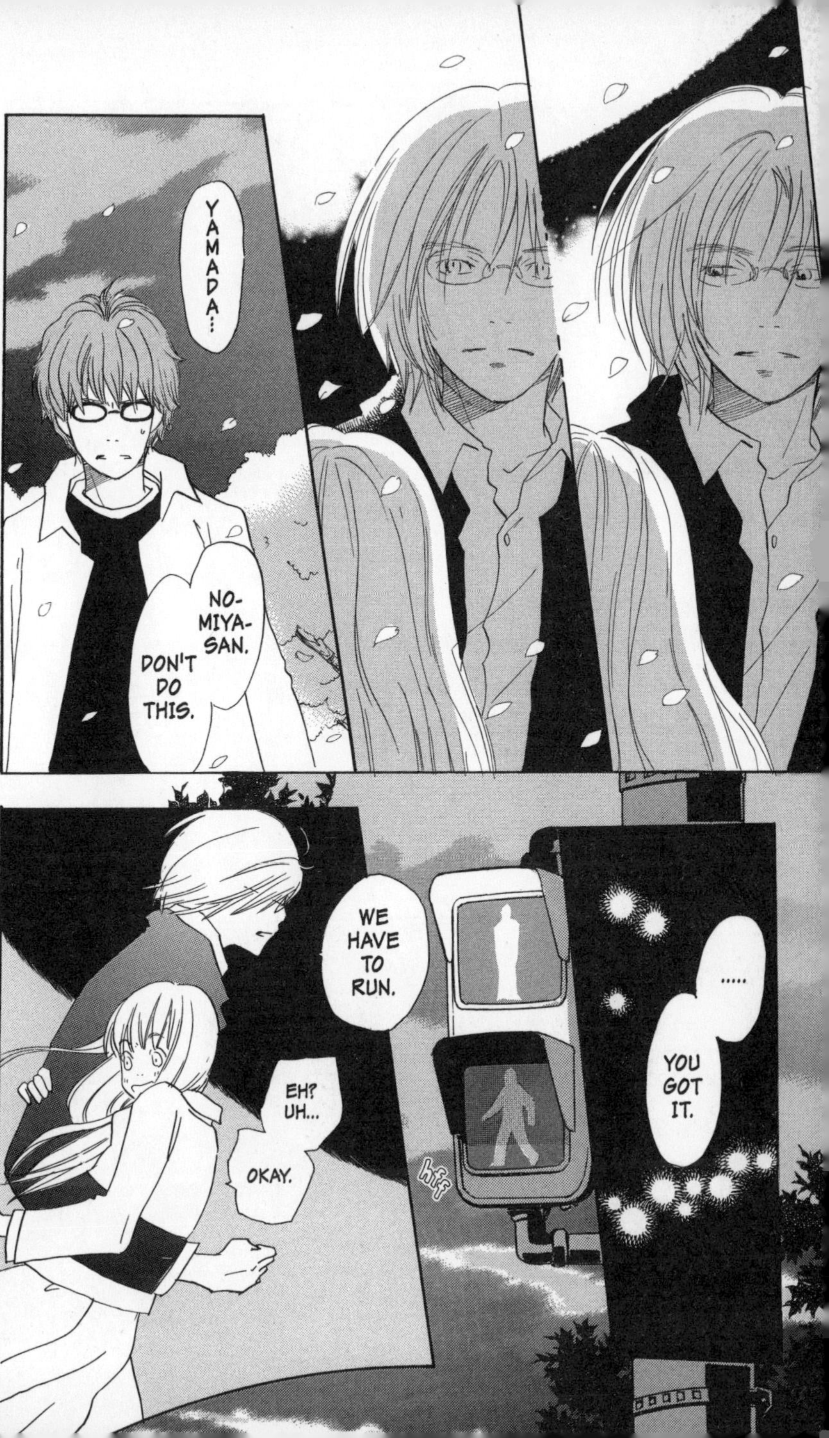
YAMADA...
NO-MIYA-SAN. DON'T DO THIS.
.....
YOU GOT IT.
WE HAVE TO RUN.
EH? UH...
OKAY.
hff

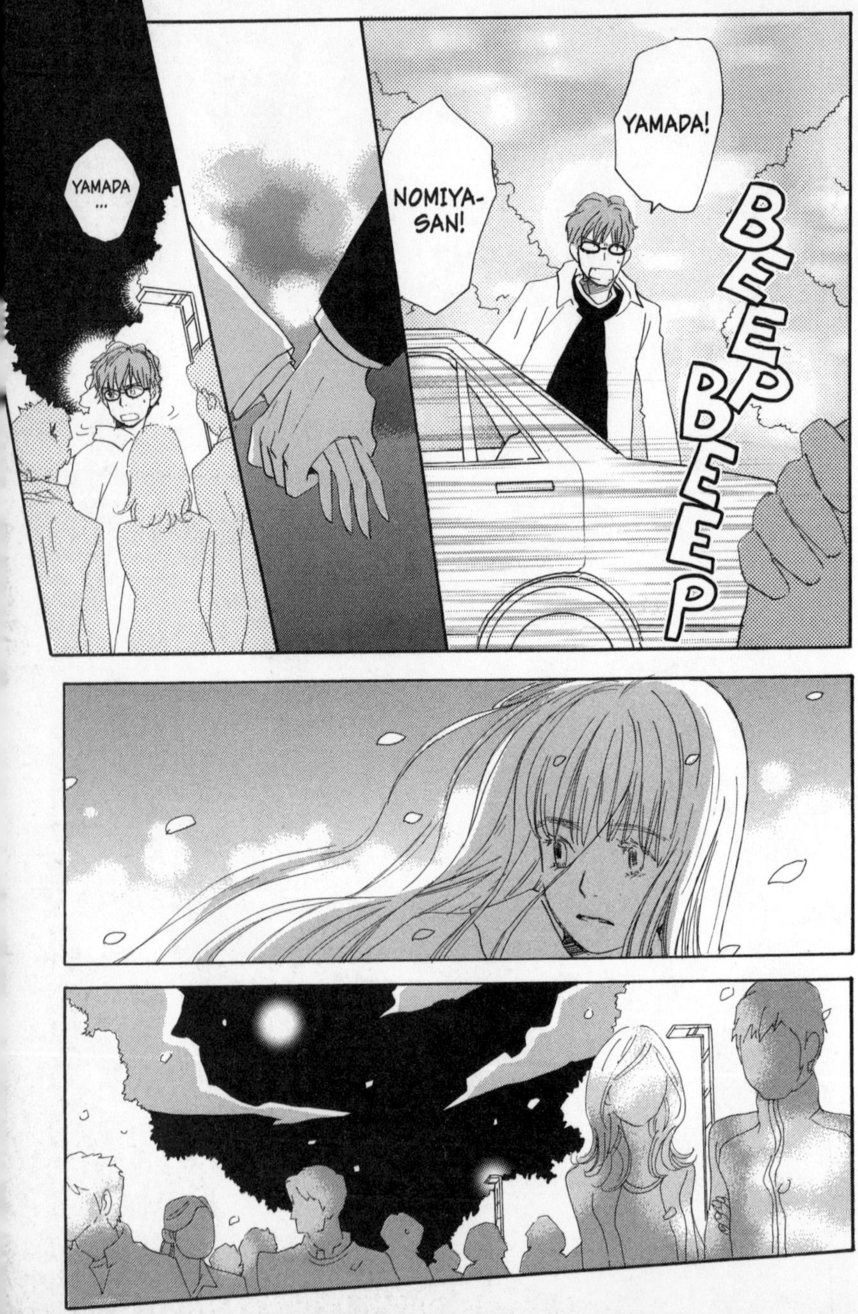
YAMADA!
NOMIYA-SAN!
BEEP BEEP
YAMADA ...

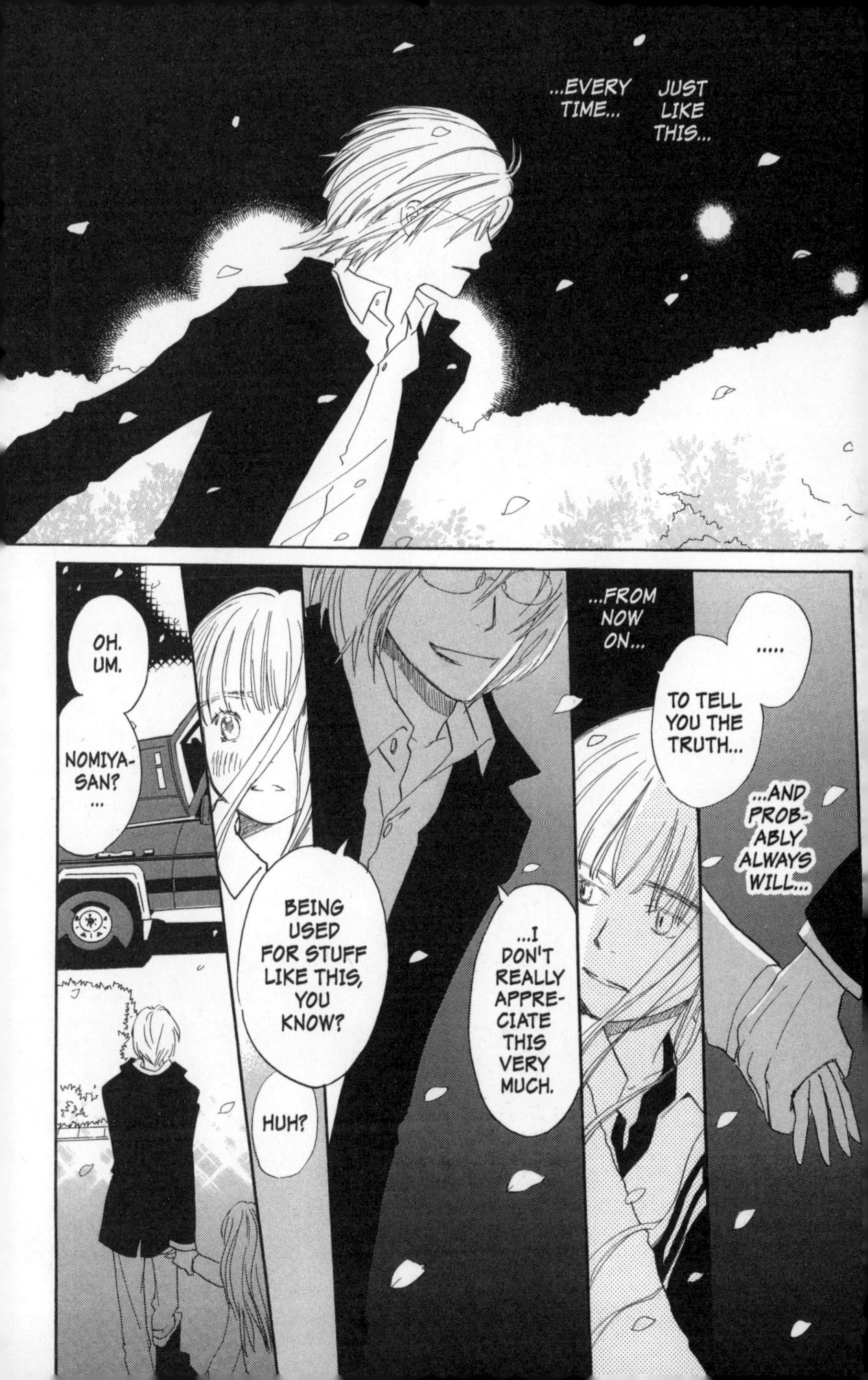
JUST LIKE THIS...
...EVERY TIME...
...AND PROBABLY ALWAYS WILL...
.....
TO TELL YOU THE TRUTH...
...I DON'T REALLY APPRECIATE THIS VERY MUCH.
...FROM NOW ON...
BEING USED FOR STUFF LIKE THIS, YOU KNOW?
HUH?
OH. UM.
NOMIYA-SAN? ...

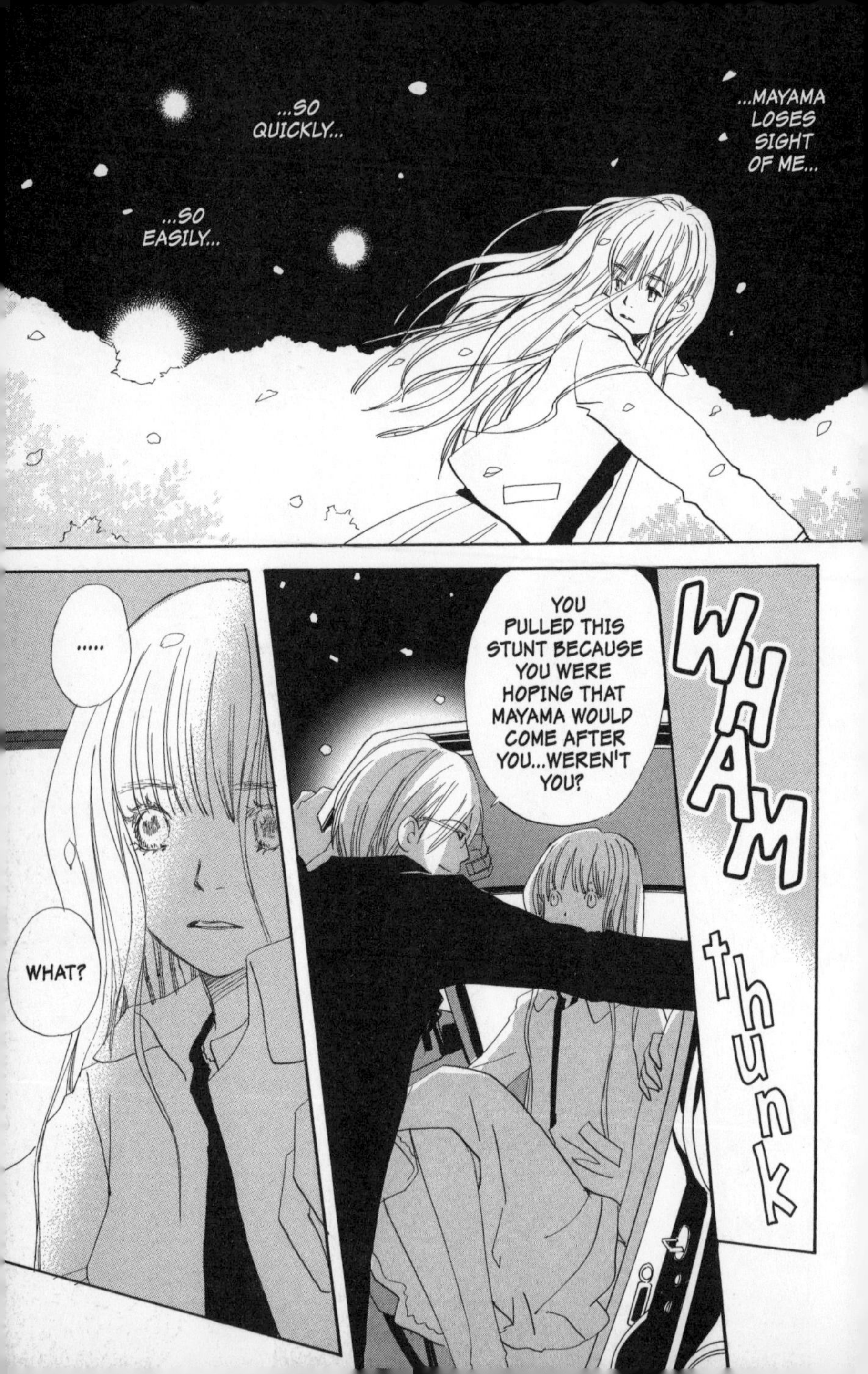
...MAYAMA LOSES SIGHT OF ME...
...SO QUICKLY...
...SO EASILY...
WHAM
YOU PULLED THIS STUNT BECAUSE YOU WERE HOPING THAT MAYAMA WOULD COME AFTER YOU...WEREN'T YOU?
thunk
......
WHAT?

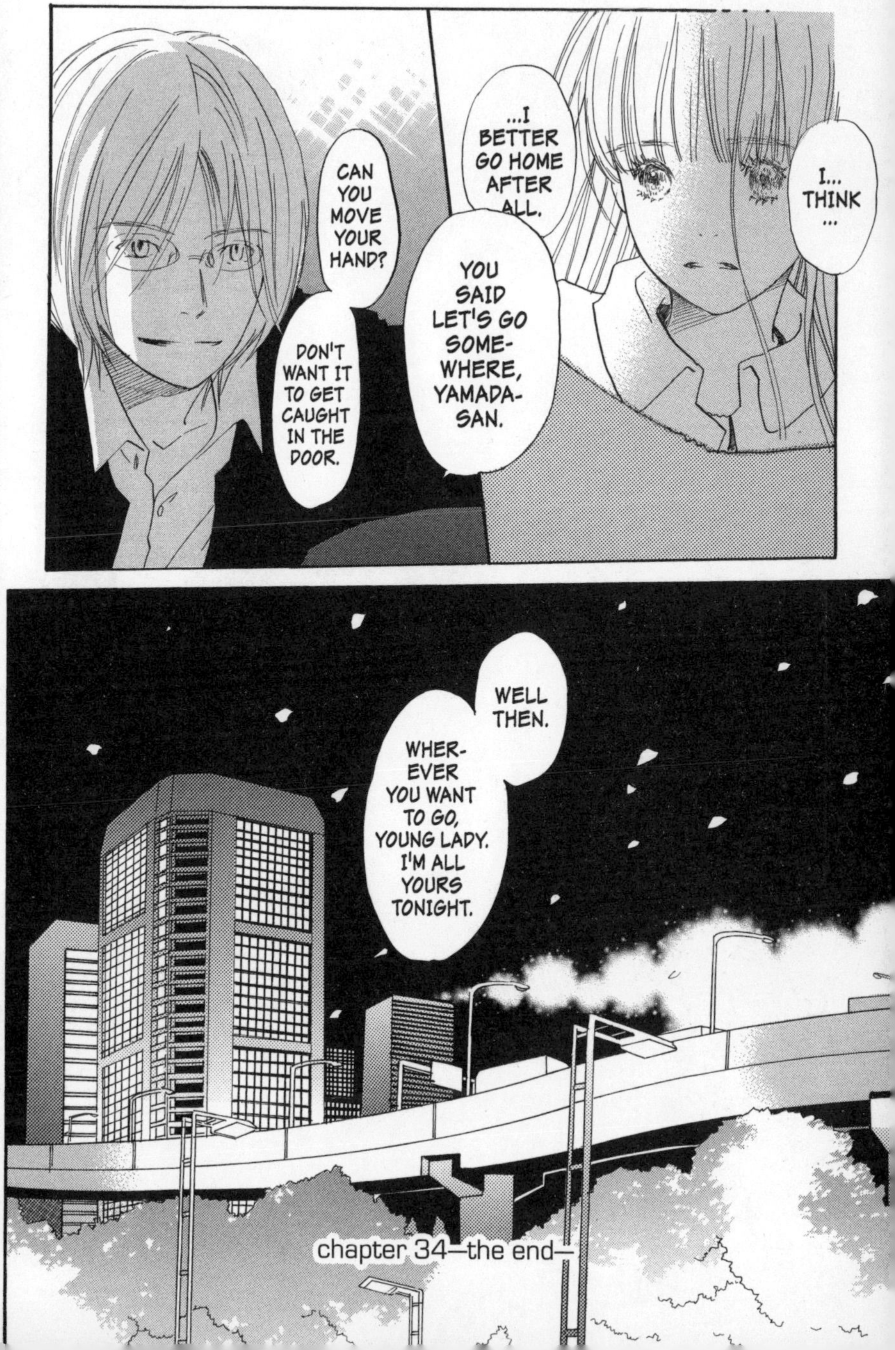
I... THINK ...
...I BETTER GO HOME AFTER ALL.
YOU SAID LET'S GO SOMEWHERE, YAMADA-SAN.
CAN YOU MOVE YOUR HAND?
DON'T WANT IT TO GET CAUGHT IN THE DOOR.
WELL THEN.
WHEREVER YOU WANT TO GO, YOUNG LADY. I'M ALL YOURS TONIGHT.
chapter 34—the end—

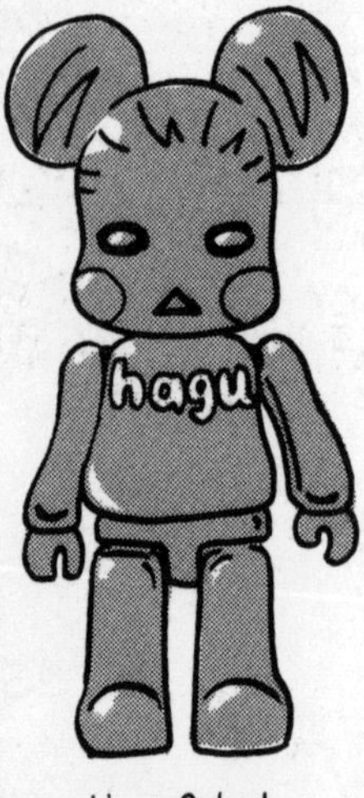
hagu

Hagu Robot
produced by Shinobu Morita
(available in 38 colors)

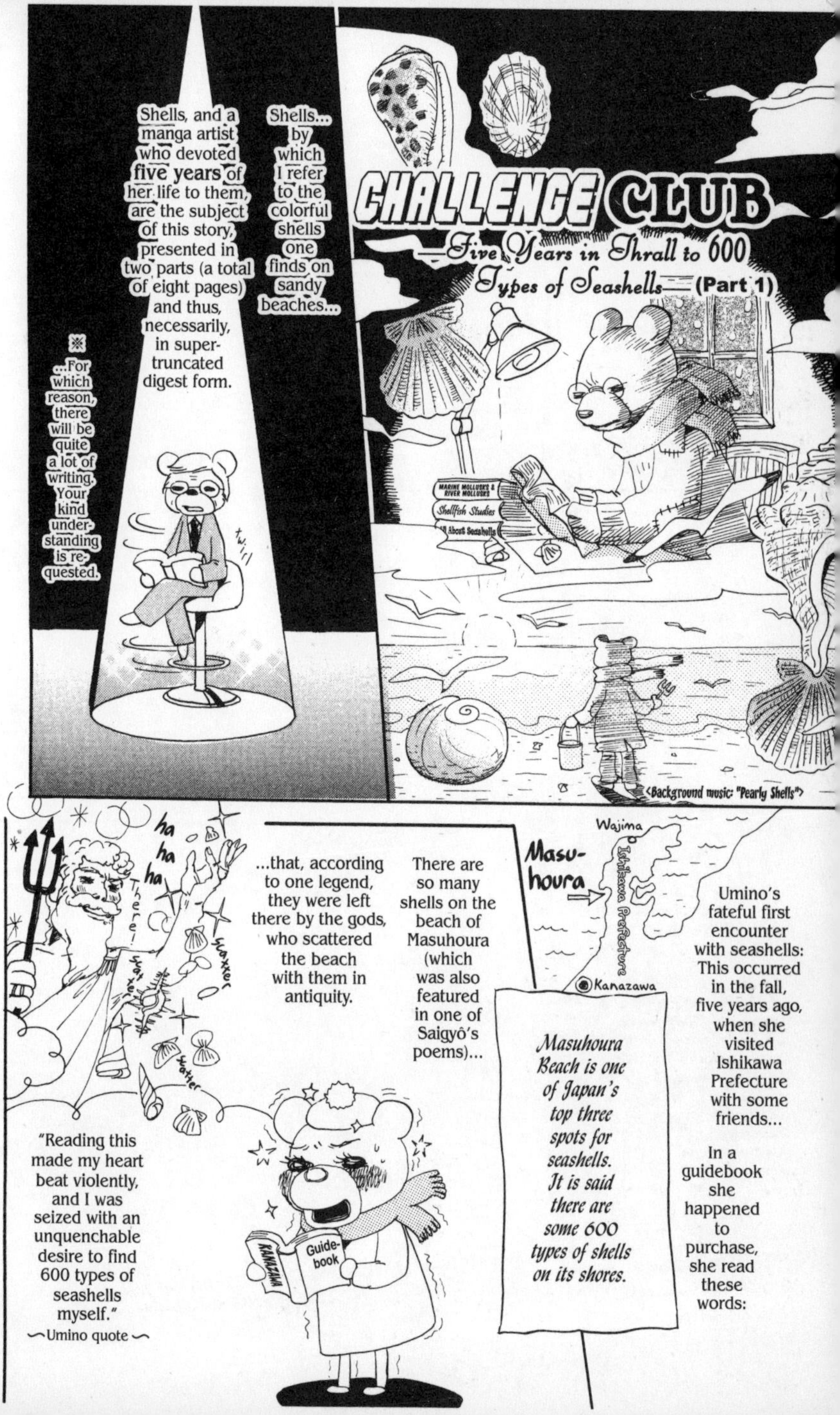
CHALLENGE CLUB
—Five Years in Thrall to 600 Types of Seashells— (Part 1)
MARINE MOLLUSKS & RIVER MOLLUSKS
Shellfish Studies
All About Seashells
<Background music: "Pearly Shells">
Shells... by which I refer to the colorful shells one finds on sandy beaches...
Shells, and a manga artist who devoted **five years** of her life to them, are the subject of this story, presented in two parts (a total of eight pages) and thus, necessarily, in super-truncated digest form.
※ ...For which reason, there will be quite a lot of writing. Your kind understanding is requested.
Twirl
Umino's fateful first encounter with seashells: This occurred in the fall, five years ago, when she visited Ishikawa Prefecture with some friends...
In a guidebook she happened to purchase, she read these words:
Wajima
Masuhoura
Ishikawa Prefecture
Kanazawa
Masuhoura Beach is one of Japan's top three spots for seashells. It is said there are some 600 types of shells on its shores.
There are so many shells on the beach of Masuhoura (which was also featured in one of Saigyô's poems)...
...that, according to one legend, they were left there by the gods, who scattered the beach with them in antiquity.
ha ha ha
There!
Skatter
Skatter
Skatter
KANAZAWA
Guide-book
"Reading this made my heart beat violently, and I was seized with an unquenchable desire to find 600 types of seashells myself."
~Umino quote~

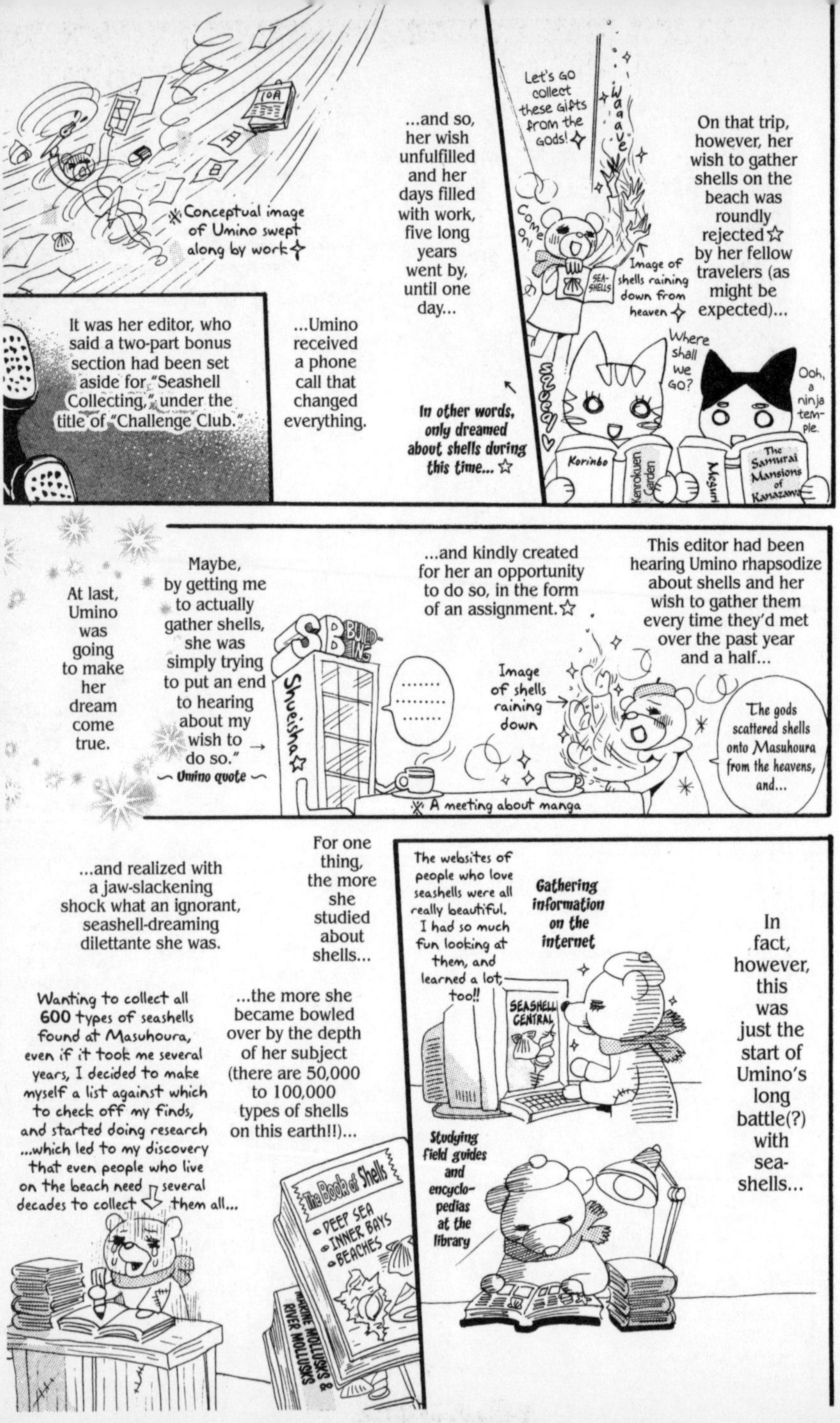
On that trip, however, her wish to gather shells on the beach was roundly rejected☆ by her fellow travelers (as might be expected)...
Let's GO collect these Gifts from the Gods!
Waaave
Come on!
SEA-SHELLS
Image of shells raining down from heaven
Where shall we GO?
Ooh, a ninja temple.
Korinbo
Kenrokuen Garden
Meguri
The Samurai Mansions of Kanazawa
In other words, only dreamed about shells during this time...☆
...and so, her wish unfulfilled and her days filled with work, five long years went by, until one day...
※Conceptual image of Umino swept along by work
...Umino received a phone call that changed everything.
It was her editor, who said a two-part bonus section had been set aside for "Seashell Collecting," under the title of "Challenge Club."
This editor had been hearing Umino rhapsodize about shells and her wish to gather them every time they'd met over the past year and a half...
The gods scattered shells onto Masuhoura from the heavens, and...
Image of shells raining down
...and kindly created for her an opportunity to do so, in the form of an assignment.☆
....
SB BUILDING
Shueisha☆
※A meeting about manga
Maybe, by getting me to actually gather shells, she was simply trying to put an end to hearing about my wish to do so." → ~Umino quote~
At last, Umino was going to make her dream come true.
In fact, however, this was just the start of Umino's long battle(?) with sea-shells...
Gathering information on the internet
The websites of people who love seashells were all really beautiful. I had so much fun looking at them, and learned a lot, too!!
SEASHELL CENTRAL
Studying field guides and encyclopedias at the library
For one thing, the more she studied about shells...
...the more she became bowled over by the depth of her subject (there are 50,000 to 100,000 types of shells on this earth!!)...
...and realized with a jaw-slackening shock what an ignorant, seashell-dreaming dilettante she was.
Wanting to collect all 600 types of seashells found at Masuhoura, even if it took me several years, I decided to make myself a list against which to check off my finds, and started doing research ...which led to my discovery that even people who live on the beach need several decades to collect them all...
The Book of Shells
DEEP SEA
INNER BAYS
BEACHES
MARINE MOLLUSKS & RIVER MOLLUSKS

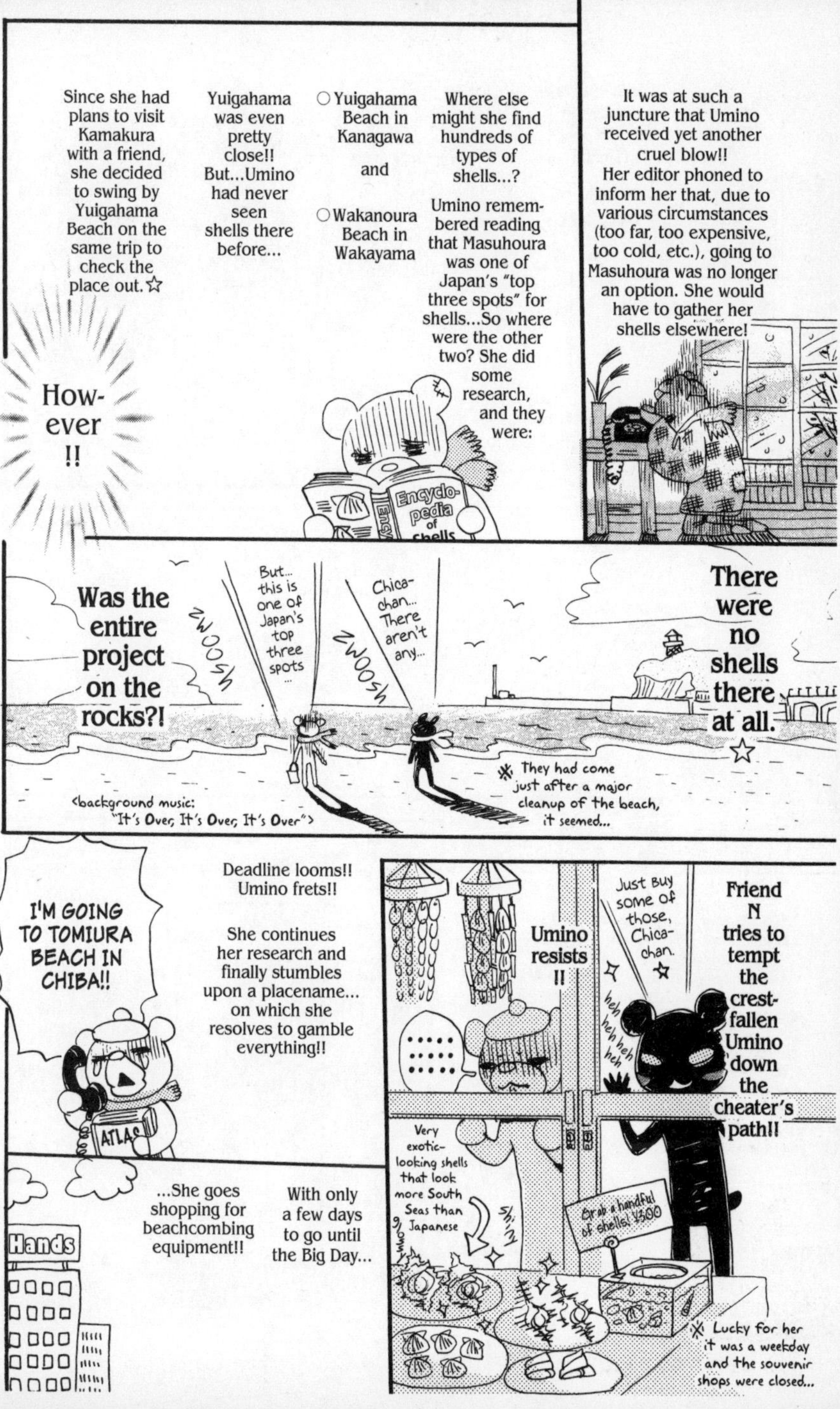

It was at such a juncture that Umino received yet another cruel blow!! Her editor phoned to inform her that, due to various circumstances (too far, too expensive, too cold, etc.), going to Masuhoura was no longer an option. She would have to gather her shells elsewhere!
Where else might she find hundreds of types of shells...?
Umino remembered reading that Masuhoura was one of Japan's "top three spots" for shells...So where were the other two? She did some research, and they were:
○Yuigahama Beach in Kanagawa
and
○Wakanoura Beach in Wakayama
Encyclopedia of Shells
Yuigahama was even pretty close!! But...Umino had never seen shells there before...
Since she had plans to visit Kamakura with a friend, she decided to swing by Yuigahama Beach on the same trip to check the place out. ☆
However!!
There were no shells there at all. ☆
Chica-chan... There aren't any...
ZWOOSH
But... this is one of Japan's top three spots...
ZWOOSH
Was the entire project on the rocks?!
※They had come just after a major cleanup of the beach, it seemed...
<background music: "It's Over, It's Over, It's Over">
Friend N tries to tempt the crestfallen Umino down the cheater's path!!
Just buy some of those, Chica-chan. ☆
heh heh heh heh
Umino resists!!
......
Very exotic-looking shells that look more South Seas than Japanese
shiny
shiny
Grab a handful of shells! ¥300
※Lucky for her it was a weekday and the souvenir shops were closed...
Deadline looms!! Umino frets!!
She continues her research and finally stumbles upon a placename... on which she resolves to gamble everything!!
I'M GOING TO TOMIURA BEACH IN CHIBA!!
ATLAS
With only a few days to go until the Big Day...
...She goes shopping for beachcombing equipment!!
Hands

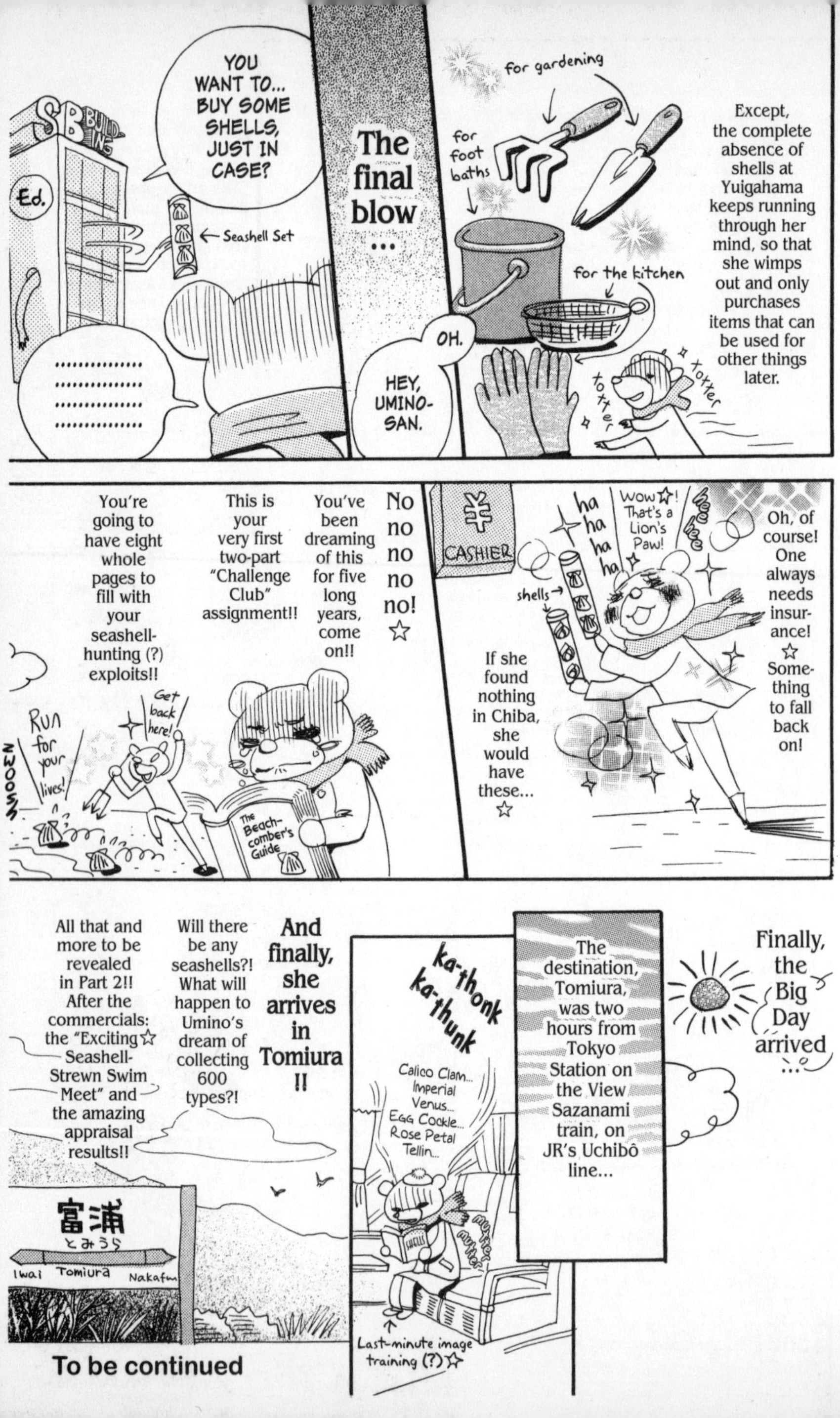
Except, the complete absence of shells at Yuigahama keeps running through her mind, so that she wimps out and only purchases items that can be used for other things later.
for gardening
for foot baths
for the kitchen
totter totter
The final blow...
OH.
HEY, UMINO-SAN.
SB BUILDING
Ed.
YOU WANT TO... BUY SOME SHELLS, JUST IN CASE?
← Seashell Set
....
....
....
....
Oh, of course! One always needs insurance! ☆ Something to fall back on!
Wow☆! That's a Lion's Paw!
hee hee
ha ha ha ha
CASHIER
shells
If she found nothing in Chiba, she would have these... ☆
No no no no no! ☆
You've been dreaming of this for five long years, come on!!
This is your very first two-part "Challenge Club" assignment!!
You're going to have eight whole pages to fill with your seashell-hunting (?) exploits!!
Get back here!
Run for your lives!
SWOOSH
The Beach-comber's Guide
Finally, the Big Day arrived...
The destination, Tomiura, was two hours from Tokyo Station on the View Sazanami train, on JR's Uchibô line...
ka-thonk ka-thunk
Calico Clam... Imperial Venus... Egg Cockle... Rose Petal Tellin...
SHELLS
mutter mutter
Last-minute image training (?)☆
And finally, she arrives in Tomiura!!
Will there be any seashells?! What will happen to Umino's dream of collecting 600 types?!
All that and more to be revealed in Part 2!! After the commercials: the "Exciting☆ Seashell-Strewn Swim Meet" and the amazing appraisal results!!
富浦
とみうら
Iwai Tomiura Nakafu
To be continued

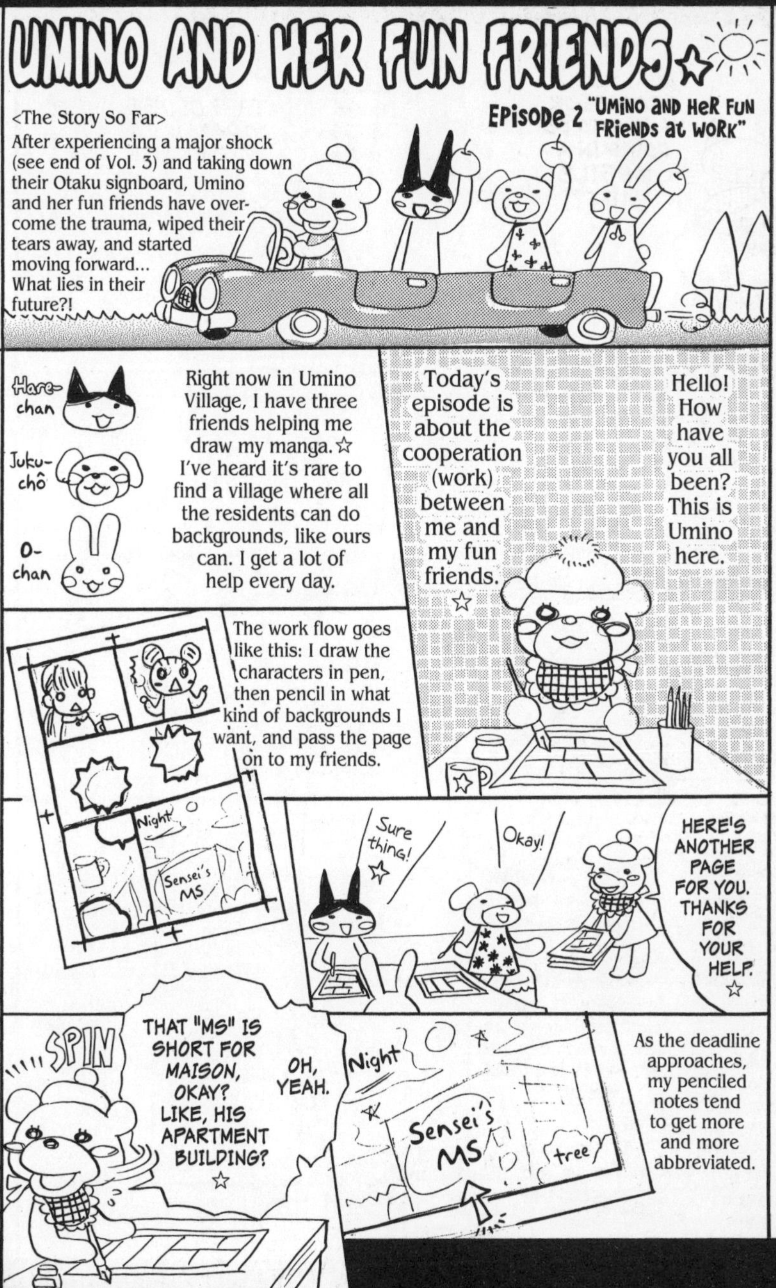
UMINO AND HER FUN FRIENDS☆
Episode 2 "Umino and Her Fun Friends at Work"
<The Story So Far>
After experiencing a major shock (see end of Vol. 3) and taking down their Otaku signboard, Umino and her fun friends have overcome the trauma, wiped their tears away, and started moving forward... What lies in their future?!
Hello! How have you all been? This is Umino here.
Today's episode is about the cooperation (work) between me and my fun friends. ☆
Right now in Umino Village, I have three friends helping me draw my manga.☆ I've heard it's rare to find a village where all the residents can do backgrounds, like ours can. I get a lot of help every day.
Hare-chan
Juku-chô
O-chan
The work flow goes like this: I draw the characters in pen, then pencil in what kind of backgrounds I want, and pass the page on to my friends.
Night
Sensei's MS
HERE'S ANOTHER PAGE FOR YOU. THANKS FOR YOUR HELP. ☆
Okay!
Sure thing! ☆
As the deadline approaches, my penciled notes tend to get more and more abbreviated.
Night
Sensei's MS
tree
OH, YEAH.
THAT "MS" IS SHORT FOR MAISON, OKAY? LIKE, HIS APARTMENT BUILDING? ☆
SPIN

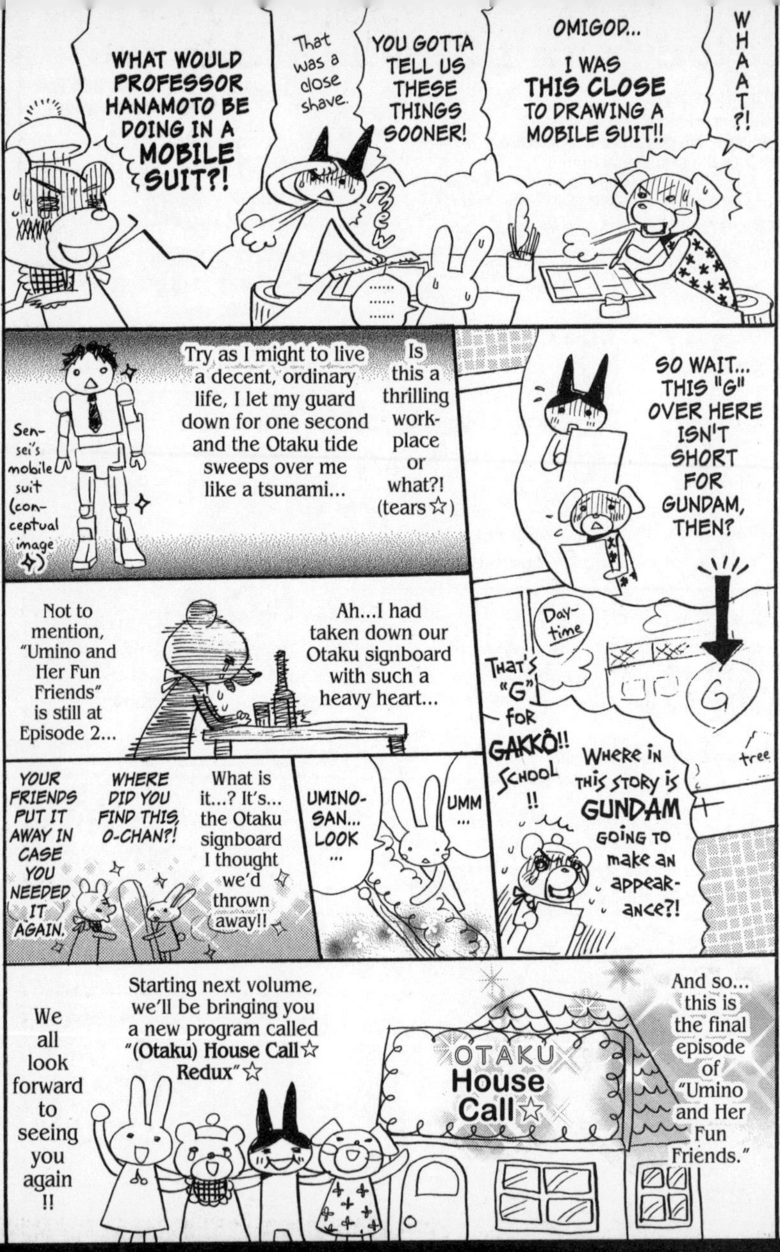
WHAAT?!
OMIGOD... I WAS THIS CLOSE TO DRAWING A MOBILE SUIT!!
YOU GOTTA TELL US THESE THINGS SOONER!
That was a close shave.
Phew
WHAT WOULD PROFESSOR HANAMOTO BE DOING IN A MOBILE SUIT?!
......
......
......
SO WAIT... THIS "G" OVER HERE ISN'T SHORT FOR GUNDAM, THEN?
Is this a thrilling work-place or what?! (tears☆)
Try as I might to live a decent, ordinary life, I let my guard down for one second and the Otaku tide sweeps over me like a tsunami...
Sen-sei's mobile suit (con-ceptual image ✧)
Day-time
G
THAT'S "G" FOR GAKKÔ!! SCHOOL!!
tree
WHERE IN THIS STORY IS GUNDAM GOING TO MAKE AN APPEAR-ANCE?!
Ah...I had taken down our Otaku signboard with such a heavy heart...
Not to mention, "Umino and Her Fun Friends" is still at Episode 2...
UMM...
UMINO-SAN... LOOK...
What is it...? It's... the Otaku signboard I thought we'd thrown away!!
WHERE DID YOU FIND THIS, O-CHAN?!
YOUR FRIENDS PUT IT AWAY IN CASE YOU NEEDED IT AGAIN.
And so... this is the final episode of "Umino and Her Fun Friends."
OTAKU House Call☆
Starting next volume, we'll be bringing you a new program called "(Otaku) House Call☆ Redux"☆
We all look forward to seeing you again!!

★END★

I'm keeping a rental diary.
http://www2.diary.ne.jp/user/162279/

Honey and Clover Study Guide

Page 24, panel 4: If you love your child...
A Japanese proverb that means don't be overprotective, and let your child experience some hardships for their own good.

Page 33, panel 1: Omiki
Sacred sake served at Shinto rites. At weddings, the bride and groom drink three times from three different cups of sake in a ritual called *san san ku do* (三々九度)。

Page 41, author note: Yakisoba-bread
Yakisoba is a stir-fried noodle dish similar to chow mein. When it is served in a bun, it is called *yakisoba-pan*. The Portuguese were the first to introduce bread to Japan, and the Portuguese word (*pan*) is still used to this day.

Page 61, panel 3: Ume
Prunus mume, a type of Asian plum, also called Japanese apricot. Ume are considered to be effective against parasites and ulcers, and to promote a healthy digestive system.

Page 61, author note: Takikomi gohan
Rice boiled or cooked with meat or seafood, vegetables and seasonings, somewhat like a rice pilaf. it is sometimes also called *gomoku gohan*.

Page 130, panel 1: Don Quijote
A chain of over 159 discount stores in Japan, with four locations in Hawaii. The chain is so well known in Japan that it is often abbreviated to Donki. Don Quijote carries a wide range of goods, from groceries to electronics.

Page 141, panel 5: Cover his face
In Japan, the face of a deceased person is sometimes covered with a white cloth. Plus, the bowl and flower behind Professor Tange look like offerings at a wake.

Page 142, panel 1: Goddess Benten
Also called Benzaiten. The Japanese version of the Indian goddess Sarasvati. She is the goddess of eloquence, music, words, love, and the arts. She is also one of the Seven Gods of Fortune.

Pg 165, panel 2: Shikoku:
The Sanuki region of Shikoku is famous for udon. Shikoku is the smallest of the four main Japanese islands.

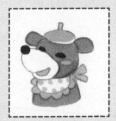

Honey and Clover has won the 27th Kodansha Manga Award, a very wonderful honor indeed. It made me very happy and filled me with a renewed resolve to keep working hard... From the bottom of my heart I thank all the people who have picked up this manga. Please watch over me from now on, too, as I'll be doing my best.

-Chica Umino

Chica Umino was born in Tokyo and started out as a product designer and illustrator. Her beloved *Honey and Clover* debuted in 2000 and received the Kodansha Manga Award in 2003. *Honey and Clover* was also nominated for the Tezuka Culture Prize and an award from the Japan Media Arts Festival.

HONEY AND CLOVER
VOL. 5
The Shojo Beat Manga Edition

This manga volume contains material that was originally published in English in *Shojo Beat* magazine, November 2008-January 2009. Artwork in the magazine may have been slightly altered from that presented here.

STORY AND ART BY CHICA UMINO

English Translation & Adaptation/Akemi Wegmuller
Touch-up Art & Lettering/Sabrina Heep
Design/Yukiko Whitley
Editor/Pancha Diaz

Editor in Chief, Books/Alvin Lu
Editor in Chief, Magazines/Marc Weidenbaum
VP, Publishing Licensing/Rika Inouye
VP, Sales & Product Marketing/Gonzalo Ferreyra
VP, Creative/Linda Espinosa
Publisher/Hyoe Narita

Printed in Canada

Published by VIZ Media, LLC
P.O. Box 77010
San Francisco, CA 94107

www.viz.com

Shojo Beat Manga Edition
10 9 8 7 6 5 4 3 2 1
First printing, March 2009

RATED T+ FOR OLDER TEEN

PARENTAL ADVISORY
HONEY AND CLOVER is rated T+ for Older Teen and is recommended for ages 16 and up. This volume contains adult situations.

ratings.viz.com

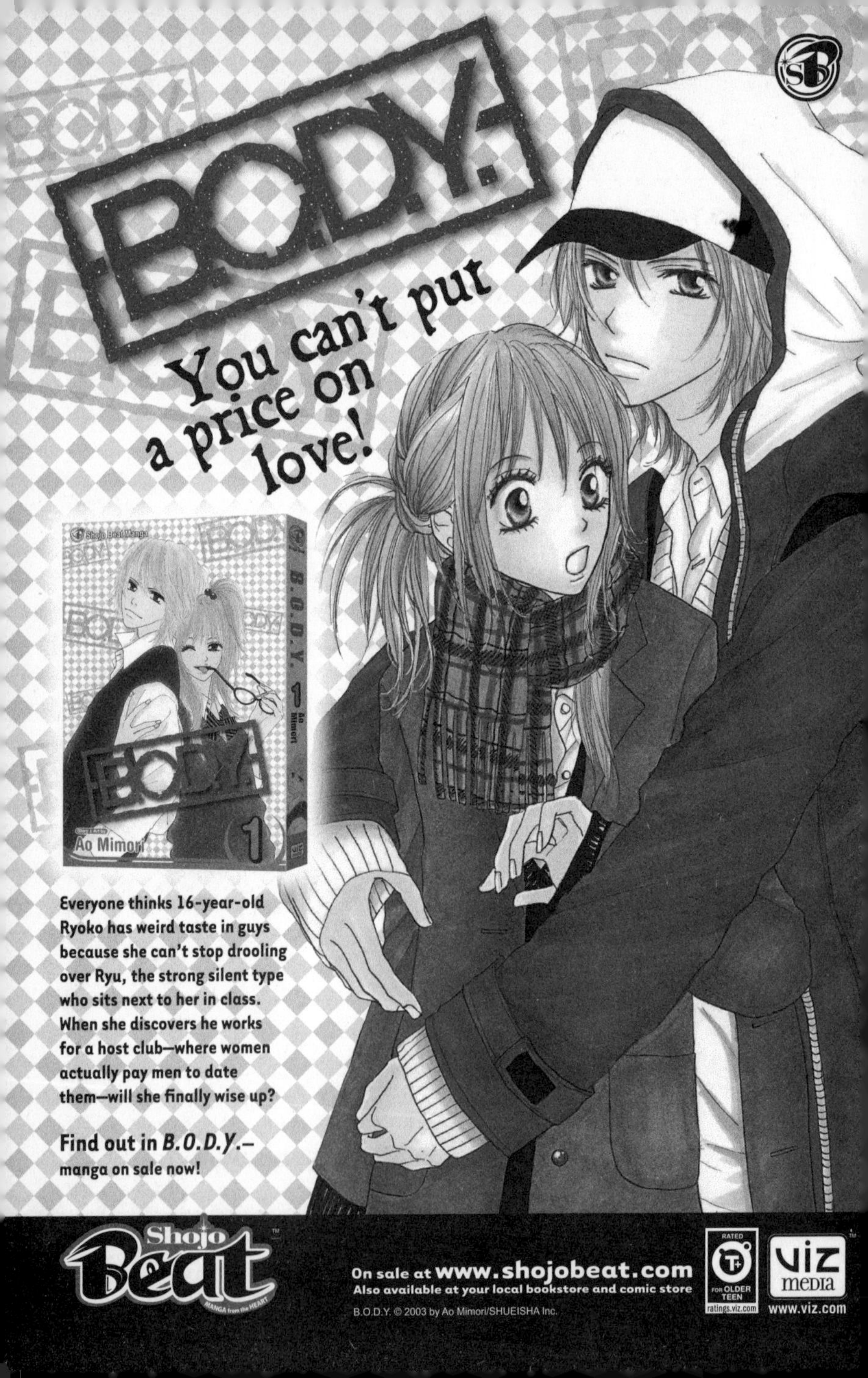
B.O.D.Y.
You can't put a price on love!
Shojo Beat Manga
B.O.D.Y.
1
Ao Mimori
Everyone thinks 16-year-old Ryoko has weird taste in guys because she can't stop drooling over Ryu, the strong silent type who sits next to her in class. When she discovers he works for a host club—where women actually pay men to date them—will she finally wise up?
Find out in B.O.D.Y.– manga on sale now!
Shojo Beat
MANGA from the HEART
On sale at www.shojobeat.com
Also available at your local bookstore and comic store
B.O.D.Y. © 2003 by Ao Mimori/SHUEISHA Inc.
RATED T+ FOR OLDER TEEN
ratings.viz.com
VIZ media
www.viz.com

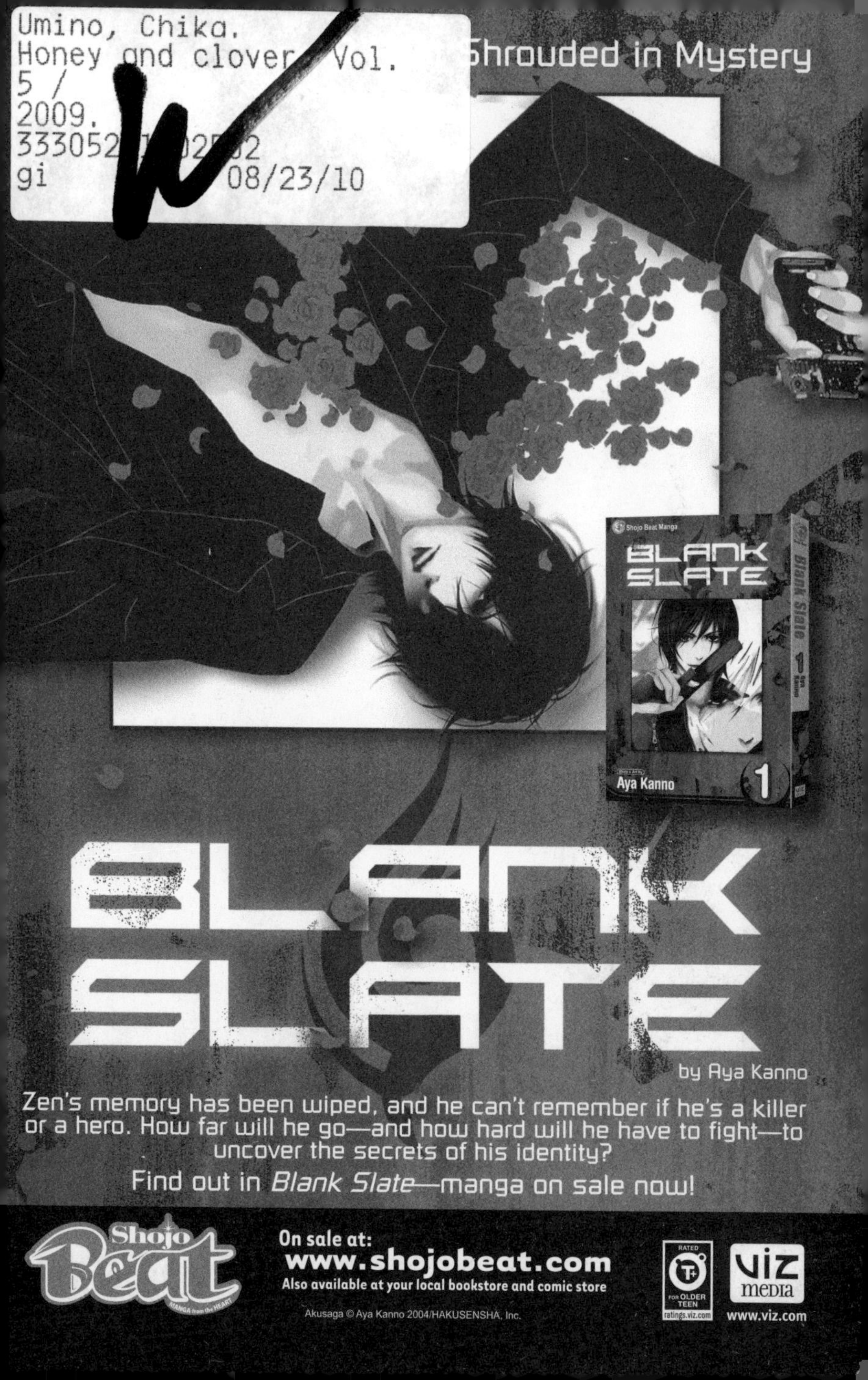
Shrouded in Mystery
Shojo Beat Manga
BLANK SLATE
Aya Kanno
1
BLANK SLATE
by Aya Kanno
Zen's memory has been wiped, and he can't remember if he's a killer or a hero. How far will he go—and how hard will he have to fight—to uncover the secrets of his identity?
Find out in Blank Slate—manga on sale now!
Shojo Beat
MANGA from the HEART
On sale at:
www.shojobeat.com
Also available at your local bookstore and comic store
Akusaga © Aya Kanno 2004/HAKUSENSHA, Inc.
RATED T+ FOR OLDER TEEN
ratings.viz.com
VIZ MEDIA
www.viz.com

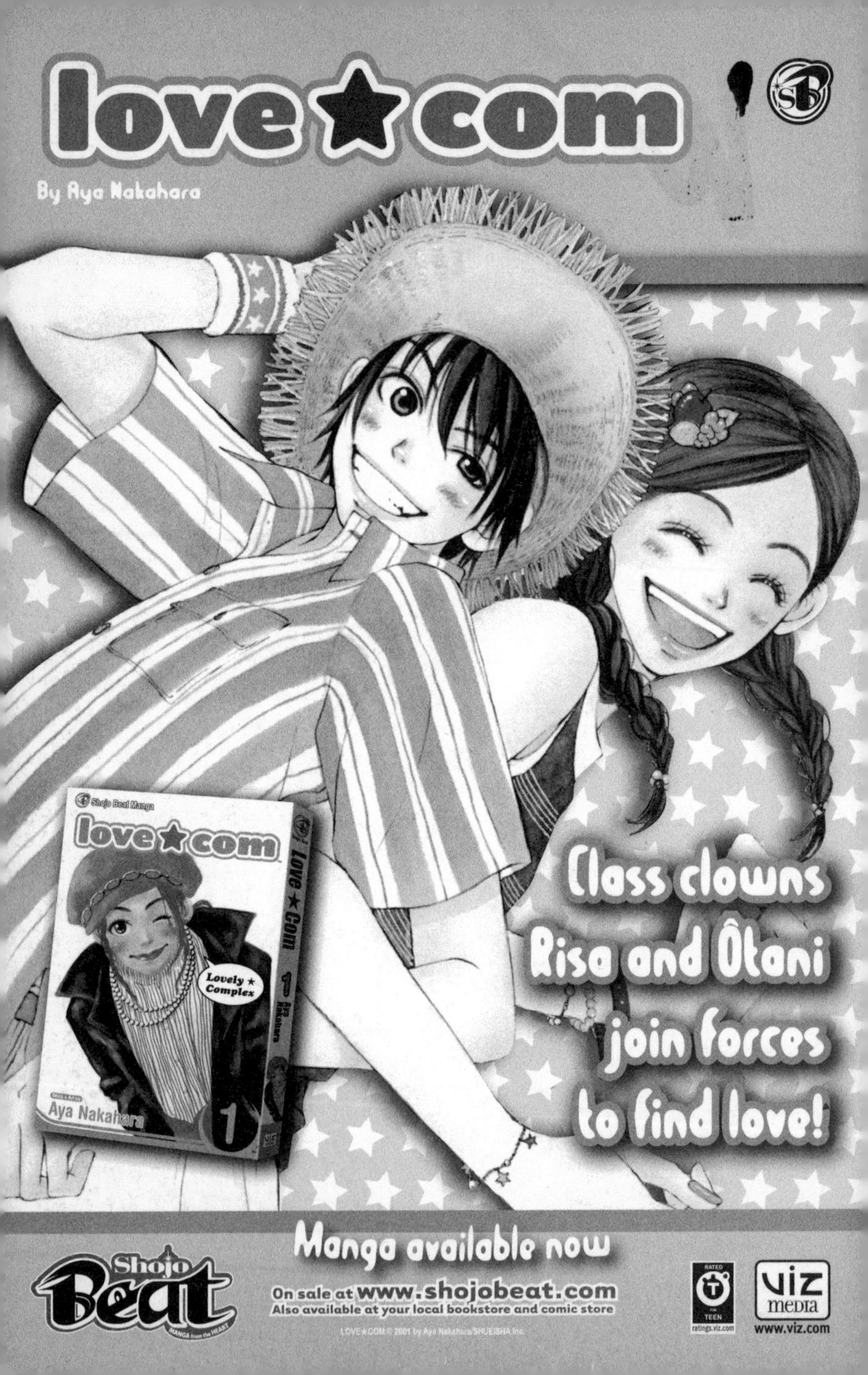
love★com
By Aya Nakahara
Shojo Beat Manga
love★com
Lovely★Complex
Aya Nakahara
1
Class clowns Risa and Ôtani join forces to find love!
Manga available now
Shojo Beat
On sale at www.shojobeat.com
Also available at your local bookstore and comic store
LOVE★COM © 2001 by Aya Nakahara/SHUEISHA Inc.
RATED T FOR TEEN
ratings.viz.com
VIZ MEDIA
www.viz.com

Tell us what you think about Shojo Beat Manga!

Our survey is now available online. Go to:

shojobeat.com/mangasurvey

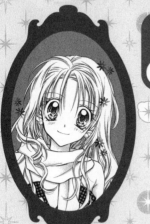

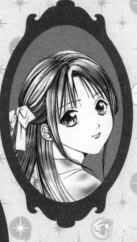

Help us make our product offerings better!

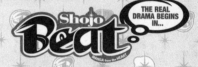

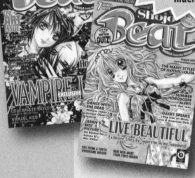
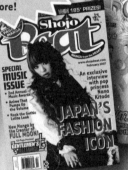
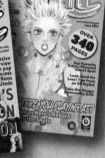

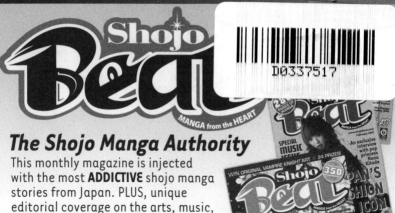